DESIGNING EDUCATION FOR THE FUTURE, NO. 3

Planning and Effecting Needed Changes In Education

Edited by EDGAR L. MORPHET, *Director, and* CHARLES O. RYAN,
*Associate Director, Designing Education for the Future: An
Eight-State Project, Denver, Colorado*

Citation Press • New York • 1967

Library of Congress Catalog Card Number: 67-24865

*Copyright © 1967 by Scholastic Magazines, Inc. Published by Citation Press,
Educators Service Division, Scholastic Magazines, Inc.*

1st printing, July 1967
Printed in the U.S.A.

PREFACE

At the close of the American Revolutionary War, the statement "Eternal vigilance is the price of liberty" became popular. After World War One, H. G. Wells expressed the same basic idea, with a modern application, when he said, "Human history becomes more and more a race between education and catastrophe."

During my many years in school teaching and administration, and more recently in educational publishing, these two statements, always vivid in my memory, never ceased giving me a deep sense of urgency in proceeding with the great task of vastly improving education and universalizing it in this country.

Seldom, if ever, has anyone given more meaning to the term "education" in so few words as did Mr. Wells. He was talking about the fast-moving accumulation of unprecedented power born of a technology never known to man in all history and capable of annihilating the slowly developed culture of the ages.

Against such a background of admonition and prophecy, it is indeed heartening to learn of the initiative taken by eight State Departments of Education in developing an Eight-State Project entitled "Designing Education for the Future" and supported generously by the U. S. Office of Education — a deliberate effort to keep education ahead in the race.

The initiators of the four-year project, launched in 1965, secured 16 carefully prepared papers by 24 authorities in various technical fields indicating what they believe will be the nature of many important facets of our society in 1980. These papers are published in *Prospective Changes in Society by 1980,* volume one in the "Designing Education for the Future" series.

The papers of the first volume were studied by 21 eminent educators who in turn prepared their respective statements of *Implications for Education of Prospective Changes in Society* for the second volume.

The third volume, entitled *Planning and Effecting Needed Changes in Education,* presents papers by other experts who have examined strategies and procedures for implementing changes in individual schools, school systems, and state educational agencies.

It should be stated that during the progress of the entire Project there were many conferences in which the writers thoroughly discussed the predictions and the implications.

JOHN W. STUDEBAKER
Chairman of the Editorial Boards
Scholastic Magazines, Inc.

DESIGNING EDUCATION FOR THE FUTURE:
An Eight-State Project

Policy Board and Project Staff

Sponsoring States	*Chief State School Officers (Policy Board)*	*State Coordinators*
ARIZONA	Sarah Folsom	Robert L. Pickering
COLORADO	Byron W. Hansford, *Chairman*	Russell B. Vlaanderen
IDAHO	D. F. Engelking	Robert S. Gibb
MONTANA	Harriet Miller	Wayne Grames
NEVADA	Burnell Larson	Lamar LeFevre
NEW MEXICO	Leonard J. De Layo	Thomas B. Bailey, Jr.
UTAH	Terrell H. Bell	Jay J. Campbell
WYOMING	K. Harrison Roberts	Paul G. Graves

Edgar L. Morphet, *Project Director*
Charles O. Ryan, *Associate Director*

Financed by funds provided under the
Elementary and Secondary Education Act of 1965
(Public Law 89-10, Title V, Sec. 505)
and
the Sponsoring States

Project Office:
1362 Lincoln Street
Denver, Colorado 80203

FOREWORD

DESIGNING EDUCATION FOR THE FUTURE, an eight-state project, involves a study of society as it may exist in 1980, in an attempt to identify needed changes in education and to examine the planning and change processes whereby these improvements may be brought about.

In designing the project, the policy board adopted the procedure of asking outstanding scholars from various disciplines to develop papers representing their best thinking regarding projections for the future. In addition, educators were asked to relate these projects to education and to draw implications for the future of education. Finally, other individuals were asked to analyze the planning and change processes and how society should go about making changes in education to meet the needs of the future. Each participating state appointed a project coordinator, an advisory committee and study committees to carry out related activities of the state and to help assure the effective planning and conducting of the project.

Reports of the first conference held in Denver, Colorado, June 29-30 and July 1, 1966, are contained in the publication, *Prospective Changes in Society by 1980.* Reports of the second conference held in Salt Lake City, Utah, October 24-26, 1966, are contained in the publication, *Implications for Education of Prospective Changes in Society.* This document includes the reports of the third conference held in Scottsdale, Arizona, April 3-5, 1967.

This project continues to be one of the most exciting and significant projects of our time. It is my sincere hope that it will be of value to the citizens of this country in helping to bring about the needed improvements in education.

Byron W. Hansford
Chairman, Policy Board

CONTENTS

xi

INTRODUCTION

Is it feasible—or even desirable—to plan for changes that may be needed in education by 1980? Questions along this line have been asked, or implied, by many people during the course of this project. Some educators and laymen have frankly stated that the problems of today are so complex and demanding that it is fruitless to devote time and effort to prospective problems of the future. Others point out that, in a fundamental sense, the future is with us now; that the children presently enrolled in kindergartens will have graduated from high school by 1980 and will be legally qualified to vote soon thereafter; and that the kind of educational program provided during the next few years will have significant implications for the kind and quality of decisions made by the citizens of the nation during coming years.

This project is not concerned with the development of a detailed plan for education in 1980 in the participating states; instead it is devoted to the process of assisting each of the states to attempt to determine the changes (improvements) that should be made and to develop appropriate plans to meet those needs. *It is concerned with the process of planning for the future,* and of establishing priorities to help to assure not only that present problems and needs are met but also that the states will be better prepared to meet emerging needs. The ultimate focus is on improving the organization and operation of the state agencies for education, but this cannot be done without ascertaining changes that are needed in the educational program, in instruction and learning, and in local school organization and operation—since the state agency must be prepared to provide the leadership and services required to meet these emerging developments.

Planning is *not* a process of speculating on probable developments and preparing a theoretical blueprint for meeting needs. Rather it is a process of attempting to determine appropriate goals and objectives, obtaining and analyzing pertinent information that will bring into focus present and emerging problems and needs, and obtaining agreement on steps and procedures that are designed to meet those needs so the objectives can be attained.

The process of effecting needed changes is equally difficult. Unless the citizens understand the need for making changes, and are convinced that the changes will result in improvements in education, these changes —regardless of their importance—are not likely to be made. This report, including papers prepared for the third conference, is devoted basically to the process of planning and effecting needed changes in education.

The basic design for this project, including both the area and individual state aspects, was briefly explained in chapter 1 of the first conference report; further information was provided in the Introduction (pp. XIII, XIV) to the second report. Briefly the area aspects provided for three major conferences primarily for—but not restricted to—lay citizens and educators from the participating states. The first conference was devoted to *Prospective Changes in Society by 1980* (the title of the report published in July, 1966). The second was concerned with *Implications for Education of Prospective Changes in Society* (the report, with that title, was published in January 1967). The third and final conference in this particular series was concerned with *Planning and Effecting Needed Changes in Education,* the title of this report.

Leading authorities were selected to prepare the papers included in each of these publications.

During the second phase of this project, each of the participating states expects to complete the process of planning needed changes in education for the future, establishing priorities and implementing some of the most urgent changes. As a means of further assisting the states, reports will again be prepared by leading authorities and conferences held in the area and in the states on important aspects of planning and change such as: "The Educational Program of the Future"; "Local Schools and School Systems of the Future"; "State Educational Organization and Operation in the Future"; and "The Economics and Financing of Education in the Future".

Edgar L. Morphet
Project Director

CHAPTER 1

Strategic Variables in Planning

LEONARD A. LECHT*

It is appropriate that a project involved in designing education for the future should be concerned with planning in all its aspects—economic, political, and social. Much has been written by educators, sociologists, economists, and others about *planning*—a term which has carried over into our everyday speech. We "plan" our lives as individuals; as communities we "plan" our local school systems; nationally we strive to "plan" our economy to provide expanding employment opportunities sufficient to absorb the 1.5 million Americans who will be added to the labor force each year in the next decade.

As an economist, I am naturally most concerned with economic planning and with the social consequences of economic planning. Yet a great deal of contemporary economics is also relevant for educational planning and many of the new programs under way, or under consideration, in education have significant economic implications. The kinds of educational systems we can successfully plan, and the future our students will face after leaving school will depend, to a large extent, on the growth of the economy's resources, and on the wisdom we exercise in utilizing these resources. In turn, *the capacity of the economy to grow is very much affected by the skills and attitudes we develop in our young people as persons, as citizens, and as future members of the labor force.*

The subject of economic planning and its relationship to education can be approached in several different ways. One might be called the "social engineering" approach. The objective in this way of getting at planning is to describe how planning can be done—the institutional machinery required, the roles of the persons and the groups involved in planning, the strategies with the greatest probability of yielding a successful outcome—and to select and utilize effectively the best procedures in the planning process. An alternative route for an analysis of planning might be called the "strategic variables" approach. The aim in this approach is to get at some of the underlying problems in economic planning. Thus we should be able to develop insights into the relationship between economic planning and educational planning which can help to explain a variety of problems common to both.

Either of these two ways of discussing planning can be useful. This

* Director, Center for Priority Analysis, National Planning Association, Washington, D. C. Chairman, Department of Economics and Sociology, Long Island University (1954-1962). Publications include: *Goals, Priorities, and Dollars—The Next Decade* (1966); and *The Dollar Cost of Our National Goals* (1965).

1

paper will largely follow the "strategic variables" approach because it offers an opportunity for raising some of the underlying problems in designing the educational systems of the future: what the educational objectives we accept are likely to cost, the resources that are likely to be available to support them, and possible routes for narrowing the gap between our resources and our aspirations in education.

PERFORMANCE PLANNING AND ACHIEVEMENT PLANNING

"Planning", like "capitalism", is a value-loaded term calculated to induce a reaction of warm approval—or of hostile negation—in the person who encounters it. To those who dislike the term, planning conjures up the image of a totalitarian society in which all men are equal but "some are more equal than others". Soviet Russia in the Stalin period or contemporary China are the stereotypes which come to mind. To those who react favorably to the term "planning", the contrary images are produced. Planning, in this context, calls forth the stereotype of a society such as Sweden with perpetual full employment, a high level of educational attainment, absence of extremes of wealth or poverty, and a highly developed social welfare system. To the persons who react in this manner, planning is synonymous with economic efficiency, social justice, and political rationality.

If we are to escape from this semantic mirage, *the planning which is relevant for the United States should be related to underlying problems which continually recur in different circumstances requiring redefinitions of objectives and new solutions.* As seen by an economist with a sociological bent, these problems can be summarized in terms of two types of economic planning. One can be called "performance planning". The problem in this kind of planning is to translate the potential capacity of the economy to grow into high and rising levels of production and employment. The other type of planning can be called "achievement planning". The problem in achievement planning is to make wise use of the output our economic machine produces.

A brief digression into recent history can serve to illustrate the differences between the two types of planning. Our economic planning in the 1930's was largely an experiment in performance planning. The main thrust of the planning in that decade was directed at alleviating economic hardship and, especially, at ending mass unemployment by improving the overall performance of the economy. As a result of the experience of the Great Depression and of World War II, *full employment, economic growth, price stability and international economic balance have emerged as national objectives* supported by a consensus embracing a broad range of opinion and interest groups. The most striking manifestation of the nation's concern with its performance goals was the enactment by Congress of the Employment Act of 1946 which created the President's Council for Economic

Advisers. The tax cut of 1964 was another, and a more recent, instance of planning to improve the economy's performance.

Since World War II, our economy has avoided a recurrence of major depressions. For much of this period it has typically been taken for granted that our standards of living—and our standards in education, or in health and research and development—were generally superior to those of other nations, and that our attainments in these areas could be expected to make substantial progress from one decade to the next.

A series of events in the past decade has shaken this belief in the inevitability of our progress. Confidence in our educational, scientific, and technological superiority has been shaken by Soviet accomplishments such as the events associated with Sputnik in1957.[1] The civil rights movement and the research of social scientists have made the nation aware that *large numbers of Americans have shared neither the material well-being, nor the political and social rights which generally characterize our society.* With over seven-tenths of Americans living in urban areas in the 1960's, our everyday experience with highway congestion, decaying central cities, smog, inadequate mass transit, or with water shortages, have moved the problems of urban development into a prominent place in our national consciousness.

The problem these issues raise is one of *priorities*—the question of "what comes first" as a claim on our resources. Such problems make up the substance of achievement planning—of determining how we should use the enormous output our economy produces to cope more effectively with individual and national needs.

PLANNING AND NATIONAL GOALS IN A PLURALISTIC SOCIETY

The importance of performance planning—of assuring dynamic growth in the economy—is underscored by a brief consideration of the alternatives. In 1962 and 1963, for example, the economy was growing at a sluggish pace, and we were unable to utilize fully our manpower and our plant capacity. The gap between our actual output and the output the economy could have produced with reasonably full use of our resources has been estimated by the President's Council of Economic Advisers[2] at $30 billion a year in 1962 and in 1963. What this loss of output meant for the nation's ability to implement its plans in education, or in health and housing, can be indicated by comparing the $30 billion loss of potential output with the total public and private expenditures in these three areas in 1962. The comparison is summarized in Table 1.

---

[1] President Eisenhower's Commission on Education Beyond the High School expressed this sentiment in its observation that "Our institutions of higher learning, despite the remarkable achievements in the past, are in no shape today to meet the challenge. Their resources are already strained, their quality standards are even now in jeopardy, and their projected plans fall far short of the indicated need". *President's Commission on Education Beyond the High School, Second Report to the President,* 1957, pp. 3-4.

[2] *Annual Report of the Council of Economic Advisers* (January, 1964), p. 37.

TABLE 1

PUBLIC AND PRIVATE EXPENDITURES FOR EDUCATION, HEALTH AND HOUSING IN 1962
(in millions of 1964 dollars)

Item	*Expenditure in 1962**
Education	$31,150
Health	$34,000
Housing	$30,850

* Derived from Leonard A. Lecht, *Goals, Priorities, and Dollars—The Next Decade* (New York, N. Y.: The Free Press, 1966), p. 36.

If all of the loss of potential output had been avoided in 1962, our society—if it had so planned—could have divided its greater output among the three. Allocating our additional resources in this manner would have made it possible to increase the expenditures for education, health and housing by close to one-third, or by $10 billion in each area.

Planning for economic growth has become familiar and generally accepted in our society, although we frequently prefer to use names for it other than "planning". Planning to establish our *priorities* is a less generally understood process in the United States. Some important recent developments, however, have led to greater recognition that *many major public policy decisions—and many private decisions—essentially concern the nation's choice of priorities.*

Priorities are the major issue, to cite a leading instance, in the continuing debate concerning the desirability of landing a man on the moon by 1970. Critics of the 1970 deadline contend, and its advocates deny, that concentrating a large share of our research and development resources on the manned lunar landing has made it difficult for us to increase substantially the scientific and engineering resources available to rebuild our cities by devising new and more effective mass transit systems, or by increasing productivity in technologically less advanced industries such as residential construction. The priorities problem has also come to the fore in the recent controversies as to whether the larger spending for the military action in Vietnam should lead to reduced expenditures for the War on Poverty. As citizens, we are, in effect, passing on community (and state) priorities in the many local (and state) elections to decide whether bond issues should be floated to enlarge educational facilities, or taxes increased to provide better education, to raise teachers' salaries, or for other purposes.

In a decentralized, pluralistic society such as our own, the mechanisms by which priorities are established and implemented are frequently obscure. Goals in a totalitarian society—Soviet Russia serves as an illustration—are defined by a national authority as part of an overall national plan, and this definition has the force of law. The production of steel in 1970, the number of new secondary schools and their location, and the quantity of steel to be used in building these schools are spelled out in a plan presumably binding on the entire nation.

In our society, many groups, public and private, participate officially and unofficially in determining what our *objectives* are to be and in implementing them. Numerous voluntary associations influence priorities in both the public and private sectors by publicizing, educating, and lobbying for more spending for mental health, to preserve our parks and wilderness areas, or to increase educational opportunity. In major segments of the economy the role of public authority is minimal. For example, consumers spend the incomes they earn according to their individual preferences. In some areas—as in national defense—public authority alone makes the decisions controlling expenditures. In many fields—education is an important example—the federal government makes use of its revenues to encourage state and local governments to expand their educational plant, to use new or more effective teaching materials and technologies, and to provide greater opportunities for students from low-income areas.

Concern with the nation's objectives is, of course, nothing new. What is new is the extent of concern with our society's purposes and with the directions in which we are moving. The report of President Eisenhower's Commission on National Goals represents a landmark in articulating this concern.[3] The report identified and discussed goals in 15 areas affecting most aspects of American life. The goals considered were significant because they indicated a broad agreement in American opinion in defining the areas in our society where changes are needed.

To spell out the implications of the kind of planning at which the thinking represented by the Goals Commission's report was directed, the National Planning Association has undertaken a two-year study of the probable cost of achieving our objectives in the 15 goal areas in the mid-1970's. Needs and standards of achievement in the different areas were formulated from special studies, legislative hearings, legislation and general national policy. The standards for the goals reflect current developments in each area, and represent levels of achievement regarded as individually reasonable and within reach in a free enterprise system on the basis of present knowledge. Along with the goals considered in the Commission's report, space goals were added as a sixteenth area after the late President Kennedy proposed in 1961 that it become a national objective "to put men on the moon and bring them back". This we interpret to mean the goal of embarking on a sustained space research and development program.

The 16 goals are listed in Table 2 which gives the actual expenditures in each of the goal areas in 1962—the base year for the NPA study—and the estimated expenditures for the "aspiration goals" (that is, for achieving the standards) in 1975.

The projections for the education goal suggest changes in the nation's priorities favoring a greater emphasis on objectives in education. Total spending for education amounted to $31 billion in 1962 (in dollars of

---

[3] *Goals for Americans, The Report of the President's Commission on National Goals* (Englewood Cliffs, N. J.: Prentice-Hall, Inc. 1960).

1964 purchasing power). To realize the aspiration goal for education in the next decade—the increases in the ratio of professional staff to students, the growth in enrollments, the needed construction of educational plant and facilities, the desired changes in curriculum and in methods of teaching, plus a substantial increase in compensation for teachers—is estimated to require annual expenditures for education rising to $86 billion by 1975. This would amount to an increase of 176 percent over 1962. In 1962, education ranked eighth among the sixteen goals in the order of its expenditures. By 1975 the spending anticipated for the education goal would move education to sixth place on the list. A shift of this nature would be consistent with historical trends since World War II. In 1950 public and private spending for education reached 3.5 percent of the gross

TABLE 2

EXPENDITURES FOR INDIVIDUAL GOALS, 1962, AND PROJECTED 1975*
(in millions of 1964 dollars)

Goal Area	Expenditures in 1962	Projected Expenditures for Aspiration Goals in 1975	Percent Increase, 1962 to 1975ᵃ
Consumer Expenditures	$364,750	$674,400	85
Private Plant and Equipment	50,050	155,050	210
Urban Development	67,700	136,700	102
Social Welfare	39,050	94,400	142
Health	34,000	89,800	164
Education	31,150	85,950	176
Transportation	39,950	76,650	113
National Defense	53,750	70,700	31
Housing	30,850	65,000	111
Research and Development	17,350	40,000	131
Natural Resources	6,050	17,100	185
International Aid	5,550	12,550	127
Space	3,400	9,550	183
Agriculture	7,350	9,300	27
Manpower Training	100	3,050	2,750
Area Redevelopment	350	1,000	171
Gross Total	$747,400	$1,541,200	
Minus Double Counting and Transfer Adjustmentsᵇ	174,100	379,600	
Net Cost of Goals	$573,300	$1,161,600	

* Derived from Leonard A. Lecht, *op. cit.*, pp. 36, 38.
ᵃ The numbers in the table have been rounded. The percentage increases refer to the unrounded totals.
ᵇ The adjustment for double counting occurs because parts of the cost of some goals are also parts of the cost of other goals. Spending by families for tuition in colleges and universities is included as part of the total expenditures for the consumer expenditures goal. It also makes up part of the spending listed for the education goal.

national product (GNP). These expenditures had risen to 5.5 percent of the considerably enlarged GNP in 1962 and to nearly 6 percent in 1964.[4]

THE ECONOMIC FRAMEWORK FOR THE 1970's

Planning for national—or state—priorities refers to the future, to what we aspire to achieve as individuals and as a society five, ten, or twenty years from now. The point of departure for a consideration of the relationship between our resources and our aspirations, therefore, is a consideration of the economic framework which is likely to characterize our society in the coming decade.

The limiting factor in realizing the nation's objectives in the next decade will be the volume of output the economy can reasonably be expected to be capable of producing. Assuming optimistic but feasible growth in GNP over the next ten years—growth at a sustained rate of about 4.5 percent a year—the gross national product should increase (in dollars of 1964 purchasing power) to just over a trillion dollars by 1975. A 4.5 percent annual increase in GNP is considerably larger than the average increase of 3.8 percent a year for the entire period since 1947, although it is somewhat smaller than the 5.5 percent growth in output of the past two years.

The gross national product and the other basic ingredients in the economic framework anticipated in the mid-1970's are described in Table 3.

TABLE 3

ESTIMATED GNP, POPULATION, AND FAMILY PERSONAL INCOME, 1962, 1964 AND 1975
(dollar estimates are in 1964 dollars)

	Actual		Projected
Item	*1962*	*1964*	*1975*
GNP (in billions)	$ 573	$ 622	$ 1,010
Population (in millions)	187	192	226
Civilian Labor Force (in millions)	72	74	91
Average Family Personal Income*	$7,450	$7,800	$10,350

* This estimate of average family personal income refers to "consumer units"—i.e., to families and unattached individuals. The figures cited represent the arithmetic means. For the source of the 1962 estimates see *Survey of Current Business*, July, 1964, Table 17, p. 18. The 1964 figure is an NPA estimate.

A gross national product of a trillion dollars in 1975 would be about $435 billion greater than in 1962 and almost $400 billion greater than in 1964. Increases in output of this magnitude may appear to be so enormous as to suggest that as a nation, we could do whatever we thought desirable to improve education, to develop space research, to raise living standards, or for other purposes. However, between 1962 and 1975 the population is expected to grow by 39 million. There will be 19 million more persons in the civilian labor force. Elementary and secondary school enrollments, according to the U. S. Office of Education, will probably

4 *Health, Education, and Welfare Trends,* 1965 Edition (Washington, D. C.: U. S. Department of Health, Education and Welfare), p. S-61.

increase by some 10 million, and enrollments in higher education are projected to grow by 5 million. Roughly one-half of this increase of $435 billion—an amount three-fourths as great as the entire GNP in 1962—will be required to maintain existing standards of living, housing, or health for a larger number of families, to provide current standards of education for an additional 15 million students, and to provide the additions needed to our productive capacity to make possible the trillion-dollar economy expected in the mid-1970's.

On this basis, about $200 billion a year would be at our society's disposal in the 1970's to raise standards of living, to improve the quality of life, and to make progress in reducing the nation's agenda of unfinished business in education, health, social welfare, research and development, in rebuilding our cities, and in other areas. This is about $150 billion less than the costs of the improvements included in the 16 aspiration goals. The claims on output represented by the cost projections for the aspiration goals would be 15 percent greater than the anticipated trillion-dollar GNP. With the available resources, we could make progress toward achieving all of our goals—and *substantial* progress for many. However, we could not achieve all of our objectives at the same time.

IMPLICATIONS FOR EDUCATION

It is by no means a novel conclusion to suggest that our society's goals exceed its present reach. What is significant in this conclusion for education is the possibility of indicating a context for viewing planning in education in relation to planning in a host of other areas. This context helps to make it apparent that *educational planning is concerned with defining the nation's (or a state's) priorities in education, and with designing programs which could achieve them.* The extent to which we are likely to implement our educational priorities depends on how rapidly the economy grows, and on the competing claims for resources arising from the pursuit of other goals in the public and private sectors of our society. From this viewpoint, *the task of policy, and essentially of politics, is to reconcile these claims, and to keep a multitude of competing claims within the constraints set by the available or the anticipated resources.*

We are currently spending about 6 percent of the GNP for our entire national educational effort, public and private. In order to achieve our objectives in education, with a GNP growth rate of 4.5 percent a year over the next decade, we would have to be spending something more than 8 percent of the gross national product for education in the mid-1970's. We are currently spending an amount equal to 7 percent of GNP in public and private expenditures for programs which promote social welfare. Attaining the objectives considered for the social welfare goal is expected to require expenditures reaching close to 9.5 percent by 1975. Similarly, before the current capital goods boom, we were spending about 9 percent of the GNP to replace, modernize, and expand our stock of private plant and equipment including the facilities utilized by non-profit organizations such as private hospitals and universities. Creating the productive plant and the facilities for non-profit organizations needed in the 1970's is projected to involve spending something close to 15 percent of the GNP.

Priorities in education, like priorities in social welfare—but unlike our priorities for private plant and equipment—are largely implemented through the use of the government's resources. In the mid-1960's, almost four-fifths of all expenditures for education were public expenditures.[5] These resources are primarily made up of state and local government revenues, although they have been increasingly supplemented by revenues from the federal government in recent years.

On the national scene, our educational priorities are translated into educational services and facilities through the expenditures authorized in the federal government's annual budget. The budget authorizations determine the weight to be assigned in distributing the federal government's resources between spending for educational priorities, and spending for our objectives for national defense, for research and development, for health, for social welfare, for urban development, and for other purposes.

The National Planning Association has prepared estimates of the federal government's expenditures by program objective in the 1970's *taking into account recent trends in government spending, population growth, rural-urban population shifts, and the impact of recently enacted legislation such as Medicare and the Elementary and Secondary Education Act.* These projections are "probabilistic" estimates since they attempt to show what *is likely to happen* in the next decade *rather than what ought to happen,* to achieve our objectives. Together with the comparable estimates of state and local government expenditures, and of private spending for education, the projections provide a basis for appraising the extent to which, in the light of recent developments, we are likely to achieve our goals in education in the next decade. The estimates for the federal government expenditures in 1975, and the actual expenditures in the base year for this study, 1964, are given in Table 4.

The estimates in the table indicate that federal spending for education, like the related spending for job preparation, is expected to increase at a considerably more rapid rate than for other federal programs. In education, the projected expenditures in 1975 represent more than a 400 percent increase over 1964. Viewed in relation to total federal spending, the resources allocated for implementing our educational priorities would still account for a small share of the federal budget—increasing from about 1 percent of the total in 1964 to 3 percent by the mid-1970's. The federal government's expenditures are likely to be especially significant in assisting colleges and universities to expand their facilities, in encouraging research in education, in aiding young people to enter "shortage" fields such as the health occupations today, and as grants-in-aid to state and local

---

[5] Derived from *Health, Education, and Welfare Trends,* 1965 edition, *op. cit.,* p. S-61.

governments to develop programs to offset the effects of poverty and cultural deprivation in low income areas.

TABLE 4

ESTIMATED FEDERAL GOVERNMENT EXPENDITURES BY PROGRAM OBJECTIVE,
1964 AND 1975*
(in millions of 1964 dollars)

Program Area	Actual 1964	Projected 1975	Percent Increase, 1964 to 1975
1. Education	$ 1,100	$ 5,700	418
2. Job Preparation	700	4,700	571
3. Health	4,400	11,600	164
4. Social Welfare	25,200	48,200	91
5. Natural Resources Conservation and Development	2,900	6,500	124
6. Research and Development	13,700	17,900	31
7. Housing, Area Redevelopment, Transportation, Communications	8,800	18,700	112
8. Defense, AEC, Space, International	48,600	51,000	5
9. Farm Income Stabilization	4,100	3,300	–20
10. General Government Operations	10,800	12,700	18
Total	$120,300	$180,300	50

* Derived from *National Economic Projections to 1976/77* (Center for Economic Projections, National Planning Association, 1966), p. 18. The figures listed refer to fiscal years 1964 and 1975. They represent the federal consolidated cash budget expenditures.

Education in the United States is primarily the responsibility of state and local governments. Spending for education, accordingly, is the largest single element in state-local government budgets—accounting for over 35 percent of their total expenditures in 1964. State and local governments also figure prominently in the pursuit of national objectives in transportation, health, social welfare, and in natural resources conservation and development. The claims on state and local governments arising from these objectives in 1964, and the anticipated expenditures in 1975 are summarized in Table 5.

While state and local spending for educational objectives is expected to increase by almost three-fifths between 1964 and 1975, this increase would represent a less rapid rate of growth than the percentage growth anticipated for most of the other program areas supported by state-local government revenues. As a claim on the budgets of these units of government, the educational expenditures are projected to diminish from the 36 percent of the total they represented in 1964 to 29 percent by 1975. However, in terms of dollars, the $15 billion increase listed for educational spending exceeds the comparable increases for other objectives.

The lesser percentage increases projected for state-local government spending for education reflect the probable slowing down in the growth of enrollment in elementary and secondary schools. Between 1954 and

TABLE 5

ESTIMATED STATE AND LOCAL GOVERNMENT EXPENDITURES BY PROGRAM OBJECTIVE,
1964 AND 1975*

(in millions of 1964 dollars)

Program Area	Actual 1964	Projected 1975	Percent Increase, 1964 to 1975
1. Education	$26,100	$ 41,200	58
2. Job Preparation	400	1,200	200
3. Health	8,000	13,600	70
4. Social Welfare	8,600	13,200	53
5. Natural Resources Conservation and Development	2,800	6,700	139
6. Housing and Area Redevelopment	600	2,000	233
7. Transportation, Communications, and Public Utilities	11,600	24,000	107
8. Defense, AEC, Space, International	400	500	25
9. General Government Operations	13,900	40,100	189
Total	$72,400	$142,500	97

* These estimates, other than the projection for general government operations, are derived from *The National Program for Domestic Progress: Its Character, Cost and Economic Consequences* (Center for Economic Projections, National Planning Association, 1966), p. 104. The figures listed refer to fiscal years 1964 and 1975.

1964, enrollment in all schools through grade 12 grew by over 14 million—an increase of over 40 percent. Between 1964 and 1974, enrollments are expected to grow by only 6½ million—an increase of less than 15 percent.[6] In addition, the projections take into account the fact that state and local governments are just beginning to spend on a large scale to cope with such problems as inadequate mass transit, smog, insufficient recreational facilities, or water pollution. Rapid growth in the claims on state and local revenues for these purposes can reasonably be anticipated in the next decade.

The "probabilistic" estimates overlook the role of the private sector in contributing resources to attain our educational goal. In 1964 private expenditures for education by individuals and non-profit organizations amounted to over one-fifth (22 per cent) of the total spending for education. If this proportion were to continue through 1975, what share of the $86 billion estimated as the cost of the education goal would be accounted for by the budget estimates in the public sector and in the corresponding private expenditures?

To make this comparison, we must first refine our statistical net to eliminate double counting; that is, the federal grants-in-aid to states for education. We must also allow for the cost of programs included in the education goal which are listed as parts of other program areas in the budget estimates (for example, the spending for education in health fields

---

[6] *Health, Education, and Welfare Trends*, 1965 edition, *op. cit.*, p. S-42.

included as part of health rather than as education). These excluded elements are reckoned at the same percentage of total educational expenditures in 1975 as in the mid-1960's, that is at 5 percent of the total. Taking into account these adjustments, we would be providing an estimated seven-tenths of the financial resources needed to achieve our goal in education in the mid-1970's. The calculations entering into this projection are presented in Table 6.

TABLE 6

PROJECTED EDUCATIONAL EXPENDITURES AND COST OF EDUCATION GOAL IN 1975
(in millions of 1964 dollars)

Item	Expenditures and Adjustments	Goal Cost and Deficit
1. Cost of Education Goal		$86,000
2. Expenditures for Education		
a. Federal expenditures	$5,700	
Minus grants-in-aid	$3,100	
Net federal expenditures	$2,600	
b. State and local government expenditures	$41,200	
c. Private expenditures	13,200	
d. Allowance for items included in other program areas	3,000	
Total educational expenditures		$60,000
3. Deficit in Expenditures to Achieve Education Goal		$26,000
4. Educational Expenditures as Percent of Cost of Education Goal		70

By 1975, according to our estimate, the nation would be spending $60 billion for education. This would amount to close to double the 1962 level of spending, or $29 billion more, and $24 billion more than in 1964 (all in 1964 dollars). However, we would be $26 billion short of the financial resources estimated as the cost of achieving the education goal.

NARROWING THE GAP BETWEEN RESOURCES AND
ASPIRATIONS IN EDUCATION

The overall bearing of this presentation is to *emphasize the alternatives likely to affect the balance between our resources and our aspirations in education.* The projection of a $26 billion deficit for achieving our goal in education in the next decade represents an extension in time of one of these alternatives—the changes of the recent past. *If the future were to continue along the lines suggested by the recent past, the problem of planning in education would center on the design of the educational systems which would be feasible with resources limited by a growing gap between the revenues and expenditure needs of state and local governments.*

Larger populations, greater urbanization, and rising demand for more and better public services are causing the expenditures of state and local governments to rise more rapidly than their tax revenues or non-tax receipts. These units of governments depend largely on revenues from property and sales taxes, and revenues from the two sources have grown more slowly than expenditures. By 1970, according to a study by Professor George Break of the University of California, state and local governments will probably have a gap between revenues and expenditures ranging between $30 billion and $56 billion a year.[7]

What changes could be made to help bridge the gap between resources and aspirations sufficiently to enable us to achieve, say, 90 percent of our goal in education by 1975 rather than the 70 percent anticipated on the basis of recent developments? This would require expenditures for education reaching $77.5 billion, or an additional $17.5 billion a year beyond the $60 billion expected on the basis of the budget estimates and the comparable private expenditures.

Changes in our priorities affecting expenditures within the public sector could help to release additional resources for education. Expenditures for highway construction and maintenance, for example, are the second largest items in the budgets of state and local governments, and they are exceeded only by spending for education. By 1975 it is likely that state and local governments will be spending $18 to $20 billion a year for highways.[8] If more and more adequate mass transit facilities could induce Americans to transfer their allegiance from the private automobile to mass transit in commuting to and from the central city, a substantial saving in expenditures would probably result which could be allocated to other purposes such as education. To illustrate these possibilities: If investing $1 billion a year in mass transit facilities could reduce the highway expenditures by one-fifth, there would be an additional sum of close to $3 billion potentially available for education. Realizing these savings would also involve an equivalent change in the federal grants-in-aid programs from the present emphasis on highway construction to greater emphasis on education.

Recognition of the need of state and local governments for larger revenues has led *many economists and public figures in both parties to favor the sharing of federal revenues with the states for programs to be determined by the states* in addition to grants-in-aid for specific purposes. The revenue sharing plans are based on the idea that federal revenues from the individual and corporate income tax grow automatically as the economy

---

[7] George F. Break, *Intergovernmental Fiscal Relations in the United States* (Washington, D. C.: Brookings Institution, 1967).

[8] Derived from *National Economic Projections to 1976/77* (Washington, D. C.: Center for Economic Projections, National Planning Association, 1966), p. 51.

grows and they tend to grow more rapidly than the GNP. *If these greater revenues are not returned to the income stream through larger public expenditures or by tax reduction, they constitute a "fiscal drag",* depressing purchasing power in the economy. As one way of offsetting this fiscal drag, Congressman Henry Reuss of Wisconsin has introduced legislation in the current session of Congress proposing that the federal government make bloc grants of $5 billion a year to states which qualify by modernizing their tax structures and administrative machinery and by cooperating with other states on common problems such as water use.[9] If the bloc grant program were adopted, and the grants were to increase roughly in line with the GNP, by 1975 they would add as much as $7 billion (in 1964 dollars) to the resources of state governments.

A more direct solution to providing additional resources to education would be to undertake a modest shift in emphasis in our priorities from private consumption to public services. With the trillion-dollar GNP anticipated in 1975, personal consumption expenditures are expected to reach $615 billion. A decrease in private consumption of slightly more than 2.5 percent, achieved by increasing state and local income taxes and making them more progressive, could provide $17.5 billion in additional resources for education or for other goals. These higher taxes would be imposed in an economy with family consumption spending adapted to average family incomes of close to $10,400. Together with the bloc grant revenue sharing plan, they would add approximately $25 billion to the resources of state and local governments by the mid-1970's.

The three possibilities considered constitute "what if" explorations of the future which, in some respects, run contrary to the course of recent events. The bloc grants legislation, for example, is unlikely to be enacted by Congress in a period, as at present, when the federal budget shows a deficit and prices are rising. Yet proposals which appear to be visionary in 1967 may appear as feasible alternatives in a changed economic environment, one, three, or five years from now. President Johnson, in his 1967 *Economic Report,* to cite a leading instance, points out that it is impossible to predict how long the military action in Vietnam will continue. However, the President also observed that "peace will return —and it could return sooner than we dare expect". When the hostilities end, "the resources now being claimed by the war can be diverted to peaceful uses . . . and can hasten the attainment of the great goals upon which we have set our sights".[10] The military activities in Vietnam are estimated to add $22 billion to expenditures for national defense in the coming fiscal year. *A relaxation of international tensions sufficient to permit our nation to release many of the resources currently required for national defense offers the most favorable circumstance for narrowing the deficit in resources for our goal in education in the next decade.*

---

[9] *Congressional Record* (Washington, D. C.: January 11, 1967), pp. 107-110.
[10] *Economic Report of the President,* January, 1967, p. 23.

EDUCATION AS A DIMENSION OF ALL OUR GOALS

This analysis of planning in terms of the priorities problem has discussed education as one of a group of competing claims on the nation's resources. At best, such a point of view contains only a partial truth. *Education also increases the supply of resources for the pursuit of all our goals.* Assuring our future manpower needs for doctors and teachers, scientists and social workers, or for electricians and secretaries will depend largely on progress in education. The feedback effects of additional expenditures for education increase output by raising the skills of the labor force and by encouraging our technological dynamism. *Widespread diffusion of educational opportunity is also our main channel for diffusing social and economic opportunity.* Education, from this perspective, is an important dimension of all of our goals.

Since progress in education increases the nation's capacity for pursuing all of its goals, narrowing the gap between the resources allocated to education and educational needs concerns both professional educators and the public. Where and how the nation assigns its priorities in the next ten years will be determined, as in the past, by the decisions of consumers, business firms and trade unions, and by legislation enacted by national, state and local governments. Research and analysis can contribute significantly to these decisions—in education and in other fields—by identifying emerging problems, defining their dimensions, and by pointing to important implications and consequences of alternative courses of action. Yet technical analysis alone cannot "scientifically determine"—even with the aid of super-computers—what our society's priorities ought to be. In the broadest sense of the term "politics", these choices are essentially political. They involve many value judgments and differing interpretations as to what is most important and best for our future growth as individuals, as state and local communities, and as a nation.

Our choices in defining objectives in education, and in planning the social technology for pursuing them, are more likely to reflect the knowledge gained through research if a substantial number of persons are involved in educational planning in meaningful ways. *Helping more people to understand the problems and needs in education, and to participate in effecting the changes which can move the educational system to a much closer approximation to our aspirations is an important part of the planning process.* This participation is facilitated by projects such as *Designing Education for the Future.*

Strategies and Procedures in State and Local Planning

ROBERT P. HUEFNER*

Everyone plans—but not very well. Most of our actions are influenced by expectations of the future and a written—or at least a mental—"plan" of how that future can be improved. But seldom have these plans been subjected to a critical evaluation of assumptions and objectives, a rigorous questioning of internal consistency, a useful analysis of realistic alternatives, or a careful coordination with other plans to which they must relate. The complex and rapidly increasing demands facing our governments have been answered with plans that have been little more than "wish-lists"— when hard-headed strategies of development have been needed and could have been provided through modern planning techniques.

Good planning, as a management tool, should identify potential program conflicts before financial and emotional commitments make resolution impossible. *Planning should improve the analysis of alternative courses of action so the processes of selecting are better guided toward long-range goals.* It should show the immediate and long-range budgeting implications of alternative actions. It should outline objectives in advance in order to increase local guidance and control of local and federal programs.

Governors and legislators are no longer satisfied by "wish-list" planning and are requiring, from planning, defensible justifications of priorities before financing programs. The federal govenrment is also requiring careful analyses of priorities and strategies by extending its Planning-Pro-gramming-Budgeting-System (PPBS) beyond the Defense Department to domestic programs, with their more elusive objectives. The "Comprehensive Health Planning and Public Health Service Amendments of 1966" (P.L. 89-749) *may be the beginning of an entirely new approach to federal grants-in-aid, in which categorical grants are replaced by broad-program block-grants which are allocated to various projects in accordance with state plans;* with federal control restricted to the assurance of high standards in the state planning process.

The following comments are a planning practitioner's views of some of the means by which the *quality* of planning can be improved.

THE PLANNING PROCESS: CONCEPTS AND CONFLICTS

The planning process can be described as research, goal-setting, and plan formulation. But before describing this process, four concepts which the process is expected to implement should be identified. These concepts, for far too long, have been recited as platitudes. They deserve more careful consideration because each requires a balancing and reconciliation of two not entirely compatible purposes.

---

* *Utah State Planning Coordinator, Office of the Governor.* Member of the American Institute of Planners' Committee on State Planning; member of the Board of Directors, Association of State Planning Officials.

FOUR BASIC CONCEPTS

A Management Tool. The planning process should provide a management tool whose purposes are: (1) to support our democratic decision making process by improving the selection of goals and policies; and (2) to guide administrative action to implement these goals and policies.

Coordinated Programs. The planning process should (1) better coordinate elements of the program being planned, as well as (2) better coordinate the total program with other programs outside the scope of the plan.

Up-to-Date Guidance. The planning process should (1) maintain a current plan, flexible to changing conditions and goals, but (2) provide a firm enough plan that it maintains its integrity and provides real guidance.

Competent Analysis. The process should provide the best information and the most competent skills available for each step of the decision making process. This includes: (1) the general planning information and skills, such as population projections, pertinent to most elements of the plan; and also (2) specific program information and skills—such as an understanding of new teaching techniques—pertinent only to specific elements of the plan.

THREE KEY CONFLICTS

Designing a planning process requires choices between several conflicting approaches which emphasize some purposes more than others. Three key conflicts are identified here before beginning a description of the author's views of the planning process and the way this process should resolve these conflicts.

Centralization Versus Decentralization. Planning involves all levels of administration but key responsibilities may be centralized or decentralized. Centralization strengthens control and support of the planning by the governor—or any other top administrator served by the planning program—because the planning more accurately reflects his goals and interest. It similarly strengthens the central planning agency's control of the planning and thereby more easily coordinates the various program plans. It also assures the use of basic planning information and skills.

Decentralization results in wider participation in the planning process and, thereby, wider commitment to the plan from those who ultimately must administer and implement the plan. Decentralization takes better advantage of detailed program information and skills. It also improves staff-line relationships by reducing the threat felt by line administrators that the central planning staff is assuming program control.

Consultants Versus Staff. The recent growth of state planning programs is demanding many more skilled and experienced planners than will be available for some years. Development of a planning staff therefore requires substantial investment in training and experience. An alternative is partial—or full—dependence upon consulting services. Consulting services can provide a wider range of skills, and greater certainty of maintaining program schedules, but the experience of the consultants is also limited and a considerable portion of their fee will probably be an investment in the consultants' future capability. Use of a staff is likely to produce a less-sophisticated program but more assurance of coordination of detail, internal understanding and interpretation of the planning program, and continuity of the program.

Plan Versus Planning. A written plan serves as an instrument of communication—directing action and coordinating programs. By providing *the* plan it serves to focus criticism and when such criticism justifies change, the new plan serves to speed the necessary changes by all those using the plan. *Care must be taken, however, to prevent the plan from becoming a permanent or outdated document.* An equal problem is the difficulty of producing a plan which is reasonably comprehensive and defensible. To provide a good working instrument, several recent planning programs have produced a "policy plan" which outlines basic strategies and may be supported by separately-published project plans which can be independently updated. Other planning programs have never produced a comprehensive plan, relying instead upon the personal involvement of the planning staff in daily decisions to direct those decisions toward long-range needs. Some planners even suggest that the focusing of criticisms, made possible by a published policy plan, is too threatening to the planning program and is better avoided.

The following sections discuss the elements of the planning program, suggest means to implement the above concepts, and propose means of resolving the conflicts.

RESEARCH FOR SOUND PLANNING

The most frequent fault of planning programs is that they are too centralized. But in the area of research—where centralization has the most certain advantages—planning programs are uselessly and inefficiently decentralized. We would not think of asking each Ford dealer to finance independently the design of next year's Ford; yet planning programs are often expected to be internally self-sufficient by providing all their own research. Thus, an attempt to make a planning program "complete" usually results in an embarrassingly inferior duplication of scientific research efforts. The most needed and apparently least-asked question when outlining research is: If a research project can be financed by a single program plan, can it be any good?

State—and even local—planning for education can use much national research and information, a surprising amount of which relates specifically to the plan in question. The reports of *Designing Education for the Future* have identified much of this material, such as the efforts of Dr. Selma Mushkin for the State-Local Finances Project and of the National Planning Association. The identification of additional national sources of information will be a principal task of the staff of this eight-state project. The work of the U. S. Office of Education should be extremely valuable—particularly the planning-programming-budgeting efforts now underway, which Dr. Mushkin is attempting to make more readily adaptable to state and local governments.

The advantage of centralization at the state level may be more difficult to achieve because the comprehensive state planning programs, through which such centralization can be achieved, are just being established. But the advantages are substantial.

By combining efforts of population analysis and projection, Utah is replacing crude and conflicting projections with computer-programmed models of population shifts, based upon analysis of birth rates, age and sex distributions of migration, labor force participation ratios, and disaggregated employment models for each county. By combining efforts of economic analysis, a forty-sector input-output table will be completed this spring for analysis of the dynamics of the state's economy. These and other similar efforts are making available analyses whose duplication would require the entire budget of some single agency planning programs.

Centralization of research also provides a focus for criticism and refinement to assure that all programs are based upon the most broadly considered and most recently updated findings. For example, if educational planning is based upon central projections of the economy and labor force, it will most likely reflect the state employment office's understanding of future skill requirements.

Where a central state planning agency does not exist it is important that the agencies themselves establish relationships with each other. Every state has recently completed or now has underway plans for mental health, mental retardation, vocational education, and unemployment compensation which have direct relationships with educational plans. Every state has underway a number of other planning programs, including highway and outdoor recreation plans, which require economic and population analyses and which indirectly affect education through their effects upon the state's economy and population distribution.

This does not deny the need for some decentralized research and analysis, the stimulation of which is one of the basic advances in program management achieved by a planning program. The quality of planning depends more upon the depth and continuity of understanding of conditions and problems unique to the program being planned than upon the quality of general research such as population and economic analyses. The quality of specific program research depends, in part, upon avoiding inefficient duplication of central research and concentrating upon analyses of specific problems that offer the most promise to improved program management. The quality of such research also depends upon the use of modern scientific skills and tools, even though this may require outside assistance. Particularly distressing are surveys and statistical analyses which must be dismissed because the planning agency failed to use scientific methods of survey design and sampling, or meaningful statistical procedures. The quality of research also depends upon its success in establishing sources of regularly updated information useful for decision making and useful to evaluate the results of decisions made.

GOALS FOR PROGRAM PLANNING

Although every planning program vigorously proclaims that it is guiding action by careful consideration of goals, the consideration of goals is usually an isolated and academic exercise not really used to direct the plan. *The goals should provide the common objectives by which the merits of alternative programs are weighed and by which conflicts between programs are resolved.* The goals also should provide the relatively stable basic direction for the plan, around which programs can be adjusted to meet changing circumstances without jeopardizing the basic integrity of the plan. To serve these functions, the goals must be specific, well-considered, and consistent selections from realistic alternative goals. And they must be understood and accepted by those expected to implement the programs designed to achieve the goals.

Making the goals an effective guide to the plan is concerned not so much with the question of centralization versus decentralization as it is with the need for much more involvement of all levels of administration. It is also important that the consideration of goals continue throughout the preparation of the plan. But such involvement and consideration cannot be achieved if it is not deserved, and it is not deserved if the goals statements are platitudes. To deserve such attention, *the goals statements must be concerned with the key questions regarding the purposes of the programs being planned.* And the goals statements must answer such questions in terms specific enough to guide program development where technical analysis does not provide a set of answers and where value decisions must be made.

The planning program should make goal formulation the focus of management decision making. The role of top policy makers is to continuously consider the program goals—initially to identify the key questions as a guide to the researcher in developing information useful for decision making; then, to re-evaluate the goals to guide the development of preliminary plans; and finally to revise the goals in order to resolve problems uncovered in the planning process and to direct the further refinement of the plan. Advising policy-makers in these matters should be the primary concern of a policy advisory committee, if its purpose is policy advice —as it should be—and not just citizen involvement to establish citizen commitment.

The planner's greatest challenge is to formulate meaningful alternatives meriting the consideration of top policy-makers. He must also assure that all research and plan formulation efforts are developing the information useful in considering these alternatives, and that the plan reflects the goals finally adopted. The role of the plan itself is to state the goals—and thereby provide the common guide for all parts of the program—and to stimulate discussion which can lead to improvements when the plan is refined or updated.

A PLAN WHICH DIRECTS CHANGE

To be effective a plan must effect change. To effect change the plan must be a strategy for development—outlining available resources, how these resources will be marshalled, for what purpose they will be used, how they will be used, and who will use them. Analysis of alternatives is the basic difference between a plan as a management tool and wish-list planning; analysis of how effectively each alternative accomplishes the various goals and what inputs are required for these returns; and analysis resulting in outlines of priorities rather than listings of actions which might be helpful if resources were only available.

A centralized planning effort, which can take a broad overview of the many interests involved and which is least likely to be biased toward a particular program, may appear to be the judicious approach to comprehensive planning which is expected to coordinate various programs. But two serious problems develop if this inclination toward centralization is not restrained.

First, *it is unrealistic to expect a central staff to match the specialized knowledge of the various program staffs.* An attempt by a central staff to out-plan the program staffs often results in crude reports by the central staff which do little more than provide a limited education to those preparing the reports.

The second consideration is that *program staffs cannot be expected to properly implement a plan which they do not understand and appreciate.* Even if the central staff could understand the program details better than the program staff, the program staff would not believe it. Because involvement leads to commitment, agency understanding and appreciation of the plan depends upon participation in the preparation of the plan and in the compromises which are necessary between competing interests.

The preparation of the plan, therefore, requires much greater decentralization than has usually been the case. *The staffs responsible for executing various elements of the comprehensive plans should be given the responsibility for proposing the plans for their programs.* The responsibility of the central planning staff is to set the basic guidelines for such planning; review and direct adjustment of the parts of the plans to insure their mutual compatability; review the parts of plans for quality of planning technique and achievement of basic goals; and—if the plans are found wanting in these respects—to direct refinement, if possible, by the program staffs concerned but, if necessary, by the central staff.

For the very reasons that planning should use program staffs, major dependence upon consultant staffing should be avoided. On the other hand, outside consultants can provide an invaluable service in guiding the program, helping to avoid pitfalls, and in contributing highly specialized skills such as certain types of survey and statistical techniques.

The plan must not become the end product of the planning process—an end to the planning function. But a plan should be prepared and published as a tool of communication and a tool to clarify strategy. The plan should be revised and updated at regular intervals corresponding with the meeting of the legislature, or other significant periods in the basic decision making process to which the planning programs should relate. The published plan is needed to publicly articulate the goals and programs envisioned by the public agencies. It becomes a clear and firm direction for the program; describes the alternatives and explains the reasoning behind the selections from these alternatives; provides a reliable framework to which other programs can relate and, thereby, within which they can be coordinated; and focuses comment and criticism for a more effective and informed discussion of future adjustments. The attempt to develop such a public plan will reveal problems in the heretofore unwritten plans of chief executives and force a resolution of problems which otherwise might be allowed to grow to crisis proportions. A plan is necessary, but it should be viewed as a part of the long-range planning process.

LOCAL PLANNING

Although these comments have been concerned with state-level planning, they also apply to the local level. Local planning can usually involve more directly and fully the public it serves and can be less concerned with institutionalized government. Of course, the primary agencies involved are different, including the local boards of education and the city and county planning commissions. But the emphasis upon efficient research, meaningful goals, and a strategy of development is the same.

IN CONCLUSION

This paper suggests that consideration of goals could—and should—be the basis of decision making by discarding the platitudes frequently proposed as goals, and instead, discussing realistic alternative program objectives as related to defensible long-range objectives.

The most important contribution of initial state plans should be the establishment of a *planning process* as a management tool. The initial planning project should establish the communications necessary to coordinate the various programs of development; identify the outside sources of information which will provide the continuing input to strategy development; initiate the internal research to complete this input; and establish the process by which goals and programs are tested, evaluated and synthesized as a plan. The planning process should finally strengthen the democratic process, not only by making it more rational and better coordinated but also by making the analyses, goals and programs more public and therefore more responsive to the public.

CHAPTER 2

Planning for Changes in Education

KENNETH H. HANSEN*

Planning for educational changes must always take place in and among a number of cultural settings, including the social, the political, the economic, the psychological, and the philosophical. When one has been assigned a subject of such tremendous scope as this one, there is always a temptation to devote most of one's attention to the various settings as background for the change-planning that is necessary and desirable. Recognizing and resisting this temptation to discuss broad cultural issues becomes my first task.

Although planning for change must take place in a multiplicity of settings—each of which is of crucial importance—the fact should be recognized that *educational change as conducted by state and local authorities is itself fundamentally a form of institutional change.* Granted that education is a social function, and must take cognizance of societal changes of all sorts, nevertheless it is true that the educational enterprises are carried forth through the institutions of education. Educational institutions are not just some vague, amorphous "social force," but are actually educational organizations. Therefore, planning for educational change—although it involves changing people and society and outlooks—is essentially a matter of planning for organizational change.

CONDITIONS AFFECTING ORGANIZATIONAL CHANGE

Some of the conditions affecting organizational change are discussed briefly in the following paragraphs.

Social Interaction. Any organization—in this case the educational institution of any sort (whether it be an individual school system, a state department of education, or whatever)—must be recognized as a subpart (or subsystem) of a larger society (or social system). Hence it is inevitably subject to influence by changes already going on in the world outside the organization.[1] This is equally true whether the change is an *involuntary reaction* or a *planned response* to these outside forces.

* Director of Program Development, Education Commission of the States, Denver, Colorado. Coordinator, NEA Development Project (1965-67); Director, School of Education, Western State College of Colorado (1949-65). Participated in education surveys in Africa (1964, 1966, 1967) for the U. S. Department of State. Publications include: *Public Education in American Society; High School Teaching;* and *Philosophy for American Education.*

[1] See previous volumes prepared by the Eight-State Project, Designing Education for the Future: *Prospective Changes in Society by 1980* and *Implications for Education of Prospective Changes in Society.*

The recent history of changes in educational institutions and enterprises demonstrates clearly this interrelationship between the educational organization and the outside society. Current advances and emphases in mathematics and science, widespread popular support for vocational-technical education, the school's growing concern for the educationally and socially disadvantaged, and the sheer increase of numbers of children and youth and adults engaged in educational pursuits—all of these and many other developments illustrate how quickly and how deeply the educational organization finds itself reacting to changes in the society of which it is a part. Thus, one of the conditions affecting change in any organization—whether in education or in other enterprises of our society—is the inevitably dependent position of that organization as a subpart of a larger society.

The Strain of Change. Another condition affecting organizational change is the plain fact that no organization changes easily. The shock of changing organizational habits ranges in intensity from the merely annoying to the psychologically devastating. Such factors as jealousies and multi-loyalties, preoccupation with organizational charts and managerial problems, and, most of all, a lack of top-level climate hospitable to change—all make it difficult to plan for change, much less actually to bring it about.

The Primacy of People. We should not, however, make the common mistake of thinking in terms of the "psychological readiness" of an organization to change or not to change. To ascribe feelings or emotional reactions to organizations is a good example of the classic figure of speech known to all English teachers as the "pathetic fallacy," in which pathos or feeling is assigned to an inanimate object. Only people within an organization have psychological reactions. Thus, it is with the people and not the organization itself that we must concern ourselves.

Resistance and Readiness. Multiple forces are always operating either to facilitate or to inhibit change. Since the educational organization, as pointed out above, operates in a complex constellation of forces, it is always necessary to analyze the field of influences which these forces are exerting upon the organization and the people in it; hence there is a necessity for what certain psychologists and sociologists call "force-field analysis" as a first step in the strategy of planning for change.

Planning and Prodding. Some changes do not have to be planned; they just happen. But the ones that just happen are not likely to be particularly useful or effective; they may actually be harmful to the organization. So change not only has to be accepted but actually has to be consciously brought about. But a paradox emerges here: Although change has to be brought about—often by outside forces—*the most desirable change and the most effective change remains that which is self-generated within an organization, or by the people involved.* Change readiness, like reading readiness, is not something that one just waits for; it has to be encouraged and prodded into being. While we would like to think of the best change as that which is self-generated, it can by no means be expected to be spontaneous.

Therefore, even in *planning for change there must also be planning for how to bring about or implement the change.* The planners have to think almost in terms of mechanics or engineering: How do we get the change machine running and keep it going? That is why the change-planner puts so much emphasis on seemingly rather mechanical concepts such as "points of entry and leverage," "multiple entries," and "temporary systems". Each of these terms—which I shall discuss briefly at a later point—is a way of describing how to get the planning started, keep it going, and transmute it eventually into change itself.

Because of this necessity for judicious prodding of the educational organization or its subparts (in the terms of change-agentry, the "client system"), the change process sometimes gets bogged down when excessive reliance is placed on non-directive methodologies. Non-directiveness as a basic psychological theory can check excessive authoritarianism, encourage desirable creativity, and cause the personality to develop—*but non-directiveness can also result in non-direction for change.*

STRATEGIES, PROCEDURES, AND METHODOLOGIES

There are almost as many strategies, procedures, methodologies and approaches to planning for change as there are scholars in the field and practitioners of the art. No one of these "models," as they are often called, is without merit; yet no one of them can arrogate to itself all possible virtues. The particular pattern that I propose to discuss at this point is not, therefore, set forth as original or uniquely valuable. It is a hybrid pattern which has been recently employed in a planning study of a large-scale, voluntary-membership educational organization.[2] It will serve here primarily as a basis for tying together some later comments about the basic principles which underlie planning in all change-development systems.

This pattern is a very simple one, involving six sequential steps: (1) identification of problems; (2) diagnosis of the problem-situation; (3) clarification of the diagnostic findings; (4) search for solutions; (5) mobilizing for change; and (6) making the actual change decisions.

There is certainly nothing new or innovative or startling about such a procedure in planning; it is essentially a variant of the normal problem-solving methodologies. But it does serve to illustrate exactly what might be expected to happen when such a sequential approach is used.

IDENTIFICATION OF PROBLEMS

There really is not much point in doing any planning for change unless there is some necessity for change—some problem that needs

---

[2] I am indebted to my colleagues in the NEA Development Project for much of the explication of this pattern for planning.

solution. At this first step, it is very easy to get waylaid at the obvious symptomatic level, instead of examining the real basis of the problem, or even verifying its existence.

A problem is likely to exist in an educational organization when any one or a combination of these conditions is found:

Vague Purposes. When the purposes and policies of the organization are simply not clear or consistent, there is a problem. For example, if the states represented in this project knew exactly what they wanted to do in the provision for state support of education, say, or in the aims of professional education or of technical education, or in the objectives for coordination of systems of higher education, there would be no problem and hence no need for considering change. But if the educational aims and policies are lacking in explicitness or internal consistency, a problem does exist.

Operational Procedures Inconsistent with Policies. When stated policies, once developed and made explicit, are not matched by the operational procedures of the educational organization, a problem again exists. That is, when we intend to do one thing and find ourselves actually doing another—for whatever reason this inconsistency may be present—there is an organizational problem which needs clear identification. Why is it that our actions are not matching our stated policies or objectives?

Complacency. A problem also exists in the educational enterprise when the people within the organization see no possibility of operating differently, or have no vision of any other way to do things than the way they are now being done. Whenever an educational enterprise reaches the point at which there cannot be envisioned another mode of activity, it has an organizational problem.

Leaders Do Not Know How to Effect Change. The final condition which is indicative of the existence of a problem is found when those who operate the organization want to change, but simply do not know how to go about it. This is, perhaps, the point at which they are most likely to turn to some form of systematic educational planning.

DIAGNOSIS OF PROBLEMS

The second step in this approach to planning for change is that of analysis and interpretation of information available regarding the history, causes, and ramifications of identified problems. This step may seem to be taking us backward rather than forward; planning should always be forward looking. But until the educational problem situation is understood —until all the data of informational, statistical, and even psychological nature are fed into and utilized in the diagnostic process—intelligent planning is not possible. A special emphasis must be placed on finding out how people *feel* and what they *think* about the various aspects of the problem being studied. The favorite phrases of the professional change-agent—"Tell me how you feel about it," and "Why do you think you feel that way?"—may become pretty stilted; nevertheless, finding out how people feel about the problem is an important step in problem diagnosis which itself is a stage in the strategy of planning.

CLARIFICATION OF PROBLEMS

The process of clarifying the problem is a third step. Getting what is perhaps unfortunately known in the jargon of change-agentry as "feedback" to and from the "client-system" is another often cumbersome and ponderous step. But there must be recurring cycles of feedback *to* those involved in the problem-solving process and, in turn, feedback *from* these people. The comment—"I heard you say" may become artificial and tiresome as the way of trying to get at clarification of the problem issue, but a phrase remains a constant and open invitation to correction and clarification of data being received.

SEARCH FOR SOLUTIONS

Once the steps of identification, analysis and clarification of the educational problem (or problems) have been at least minimally accomplished, the more constructive phases of planning should begin. The heart of the matter is the search for solutions to the problem. This search involves, first of all, derivation of all possible tentative (alternative) solutions from the data available. It is almost inconceivable that there would be only one "right" solution to any educational problem. Neither is it likely that there will be a single sequence or pattern of solutions leading from one clearly-ordained step to the next. Rather, the possible solutions tend to formulate themselves into recurring sets of alternatives—the exact sequence depending on which way it seems most feasible to move. In other words, deriving possible solutions is less like linear (Skinnerian) programming than branching (Crowderian) programming. At any given point in deriving alternatives, further alternatives emerge which must be explored for their consequences.

The search for solutions, however, remains a dead-end process unless there is some way of trying out the proposed alternatives. Since problems which are being subjected to educational planning rarely have multiple solutions all of which can be tried out at once, solutions must of necessity be tested for *apparent* feasibility and *probable* consequences. At this stage, consequential analysis—analysis of the details of the probable consequences of a proposed solution—is an extremely necessary step.

One way to determine the probable consequences of a given solution to an educational problem is to seek out and check out related educational changes (innovations) which have been used, adopted, or adapted as alternatives to the solution which is being proposed. Thus, although the solution may not be amenable to being tried out on a large scale, some small-scale version of the solution may be subjected to scrutiny based on its actual innovative—if not yet widespread—use.

MOBILIZING FOR CHANGE

All of the planning steps suggested up to this point are essentially preliminary. In fact, all of them are useless unless the educational organization is actually able to mobilize for change. This step involves three substeps: setting goals, establishing priorities, and developing change strategies.

Goal-Setting. It might appear that goal-setting should be one of the very first steps in planning for change, rather than one that occurs at the time that mobilization for actual change is taking place. It may seem perfectly logical just to try to determine the basic principles first, find out where you are, find out where you want to go, and then develop ways to get there.

But in actuality, *goal-setting cannot be done in a vacuum.* Only after the situation has been analyzed, diagnosed, and clarified, and certain alternative solutions to the problem-situation have been suggested, can fully tangible goals be set. At this point, goals are of the utmost importance. For *if change is to have any real thrust, it must have both force and direction.* That is, the change must come out of the constellation of forces that necessitate or demand change, but it must be given the direction that only clear-cut goals can provide.

Establishing Priorities. Establishing priorities when the choice is clearly between "the good" (beneficial) and "the bad" (harmful) presents no real problem, but establishing priorities among various "good" alternatives is always difficult. It is when there is a necessary choice among valuable and worthwhile priorities that the planning process becomes most complex.

You may recall that in making plans for the establishment of his first academy, Benjamin Franklin remarked wistfully that it would be well if his students could be taught all things that were useful and all things that were ornamental. But, he continued, art is long and their time is short; therefore, it is proposed that they be taught those things which are *most* useful and *most* ornamental.

Some priorities can be established on more or less empirical bases, or on one subject at least to rational analysis. Such considerations as the likelihood of success for a given change, its viability, the chance that it will spark further changes, the cost-effectiveness ratio of a proposed change —all of these can be assessed with some degree of assurance that the results desired are at least *likely* to ensue.

But of greater importance in setting priorities is the question as to *what is most worthwhile* in terms of accepted goals. This—like all value judgments—is ultimately a subjective one. But "subjective" does not necessarily mean "personal." In education, these subjective judgments must be made by the general public, by legislative authorities, by state education authorities, by school boards, and by professional workers in education. Such choices—as with all value judgments—are susceptible to a very wide margin of error. Yet in the final analysis, the *importance of the proposed educational changes to the educational goals of society is a determination that must be made on a subjective basis.*

Developing Change Strategies. The actual strategies of mobilizing for change are topics largely within the purview of later papers in this series. Three or four very important strategies, however, might well be mentioned here.

The first is that of finding points of multiple entry. This simply means that in any strategy of change the possibility that there is more than one way to approach the solution to a given problem has to be accepted. A previous multi-state project in this area, Western States Small Schools Project, has rather conclusively demonstrated, for example, that if one is to improve the quality of education in the necessary existent small high schools, there have to be many different kinds of approaches to the problem-solution, rather than a single one. Those of us who worked on this project sought "entry" to the problem at many points: upgrading teachers, reorganizing class schedules, using new instructional materials, providing new grouping patterns, and encouraging interschool cooperation.

Once it has been agreed that there must be multiple entries into the problem-solution, the next step is that of finding the exact points of entry and leverage. In simple terms, where can we get a handhold or a toehold; where can we get a pry bar under, with leverage enough to get something moving? Finding these places to push or pry is not so much a matter of formal research or even rational analysis as it is a matter of thorough understanding of the situation and the people involved in the educational issue so that a testable hypothesis can be formed about where we can begin to get things started.

It is important, too, that the strategy of mobilizing for change must not wait until the ultimate can be accomplished. The concept of "temporary systems" is most useful here. Often all that we can bring about is a little bit or piece of the desired educational change; a new way of doing things—whether in finance, coordination, or administration—that will allow a system to be set up temporarily that, while far from being the ultimate desired, is better than what we now have.

CHANGE DECISIONS

The final step in this process of bringing about change through planning-for-change is that of making the decisions, including specifying the necessary actions, so that change actually is effected. Often the "decisions" *will require primarily the instilling of new outlooks,* rather than the immediate passing of new educational legislation or even the undertaking of new educational activities. *Change of attitude is clearly the key to effective educational change.* When the change-decisions are being made, there must always be a pragmatic approach and a pragmatic test: what difference will it make in the way things work? But even that question is not sufficient, for real pragmatism does not base its value judgments on whether or not a thing "works"; those making the judgments must ask and answer the question, "works to what end?" Even the "pragmatic" decision involves value judgments.

PLANNING: TENSIONS AND PARADOXES

Now that we have outlined one representative example of a planning system, let us look at some difficulties that will emerge with this or any other approach to planning for educational change. Such planning is becoming more and more a rational, scientific, systematized, and sequential process; but there remain some clearly unsolved problems, some inherent tensions and paradoxes.

THE INDIVIDUAL AND THE GROUP

In the writing about the practice of planning for educational change, a great deal of confusion regarding the necessity of group involvement in all aspects has been engendered. I comment on this problem with some trepidation, for I know that the generally accepted theory today is that the group process is a superior way of organizing for and conducting educational planning. Unfortunately, however, *preoccupation with the group process, and preoccupation with "process" itself, may limit or delay needed action.* It can be readily granted that most of what we know about how people function strongly supports the idea that *involvement of all persons concerned with a given change operation does lead to better acceptance and more self-identification with the process of change.* Nevertheless, "involvement" itself must not be accepted uncritically merely because it is a fine democratic ideal. *It must be seen as valuable only insofar as it provides a necessary way to get as much insight, knowledge, and creativity as possible from the group and to lessen the likelihood of the automatic rejection of new ideas which often occurs when the people involved are not really "involved."*

But *there are at least two points in planning for change at which much of the work must be done on a highly individual basis,* group process or no. One is *the point at which specified detailed information needs to be sought out, ordered, analyzed and reported.* There is more than a little truth to the statement that, with the exception of the King James version of the Bible, no good book was ever written by a committee. The same is generally true of analytical and diagnostic reporting. Some *one* person has to do this job.

The *second point* at which the group may be less helpful than the individual is *that of specific decision making.* While the group process and the group involvement are always desirable in setting forth basic principles and premises, in examining possible alternatives, and suggesting priorities, there comes a time when an administrative or executive decision has to be made. At this moment—whether we like it or not—the individual comes into his own. For while formulation of principle and enunciation of policy can be a group operation, decision making rests with the individual. Even ostensibly "group" decisions on educational matters—such as those made by a vote of a legislature, a state or local board of education, or the staff of a school system—are really composites of individual voices and wills. The "group" cannot decide; *individuals—whether operating indi-*

vidually or in concert—make the ultimate decisions. And decision making, unfortunately, is often a very lonely business.

ENDS AND MEANS

A major source of tension and paradox in educational planning is the tendency to mistake the nature of the interrelationship between ends and means. The first and most obvious mistake, of course, is to fail to distinguish between the two and to mistake one for the other. Ends and means are inextricably interrelated, but they are not identical.

They cannot be thought of as separate entities, yet they must not be confused. Very frequently in educational planning, *confusion between desirable means and the end being sought results in putting too much emphasis on the means by letting the means become the end.* Encouraging the very desirable and productive involvement of groups in the planning process because of the mystical or ineffable ideal that group work is in itself a "good thing" is a case in point. So also is assuming that equalization programs are good in themselves—or educational parks, or computerized instruction. They may be "goods", but primarily as means rather than ends.

But the second mistake often made in dealing with ends and means is that of separating them too far. There needs to be a distinction without a separation. Very rarely are ends uncontaminated by means, or means effective or valuable except in relation to ends. This erroneous separation of ends and means has been the downfall, for example, of most totalitarian governments. The seductive argument that you can achieve a good end by bad means—either in government or education—we know to be totally false.

The third confusion between ends and means is a little more subtle—even controversial. It finds its expression largely in the easy assumption that in American education we all agree on ends and find ourselves differing only on means. I would submit that quite the opposite is true. *We do not yet have, in any one state or group of states, or in the nation as a whole, any fundamental agreement about the ends of education.* Many of the *means,* however, we do agree upon. We may not agree, for example, on what "good learning" is; but we do tend to agree on at least some of the means by which learning may be encouraged: financial support, classrooms, teachers, and textbooks. Thus, we may come a lot closer to agreement on the means of education than we do on educational ends.

RESEARCH AND PHILOSOPHY

In educational planning, an unfortunate tension often arises between those who support the preeminence of research and those who support the preeminence of philosophy. Neither group, actually, lacks respect for the other; the problem really has more to do with starting point than it does with procedure. The research-oriented person is likely to say that we must of necessity first get all the facts—find out exactly where we are, and determine the baseline data and the outlines of the parameters within which we are operating—before we can even begin to plan for change or redirection of our efforts.

On the other hand, the philosophy-oriented person says that we surely must first of all determine our goals before we have any basis or touchstone for determining the meaning of either where we are or where we want to go, much less determining ways to get there.

I would submit that both the scientist and the philosopher who take these extreme positions may do us a disservice in planning for change. If, with the scientist, we wait until we have gathered, collected, analyzed, and interpreted all of the data, we will never get under way. If, with the philosopher, we wait until we have developed a comprehensive, universally agreed-upon philosophical framework, we are equally inhibited from action.

So we stand transfixed, baffled by the unmanageable scope of our task; or, if we move, we find ourselves spending all our efforts in trying to steer a course between Scylla and Charybdis (or, in the language of this area, we are caught between a rock and a hard place!).

Perhaps the enunciation of this paradox sounds defeatist, but my intent is just the opposite: I intend to convey a strong plea for optimism and activism in planning for educational change.

We should assemble and even create as much relevant data as we can and then analyze, interpret, and project from that. At the same time, we should set forth as clearly and convincingly as possible the educational and social goals we desire. But, *within a framework known to be incomplete,* both in terms of data and principle, I suggest that we move ahead —a step or a jump or a leap at a time—on the basis of as much data as is available, toward the goals as they can be most clearly seen. *Waiting for the ultimate, in data or goal-agreement, is a sure way to bog down in planning for educational change.* We must always compromise between the ultimate and the achievable.

THE ULTIMATE AND THE ACHIEVABLE

Anyone who would seem to advocate embarking on educational planning on the basis that I have just suggested is likely to be charged with encouraging an uncritical, hurried, and expediential approach. But what I actually am suggesting, though perhaps not wholly defensible, is really a little better than that. I am suggesting that our planning must move ahead on the basis of *consent, consensus,* and *compromise.*

For any change to be effective, or even for planning-for-change to be effective, the people involved—though they may not have all the data or agree on all the principles—must reach at least some minimal level of consent to the change. Saint Augustine, authoritarian moralist though he was, once commented that "No man does well against his will, even though that which he does be good." Even "good" educational change, carried out against the will of those involved, is not likely to bring about very good results.

There must be some consent, then, in trying to move toward the ultimate by way of the achievable, and this consent always requires a degree of consensus. The term "consensus" has unfortunately acquired, in these days, a slightly unsavory connotation; but it is still a good word! For consensus is a limited kind of operational agreement—not whole-hearted agreement—but enough to serve as a basis for moving ahead. Consensus serves as a kind of bridge between opposed positions—perhaps a temporary structure, neither sturdy nor durable, but one that does permit passage. Across the bridge—if we may risk stretching this metaphor a little further—persons and ideas and actions can pass back and forth between widely disparate positions, positions nevertheless held together by this thin linkage of a limited agreement for limited purposes.

Obviously, gaining even minimal consent and limited consensus involves some degree of compromise. Our Judeo-Christian ethic has long told us that compromise is another dirty word—or at best a faintly immoral concept. However, long-rang educational planning—like the daily operation of local and state systems of education, and even individual schools and individual classrooms—is ultimately based on a series of compromises most of which I submit to be moral—rather than immoral—because they allow us to achieve certain social goals; that is, to strengthen our educational system, to preserve our democracy, and to educate our children. But only when compromise is employed to lead us directly to the accomplishment of these socially valuable goals can it be said to have commendable moral qualities. Educational compromise which is timid, self-serving, or backward-looking continues to deserve our professional scorn; compromise which is imaginative, unselfish, and goal-oriented can serve as one of the most effective ways known to bring to fruition our ultimate educational purposes.

The examples of how we can work toward the ultimate only through the achievable are widely visible in educational practice familiar to all of us —both positive examples and negative examples.

I was visiting with a faculty not long ago in a school where a potentially exciting and innovative program in education had seemed to be inordinately slow in getting off the ground. Members of the faculty explained to me—with a kind of resigned cheerfulness—that they had decided to start out by "taking a year, if necessary" (and it had) to reach agreement on a philosophy of education. I was tempted to tell them that they doubtless could have saved a lot of time and advanced the cause of education in their district considerably if they had simply conceded at the outset that they probably would never reach real agreement on all aspects of the basic philosophical undergirding of their innovative program. "Agreements" about many concepts—such as the nature of good and evil, of the good society, of intellectual values, and of the human condition and the learning process—can never represent more than limited compromise and limited consensus. But within these limits we can go ahead— planning, organizing, administering and teaching.

Some states have delayed for years needed changes in teacher certification laws because the experts could not agree on what constitutes the "complete" education of teachers. Others have moved ahead—far ahead—in raising teacher certification standards on the basis of limited agreements and recognized compromises.

Some states have put off revision of the structure of educational finance because experts disagree on details of an equitable tax base or a workable distribution formula. Others have continued to plan and research—but have gone ahead with limited improvements.

I suggest—with considerable caution but nonetheless with conviction—that in educational planning we must ultimately move ahead on the basis of consent, consensus, and compromise, using multiple approaches and employing admittedly temporary systems if we ever hope to come up with any reasonably defensible design for education before the future has caught up with us.

*   *   *

SUPPLEMENTARY STATEMENT

J. CLARK DAVIS*

Before discussing some strategies and procedures relating to educational planning, let us consider briefly some of the characteristics of the society in which our planning will be operational.

Margaret Mead, in a recent article, made this analysis:

Americans as a people have always been optimistic. We have built a whole civilization on our belief in progress and our conviction that whoever came to this country could learn to accept change and adopt the way of life common to our citizens. But what grounds for optimism do we have now when we realize that all of us, even those Americans who have had the greatest advantages, wonder how we are going to cope with the changes that lie ahead?

. . . The acceleration of change is such that good communication between grandparents, parents, and children is becoming difficult, even among the well educated. In the scholarly fields, humanists trained in traditional forms are losing contact with scientists breaking old bounds. The few who pioneered a new technology find themselves separated from the many who are now turning the pioneering visions into practice.[1]

Against this backdrop of tremendously accelerated change, let us consider that man is often frustrated about his ability to produce—or to control—change, by his traditions, his environment and his own limitations.

The extent of worthwhile planning for any endeavor—whether it be education, research, buying a new home, or writing a book—is proportionate to man's ability to analyze the problem and make a sound decision. Obviously, however, the previous and present environment greatly influence man's decision making process. Family, religion, superiors, job, and associates limit his outlook toward change. Likewise, *history* is a restrictive

* *Associate Professor of Education, Department of School Administration, College of Education, University of Nevada;* Director of Small School Planning Laboratory, and of Research Coordinating Unit for Nevada; Member, Executive Panel, Far West Regional Laboratory.

[1] Redbook (Feb., 1967), pp. 46-50.

influence. Our society places great value on continuing what has proven successful in the past. Therefore, many times we are bound by limiting our planning to copying old patterns of change.

What, then, of the strategies and procedures for educational planning in the society we have briefly considered? No longer can we depend upon the pat answers for education utilized in the past. We must become involved in making history by structuring strategies and procedures that will prove successful in solving the problems of our rapidly changing society.

In this supplementary paper I would like to focus on two important components of planning and strategy which must be given adequate consideration. They are the processes of: (1) changing attitudes, and (2) communication.

CHANGING ATTITUDES

Desirable change cannot be shaped by outside forces alone; it must be internalized and activated by those directly affected by the change. Recognition of this principle is evident in the strategy of the eight-state project to involve in its planning and conferences those people who are capable of implementing educational change in their respective communities and states.

Many people are rather reluctant to become members of a planning group which may well change their own behavior; however, most will accept, to some degree, the concept of being "exposed to new ideas."

Most of us have developed a variety of attitudes as responses to our environment. These attitudes are usually developed over a long period of time. Occasionally, a traumatic experience can radically change a person's attitude, but in general, attitude change does not occur overnight. A person who has a negative attitude toward change will be less likely to change than one with no clearly defined attitude, or who tends to be favorable.

The following are a few important guidelines for attitude change in educational planning.

The leader must help, by his status, to provide prestige for his group. The exposure of group planning members to people of prestige and credibility with preferred attitudes is many times influential in bringing about change.

A strong sense of belonging should be developed within the group. Cohesiveness—the we-feeling—tends to support any influence or movement for change.

Desired changes in attitude should be relevant to the tasks to be performed by members of the team.

A clear cut reason for the need for change should be established so that the planning group will generate its own pressure for change.

Basically, attitudes are reinforced—or changed—by approval or acceptance by another person or by a particular group.

Dissemination of information relevant to the needs and plans for change is vital.

These guidelines offer a few ideas which have evolved from research relating to the changing of attitudes. Certainly, there are additional strategies which must be investigated to determine their usefulness for planning.

COMMUNICATION

Change may be delayed or prevented because many people who make the decisions for change in education lack exposure to—or fail to utilize—useful information. I have in mind the log jam of information derived from research that remains immobile because a communication system has not been devised, in most instances, to allow an adequate flow of information to educational decision makers.

DISSEMINATION OF INFORMATION

Over the years, the U. S. Office of Education has recognized the fact that information dissemination is imperative for change to occur. Great significance has been attached to the idea that a prime responsibility of the government sponsored Research and Development Centers is to relate (communicate) to as many as possible what they have found of value in their research. To relate means to write, speak and utilize means that will clearly communicate to all concerned—especially to the educational decision makers—the results of the researcher's work.

Recently another educational institution was created under the provisions of Title IV of the Elementary and Secondary Education Act of 1965. It, too, is the offspring of federal law and of U. S. Office of Education policy. I am referring to the Regional Laboratories for Educational Research and Development. According to the regulations and provisions of this title, regional laboratories are to accept the responsibility of communicating directly with school districts so that information of interest and value to educational decision makers reaches them. It is pertinent that a communication net be developed which will allow the education decision makers on the local level to make known the kind of information they need. Receiving information just for the sake of information is generally of little value.

A strategy of significance in local planning is the establishment of this communication net which permits a direct flow of communication to and from the established Research and Development Centers, the Regional Laboratories, and other resource centers.

What about our colleges and universities as communication components? Certainly there have been some lighthouses among colleges and universities but these have been in the minority. For decades, most colleges and universities have neglected to communicate their discoveries and pertinent information to educators on the local level. There does not appear to be much prospect of any significant change of attitude and behavior on their part in the near future. The establishment of Research and Development Centers as well as Regional Laboratories has finally provided a major breakthrough for research and development information to flow to people at the state and local school level who are interested in bringing about needed change in educational programs.

COMMUNICATION OF INFORMATION REGARDING ALTERNATIVE SOLUTIONS

The planning group should be motivated by a strong desire to learn about a variety of ways to solve problems (alternatives). Therefore, an efficient system to gain access to the relevant information must be developed. An important procedure in planning is the provision of extensive information about possible answers to problems rather than trying to influence certain decisions by communicating only selected information. An important criterion for the effective use of communication is not the educational change itself, but rather how the decision was made in view of exposure to all available information. Certainly there will be times when, after a thorough study of a particular problem, the data will indicate that certain changes would be undesirable, or even that no change is needed.

COMMUNICATION OF FACTUAL INFORMATION

There is a clear need, when developing a communication strategy for planning, to provide and utilize all pertinent information. It is possible to develop a communication network that disseminates words, sentences, and paragraphs with *no* utility because they distort or confuse the situation. It is imperative that all information be checked and double checked for validity. One wrong statement or misrepresentation of a concept can undermine months of effective planning.

This writer is reminded of an effective communication plan established by the Nevada Parent Teacher Association some years ago to support the adoption of a 2 percent sales tax. There is no doubt that the able support of this effective association heavily influenced the acceptance of the sales tax by the voters of the state. However, at present, a large number of people in the state are strongly opposed to the addition of another cent to the sales tax primarily because they were led, by a few misinformed communicators, to believe that the money derived from the initial tax would be earmarked for education instead of being placed in the general fund. This example illustrates the point that the strategy of communicating factual information germane to the problem at hand should have priority in planning.

COMMUNICATION EVALUATION

Each of us should develop a criterion for evaluating our communications. We should ask questions such as: (1) What does this mean? (Clarification of a statement is often helpful); (2) Who made the statement? (Identification of the source provides a way to authenticate the statement); (3) What is the communicator's authority? (Is he responsible? Is he knowledgeable? Where did he get his information?)

Utilizing the above should *provide a clearer understanding of the importance of valid communication to the receiver.*

COMMUNICATION FOLLOW UP

It is not sufficient just to "give the good word", but intensive effort must be made to ascertain that the listener—the receiver—is really hearing and understanding what is said.

A classic example is the following modern version of the story of John Paul Jones. His crew, fighting a tough naval battle, was virtually decimated; the ship was battered and torn; his marine gunnery sergeant was severely wounded. At this point, John Paul Jones shouted his historic "We have just begun to fight." The gunnery sergeant turned to another wounded mate and said, "There is always someone who never gets the word."

In communication planning, ways must be devised to sample the people involved or concerned to determine whether they are receiving and correctly interpreting the information.

IN SUMMARY

Education has been expected for decades to be one instrument in our society to bring about appropriate changes. Today, education has a greater opportunity than ever before to provide a sound basis for helping people to plan and prepare for change. We are faced with the necessity of capturing and controling the extensive knowledge that emerges through the efforts of man's research. We will not utilize this vast store of knowledge effectively if we continue to plan for education in the same way we have planned in the past.

Writers have developed new strategies for planning, but few of us have had the courage to read, listen, and then become involved in field testing the innovations that grew out of planning. We are usually content to drive down the same old road each day which always leads us, incidently, to the same old place.

I have offered in this paper a few guidelines concerning: (1) the strategy of changing attitudes, and (2) the strategy of planning for a viable communication network. These, though they are only a part of a whole, must be considered in the overall strategies and procedures in planning for education.

CHAPTER 3

Basic Strategies and Procedures in Effecting Change

ROBERT CHIN*

If I were to attempt to discuss everything implied by the title of this paper, I would find it necessary to cover much of the recent literature in the social and behavioral sciences. Since this project is concerned primarily with planning and effecting needed changes in education, and since the space allotted to this paper is necessarily limited, I will discuss the topic chiefly in the context of the needs of education; that is, of a system that comes under the scrutiny of more and more people who have the intention of "making changes"—or of helping to bring about change.

First of all, I shall limit myself to those changes which are planned— where there is a deliberate attempt to bring about change. Second, I shall classify and categorize programs and procedures which may have one or a few common elements but, in fact, differ widely in many other respects. Third, I shall look beyond the forms and procedures in the common sense terms ordinarily used, in favor of some genotypic characteristics.

How seriously should we take the word *strategy?* The use of this word can give aid and comfort to practitioners, since it implies a campaign— a battle to be won—with the leadership in one's hands. It also implies a rationale for maneuvers and tactics that fit with each other in some grand design to accomplish the objective. And, finally, the word "strategy" seems to some people to justify the use of stratagems and artifices—perhaps even wiles and deceptions—rather than a defensible plan or method for achieving an appropriate goal or goals.

In game theory and simulations or inter-system relations, the concept of strategy is found in the analysis of situations involving a conflict of interest between the two parties. A strategy is used by one party to gain a desired outcome when the behavior of the opponent is known—to prescribe a possible decision for each situation that may arise.

I suppose that the use of the concept strategy in the analysis of programs and procedures of changing is simultaneously a search for a viable and evocative concept as well as a search for an orientation which

* *Professor of Psychology* and *Research Associate of the Human Relations Center, Boston University.* Editor, *Journal of Social Issues* (1960-1965); Co-editor (with Warren G. Bennis and Kenneth D. Benne) of *The Planning of Change* (1961); Author of: "The Utility of Systems and Developmental Models for Practitioners," "Models and Ideas About Changing," "Human Relations and the Elementary School Principal," and "New Directions in Research on Adolescent Education and Citizenship."

characterizes programs and procedures for effecting change. I suspect that the very ambiguity of the concept has some appeal.

In the preliminary literature prepared for this report, I find the following suggestion about what to include in "strategy".

> *Strategies of Change* is interpreted as including, but not limited to, dissemination and provisions for utilization of pertinent information regarding all aspects of the proposed plan; ways of identifying and dealing with internal and external (environmental) constraints as well as facilitating influences; ways of identifying potential opposition, conflicts and tensions and of resolving them advantageously; appropriate means of helping individuals, organizations and agencies to effect needed change in their perspectives; and procedures (guidelines) for implementing proposed change.[1]

This paper, because of space limitations, can give adequate attention only to certain aspects of this broad area. In the first section, I shall examine the major groups of programs and procedures now in use in effecting planned change. Second, I shall categorize the strategies into three types: the empirical-rational, the normative-reeducative, and the power strategy of effecting change. Then, I shall tie together the formulations of strategies with the conditions and requirements of practitioners.

General strategies and procedures of effecting change can be classified in several ways: according to frequency of use, size and kind of effects intended to be achieved, by target populations and goals, or by some conceptual categorization of the strategy or approach. I shall undertake the last method. The target, goals, and other complexities are cross-sliced rather than emphasized.

This paper is purposely scanning programs, procedures and strategies of change in a variety of disciplines, fields and targets of change. The direct applicability of each of these strategies to the field of education will not be assessed here. Indeed, one of the purposes of this paper will be well served if some of the available procedures and approaches in other fields which probably have implications for education can be identified.

PROGRAMS OF UTILIZING KNOWLEDGE TO EFFECT CHANGE

I shall examine in later sections those strategies of deliberate changing which have some basis of "valid knowledge".[2] By valid knowledge, I mean the body of ideas emerging from a refined examination of experience and from the findings of theory and research in behavioral and social sciences. In short, valid knowledge to me means research findings, concepts and theories, ideologies and utopias, deductive systems of thought and heuristic systems of analysis—those refined ideational products used to guide men's actions. I confess to some feelings of uneasiness in such an inclusive proposition and would much rather define valid knowledge solely as that created by social and behavioral scientists, but I am aware of the fact that

[1] "Suggestions Relating to Topics for Third Area Conference on Strategies for Planning and Effecting Needed Changes in Education" (Denver, Colorado: Designing Education for the Future: An Eight-State Project, Oct. 1966).

[2] Edward G. Bennis, Kenneth D. Benne and Robert Chin. *The Planning of Change* (New York: Holt, Rinehart, Winston, Inc., 1961).

proven conclusions of fact and invariant relationships from the behavioral sciences are too sparse to use as a basis of strategies of action. Obviously, we have had strategies and rationales of action which have been proven "effective" prior to their examination by the behavioral or social sciences. In any event, I shall lean to researched knowledge, using as a criterion some sort of consensual validation, and some form of willingness to "test" the statements and propositions in order to make them more adequate. The essential quality of valid knowledge is that the holder "knows", as a "proven" relationship, some statements about the social and human processes that are being acted upon, or utilized in the process of change.

The experienced administrator or change agent may not have the same kind of theory or valid knowledge as the researcher. Insofar as the practitioner moves beyond the immediate "case" and makes sound generalizations, and with orderly formulations of the principles lying behind the empirical generalizations, he is probably creating, sharing, and using "valid knowledge."

Programs of utilization of knowledge have evolved and various summaries of these are available. These listings of programs give us some idea of how knowledge is put into use, or how it is introduced into the target organization for purposes of effecting change.

Bennis has surveyed the ways in which industrial organizations traditionally "apply" knowledge.[3]

Exposition and propagation, perhaps the most popular type of program, assumes that knowledge is power. It follows that the men who possess "Truth" will lead the world.

Elite corps programs grow from the realization that ideas by themselves do not constitute action and that a strategic role is a necessity for ideas to be implemented (e.g., through getting scientists into government as C. P. Snow suggests).

Human Relations training programs are similar to the elite corps idea in the attempt to translate behavioral science concepts in such ways that they take on personal referents for the men in power positions.

Staff programs provide a source of intelligence within the client system, as in the work of social anthropologists advising military governors after World War II. The strategy of the staff idea is to observe, analyze, and to plan rationally.[4]

Scholarly consultation, as defined by Zetterberg[5] includes exploratory inquiry, scholarly understanding, confrontation, discovery of solutions, and scientific advice to client.

Circulation of ideas to the elite builds on the simple idea of influencing change by getting to the people with power or influence.

Developmental research has to do with seeing whether an idea can be brought to an engineering stage. Unlike Zetterberg's scholarly confrontation,

3 Warren G. Bennis, "Theory and Method in Applying Behavioral Science to Planned Organizational Change," *Journal of Applied Behavioral Science*, Vol. I, No. 4 (1964), pp. 337-60.
4 Gunnar Myrdal, *Value in Social Theory* (New York, N. Y.: Harper and Row, Publishers, Inc., 1958), p. 29.
5 Hans L. Zetterberg, *Social Theory and Social Practice* (Bedminister, N. J.: Totowa Press, 1962).

it is directed toward a particular problem, not necessarily a client, and is concerned with implementation and program. (I would wager that little developmental research is being done today in the behavioral sciences.)

Action research, the term coined by Kurt Lewin, undertakes to solve a problem for a client. It is identical to applied research generally except that in action research the role of researcher and subject may change and reverse, the subjects becoming researchers and the researchers engaging in action steps.

Bennis goes on to point out the four types of biases which weaken the full impact of these programs: (1) *the rationalistic bias* or the assumption that knowledge about something leads automatically to intelligent action; (2) *the technocratic bias,* which ignores people and their concerns; (3) *the individualistic bias*—lack of appreciation of situations and structures; and (4) *the insight bias,* leading to no action and showing no manipulability of the situation.

A survey by Grenier, as reported in a forthcoming publication by L. B. Barnes[6] found seven approaches in frequent use in organizational change: (1) *the decree approach*—a person or group in authority orders a change to be made; (2) *the replacement approach*—a new person is brought in or at least someone is removed from his position; (3) *the structural approach*—reorganizing the required relationships in the organization, changing the roles and job definitions, the contacts and other organizational variables; (4) *the group decision approach*—members of the organization or group decide on a plan and elect to do it together; (5) *the data discussion approach*—where data about the organization and its functioning are brought to the members for review—in general, the feedback procedures; (6) *the group problem-solving approach*—where internal groups diagnose and collect relevant data about the problem; and (7) *the T-group approach* —where the emphasis is upon the nature of the relationship of the organizational and interpersonal environment, the quality of trust, openness, power balance, and other such factors.

There is a gradation of power and involvement in these typical approaches to change in organizations. In an earlier paper, I listed several different forms of deliberate changing which subsumed a variety of different programs. The most frequent approach is that of education, and the use of specialists in the technical content under change. The second form was identified as innovation and diffusions; the third was communication and influence patterns, then came money and inducement patterns, and finally collaborative planned change.

I suppose we could find more listings of forms of action to bring about change. Is there not some orderliness to the list—an orderliness which can show us some affinities among the variety of procedures? I shall be bold enough to pigeon-hole a large variety of action programs into simple classes of strategies.

---

6 Louis B. Barnes, "Research Methods in Organizational Change," in V. Vroom (ed) *Research in Organizations* (in press).

Types of Strategies

It is indeed a perilous task to cast into a mold the complex activities and orientations which are in use in prescribing actions in effecting change. But without venturing some such effort, we cannot progress beyond the surface phenomena.

My formulation is similar in some respect to those of several other writers. Garth Jones, in his classification of strategies and tactics of change, worked out a large-scale coding system for planned change programs which noted a large number of strategies and tactics.[7]

Equally relevant is the classification by Miles.[8] Miles saw the strategies as being (1) power oriented and solution oriented approaches; (2) relationship oriented and attitude change oriented; and (3) problem-solving and process-oriented approaches.

Richard Walton[9] proposed a slightly different way of classifying processes of planned change: that based on power, that on love and trust, and that of problem solving. He sees these three approaches as related to the question of scarcity of resources in conflict situations.

My own classification has been heavily influenced by my colleagues Kenneth D. Benne and Warren G. Bennis. Benne's pioneering work in educational change is well-known. He sees planned change in education as basically issues of practical judgments, with constant attention to the value issues in making these judgments with other people.[10] Bennis' work on organizational change has previously been cited. He identified the three variables that distinguished collaborative planned change as: valid knowledge, mutual goal-setting and the balancing of the distribution of power in the relationship between the change agent and changee.

For my own classification of change, I have attempted to cover a wider variety of programs for effecting change than presently covered in other formulations. For simplicity, I have classified these programs into three major groups or types.

The first major group of strategies, and probably the most frequent, includes those I call the *empirical-rational type*. The fundamental process is based on reason and utilitarianism. The change to be effected is demonstrated to be desirable and effective and then brought to the attention of the potential changee. Because the changee is reasonable or because he sees he can gain from using this new form of action, he adopts it. The second group of strategies is the *normative-reeducative type* with the funda-

---

[7] Garth Jones, "Planned Organizational Change, a set of working documents" (Center for Research in Public Organization, School of Public Administration, University of Southern California, Los Angeles, 1964).

[8] Matthew B. Miles, in "Symposium on Planned Change," Robert Chin, Matthew B. Miles, Donald Orto, and Elmer Van Egmond, chmn. (Boston, Mass.: New England Psychological Association, November, 1965).

[9] Richard Walton, "Two Strategies of Social Change and Their Dilemmas," *Journal of Applied Behavioral Science*, Vol. 1, No. 2 (1965), pp. 167-179.

[10] Kenneth D. Benne and Bozidar Muntyan, *Human Relations in Curriculum Change*. Illinois Secondary School Curriculum Program Bulletin No. 7 (1949).

mental process of attitude changing. The third group of strategies is based on *power in some form with compliance* as the fundamental process. For convenience and some sense of historical development, I have created a chart (see figure 1, p. 47) on "Strategies of Deliberate Changing."*

Throughout the discussion of strategies and procedures, we shall not differentiate these according to the size of the target of change. We shall assume there are similar procedures for the individual, small group, organization, community and culture. In addition, we are not attending to the differences between objects and materials being changed—curriculum, audio-visuals, new curriculum, PSSC, BSBS, New Math, team teaching— or to the differences between people and the relations aspects and social functioning processes. Because many of the changes in communities, in organizations or in groups start with the individual or the small membership groups of which he is a part, the general focus in this paper will tend to be on strategies starting from individual change. The target is the learner and his progress, of course. However, some of the factors—such as teachers, administrative procedures and the arrangements for conducting the teaching of children—are variables in their own right. The criterion variables, the immediate and long-range effects, and the intermediate and intervening factors need to be put into the perspective of the change objectives.

The issue of defining "change" is sidestepped in this paper.[11] As further conceptual and theoretical work progresses in the field of planned change, we shall have to examine how the different definitions of change relate to the strategies and procedures for effecting change.

These neglected issues, of size and type of target, objects and people, mode of entry, the immediate and long-range effects, and the very definition of change (and probably some others not yet foreseen) will have to be introduced into the analysis before we can confidently emerge with the practical strategies.

EMPIRICAL-RATIONAL APPROACHES

Many types of strategies for effecting change are included in the empirical-rational approach. The primary rationale lying behind most of these is the assumption that man is reasonable and will act in some rational calculus in changing a mode of behavior. *The primary task is seen as one of demonstrating through the best known method the validity of the new mode (the proposed changes) in terms of the increased benefits to be gained from adopting it.*

The first two approaches (at the right of the figure) should be mentioned briefly, even though they do not fit directly into this set of assumptions.

---

* The accompanying chart (figure 1, p. 47) on *Strategies of Deliberate Changing* lists the three types. It attempts to show family resemblances and to indicate a few of the persons whose names are closely identified with the procedure of deliberate changing. There are areas of overlap, pointing to the need for some combined categories.

11 For further discussion of this crucial theoretical problem, see Robert Chin, "Concepts of Change in Educational Programs," a paper prepared for the National Institute for the Study of Educational Change (Bloomington, Indiana, January, 1967).

Basic Knowledge. Basic knowledge is the strategy of conducting more basic research and theory-building—the preferred way of the traditional man of knowledge in the humanities and of the social critic.

Personnel. The advantages and disadvantages of the selection, replacement, and training of personnel as a strategy for effecting change are well enough known that we do not need to evaluate them. Presumably, however, these procedures have not been fully satisfactory in terms of the immediacy of needs of planned change. Indeed, it is precisely the failure of both these approaches to effecting change that has contributed to the crisis that is upon us.

Applied Research. Applied research has been a continuing and honored approach to changing. In product development in education, the curriculum materials in science instruction have had good "research" in their construction. In other areas, mixed consequences have followed when a researched product is made available. When we assess the situation to find the reasons why these researches have not been effective, the answer seems to be that the barriers lie both in the design of the studies and in the potential users of the findings. The recent spurt of concern over evaluation research may result in disappointment also, since, I would point out, much of the work in it is not focused to communicate to a relevant audience or the consumer. Evaluation research conducted in the spirit of justifying the program does not help guide the practitioner whose concerns have not been taken into account.[12]

Linking Systems. The linking of research and development with innovation-diffusion has been steadily gaining way in the field of education: research and development centers, inter-agency centers and consortia, and development institutes. *The strategy of change here includes first of all a well-researched innovation that is palatable and feasible to install.* Attention in this strategy is directed to the question as to whether the innovation will bring about a desired result, and what can be accomplished if it is given a trial. The question as to *how* to get a fair trial and *how* to install an innovation is not ordinarily built into the strategy. The rational assumption is that if it works, consumers will, if it is properly disseminated, adopt it. In the Research and Development formulations of Miles[13] and Wiles[14], Lippitt and Jung[15], Benne and Havelock[16], they have analyzed the necessary roles and processes for innovation and diffusion. More recently, D. Clark and E. Guba formulated very specific processes related to and necessary for change in education following upon research. For them, the necessary processes are: *development,* including invention and design; *diffusion,*

12 Robert Chin, "Research Approaches to the Problem of Civic Training," Ch. 9 in Franklin Patterson (ed) *The Adolescent Citizen* (Glencoe, Ill.: Free Press of Glencoe, Inc., 1960).

13 Matthew B. Miles, "Some Propositions in Research Utilization in Education," March, 1965 (in press).

14 Kenneth Wiles (unpublished paper for seminar on Strategies for Curriculum Change).

15 Charles Jung and Ronald Lippitt, "Utilization of Scientific Knowledge for Change in Education" (Center for Research on Utilization of Scientific Knowledge, Institute for Social Research, University of Michigan, 1965).

16 Ronald Havelock and Kenneth D. Benne, "An Exploratory Study of Knowledge Utilization" (COPED working paper, Center for Research on Utilization of Scientific Knowledge, Institute for Social Research, University of Michigan, 1965).

including dissemination and demonstration; *adoption,* including trial, installation and institutionalization.[17] Clark's earnest conviction is best summed by his statement: "In a sense, the educational research community will be the educational community, and the route to educational progress will self-evidently be research and development."[18]

The approach of Benne and cohorts is concerned with the inter-system relationship, with the role requirements and the role conflicts that ensue from linking the processes together. Their general orientation is salutary in designing arrangements since the realistic role conflicts are confronted. These conflicts are important because they illuminate the issues at stake.

The behavioral science theories and concepts underlying these discussions come from two traditions: studies of cultural diffusion of traits initiated by F. Boas, and carried on by E. Rogers, and studies of mass influence patterns in communications by Lasswell, Lazarsfeld, and Katz. Both traditions of study, I want to point out, assumed a *relatively passive recipient of an input!* The actions are seen from the point of view of the observer of the process. Bauer has pointed out that we have exaggerated the effectiveness of these mass persuasions in that we confused the total number of people persuaded with the proportion of the audience. The large number does not mean a large proportion of the audience successfully persuaded, but rather the product of a small percentage of a large number in the audience.[19]

Expert Consultants. These specialist roles are closely allied to another class of procedures and strategies for changing. The changee, or client system, engages experts or technical consultants to serve special tasks because of their special knowledge about a new area. Some behavioral scientists have insisted that we already have more knowledge than is being applied, and that we need a retrieval system and a re-analysis of accumulated data, in the forms of secondary analysis, for direct application to the confronting problems of action. The expert is used both in processing and in squeezing data for their implications.

It is interesting to note that the role of the expert is becoming embroiled in the discussion of whether or not behavioral science research should contribute *concepts* to "sensitize" administrators to new perspectives and new orientations, or should be a *body* of substantial findings. Indeed, in the challenging article by Jean Hills,[20] the question is raised as to how applied behavioral science perpetuates ideology and the *status quo* because of the blinders imposed by being "problem centered" and as to what is meant by defining "a problem".

Among the emerging new experts is the systems-engineer who views

[17] David Clark and Egon Guba, "An Examination of Potential Change Roles in Education" (Seminar on Innovation in Planning School Curricula, October, 1965).

[18] David Clark, "Educational Research and Development: The Next Decade," Ch. 10 in *Implications for Education of Prospective Changes in Society* (Denver, Colo.: Designing Education for the Future: An Eight-State Project, 1967).

[19] Raymond Bauer, "The Obstinate Audience: The Influence Process from the Point of View of Social Communication," *American Psychologist,* Vol. XIX, No. 5 (May, 1964).

[20] Jean Hills, "Social Science, Ideology and the Professors of Educational Administration," Education Adminstration Quarterly, Vol. I, No. 3 (Autumn, 1965), pp. 23-40.

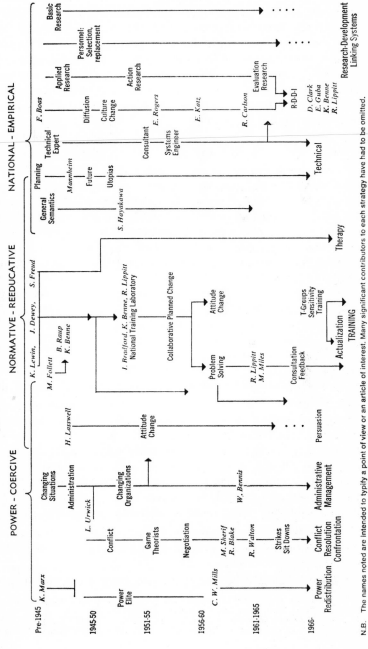

Figure 1: *Strategies of Deliberate Changing*

N.B. The names noted are intended to typify a point of view or an article of interest. Many significant contributors to each strategy have had to be omitted.

the problem of change and changing as a wide-angled problem, one in which *all* the input and output features and components of a large-scale system are considered. It is foreseeable that with the onset of modern high-speed high-capacity computers, and the growth of substantial theory and hypotheses about how parts of the educational system operate, we shall find more and more applications for the systems-operations research. In fact, it is precisely the fact that these orientations, including their mathematical and quasi-mathematical quality, can handle data about mass cohorts of students in the educational system that make them adaptable to planning for massive poverty programs, educationally deprived programs, and other such large and multi-phased operations. I see no incompatability between the ideology of the individuality of the student and the use of the computer in strategizing the operations of the total systems.

Prophesying a Future. It may seem odd to include under rational-empirical strategies the use of prophecy and utopias as strategies of changing. *Inventing and designing the future by extrapolating from the present is to envision the direction of the future and provide a sense of goals to the present. If the future is convincing and rational, then action leading toward it, effecting change to make it come about, also seems reasonable.* The title for the Eight-State Project, "Designing Education for the Future" and the papers of the three conferences show the practical application of the strategy of prospecting the future. At the same time, it is interesting and somewhat disheartening to note the relative absence of out-and-out ideology, the rousing and beckoning normative statements of what ought to be, and the visions and utopias—whether these are based on psychology and on personality theory, or on political or philosophical assumptions. *The absence of ideology in current society has led to the presentation of future directions as "technical" questions, not as matters of values and preferences.*

Perceptual and Conceptual Reorganization. Programs and strategies for "rectifying" the names of things for semantic clarifications have been seen as not only therapeutic but also as bringing about change of the system. People will see more correctly and communicate more adequately because of the common language and common meaning of symbols. The general semantics of Korzybski and Hayakawa can be taken as programs and strategies, in that strong relational elements are present in the mode of bringing about change.

NORMATIVE-REEDUCATIVE APPROACHES TO EFFECTING CHANGE

The normative-reeducative approaches to effecting change use *direct interventions,* based on a consciously-worked out theory of change and changing applied to individual behavior, in small groups, organizations and communities. The theory of changing is crude but is probably as explicitly stated as possible at the present state of our knowledge in planned change.[21, 22]

---

[21] Kenneth D. Benne and Bozidar Muntyan, *op. cit.*
[22] Warren G. Bennis, Kenneth D. Benne, and Robert Chin, *op. cit.*

The historical roots of this approach lie in Freud, Dewey, Lewin and Follett of the reconstructionist and transformationist mood, as our chart indicates. Out of the concepts and theories of these theorists have been constructed technologies and strategies for guiding the sequences of actions. The "workshop movement", "action research", "problem-solving" stages, T-group, sensitivity training, and human relations training are some well-known technologies as Bennis has pointed out.[23] These modes of effecting the change conceptualized and made explicit the diagnostic processes in relation to the client system (Lippitt).[24]

Some of the common elements that identify this cluster of methods are as follows: (1) an emphasis on the client system, the way the client sees himself and his problem; (2) the problem of change is considered to be not necessarily an absence of technical information among the members of the client system, but rather the nature of the attitudes, values, human skills and relationships of the people in the system that act to facilitate or resist change; (3) the change agent and the client system can mutually intervene by making use of learning processes which are based on experience (the here-and-now experiences provide a basis for inducing learning); and (4) some fundamental re-examinations of the concepts of motivation, morale, and productivity in small groups and organizations are necessary among the client system and changees.

These approaches center on the principle that behavior changing, or "people technology", is just as necessary as "thing technology". Put in this bald fashion, *it is obvious that the problem of values and value choices is pivotal.* In acknowledging the values of the client system, it is hoped to avoid the charges and accusations of manipulations from without.

The sub-sets of approaches to changing in the context of re-education are many, but two stand out as nodes: One set is oriented toward improving the problem-solving processes of the client; the other aims at examining the relevancy of attitude changes of the person or client system.

Problem-Solving Approaches. These focus on such forms as procedures of self-study, increasing data flow within an organization, examination of the relationship of the system to its external environment, developing feedback mechanisms, and forming consultative activities for multi-faceted and multi-level problem solving in an organization. *Change is defined as activating forces within the system to alter the system.* Change is altering the methodological processes of the system, independent of the technical "content" of the problem to be solved or the innovation to be adopted. In other words, effecting change is inculcating a posture of "changingness" —a state of readiness to change, to venture and take risks. The quality of problem-solving is the ability to use ways of scanning and detecting problems, diagnosing the relevant factors and moving on to solutions with a collaborative orientation. A very direct statement of these problem-

[23] Warren Bennis, *Changing Organizations* (New York: McGraw Hill Book Co., 1966).
[24] Ronald Lippitt, Jeanne Watson, and Bruce Westley, *The Dynamics of Planned Change* (New York: Harcourt Brace and Company, 1958).

solving attributes for a problem-solving approach is contained in a chapter by Miles.[25]

Attitudes and Feelings Approaches. The procedures of scrutiny and self-confrontation of how one's own behavior impinges upon others and is experienced by these other people, focuses upon the relevancy of one's own behavior for the problem of change. Sensitivity of these factors can be learned in constructed situations where experiences can be examined. The T-group, laboratories in human relations, in organizational change, in conflict management, in personal growth, and other groups for specific occupations and work areas—such as church-related labs, education labs, higher education labs, executives labs, managers labs, etc.—are the institutions embodying these strategies.[26, 27]

Both the problem-solving approach and the attitude and human relations approach do make use of procedures of establishing "temporary systems," but not necessarily exclusively in constructed conditions.[28] Both emphasize the collaborative orientation in defining and selecting goals of change. Most importantly, both try to achieve a consistency between the *means* of effecting change and the *ends* of change itself. If the aim is to achieve openness, or problem-solving orientations, then the relationships between the change-agent and client ought not to negate these, but indeed, to role model the very ends. The normative direction seems to be in building trust between persons, achieving equal status and mutual openness in feelings and empathy coupled with the willingness to confront data and work toward procedures for problem-solving. The National Training Laboratory (NTL Institute for Applied Behavioral Science) of the NEA has spearheaded the development of experience based training.

In recent times, *there has emerged an emphasis on unshackling the creativity of the persons in organizations in such a way that innovation becomes possible.* Ways are found for creative individuals to cope with the interpersonal dynamics and to *proact* as well as *react* to the environmental forces of the system. In contrast to the approaches of the innovation-diffusion, and especially to the power approaches, the re-educative assumption here is that the growth potential of the system's members must be unleashed. Implanting of change from the outside is not necessary.

The source of influence seems to lie in the psychological processes of identification with the change agent and of internalization of the "ideal" mode of behaving. Internalization is bolstered through the formation of group norms and supports in the face-to-face contexts.

The re-educative approaches to changing through collaborative planned change are becoming more widely used in recent times. Conceptualization

[25] Matthew B. Miles, "Planned Change and Organizational Health" in *Change Processes in the Public Schools* (Eugene, Ore.: Center for the Advanced Study of Educational Administration, 1965).
[26] Leland Bradford, Jack Gibb, and Kenneth D. Benne, *T-Group Theory and Laboratory Method* (New York: John Wiley and Sons, Inc., 1963).
[27] Edgar Schein and Warren G. Bennis, *Personal and Organizational Change Through Group Methods* (New York: John Wiley and Sons, Inc., 1965).
[28] Matthew B. Miles, "On Temporary Systems" in Matthew B. Miles (ed) *Innovations in Education* (New York, Bureau of Publications, Teachers College, Columbia University, 1964), pp. 437-492.

Procedures in Effecting Change 51

is continuously going on in this field so that self-renewing inputs keep alive developments in methods and technologies.

POWER APPROACHES TO EFFECTING CHANGE

Bringing about change through the exercise of power is probably more frequent than acknowledged. Often, there are strong attitudinal feelings against the use of power strategies. In the most general of terms, *the imposition of power alters the conditions within which other people act by limiting the alternatives or by shaping the consequences of their acts, or by directly influencing and controlling actions. The basic process for the changee is compliance and submission.* The chart shows a few of the strands to be discussed here.

Ways of effecting change through power operations can be grouped into four types: situational alterations, command structure operations, power redistribution, and conflicts over the allocation of resources.

Situational Alterations. Power can be used to alter the situation in which others act through the control over job and role requirements, inducements and punishments, and aspects of the physical ecology. More recently, massive change in education is envisioned through the use of external grants of money to bring about changes in specific programs in education. Among traditional organizational and administration theorists and practitioners, there has been a search for the leadership skills thought necessary to bring about the proper alterations in structure as a means of effecting change. However, the motivational assumption of this view of behavior in an organization has been criticized by McGregor in his Theory Y. For him, the challenge is that the conventional theory of control and constraints over organizational behavior may give place to a theory of management by objectives. "The essential task of management is to arrange organizational conditions and methods of operations so that people can achieve their own goals best by directing their own efforts toward organizational objectives."[29]

Command Structure Operations. Organizations and systems have authority and command structures for getting things done. In addition, there may be a shadow system of informal power and an informal system. The strategy question is how to identify it and how to tap it. Concepts of the power elite and power structure and key persons in the influence patterns have been advanced as a favored strategy in effecting change. The power structure is usually seen as the conserving part of the system. As Klein points out, the resistor role in change situations has the positive function of testing and evaluating the proposed change in terms of the accepted values of the system.[30]

---

[29] Douglas McGregor, "The Human Side of Enterprise," *The Management Review,* 46 No. 11 (1957), pp. 22-28. Also reprinted in W. G. Bennis, Kenneth D. Benne and Robert Chin, *The Planning of Change, op. cit.*

[30] Donald C. Klein, *Dynamics of Resistance to Change: The Defender Role* (Boston University Human Relations Center, 1966).

Power Redistribution. When put into use, power itself changes through the redistribution of old power and creation of new balances. In the dynamics of changing, there is a readjustment of the power balance between the change agent and the client system so that dependency does not become excessive. One interesting speculation in this regard involves the question as to whether or not any change can be effected without a minimum amount of power on the part of the client system over its own fate. *High concentration of power in the hands of the change agent does not seem to lead to effective change.*

Conflicts Over the Allocation of Resources. Power operates in, and is a resultant of, situations where there is conflict over the differential allocation of limited resources (e.g., money, prestige or power). There are sub-strategies of building a power base and manipulating the conditions so as to obtain a maximum amount of the scarce resources. The game theorists, diplomatic strategists and students of revolution focus only on a few patterns of resolution between the conflicting parties: dominance-submission, compromise, and only occasionally upon the establishment of a problem-solving mood. The usual forms of action are bargaining, threatening, negotiating, and maneuvering to attain the objectives desired. In education, we increasingly see this strategy being used in teacher strikes, in the newly founded power bases of minority groups, of the poor, and of various other groups. In higher education, we may be witnessing the coalescing of students in pressure groups, ready and able to bargain for their rights.

This strategy of power utilization involves conflict. The goal of the redistribution of power, for many strategists of the powerless, is to achieve a better balance so that collaboration can be possible and fruitful. Yet, it is in this form of power strategy that ambivalence to power and conflict is more prevalent than in any other. For, if the parties involved think of conflict as bad and to be avoided, then participation in these power negotiations will be distasteful.

The dynamics of conflict in an inter-system power operation lead to processes of overstating one's objectives, of creating and maintaining an ambiguity about one's intention and desires, or of increasing uncertainty of others—the very opposite of the qualities usually held as necessary for harmonious working relationships.

Power strategies are present within the boundaries of the school system and in its relations with the community it serves. As more groups develop strong concerns about the schools, and as the decision making processes become more remote from face-to-face dealings, there are bound to be more power operations in effecting change. Indeed, major changes in the schools probably always involve *some* power operations. Innovations of any significance which alter the forces of the on-going system will also alter the power balance, and will inevitably require the exercise of some degree of power. The maintaining of power operations over the allocation of scarce resources will have to continue. *The concurrent strategy of converting these types of conflicts into problem-solving ones is one phase under way in educational circles.*

In any case, the operation of power strategies for effecting change has been buried under a pseudo-democratic norm. If power is influence upon others, then we shall have to face its conditions of use and abuse.

Some Important Implications

It is quite obvious that deriving statements about basic strategies appropriate to all fields is an impossible task. However, I believe there are some guidelines or criteria for the selection of strategies by the change agents. The best we can do is to clarify the bases of our selection.

Some Guidelines

1. First of all, it is apparent that the *different procedures for effecting change are geared for special users.* Each of us—researchers, academicians, administrators in state agencies, school people—has different needs for different ways to bring about changes as we see them.

"Powerless" agents, parents, teachers and minority groups may first see the need for a better power distribution before there can be collaboration. State agencies may primarily see the need for improvement in organizational administrative and command features of education. University and research people push a Research and Development (R & D) model of effecting change. A few voices are also raised for the releasing of the creativity and actualization tendencies in students, teachers, and administrators for effecting needed changes through re-educative strategies.

2. *The preference for a particular strategy for effecting change seems to lie in our various biases in seeing the educational system as "people processes," technical processes, or processes centered around things and materials.* While all three orientations have to be involved in any full strategy of changing, there are different views as to what is the primary or focal issue. These dictate the strategy while relegating the others to the manipulating means to achieve the main issue, or to background questions to be handled once the "focal" question is resolved. The emphases on one or the other aspect do seem to reflect major traditions and referent groups in educational theory and approach.

3. *The selection of an approach also depends upon some assumptions about the nature of the problem, of change and of changing.* If a gap of knowledge is diagnosed as the major problem, the tendency is to remedy that directly. On the other hand, if a lack of creativeness is sensed, then procedures designed to encourage innovativeness are utilized.

4. *The analyses of strategies of changing are more or less infused with the analyses of the value judgments.* These value issues tend, however, to become embedded into "technical" concepts in the professional field so that the implications of the assumptions are not seen. For example,

health, the educated person, adjustment, culturally deprived, and delinquent are seemingly technical concepts in a professional field, but in fact bury out of sight a host of value judgments. Because strategies depend upon the diagnoses and concepts, these terms have precluded full examination of the possible alternative constructions of the problem and of their solution.

The fact that change and changing necessarily involve differences in valuing, cannot be avoided. *Solutions must incorporate a choice of values: judgments of what we ought to do, as well as judgments of fact and judgment of effective means to employ.* These requirements for a democratic society have been conceptualized in the past and will have to be incorporated in the present opportunities.[31]

Conceptualizing the value issues must accompany the analyses of strategies and procedures. There is no necessity to arbitrarily rule out strategies in current use without detailed examination of the conditions under which they have proven useful.

Of greater import is the possible presence of unrecognized conflict of values between the change agent and the systems undergoing change. *It is an all too human error to forget that the client has values,* and instead to explain away his resistance by attributing to him all manner of psychological mechanisms.

5. *A serious question in the field of planned change is the need for more theorization.* I do not think that we shall be able to make advances in understanding techniques for effecting change unless we continuously conceptualize the issues. As an illustration of this point, let us take the seemingly innocent question of what is meant by "change". In a previous paper, I advanced the notion that we cannot call any noticeable difference "change". From a "systems" point of view, we can list at least five levels of "change": (1) simple substitution of one element for another; (2) alteration of one part without major alteration in function or activity; (3) oscillation of an element which homeostatically will be dampened out or reversed; (4) structural change; and (5) change in value orientation.[32] These differentiations in defining the level of change follow the "systems" theory; "structural change" is equivalent to "step-jump" in the parameters of a system.

Other conceptual schemes for definitions of change can also be used to elevate the primitive quality of the concept of change. Some of these are: the developmental and maturational approach to change and changing, the problem-solving and methodological processes and other models of a functioning system. All of these fit what I call definitions of change involving alterations in the changee or client system. The other two major classes of definitions of change involve the addition of some identifiable element to the changee system (as in the adoption of curriculum materials)

[31] Bruce Raup, Kenneth D. Benne, B. O. Smith and G. E. Axtelle, "The Discipline of Practical Judgment in a Democratic Society," 28th *Yearbook of the National Society of College Teachers of Education* (Chicago: University of Chicago Press, 1943).

[32] Robert Chin, "Models and Ideas About Changing" (Lincoln, Nebraska: University Extension Division of the University of Nebraska, 1963).

or the phenomenologically constructed change between the change agent and the changee.[33, 34]

The style for bringing about changes will also vary. For example, the systems approach to defining change will require such processes as that of Lewin: the three stages of changing—unfreezing, changing and refreezing. When the internal forces of a system reach a critical point of growth, there are tipping points or step jumps. By contrast, the developmental theorists see maturation as "natural", resulting in the strategy of removing the barriers and inhibitive forces blocking actualization of the potentials or achieving a higher level of functioning.

In the definitions centering on problem-solving and methodological processes, consistency in achieving these ends may be more compelling. Thus, there are determinants of the strategies and procedures which arise out of the nature of the definition of change.

The most frequent definition of change is that some material, medium or curriculum, or teaching procedure or style is to be added. Programs of support in academic institutions and research centers have focused around audiovisual, programmed instruction, science and mathematics curriculum units, social studies and so forth. This definition pays relatively little attention to the internal characteristics of the client system.

The relational models of re-education have a close affinity to the definition of change which is existentially built between the change agent and the client system.

REQUIREMENTS FOR A THEORY OF CHANGING

Words can miscommunicate. In a sense, the discussion of a strategy for effecting change is the same as a theory of changing. A theory of changing is oriented to the needs of the practitioner. *A substantively complete theory would include the goals, value judgments, and the means of attaining these desired ends.* I have also argued that in collaborative planned change, there are both technical and value requirements. The requirements for a theory of changing or strategy of effecting change can be specified, though the theory or strategy itself is not in sight. If we can agree what it must contain, then perhaps we can see how to build it. Let me cite Bennis' illustrations of the requirements for collaborative planned change that I have outlined previously:

1. It must provide levers or handles for influencing the direction, tempo, and quality of change and improvement, i.e., variables that are accessible to control. Variables which "explain" and are causal may be the least alterable; hence, a science of "causes" may not be adequate for a theory of changing. For example, we do know that urbanization causes population explosion, but the applied demographer can do little to reduce the birth rate by manipulating the degree of urbanization. Demographers can, however, control contraceptive materials

---

33 Robert Chin, *op. cit.* in footnote #11.
34 For a further conceptualization of these issues, there are two papers of relevance: Kenneth Boulding, "Expecting the Unexpected: The Uncertain Future of Knowledge and Technology," in *Prospective Changes in Society by 1980* (Denver, Colorado: Designing Education for the Future: an Eight-State Project, July 1966), and C. H. Waddington, "Progressive Self Stabilizing Systems in Biology and Social Affairs," *Ekistics,* Vol. XXII, No. 133 (Dec. 1966), pp. 402-405.

and information. So, most of all, a theory of changing must include manipulable variables.

2. It must take into account the roles of a change-agent and a client-system, each with its own system of values, perceptions, and rights of self-determination; e.g., in the preceding example, it may be that the use of contraceptives in a Catholic country will render this independent variable virtually useless because it conflicts with the client-system's values. In addition to manipulability, then, the variable must not violate the client-system's values.

3. It must take into account the cost of usage. Prohibitive costs may again rule out a highly controllable and value-resonant variable.

4. It must provide a reliable basis of diagnosing the strength and weakness of the conditions facing the client-system.

5. It must account for phases of intervention so that the change-agent can develop estimates for termination of his relationship with the client-system, "self-take-off" points, etc.

6. It must be able to be communicated with a minimum of distortion to the client-system without destroying its effectiveness.

7. It must be able to assume its own appropriateness for different client-systems.[35]

These requirements for a theory of changing are premised upon a role relationship between the man of knowledge or the change agent and the client system. The fact that we have no approximations of such formulations does not prevent us from specifying what we might go after.

CONCLUDING COMMENTS

We are in a primitive stage in creating a body of knowledge for effecting change that is relevant to the existing conditions and problems, that includes the processes for arriving at mutually constructed goals, that has spelled-out methods and procedures, and that advances the problem towards these directions.

The sources of these procedures for innovations are in contrapuntal balance among the practitioners, the crystallizers of theory of practice and the academicians and scholars. As massive needs become more apparent, and as funds for innovative programs become available, attention is focused increasingly on a programmed model of the idea applied to invention and then to practice.

To reiterate a truism at this point may only provoke dismay. Leaders in educational agencies, in state agencies in consortia, and in universities charged with the mission of effecting educational change, will need to consider the multiple strategies I have identified in this paper. Does this truism pose any difficulties? I think so. Some of the strategies are not compatible. For example, the conflict over resources in the power model leads to inter-group and inter-system consequences which are not compatible with the model of re-education and attitude-change, of achieving openness, trustworthiness, and readiness to change. Given these incompatabilities and given the nature of multi-faceted change, it seems impossible for one person to be so flexibly oriented. He could easily be

[35] Warren G. Bennis, *op. cit.* (footnote 23), p. 100.

misunderstood. It may be necessary to think of having a change-agent team with special skills in a variety of these procedures and skills. At present, there seems to be a segregation of skills and models of strategy in separate organizations. We need a full and rounded consulting organization to help in the processes of change. The design of such teams and their relations with each other and with the client is the most urgent program ahead. Let me be clear. I do not think that evaluation research will resolve this question. I assume that the blending of these approaches in concrete situations will be necessary. Indeed, since the input from the environment of the educational system is becoming so insistent, I suspect that there is justification for a rounded consultation team—from the state, from universities or from some other appropriate organization—to maintain the self-renewing properties of the school system.

* * *

SUPPLEMENTARY STATEMENT

STEPHEN P. HENCLEY*

Chin has suggested three general change strategies that appear to have relevance in social institutions of all kinds, including educational institutions: (1) the empirical-rational types; based on reason and utilitarianism; (2) the normative-reeducative types; based on attitude change; and (3) the power types, based on compliance. The purpose of this paper is to indicate the relevance of each of these change strategies to the milieu of education, and to propose appropriate recommendations for promoting educational change in local, state, regional and national settings.

EMPIRICAL-RATIONAL STRATEGIES

Empirical-rational strategies appear oriented primarily toward strengthening the capability and effectiveness of the educational enterprise in mounting the basic processes underlying educational change—that is, research, development, diffusion and adoption. Attention to these basic processes is important for a number of reasons: (1) the knowledge base undergirding education is relatively weak—great expansions in basic knowledge appear necessary; (2) specialized roles in the areas of research, development and diffusion are relatively undefined—training programs for specialized roles require extensive development; (3) provisions for experimental innovation in education are scanty—the development of effective linkages among specialized change roles requires intensive attention; (4) since developmental activities lack system, educational inventions often remain invisible, undocumented and inaccessible; (5) there is a lack of a professional network of trained and competent change agents and communicators in education and, consequently, dissemination activities lack effectiveness; (6) specialists in education lack extensive creative working relationships with social scientists—the disciplinary base of par-

* *Dean, State College of Education, University of Utah.* Formerly, public school principal and superintendent; Associate Director of the University Council for Educational Administration; and Professor of Educational Administration, University of Illinois.

ticipation in educational research has typically been narrow, and has often been restricted to educational psychology; and (7) the research roles of various educational agencies at local, state, regional and national levels have tended to remain unclear. Role confusion has resulted in broken front approaches to educational research. The quality of research produced under such circumstances has failed on more than one occasion to reflect credit upon the sponsoring agencies.

The challenges posed by such problems are many and varied. Strategies and recommendations to meet the challenges and to strengthen the capabilities of educational institutions to effect changes are beginning to emerge.

RESEARCH STRATEGIES

First, let us consider some recommendations and strategies related to research processes that will be essential to the development of a sound knowledge base in education.

1. *There is a need to develop appropriate institutional and individual rewards for excellence in basic research processes.* Two types of rewards appear essential: one is financial, the other attitudinal. Institutions of higher learning, and researchers in general must perceive that educational research is highly valued and adequately rewarded. To support such an orientation, the federal government and other funding agencies must greatly expand support for institutional and individual research programs related to education. Universities and schools and colleges of education generally must receive support to the point where they can elevate research processes to the same level of importance that is currently enjoyed by programs for the preparation of professional personnel, without detracting from the latter.

2. *There is a need to develop an adequate taxonomy of generalist-specialist roles as they relate to research, development and diffusion.* Current patterns of training for research in the universities are still oriented for the most part toward the preparation of research generalists. If we are to improve basic research processes, we will need better definitions of what researchers do in terms of functions associated with producing new knowledge, with developing it and with diffusing it.

It would appear that at least six roles are likely to be salient in the taxonomy of research roles that is currently emerging: (1) there will be researchers with strong disciplinary orientations who will see their function as that of producing new knowledge through basic research and theory building; (2) there will be institutional researchers who will see themselves primarily in quality control research; (3) there will be research administrators who will combine management skills with research skills; (4) there will be researchers whose primary orientation will be toward social bookkeeping; (5) there will be design engineers who will identify and package applied solutions to operating problems; and (6) there will be those who will concentrate on the diffusion of packaged applied solutions. As yet, we have not clarified nor defined the roles and functions of these taxonomic types to the point where we can conceptualize programs appropriate to their preparation.

3. *There is a need to mount preparation programs whose objectives are consistent with emerging role definitions.* As the taxonomy of research roles is clarified, the characteristics and salient behaviors of each of the various research roles will require identification. Program elements and experiences will need to be oriented toward the development of competence in relation to these identified behaviors. It is quite possible that—as universities move toward definition of what is to be taught and of how it is to be taught—several independent preparation programs will emerge. It is also possible, however, that programs can be structured on a common core—with several specialized preparation routes to differentiate training on the basis of different functions.

As new programs are structured, attention will also need to be directed to a number of allied problems: (1) the need to identify trainable pools of research talent in a number of fields outside education—especially in liberal arts fields; (2) the need to bring trainees into programs at a much earlier age—possibly in their middle twenties; (3) the need to minimize or eliminate pre-professional experiences as a prerequisite for entry into research preparation programs; and (4) the need to cut down course study requirements for research careers, to provide a stimulating research environment, to immerse candidates in research activities just as early as possible, and to encourage a maximum of independent study on the part of those preparing for research careers.

4. *There is a need to generate new organizational arrangements for preparing researchers.* Buswell and McConnell, in their recent report entitled *Training for Educational Research,* have suggested several arrangements that are worthy of consideration. Among their recommendations were: (1) special interdisciplinary institutes controlled by the graduate dean, and having the authority to develop programs and to recommend candidates for Ph.D. degrees; (2) interdisciplinary committee programs—within or without schools of education—with power to recommend persons for the Ph.D. when they have completed programs mounted by the committee; (3) new special experimental research programs to be carried out in colleges of education; and (4) special training programs to be carried on in specific academic disciplines.

Support for special research fellowships—to provide research assistants to professors engaged in inquiry—is also an important factor. Moreover, movement toward institutional arrangements stressing problem-centered rather than department-centered research should be extensively encouraged. Such movement would permit the use of resources from various disciplines in the programs of graduate students.

5. *There is a need to stress interdisciplinary research approaches to educational problems.* Several of the proceeding strategies and recommendations are oriented toward facilitating multi-disciplinary approaches

to research on educational problems. The U. S. Office of Education, too, should continue to encourage interdisciplinary trends in the staffing of both research training programs and regional educational laboratory programs. Special inducements will be necessary to attract researchers from other disciplines to the study of educational problems. However, the resources of federal and state agencies, coupled with those of private foundations, can easily make this possible if the problem is accepted as one of high priority.

DEVELOPMENT AND DIFFUSION STRATEGIES

Although developments in recent years are encouraging, it is not inaccurate to say that provisions in the past for the development and diffusion of educational innovations have been both weak and discontinuous. Most usually, development activities have been centered in local school districts, with some assistance provided by individual university consultants, state department of education consultants, and university bureaus of field service. Few of these arrangements, however, have provided avenues for attacking development problems in a systematic, programatic fashion. Programatic approaches to development have appeared more characteristic of activities carried on by publishers and test builders than of formal education agencies.

Planned, massive strategies for diffusing educational innovations have also been largely absent in the past. Most diffusion activities have been directed by governmental education agencies—primarily through conference and publication routes. Demonstration and field testing (prominent for many years in the agricultural diffusion model) have been relatively underdeveloped phases of the change process in education. Moreover, there has been no accepted process for legitimizing educational innovations in education. Medicine and agriculture have special agencies for this function (that is, the Food and Drug Administration, and the Agricultural Research Center).

Several recent movements give hope that an altered pattern in relation to development and diffusion activities in education is about to emerge. We are all familiar with the role of private foundations and the National Science Foundation in the development of entire new curricula in areas such as mathematics and science. The interests of the Office of Education in other course areas has tended to make development possible on a still wider front. And, of course, the passage of the Elementary and Secondary Education Act (ESEA) made possible the regional educational laboratories, demonstration centers, and possibilities for inter-institutional partnerships. Such developments will surely lead to a strengthening of development and diffusion functions in education. However, a number of strategies and recommendations appear important to help promote development and diffusion functions in educational change.

1. *There is a need to accept developmental activities as a legitimate area of concern in universities.* Engineering, agriculture and medicine have

already accepted development as a legitimate concern in the higher education setting. Education would do well to follow their example. As many as fifty universities across the nation could be selected and funded (1) to engage in developmental work, and (2) to train educational design engineers, product testers and diffusers of applied solutions.

2. *There is a need to develop regional and national mechanisms for cooperation among demonstration centers including regional educational laboratories (REL), universities engaged in research and development (R & D), and educational agencies at the local and state level.* Compacts or consortiums need to be developed that can give attention to development activities in a wide range of areas, including teaching-learning processes, curricula, organization and management. State departments of education and local school districts should develop trained staffs to assist with development functions in individual school districts and states.

3. *There is a need to organize state and regional dissemination teams.* Such teams would require sophistication in the diffusion process and would accept responsibility for disseminating innovations in particular geographical areas. Several such dissemination teams should be available to work on call with school districts in each geographical area of the nation. Financial support for team activities could be provided from national, state and local budgets. Moreover, REL's and demonstration centers could become centers for the demonstration of educational innovations deemed worthy of diffusion by these teams.

4. *There is a need to hasten the development of the educational research information center (ERIC) so that this automated storage and retrieval system can be used as a bank of information by diffusion personnel at each level of operation.* As part of the diffusion process, USOE will need to catalog educational inventions and to disseminate information about them. USOE will also need to acquaint educational practitioners with development and demonstration activities associated with various inventions.

5. *There is a need to develop linking systems to tie research and development to demonstration and diffusion.* State and regional partnerships should be mounted among local and state educational agencies, universities, and the newly developed research and development centers and regional educational laboratories. Such partnerships, when wedded to the interdisciplinary approaches recommended earlier for staffing research agencies, would provide needed linking systems to cope with the discontinuities occurring between research, development, diffusion and adoption.

As compacts and partnerships are mounted, general divisions of labor in relation to various aspects of the change process should begin to emerge. It might be found, for example, that basic research and development would fall naturally to the universities, the R & D centers and the REL's. State education agencies could take responsibility for diffusion, while schools and school districts might concentrate on demonstration and field testing. The lines of functional demarcation would probably be structured to provide opportunities for overlap.

One of the weaknesses in the development of partnerships and compacts is that at present there is no machinery for developing coherent policies relating to educational change on the part of the various participants and levels of educational government concerned. The pattern of relationships that would need to exist between federal, state and local governments to permit these levels to work together in developing policy alternatives in relation to change is only now beginning to emerge. There is little tradition or history to go on, but there is a clear need to structure social inventions to handle this problem.

NORMATIVE-REEDUCATIVE STRATEGIES

The normative-reeducative change processes emphasize a collaborative orientation to defining and selecting goals of change. The sources of influence appear to be rooted in psychological processes of identification with change agents, and in the internalization of ideal patterns of behaving. Moreover, there is strong recognition of the axiom that group membership exerts a marked influence upon the behavior of group members. Thus, internalization of appropriate patterns of behaving is fostered through the formation of group norms and supports in face to face situations. Normative-reeducative strategies of change presuppose sensitivity to group processes, and knowledge about the diagnostic and intervention roles of change agents.

Research indicates that institution and organization groups may be viewed from the change agent's standpoint as (1) *media* of change, (2) *targets* of change, and (3) *agents* of change. All three strategies appear effective for introducing change in group contexts. Intervention strategies, however, differ in each instance. Also, elements of both problem-solving and attitude-change approaches may be involved in each of the strategies.

Employing the Group as a Medium of Change. In employing this strategy, the change agent recognizes the strong influence that groups exert upon their members. Informal pressures operating within groups may either reinforce or negate attempts to restructure the behavior of group members in new directions. The central problem in using the group as a medium of change is one of intervention; that is, of identifying group situations for certain individuals where prolonged interaction and contact with change agents will be possible.

Important to the success of this particular strategy are (1) the emergence of strong "we" feelings during the group experience, (2) the minimization of psychological distance among group members, and (3) the creation of opportunities for internalizing new attitudinal, behavioral and value patterns. Moreover, change is likely to be accelerated if group experiences lead to augmented need satisfaction, heightened prestige, or a new awareness of the significance of group goals.

Employing the Group as a Target of Change. This strategy requires a different intervention process. Here, the change agent places primary emphasis upon building channels of communication within the group, upon the creation of shared perspectives and perceptions, and upon creating desires for change within the group itself. This may be a difficult procedure, especially if communication and interaction within the group are characterized by lack of trust and hostility. In working with groups as targets of change, the change agent requires sophistication in a number of important tasks. He must help the group to face and to verbalize its problems, even though hostility and tension rise during the process. He must work toward the creation of shared perceptions and perspectives in relation to needs for change. He must be adept in helping to formulate plans with the group for desired change. Finally, he must be skilled in communicating the consequences of planned change.

Employing the Group as an Agent of Change. This change strategy is often used in institutional and organizational contexts. A committee of faculty members, chosen to study computer assisted instruction and charged with the responsibility of making recommendations to faculty and administration, might be an example of a group that is performing in the change agent's role. Recommendations for change that emanate from groups engaged in action research or in school district surveys are other examples. The goal in each example may be to initiate institutional or organizational change. The apparent pressure and motivation for change, however, is identified with an outside expert agency or with an inside faculty group.

Normative-reeducative patterns and strategies may be used in institutional and organizational settings at local, state, regional and national levels. For example, groups at one or more of these levels may serve as media of change for individuals and groups from other levels. In the operation of state educational committees, for instance, representatives of local districts are exposed to ideas from state education department officials and university consultants. The resulting interaction may cause extensive shifts in attitudes, feelings, perspectives and value frames of reference. In like manner, it would not be difficult to cite examples of the use of groups as targets and/or agents of change at each level of operation.

POWER STRATEGIES

Usually, three types of power strategies are utilized in effecting changes in organizations including those concerned with education: coercive, remunerative and normative. Ordinarily, coercive power is based on the application, or the threat of application, of sanctions. Remunerative power is based on control and manipulation of material resources. Normative power is based on leadership skill, on the manipulation of esteem, prestige, and ritualistic symbols, as well as on allocation of acceptance and positive response.

Change Strategies Based on Coercion. Despite suspicions that surrounds the use of power strategies to engineer change, it is clear that at times educational change is instituted by force or coercion. Power strategies are most frequently used either (1) to induce conformity, or (2) to change system outcomes in predetermined ways. Indeed, there is no reason for power to come into play within a system unless it is used to induce conformity or to alter system outcomes for certain of the participants. Change strategies based on coercion may be initiated either from the top or from the bottom in organizations or social institutions. Thus, these strategies may be exercised by both elites and followers and may be exemplified in such widely separated phenomena as legislative activity or teacher strikes. The goal of most coercive change strategies is to redistribute power and thus to alter the existing allocations of values within a system.

It is generally recognized that change engineered through force must often be maintained by force. Thus, change brought about through coercive strategies may not provide a satisfactory basis for building organizational effectiveness and efficiency. In organizations, coercive change through manifest power chokes communication, inhibits interaction, and induces studied formality into organizational relationships. It appears that lasting change is more likely to be built upon consent than upon coercion.

Power Strategies Based upon Remuneration. Change strategies based upon remuneration are quite common in education and can be found operating in local, state and national settings. Elites and administrators possess extensive control over many values important to organizational personnel since formal controls over reward, prestige, promotion and ratings of effectiveness are normally lodged with formal leaders. Manipulation of such power bases to induce change is not uncommon in organizations.

It should also be noted that when funds are made available at state or national levels if schools districts can meet or conform to criteria set in legislation or administrative regulations, we have a remunerative power strategy in operation. Indeed, external grants of money under legislation such as the National Defense Education Act (NDEA) and ESEA may be sufficient to trigger massive changes in education.

Power Strategies Based upon Leadership. It is important to realize that normative leadership activities, whether they are based on status, competence, or charisma are essentially a form of power strategies. Leadership skill is usually oriented in organizational settings to the initiation of needed alterations in structure as the prerequisites or co-requisites of change. Indeed, leadership activities are normally oriented toward the engineering of change—in organizational values, goals, purposes, directions and structures. Since school systems function in a milieu of community, state and national power, school leaders require competence in identifying and working with formal and informal power systems in each of these settings. Leadership in communicating the need for worthwhile educational changes to the appropriate power structures within education and at various levels of government would appear to be a task of high priority for formal leaders in education.

CHAPTER 4

Effecting Needed Changes in Education

ROBERT B. HOWSAM*

One of my colleagues at Christmas time last year dropped on my desk a copy of *Linus On Life*. One of the sections is devoted to "On Adaptability". The dialogue for the four pages goes like this:

Linus This "new math" is too much for me.
Lucy You'll get on to it . . . It just takes time . . .
Linus Not me . . . I'll never get on to it!
Linus How can you do "new math" problems with an "old math" mind?[1]

As is so often the case, Linus has come up with a profound and significant observation. Indeed, he has put his finger on what I consider to be the crux of the problem in bringing about significant educational change. Whatever we do about strategies for effecting changes, *we have to take account of the "new" problems for the "old" mind—the new behaviors that must replace the old if educational innovations are to be taken from the blueprint and the research report into the world of practice. The pace of educational innovation and adaptation depends to no small degree upon our ability to influence practitioners to modify their perceptions of reality and accompany this with performance keyed to the changed view.*

THE NATURE OF CURRENT INNOVATIONS

There is these days a good deal of attention to the development of "new math" and many other "new things". Indeed, one gets the impression that education is swept up in change and innovation. There is need for keen professional awareness of just what is actually taking place, however. It seems probable that any careful analysis of a catalog of educational change will reveal almost exclusive attention to changes in three areas:

1. Organization for instruction and for administration (team teaching; dual progress; house plan; K-4-4-4; educational parks);

2. Educational technology with major emphasis on hardware (computer assisted instruction; educational television); and

3. Subject matter content in the various curriculum areas (new mathematics; new physics; structural linguistics; Initial Teaching Alphabet; etc.).

* *Dean, College of Education, University of Houston.* Formerly, Professor of Educational Administration, Chairman of Department of Educational Administration, and Associate Dean for Graduate Studies, University of Rochester; Assistant and Associate Professor of Education, University of California, Berkeley; Principal, University Demonstration School and lecturer, University of Saskatchewan. Publications include: (author) *Who's A Good Teacher; New Designs for Research in Teacher Competence;* (co-author) *Certification of Educational Administrators;* Chapter on "Canada" in *Comparative Educational Administration.*

[1] Charles M. Schulz, *Linus on Life.* Unpaged and undated publications by Hallmark.

Far less attention to innovations in teacher behavior and instructional methodology will be discovered. The assumption seems to be either that the present instructional patterns in schools, colleges and universities are satisfactory or that they will be modified by the teacher as the new demands on them appear. There is ample evidence that neither of these assumptions is acceptable. Present teaching patterns leave much to be desired. There is little reason to believe that they will change readily in response to need. Quite the opposite may be anticipated. There is ample evidence from studies in many fields that people tend to subvert the intentions of innovators by twisting the expected new behaviors into older and more comfortable ways. Carlson has observed this phenomenon in education. He reports that teachers modify new procedures to maintain older patterns of teaching.[2] Though the pace of behavioral change in education may be accelerating, there is little reason to believe that the pace is as rapid as effective use of innovation in the other three areas would demand.

It would appear useful to attempt to categorize educational innovations in terms of the extent to which teachers would have to modify their behaviors if they are not to nullify the advantage of the innovation. When viewed in this way, three categories of change appear:

1. Changes that involve improved or different technology, organization, or content and require only superficial changes in the teacher's behavior: from 8-4 to 6-6 plan; using slides and filmstrips or overhead projectors; switching the teaching of fractions from one grade to another.

2. Changes involving organization, content or technology which, to be effective, will require basic changes in teacher behavior: teaching on a differentiated team; adopting new math; ungrading a school; using a learning resources center.

3. Changes directed at improving teacher performance as such: using a heuristic approach; making use of sociological and psychological principles in organizing and working with small groups; giving up lecturing.

Much of what we have been doing either seems to assume that no change in teacher behavior is involved or that change in the required direction would be easy. The fact is, however, that most of the recommended innovations are not simple and are not merely technical or organizational. Many involve a fundamental reorientation of teaching in directions that are alien to the teacher's inclinations. Often they involve a change in values and beliefs. Even more often they require revision in the conception of the role of the teacher and modification of the teacher's self-image.

Such change is far from simple. It is accomplished only under highly favorable circumstances and with powerful relearning opportunities. Such conditions and opportunities rarely prevail in education. In consequence many potential advantages of innovative developments are lost. Educators,

---

[2] Richard O. Carlson, *Adoption of Educational Innovations* (Eugene, Oregon: University of Oregon, Center for the Advanced Study of Educational Administration, 1965).

like everyone else, reject and subvert changes which are incompatible with their customary ways.

Though there is no valid evidence to support the view, it can be hypothesized that teachers at all levels—more than any other professional group in the society—need sophisticated in-service education. Given the present notions about teaching and learning and about the roles of teacher and student, it would be quite easy for teachers to reject the idea that they, themselves, should be "taught". Subconsciously, to many, learning may be an activity for children. If this be the case, those who would influence teachers to learn would have to be expert in strategy and have available the full range of resources and talents.

NEED FOR ATTENTION TO HUMAN RESOURCES DEVELOPMENT

As I see it, the present emphasis on the development of technology, organization, and teaching content—with its resultant or accompanying neglect of the development of people—may well be self-defeating. We may be wasting our time, our resources and our opportunity. And this is not to mention the generation of children and the future members of society who suffer the consequences of our errors and inadequacies.

Unless we are careful, present emphases may produce an educational system that pursues the *Scientific Management* tradition and leads education to the same consequences as earlier befell industry and business. In retrospect, it is now known that Frederick Taylor wasn't wrong in developing technology and management; he just wasn't right enough. His science didn't extend into the human realm. In my view we in education may be headed toward repeating errors against which history has given ample warning.

Victor Thompson[3] has pointed out the tendency in modern society to specialize in either of two directions. He refers to one of these as *task specialization;* the other as *person specialization.* His ideas seem pertinent enough to summarize here.

Task specialization means cutting work into smaller and simpler parts. Under task specialization, the worker has a less and less meaningful experience, has less and less control over what he does and how he does it, and presumably has a less satisfying experience. He is less and less important, both in his own eyes and in those of others in the society. Though what he does may be important to his organization, he is not. In addition, it has little significance to the society.

Person specialization means that the person becomes a specialist in one part of a complex activity. In doing so, he becomes one of few who have such training and so the society depends upon him. Person specialization is similar to professional training. The person works long and hard to earn his place. He has increased his worth to the society and at the same time has increased his power, since most others lack the know-how

---

[3] Victor Thompson, *Modern Organization* (New York: Alfred A. Knopf, 1961).

to make competent decisions in his area of specialization. Thus, there is a strong sense of personal and social worth. Social rewards are high. The "person" specialist draws his significance more from the society as a whole than from the particular organization for which he works.

Unless we are in a position to dispense with people in the educational process—which conceivably could be done through completely automated learning systems—we will need to ensure that what we do leads to person specialization. This will call for a great deal of emphasis on human resource development. The situation which we now confront is not yet some kind of technocratic revolution nor an organizational metamorphosis, regardless of how much of each of these elements is to characterize the education of the future. Competent "school people" will be important to all of us for a long time to come.

Thompson implies one other danger inherent in promoting technical, organizational and content changes without adequate concurrent attention to innovating in human development. He (and others) comment on the importance of interdependence among professionals (person specialists) in organizations. Argyris[4] emphasizes the natural development of personalities from the childhood state of dependence through independence to mature interdependence. Miles[5] and others have analyzed teachers as having relatively high independence and a corresponding low interdependence. If educational technology continues to develop faster than do the teachers, task specialization could result. This would tend to increase dependence and move education still further from the day when professionalization and interdependence could characterize the education work force.

It is my thesis that the strategies and processes of change must include at least as much attention to the development of professional and human competence as they do to the other supportive and enabling aspects of education. We have not been doing enough of this or doing it very effectively. Indeed, we have gone so far in the other direction as, at worst, to endanger education itself and, at least, to render our other efforts ineffective and the impact inconsequential.

You will recognize that I am greatly concerned about the difficulty of changing the behavior of teachers, and about our naivete in dealing with this problem. In my view, changing the behavior of teaching professionals in desired directions is equalled in difficulty only in a few areas (perhaps such as changing the behavior of parents in their child rearing practices). Unless we recognize this difficulty we are likely to make little progress in our efforts to define strategies for effecting educational change.

It is well established in behavioral science that people learn the accepted and expected modes of behavior in the general culture of the

[4] Chris Argyris, *Personality and Organization* (New York: Harper and Company, 1957), and *Integrating the Individual and the Organization* (New York: Wiley and Sons, 1964).
[5] Matthew Miles, "Planned Change and Organizational Health; Figure and Ground", in Richard O. Carlson and others, *Change Processes in the Public Schools* (Eugene, Oregon: University of Oregon, Center for Advanced Study of Educational Administration, 1965).

society and in the groups to which people belong and which are important to them. As Gallaher has indicated, culture is ". . . those ideas, socially transmitted and learned, shared by the members of a group and toward which in their behavior they tend to conform."[6] In essense, this is saying that people learn to behave from the culture or groups to which they belong.

Occupations differ in the source of learning of the knowledge, skills and behaviors expected of members. There seem to be at least four recognizable sources:

1. In the general culture

   • almost all members of a society would be exposed to this and given the opportunity to learn it
   • it would be learned in homes, family groups, schools, churches
   • parenthood and child rearing would be good examples

2. On the job by actual practice with little if any training

   • only some members of a modern society would learn these skills and behavior
   • driving a taxi or carpentry represent this type

3. Formal training

   • apprenticeship in nature
   • learned by a limited number depending on need
   • plumbing and electrical work would be of this kind

4. Formal education

   • highly specialized learning in college or university
   • limited to a few, depending on need and ability
   • law training would be an example

The ease of introducing change in a work group seems closely related to the source of learning and the nature of the task involved in the occupation. Where the knowledge and skill are scientific and technical in nature and learned at a college or university after a person has developed considerable maturity, the practitioner may be expected to respond to innovations in his field readily. Change will be welcomed or resistance will be light except where value or identification issues might be involved.[7] Innovation will be hardest to achieve where the behaviors are learned in the general culture beginning early in life, and where they are associated with respected groups and institutions (family and church) and beloved individuals (parent; minister, priest or rabbi; teacher).

It will be noted that in the one case the role behavior is coming largely from scientists and expert practitioners. In the other it is coming from the conventional wisdom of the society, supported and buttressed by attitudes, beliefs, and identifications. Though probably too simple,

---

[6] Art Gallaher, Jr., "Directed Change in Formal Organizations: The School System," in Carlson, *et al., op. cit.* (footnote 5).

[7] A doctor could be expected to respond readily to new methods of treating the common cold. He might balk at legalized abortion on value grounds and refuse a new heart treatment if there were controversy over a new method of treating heart disease to which some well known (both to him and the profession) specialists were party.

this analysis serves to set the stage for an examination of the sources of teaching behavior.

Almost everyone in our society has the role of student or pupil for a significant portion of his life. Each is exposed to teachers and teaching. Thus each has early and continuous knowledge of the role of teachers and of the role expectations for teachers. Correctly or otherwise a high proportion of the educated people in our society would consider themselves competent to teach in an elementary school. Similarly they would be willing to undertake secondary school teaching if they thought their academic background adequate in the particular subject to be taught. On the whole, adequately educated women in our society probably consider themselves as being as able to teach children as they are to keep house. And they consider that they learned both in the same place—in growing up surrounded by the common experiences, the mores, and the conventional wisdom of the society.

I am indebted to Kenneth Boulding, the noted economist who contributed earlier in this series (Ch. 12 in *Prospective Changes in Society by 1980*) for insight into how difficult these learnings—these folk-way orientations—are to change.[8] They tend to be value loaded and to be supported by feelings of love and loyalty to those from whom they were learned. By an unconscious process over a long period of time they were learned and internalized. They do not yield readily to relearning or to the attempts of innovators.

Teacher education, as we have known it, does little to change such behaviors. For the most part the work in professional education has tended to reinforce them. Those professors who have attempted to change them have met with little success.[9]

We behave according to what we believe to be real. Changing a person's idea of what is real about teaching is anything but easy. Carlson has pointed out the present image of appropriate behavior held by teachers:

> . . . . teachers have a somewhat compelling need to perform. "Perform" is taken to mean: to capture and hold the attention of a number of students, and to serve continuously as the mediator between the student and the information. This is what teachers seem to define as teaching.[10]

This does not seem particularly unusual in view of the experience teachers had as pupils and the kinds of experiences they probably had as student teachers. Nor is it likely that their principals and supervisors—and even most of their college professors—have any different view of teaching reality.

This, then, seems to me to be the problem facing the educational innovator. He has as his major task changing behaviors that are deeprooted in the views of reality held by pupils, parents, and educators. The

---

8 Unpublished paper presented at the University of Rochester in the early 1960's.

9 For a delightful and insightful report on the experience of a professor in a famous business school who attempted to change the perceptions of business students see James V. Clark, *Education for the Use of Behavioral Science* (Los Angeles: Institute for Industrial Relations, University of California, 1962).

10 *Op. cit.* (footnote 2).

favorite educational device of "telling" is not likely to effect much behavioral change. Only great insight and powerful means are likely to work.

Assuming that my point has been made, it will be appropriate to proceed to a discussion of strategies and procedures for achieving change. It does seem to me important that we accept the position that changes in teacher behavior are, indeed, hard to come by. Failure to recognize this can result in superficial and ineffective approaches.

MATTERS OF TERMINOLOGY AND EMPHASIS

In seeking to identify strategies and procedures for effecting change, we are concerning ourselves with a deliberate attempt to introduce change. We are saying either that the need for a change is known or that we have some specific change in mind and we wish it introduced.

The language of those who study the planned change phenomenon may be useful to us:

Innovator. The person who invents the change.

Change Agent. The person who attempts to introduce the change to a particular situation. The word "advocate" also is used in this connection.

Client system or target system. The group, organization, institution, individual or segment of society into which the change is to be introduced.

Adopter. One who accepts a changed way of behavior. "Adapter" would indicate a person who accepted the changed way of behaving but modified it to suit conditions and his needs.

Intervention. An act by a change agent designed to influence the client systems to change.

There is much semantic looseness among educators where change is concerned. The tendency is to fail to differentiate between the *innovative processes* and the *dissemination processes.* This may not be of great significance in most cases. On the other hand it appears that it may be important to those of us who are concerned with strategies for bringing about planned change.

A recent report by Ronald Lippitt[11] indicates the difference between innovation and adoption of change. He points out not only that innovation and adoption are different but also the possibility that the process of diffusion of practices in education is different from that of other areas such as agriculture and medicine. Lippitt sees innovation and adoption as representing different positions on a change continuum. His research seems to indicate that the two processes are carried out by different types of people or at least by teachers in different relationship patterns within the school. Lippitt says "These data on adoption are very different from the data on innovation."

This project is concerned primarily with "planned change". Of this, Chin says:

Planned change is defined as a deliberate and collaborative process involving

---

[11] Ronald Lippitt and Colleagues, "The Teacher as Innovator, Seeker, and Sharer of New Practices" in Richard I. Miller, ed., *Perspectives on Educational Change* (New York: Appleton-Century-Crofts, 1967).

change agent and client system. These systems are brought together to solve a problem or more generally to plan and attain an improved state of functioning in the client system by utilizing and applying valid knowledge.[12]

My own concern over the slowness with which actual teaching practice changes—coupled with the idea that we are doing better these days with promoting innovation than we are with diffusion and adoption—leads me here to emphasize strategies for bringing about more effective behavior on the educational firing line.

Perhaps a word of caution also would be in order at this point. Innovation is exciting. Recently in education we have begun to create special organizations and opportunities for those who wish to experiment and innovate. Relatively substantial funds have been made available from government and from private foundations. Higher economic awards as well as exciting opportunities, recognition, and relative freedom from restraints are going to those who qualify for appointments to positions with innovation development as the assignment. Though there undoubtedly is a much larger pool of talent than we have previously been able to tap, education should beware that in the press to increase innovation we do not disastrously deplete the talent needed for dissemination and adoption. Otherwise we will end up creating a new lag or perpetuating the existing lag between discovery and implementation of educational knowledge, insights and improved practices. Keeping the reward levels commensurate would appear to be important.

A GENERAL STRATEGY

An important general strategy is to approach change in such a way that there results a climate hospitable to continuous adaptation and change.[13] Many educational approaches to change in the past have been directed at a single change. This tends to result in thinking of change as *product introduction* rather than as a *process* of *adaptation*. This approach is dysfunctional in any long-term view since it tends to lead to an attitude of "we innovated last year".

A continuous examination of goals and their achievement through organization, behavioral norms and means is essential to a growing and adaptive system. Equally important, however, is the rather evident probability that the only suitable environment for our generation of learners is one that is, by example, adaptive to changing conditions and times.

USE OF POWER AND AUTHORITY

We are concerned with change in schools and other educational institutions and organizations. Since these are formally established organizations, there always is a hierarchy of authority to act. Some possible change strategies originate directly in this authority.

---

[12] Robert Chin, "Some Ideas on Changing", in *Perspectives on Educational Change. Op. cit.*
[13] Warren G. Bennis, Kenneth D. Benne, and Robert Chin, *The Planning of Change* (New York: Holt, Rinehart, and Winston, 1961).

Perhaps the oldest strategy is to command. The person in authority, acting as a change agent, orders subordinates to behave differently. Compliance is expected.

It should be kept in mind, however, that compliance, to a considerable extent, is a voluntary matter. Usually it lies within the discretion of the client or subordinate to decide on the extent of his compliance or cooperation. He may decide to conform overtly but covertly withhold his support. The ability of individuals and of groups to resist compliance—whether it is seen as against their best interests or just resented because of the method of application—is well known and amply documented.

The change agent who chooses to command behavior changes in the client system needs to be certain that the clients are ready to accept the changes and also will be willing to comply with the order. In the absence of this he should be ready to risk frustration and failure or resort to further use of power through application of sanctions to those who do not comply. Though command may appear to be effective in some settings, it should be kept in mind that the most creative people in the organization are likely to resent it most. Wholesome people may be expected to comply with authority on those occasions when its exercise appears necessary. The frequent use of authority will eat away at mutual respect, trust, and good will, however, and ultimately bring about a situation where the good will bank is overdrawn.

Administrative power and authority may be exercised in ways other than by command. Assignment of personnel and administration of a substantial system of rewards and sanctions are powerful control mechanism so long as discretion in their use is not removed by a system of bureaucratic rules or counterbalanced by informal power emanating from the informal organization or influential individuals.

In any system, rewards should be distributed to those who make possible achievement of organizational objectives. The system that values appropriate adoptive, adaptive and innovative behavior should communicate this value to all of its members. Then it should emphasize this criterion in its evaluation system and reward those who manifest such behavior.

It would appear that few school systems have worked out adequate means of granting rewards to innovative and adoptive personnel. Indeed, few have explicated this as a concrete objective. Teachers—like people in other organizations—respond to the formal and informal value and rewards systems of their colleges, schools and peer groups. The personnel of an educational institution or organization that is not evidencing creative behavior—and seeks to do so—should examine itself to determine what needs to be done to attain commitment to up-to-dateness. If it discovers a lack of clear institutional commitment, it should seek one. If it discovers that rewards of the system do not go to the creative, it should correct the situation. And if it finds that the informal organization is subverting the purpose of the system, it should seek means of making the goals of the informal system congruent with those of the organization. Less than this will be an inadequate strategy, no matter what else is done.

One hesitates to discuss the use of power and authority to break up undesirable situations. To do so may be necessary in some situations, however. It should be recognized that such actions probably would not be necessary if organization and leadership had been adequate. Nevertheless, such situations do exist and sometimes can best be resolved by administrative action.

Sofer[14] has made a study of change within commercial organizations. Among other things he suggests that change is more likely to occur if the organization has "adventurous and flexible leaders" or "has recently acquired a new leader who is determined to make a personal reputation by doing something different". His study also suggests that such leaders are more likely to achieve change if placed in organizations where achievement has been inadequate and where personnel are actively dissatisfied. These findings suggest considerations for administrative action. Administrators and other instructional leaders need to be innovation and change oriented if change is to occur. Further, there is evidence to indicate that this trait must characterize leaders from the top down. Placing innovative principals, for example, in poorer situations may be more conducive to their success and may thereby cause other principals to become more critical of what they are doing.

Reorganization sometimes may be used to break up undesirable situations. Any change in a system automatically brings change in the other parts of the system. Reorganization may provide the means of shifting influence and creating a more fluid situation out of which change may emerge. Such action is drastic—as is surgery in medicine—and should be taken only after careful consideration of possible consequences, both intended and unintended. Reorganization often provides opportunity for shifts of personnel and reassignments of responsibility. Changes in status may be less obvious and therefore less painful at such times. Reorganization also may provide the opportunity for introducing needed new blood.

Perhaps it should be emphasized that personnel within a school system or other organization must *perceive* that innovative and adaptive behavior is desired by the system. Otherwise reorganization and other attempts will not be understood. *Responsible change must be the norm if any consistent adaptive climate is to obtain.*

RESPONSIBILITY FOR CHANGE

A major problem and issue in decisions about change strategies lies in the area of responsibility for it. Is it better to expect the administrator to act as change agent? Or must the impetus for change come from somewhere else. The evidence on this question seems contradictory at this time.

---

[14] Cyril Sofer, *The Organization from Within* (Chicago: Quadrangle Books, 1962).

A number of observers have pointed out that impetus for change in education customarily comes from outside established educational institutions. The activities of both the federal government and several large foundations seem to be based on this assumption. Explanations of the conservative, unadaptive performance in education usually point to the bureaucratic nature of the "establishment". Pessimism is expressed over the possibility that education will be able to put its own house in order. Though there is indication of substantial innovative effort in response to outside interventions, there is little to indicate that the interventions are basic in nature or that they can survive withdrawal of the support. In any event, local and state educational institutions and organizations still face the problem *at home* of having the innovations adopted by educational personnel and integrated into the ongoing educational system; this cannot be done by outsiders no matter how serious their concerns or how good their intentions. So we are left with the local systems confronted by greater internal problems than ever. And the outside interveners, including state departments of education, have shown far too little responsibility in assisting local systems in solving the change problems with which the flood of innovations presents them.

The evidence on the role of the administrator as a change agent is not as yet clear. Brickell[15] found that such innovations as had occurred in New York State had been initiated by the administrators. Guest agrees with Brickell in principle saying ". . . complex organizations being what they are, those at the head are the primary change agents".[16] Gallaher[17] on the other hand expresses scepticism over the ability of school administrators to accept responsibility for the advocate role in the change process. He sees the administrator as being "the man in the middle", balancing the conflicting demands of local authorities and interest groups on the one hand and the professionals in the schools on the other. Since public interest groups are not likely to be in agreement on an innovative stance in general nor on any specific change, "they are not apt to permit advocacy as a part of the administrative role".[18] Other writers tend to agree with this position while recognizing individual exceptions.

Despite the logic of this position, the administrator is not likely to escape this responsibility so easily. If he does, his position will have been eroded seriously. And someone else in the school system hierarchy will be placed in the difficult but essential adoptive role.

Another factor may be expected to operate in the years ahead. Increasingly teachers are becoming professional, getting outside local school systems, and receiving cues from other professionals and professional organizations. Pressures for change from them may be expected to increase.

---

[15] Henry M. Brickell, *Organizing New York State for Educational Change* (Albany, New York: State Education Department, 1961).
[16] Robert H. Guest, *Organizational Change: The Effect of Successful Leadership* (Homewood, Illinois: The Dorsey Press, Inc., 1962).
[17] *Op. cit.* (footnote 6).
[18] *Op. cit.* (footnote 6).

One of the most promising long-term strategies is to invest more· and more in the professional development of *individual* teachers. Schools have been reluctant to do this in the past.

Lippitt and colleagues[19] have found clear indications that the perceived support of the principal is crucial to teachers who wish to introduce change and that there is more tendency to innovate when the principal is active in promoting it. Undoubtedly the principals respond similarly to cues from their superintendents.

There seems to be little doubt that—as a matter of strategy—where change is desired, administrators and supervisors favorable to change must be provided. The presence of critical elements in the community cannot be ignored but the norm of administrative leadership responsibility will have to prevail. In addition, it is increasingly important that they be the kinds of people who are well informed and who actively enter into the process of providing stimulating and support for those with whom they work. In a systems sense, this will hold true at all levels in the educational enterprise; schools, for example, are not likely to be innovative or adoptive if their state or intermediate unit level personnel are perceived as unfavorable or uncommitted to change. *The conclusion would seem to be that when administrators are seen as obstructing—or even failing to encourage— desirable change they will either have to be retooled or removed.*

Given an administrator who is favorable to change, is it more effective to leave the change agent role to him or is it better to make more specific provision for the change agent function? In many cases the latter would seem to have distinct advantage. Clark[20] has suggested that change occurs as a consequence of an *upsetting experience* in a *supportive environment.* The principal or other administrator clearly is an essential factor in the supportive environment. He may not be the best source for the upsetting experience, however. Often an outsider is better for this purpose. The widespread use of consultants attests to this need. Insiders tend to be myopic about conditions that exist in an organization. Further, since they share responsibility for what does exist they tend to be defensive about it. The outsider, on the other hand, may be brought in and given the delegated role of providing some kind of "reality shock" by bringing to light existing conditions. *Both past practice and logic indicate that a useful strategy of change is to introduce outsiders in the form of consultants.* The role may include—in addition to providing exposures of reality—assisting with the identification of problems, working out solutions, and providing ongoing support during the processes of "unfreezing", "changing", and "refreezing".

A strategy of intervention suggested in recent years and adopted by the U. S. Office of Education early this year is that of *institutionalizing the role of "heretic".* Under this strategy the institution establishes the role of heretic and includes such personnel on the regular staff. The assigned task is that of helping others in the organization to perceive things as

---

[19] *Op. cit.* (footnote 11).
[20] *Op. cit.* (footnote 9).

they really are and thereby inducing efforts at improving conditions. In a school, for example, in addition to having the usual complement of teachers, there would be one or more persons who would have no teaching, administrative, or supervisory functions. (Two such persons probably would be more effective than one since they would provide each other mutual support and stimulation.) They would have direct and ready access to everything that goes on in the school and would be expected to hold up a reality mirror to all concerned. In addition they might have the responsibility of suggesting alternative approaches, providing ideas and information, and facilitating the planning of changes and experimental approaches. They would not, however, have any responsibility for anything that was undertaken in the way of change. Clearly such an approach would not be appropriate unless a climate favorable to it exists. Where such conditions do exist, large returns might be anticipated.

A limitation in the above suggestion would be the tendency for the "heretics" to become identified with faculties or programs and to cease to function in the intended ways. This would suggest relatively short term assignments in any given situation.

SELECTING TARGET UNITS OR POPULATIONS

Consideration of change strategies inevitably leads to consideration of the target system. Is it better to direct the change effort at a whole unit, such as a state or school system? Or is it more effective to select subunits, such as individual schools or teachers, with the expectation that the change will subsequently be diffused by imitation? Another alternative is to create new units.

In the process of seeking solutions to this problem, much of the confusion over innovation and diffusion has been evidenced. What is effective for research and development probably will not be effective for instituting change in schools and other organizations. There is a growing belief that innovations should be developed and tested by organizations established for that purpose.[21] The federal government and philanthropic foundations both have moved in this direction. If this practice is followed, ideas for innovation normally will be referred to some research and development center. Requests for innovative projects by operational units will be rejected on the grounds that adequate development and testing could not be done—though such a unit could later be given preference for involvement as a field testing unit.

Assuming that innovations have been properly tested and proved valuable, introduction of them into an organization becomes a matter of having a change agent intervene to bring about adoption or adaptation by the target or client system. The object is to bring the advantage of the new behavior, organization, or equipment and materials to all who can profit from it. Selection of an individual unit to receive the change

---

[21] See Henry M. Brickell, "The Role of Local School Systems in Change", *Perspectives on Educational Change, op. cit.,* for a treatment of this subject.

would, in effect, either provide further and unneeded testing or be a tactic to facilitate the introduction of the change to the larger system.

In some cases a state institution of higher learning or school system might decide that a uniform introduction of the change was desirable. In other cases limited resources, community readiness, faculty readiness, or other factors might dictate different approaches. Ideally, where the change and adaptation orientation exists, an exercise of individual unit initiative would be expected.

One exception to the above might be envisioned. Creation of new units, such as schools, offers the unique opportunity to match buildings, faculty, community and program. In such cases it may be useful to designate the unit as commissioned to do a particular change task, and to staff and supply it accordingly. The full opportunity to do this comes only once in the lifetime of a building. Too many school systems throw the opportunity away.

HEALTHY ORGANIZATIONS

We have been considering strategies for change and searching for new solutions to an old problem. It would seem appropriate not to overlook the obvious solution. Good school systems do not need strategies for change introduction. They already have them.

State and local school systems that need a prescription for effecting change are like people who need a medical prescription. They are unhealthy. By definition healthy schools, school systems and other educational institutions and organizations can manage adaptation and change.

The only point in mentioning this obvious conclusion is to be sure that we do not overlook the importance of effective administration of schools and schools systems whether local or state. Far too few of the administrators and others in responsible positions have had the kind of preparation needed for their jobs. And almost none in the nation is given the kinds of resources needed to develop and maintain on-the-job competence. Business, industry, and the military, for example, spend vast amounts in administrative personnel development. Education does almost nothing.

Over a considerable period of time, students of organizations and organizational behavior have been attempting to understand what goes on within organizations and institutions and why it goes on. The ability to cope with change has been a primary focus of attention. Probably many of them would agree that there is no "bag of tricks" into which administrators can dip for solutions to the problems of introducing change. Manipulating the organization would be viewed largely as a superficial attempt to reach solutions to fundamental problems.

Miles has turned his attention to the question of organization health. In his paper he says:

> Thus, in a school or college, I believe that the state of something loosely termed "organization health" can tell us more than anything else about the probable success of any particular innovative effort. Even more, the school system's

capacity to go beyond an essentially passive adopting of the latest educational fashion to an active, problem-sensing, self-developmental, innovation-*inventing* stance is very crucially a matter of organization health.[22]

This school of thought would hold that there is relatively little to be accomplished by seeking the dynamics of change outside of the institutions and individuals who must effect it.[23]

Those who accept this position see the problems of change as being largely internal to the formal organizations which do the work of education (universities, state departments of education, school systems, individual schools, classrooms, research and development units). Thus they concentrate their efforts on developing the means for freeing work groups from their limitations and on releasing their creative potentials. Change agents are introduced into organizations. The people and groups within them become the targets of change.

As people work in organizations, problems of relationships and communication arise. Solutions to such problems often are grossly inadequate. Under the "organizational rug" is a host of unresolved issues and problems, swept there by people who in the very nature of things lack the insights and skills to deal with them. An unhealthy organization results. And unhealthy organizations have a hard time handling routine problems, let alone the difficult ones of innovation and adaptation.

IMPROVING THE HEALTH OF ORGANIZATIONS

There is a growing body of knowledge about, and insights into, how to help groups and organizations deal with internal conditions that inhibit them and prevent their coping adequately with their internal and environmental problems. Research evidence is growing. Both experience and evidence indicate that change agents brought into organizations can facilitate the growth of the group and its members. It may well be that the best approach to change and innovation in education is to make widespread use of this change agent or consultant process.

In essence the process of planned change involves "change agent, client system, valid knowledge, and a deliberate and collaborative relationship".[24] The process involves some form of observation and participation with accompanying feedback and deliberate interventions to bring about understanding of what really is going on. Accompanying the feedback is an attempt to interpret behavior in terms of valid information—from the social and behavioral sciences.

---

[22] Matthew B. Miles. See his *Innovations in Education* (New York: Bureau of Publications, Teachers College, Columbia University, 1964). Also see Chapter 2 in Carlson and others, *Change Processes in the Public Schools,* and "Education and Innovation: The Organization as Content", a paper delivered at Auburn University in 1964.

[23] This is not to suggest that the contributions of disciplines other than sociology or social psychology have nothing to offer to the understanding of change. Quite the opposite would be true. Understanding the inputs to school systems from the community (political science and economics for examples) is critical. These are effectively handled by the school as an institution only if there is effectiveness within the school, however. Replace the schools by other institutions and the new institutions would soon be confronted by similar problems.

[24] Warren G. Bennis, "Theory and Method in Applying Behavioral Science to Planned Change" (mimeographed).

The intended consequences are several:

1. Increased understanding of self and the impact of one's behavior on others;

2. Increased understanding of others and their behavior (each of the above both in personal terms and objectively in terms of insights from the social and behavioral sciences);

3. Bringing into the open feelings and opinions that have not been communicated and have interfered with interpersonal and behavioral effectiveness;

4. Opening lines of communication between and among members of the group;

5. Providing valid data about the group or the organization to replace subjective evidence.

A number of different approaches are used, each of which has proved effective. One of the best known is the T-Group or Sensitivity Training approach of the National Training Laboratory (which has been in operation continuously since 1947). Another is the approach developed by Blake,[25] in which "diagonal slices" (small groups) of the personnel in an organization are given encouragement and assistance to develop and implement new and promising concepts.

The writer has had several years of experience with in-service education programs with administrator groups in New York State.[26] In one of these programs all members of the administrative staffs were involved in a continuous program which included:

1. Seminars on social and behavioral science concepts relevant to organizations and organizational behavior;

2. Attendance at the National Training Laboratory summer T-Group programs with several members attending each year;

3. Semi-annual week-end retreats at which the interpersonal relations training and organizational behavior analysis were furthered.

In the absence of objective evidence, I can only report my conviction that there is indeed need for these kinds of activities and that such programs do have a marked and beneficial effect on the organization and its members.

Activities of this kind in education are rare. The few that do exist tend to be superficial and to involve only administrators. What is needed are serious attempts at innovation and adoption in the field of organizational health comparable to those now being put forth in the development of innovation. *When we are ready to invest as much in personnel development as we are in technology and program development we may begin to release the creative talents of those who work in our educational institutions.*

---

[25] Robert R. Blake and Jane S. Mouton, *The Managerial Grid* (Houston, Texas: Gulf Publishing Company, 1961).

[26] Reported briefly in R. B. Howsam, "In-service Education of School Administrators: Background, Present Status, and Problems" in *Continuing Education of School Administrators* (Albuquerque, New Mexico: University of New Mexico, 1966).

Until we are prepared to do so we will constantly be faced with efforts to develop change strategies to bring about adoption of innovations, the effects of which may be nullified by the stresses and strains which living in organizations always produces.

It is unlikely that the children in our schools will ever have the kind of education they deserve until those who teach and those who administer resolve their organizational problems and achieve interpersonal effectiveness. It would not be too much to expect that the results might appear in the classroom.

*   *   *

SUPPLEMENTARY STATEMENT

DONALD C. ORLICH*

The authorities who have prepared papers for this conference have viewed educational changes and innovations from social, cultural, political and other institutional or theoretical viewpoints. The intent of this paper is to focus attention on some problems commonly shared by the eight Rocky Mountain area states participating in this project and to offer some practical suggestions for resolving the apparent conflicts that will ensue as educators press for innovations, changes and creative approaches within the educational establishment.

Basic to successful implementation of innovation is some knowledge of the area involved. Geographically, we are somewhat isolated. Communications channels continue to be oriented from east to west, with minor north-south interaction. Seasonal weather conditions further restrict person to person communications periodically from November through March. Sparsity factors must be recognized when studying the region.

Socially, the area is marked by a comparatively homogeneous population. We tend to react in a conservative manner whether we are discussing politics or women's fashions. Our area is observably marked by conservative religious forces. The predominant religious creeds tend to neutralize or ignore many liberal currents emanating elsewhere in the nation.

Economically, the area is just beginning to develop from its agrarian antecedents. However, in such states as Nevada, New Mexico, and Wyoming, industrial development lags behind that in the other states.[1] Closely allied to the economic sector are demographic implications. The states of Montana, Idaho, and Wyoming tend to lose younger persons to other Rocky Mountain or West Coast states. In one sense we can call this a "brain drain" for included within this group are typically the better

---

* *Chairman, Department of Education, Idaho State University, Pocatello.* Director of Title I, Higher Education Act Project: In-service Education for Idaho School Trustees; and Associate Project Director, Rocky Mountain Educational Laboratory ETV Project. Author of several publications, including (with S. Samuel Shermis) *The Pursuit of Excellence: Introductory Readings in Education* (1965).

[1] U. S. Bureau of the Census, *Statistical Abstract of the United States: 1966* (Washington, D. C., 1966), Table 317, p. 226.

educated persons—especially college graduates, beginning teachers and skilled technicians.[2]

Politically, we Westerners tend to believe "that all men are created equal." In practice, the power distribution of most of these states appears to resemble an oligarchy. Montana was once described in one of the nation's leading journals as "the last of the feudal baronies." The power system is further complicated in Utah, Southern Idaho and Northern Arizona by strong religious-political-social entanglements.

Educationally (we know that education stems from the society that nurtures it) the area boasts no *great university*. To be sure, there are outstanding scholars found in the region and there are individual academic departments that are outstanding. But in actuality there is no university comparable to the University of California at Berkeley, the University of Oregon or the University of Washington on the West Coast; or the University of Chicago in the Midwest. There is no Rocky Mountain university that can approach the prestige and excellence found in Ivy League institutions.

It seems apparent that similar comparisons are applicable to the public school systems. There are no clusters of outstanding school systems or—as they are called in the trade—"light house districts". However, this condition is beginning to show signs of change. One can single out several school districts that have contributed greatly to public education. But most innovations have been developed and tested in states in other areas, with little planned experimentation and innovation taking place in our area. A brief review of the U. S. Office of Education Co-operative Research projects shows that this eight state area lags far behind other states in most other areas in utilizing this program to foster educational research, either pure or applied.[3] The one major exception is participation in Title III of the Elementary and Secondary School Act (ESEA) of 1965. There is a great deal of activity taking place which may have future consequences. However, the impact of Title III, ESEA, can only be evaluated five or ten years hence.

Finally, the state departments of education have long lagged as leaders or instigators of innovation. Although all such departments are rapidly changing in character, the impetus for change has not come from the states in most cases, but from federal agencies. It now appears that the Utah and Colorado departments of education are the most dynamic of the eight and may be playing key leadership roles for the area.

In every state, the state agency for education including staff members of the department, must be prepared to provide leadership in planning and effecting needed changes in education, and to cooperate with other agencies

---

[2] U. S. Bureau of the Census, *Current Population Reports*, "Population Estimates," Series P-25, No. 362, Table 3, March 7, 1967. See also "Americans at Mid Century" Series P-23, No. 16, January, 1966; Series P-25, No. 326, Table 2, February 7, 1966; *U. S. Census of Population, 1960, Mobility for States and State Economic Areas*, PC(2), 2B; and *U. S. Summary, General Population Characteristics*, PC(1), 1B.

[3] U. S. Office of Education, *Digest of Educational Statistics, 1963 Edition*, pp. 112-113; *1965 Edition*, pp. 147-148; and *1966 Edition*, p. 98.

and organizations—and even with other states—in the process. The state agency should—and can, if it is properly organized—develop state-wide plans for pertinent aspects of education; assemble and disseminate information on promising innovations; encourage and help to evaluate appropriate pilot projects; arrange for the cooperation of qualified college and university representatives and school systems in planning and conducting needed research and in-service programs; and facilitate the planning and implementation of needed changes in education in many other ways.

What Changes Can Be Made?

If the conditions briefly described above are realistic, as I assume, how can effectual educational changes and innovations be made within the eight states? One cannot ignore Kimbrough's discussion of power systems, Howsam's analysis of institutional and inter-personal reforms, or Chin's general strategies. To their complex analyses I would like to offer several practical—but not simple—solutions.

My suggestions are offered as a series of questions leading logically to positive methods for change. The reader will also note that my focus for change is primarily on the "formal" organization. This is not to ignore informal organizations, but to emphasize the institutionality of *status quo*.

Why Change?

In my opinion, this is the most crucial question of all. We Americans typically assume that change is automatically equated to "goodness". Some recent educational innovations have been blindly accepted by local schools to the detriment of the student population. The unplanned utilization of instructional television has already discouraged some educational leaders. Team teaching and flexible scheduling are now enjoying popularity—but, in too many cases, for the wrong reasons. For example, a district superintendent stated that his district would adopt team teaching because, "team teaching is nothing more than having one good teacher on a team with four poor ones."

Many changes are implemented because of the "band wagon" effect. Ultimately this effect causes skepticism toward many current innovations. In other words, good theory has sometimes been nullified by bad practice under conditions that were not conducive to proper implementation.

I have witnessed several abuses of sound educational planning—all made in the name of "innovation". One large district in our region offers all sixth graders *Parley Vous Francais* through the medium of educational television. But to the chagrin of the instructional staff, there are *no* foreign language experiences for these students in the seventh or eighth grades!

Too often elementary and secondary school educators ignore what scholars in academic disciplines recommend concerning the teaching of their respective specialties. For example, the Modern Language Association has released two sharply worded statements of policy concerning FLES.[4] Yet, few school districts have heeded their advice and counsel. As a matter of fact, relatively few school administrators or curriculum consultants have read the statements. The same comment may be made about modern mathematics in the elementary school. Good programs are made ineffective because the teachers are not academically qualified to teach "modern mathematics". District after district has adopted textbooks requiring the teaching of modern mathematics without having teachers who are knowledgeable about principles of mathematics. This is an indictment of administrators—rather than of teachers. If local educational administrators are not sensitive to the level of staff preparation, how can they expect to implement the tried and tested innovations?

To innovate effectively, there must be some genuine desire or need to change from that which already exists. If this statement reflects the conservatism of the region, then so be it. There is no inherent value in change, *per se.*

WHAT GOALS ARE TO BE ESTABLISHED?

In a recently completed study, we found, through an examination of hundreds of school and school board philosophies, that local schools do not usually provide a realistic or well thought out statement on educational philosophy, nor are they consciously aware of general or specific educational objectives.[5] When shortcomings are identified, it becomes necessary to establish the goals or objectives to be followed in order to resolve the problems. Albert Einstein once stated that, "Our age is characterized by the perfection of means and the confusion of goals."

The obvious implication above is that *innovation is best approached by a carefully planned, calculated and systematic procedure.* Undirected change cannot be tolerated as a systematic method. Yet, this is the typology that appears most often and usually ends with the innovation being held in disrepute. Is it any wonder that teachers are so accustomed to saying, "That won't work here!"

HOW ARE THE CHANGES TO BE EFFECTED?

Once the innovative thrust has been determined and the general and specific objectives defined, the next step is to determine the magnitude on which the innovation is to be implemented. Control and experimental groups must be established, and operated under carefully planned experimental design. Further testing can then proceed on a larger scale as each step is made operational and re-evaluated.

If a school or school system is adopting a pre-tested program, the staff must study all available literature on the subject to benefit from

---

[4] Modern Language Association, Foreign Language Program Research Center. *Foreign Languages in the Elementary School: A Second Statement of Policy.* Report of a conference sponsored by MLA, January 27-28, 1961. (New York: The Center, 1961). MLA published earlier statements in 1953 and 1959.

[5] Donald C. Orlich and S. Samuel Shermis, "Educational Philosophy as Mythology: A Critical Analysis of School Philosophies," *Administrator's Notebook,* Vol. XIV, No. 4 (December, 1965).

previous experiences. The essence of good innovation should be the same as that of good research. Application should move from the pinnacle out—not from the valleys that have been plowed and re-plowed.

The changes effected need not be minor in scope. Let us learn from the Biological Sciences Curriculum Study (BSCS). Once the three initial curricula were decided on, they were tested on ever increasing numbers of students. BSCS biology may be adopted by nearly all American high schools by 1970. In other words, in little more than one decade a radical change will have been effected on the most widely chosen secondary school science course in the nation! Every step was carefully calculated, tested, evaluated and re-tested. (The University of Colorado served as the host institution to produce the BSCS curriculum).

To this same extent, selected, needed and identifiable changes can be tested by the eight states involved in this project. Some educational innovations can be tested simultaneously in widely separated geographic areas and conditions.

I would like to stress one point strongly. *There is no clearly defined set of educational problems within any of the states participating in this project.* To be sure, inadequate financing can be mentioned as an educational problem. But all governmental agencies work with limited budgets. Therefore, educational priorities must be established. We must ask about the hierarchy of needs. What is the most urgent or pressing problem and what problems are secondary or tertiary? It appears that we tend to treat all educational problems as being of primary importance and then consider them as being equally important. If all problems are considered of equal importance, no priorities can be established and we will have no means for making practical choices.

Implementation of innovations will be accelerated when colleges and universities play a more active role in the change process. Their graduates should be given a greater understanding of promising educational innovations. All college faculties—not just those in departments of education—must accept the responsibility of working with teachers, administrators, and even students. How can we expect to implement desirable changes when those in higher education who are the most liberally oriented have seemingly established artificial communication barriers between themselves and the practitioners at the elementary and secondary levels?

When one speaks about the "knowledge explosion" he should realize that institutions of higher learning—those generating the knowledge—have not made adequate provisions for dissemination and implementation. I would suggest that we study the land grant college model with their departments of agriculture, attendant experimental stations, and county demonstration agents.[6]

---

[6] For an excellent discussion, see "What Are Innovators Like?", by Everett M. Rogers, in *Change Processes in Public Schools* (University of Oregon Press: Center For The Advanced Study of Educational Administration, 1965), pp. 55-61.

DOES THE SCHOOL SYSTEM HAVE THE ADMINISTRATIVE STRUCTURE TO IMPLEMENT CHANGE?

At the second conference held in Salt Lake City in October, 1966, program participants discussed administrative structures at great length. The administrative positions toward change can make the difference between success and failure when testing new programs. In my experience as an administrator I have observed that the faculty will ultimately reflect their "leader" if they hold compatible goals. If an administrator fosters creativity and urges his faculty to experiment, the faculty in a rather short period of time will be involved in experimentation. While creativity may not be caused by reflective administrative leadership, the conditions for creative endeavors can certainly be stimulated by sensitive and unthreatened administrative personnel.

To enhance a favorable administrative climate, it is necessary to have personnel familiar with empirical research methodology. Only in a handful of our larger school districts do we find research directors. The basic functions of such directors are to collect and disseminate information about the district, and to study continuously promising innovative programs. Practices should be thoroughly tested, explored and analyzed for their total impact on the education of youth. Complex analyses can be best made by a staff whose only commitment is to explore new ideas—and even to generate a few.

It is safe to generalize that line-and-staff patterns are the most prevalent type in this eight state area. If one man alone can stop—or encourage—innovative practices, the basic organization chart needs revising. Let me amplify. In most districts there are persons holding "staff" or advisory positions, such as consultants or supervisors. In many instances the "staff" personnel act as if they were the "line" officers by making basic instructional decisions rather than advising the designated "decision makers". Further, in the large districts the line is so long that it is almost impossible for a teacher to send anything "up the chain".

To avoid a conflict with the organization chart, the superintendent might find it advantageous to establish an advisory committee on innovations, which would be an adjunct to the research bureau. Ideally, classroom teachers would elect representatives to this committee as would the district's administrators. In this manner the superintendent would have a direct line of communication with his teachers, and they would have easy access to the opportunity to put worthwhile ideas into action.

Any successful innovation must pass the administrative hurdle. (This is not to ignore the evidence that administrators, for the most part, are the chief initiators of change at the local district level.) However, what is educationally sound must also be administratively feasible. Therefore, the program or innovation must be an integral and serious part of the entire school program.

GENERAL CONSIDERATIONS FOR CHANGE

There are at least five general aspects that must be considered if one is innovating. Questions that—if properly answered—will help to ensure that the changes can be successfully implemented are included under each of the areas. If all concerned—that is, school board members, administrators, teachers, and lay personnel—ask these questions, then any innovation should be able to stand the ultimate test—success in the classroom.

Finance. In what manner will the program be financed? Have any anticipated budget increases been discussed with the rationale that the program is to be long-range in nature? If federal funds are being used (for example, the various titles of the NDEA or ESEA) what plans have been made to phase out the federal share when that level of government withdraws categorical support? Did the school board adopt written budget policies pertaining to the program? What long term capital outlays are necessary? Will support from other projects be dropped, thereby curtailing previous commitments, when another program is being instituted?

Personnel. Does your district have personnel who are *fully* qualified to conduct or teach the program? Has the personnel officer (more than likely the superintendent) been recruiting teachers who have first hand knowledge of the anticipated innovation? Do you have adequate personnel to conduct the program on a wide scale, or will it be slowly phased into the over-all curriculum? Does your school district have a systematic in-service education program for teachers involved in the innovative practices?

Students. Have your students been fully informed as to what the program will entail? Will any analysis of student reaction account for the "Hawthorne Effect"? What impact will the addition of one or more curricular innovations have on the student's over-all program? Will any data be collected on student achievement for further research or analysis? Is any student eligible for the program, or is it another program for some "hyphenated" group? How will the new program affect other school programs? Will an adequate number of students be available to participate?

The School Plant. Will the innovation fit into the present school plant? Are there any major or minor building alterations that must be made? Can needed renovations be made during vacation periods, or will there be "interference" during the school day?

The Community. Does the school board understand the relevant aspects of the innovation, and has it adequately interpreted them to the patrons? Have pressure groups—either lay or teacher—shown interest in the curriculum change or have they seemed disinterested? How much wrath will the school board absorb from local organizations who have vested interests in *status quo?*

IN CONCLUSION

Several implications have been identified to aid the prospective change agent. The areas discussed above must be scrutinized while educational changes are being planned—not after they have been implemented.

Serious readers will note the lack of a well developed theoretical model. But, this was not intended to be the essence of this paper. The average educational practitioner does not understand theoretical models. He proceeds to attempt to implement—for better or for worse—ideas that appeal to him. One might say that this paper is grossly pragmatic. To this comment I can only offer the statement that a pragmatic solution must account for the here-and-now—the "will it work?" aspects—as well as for the consequences for the future. The latter point is my major thesis. Proposed curricular or educational changes must be analyzed primarily in terms of their implications for the future.

Changes are made while the educational machinery is in motion. The system cannot be stopped to change parts or to overhaul it. Innovations are made in viable, dynamic, organizational, and interpersonal settings. *The essence of educational change is planning*—not taking chances on spontaneous mutations. Let us build on solid foundations, thereby avoiding the errors so observable in our educational heritage.

CHAPTER 5

Research, Development, and Dissemination Strategies in Improving Education

R. Louis Bright*

Hendrik D. Gideonse**

It is most stimulating to participate in a field which has generated as much excitement as educational research has in recent months. Controversy, discussion, and debate are very much the order of the day; the gradual growth of contacts with new and informative sources of data, and of faith in the research effort are developments full of promise for the future.

In agreeing to prepare this paper, we explicitly accept the notion that it makes sense to talk about strategies of research and development for improving education. At the same time we do not make any claim to producing anything more than tentative steps in the direction of more adequately defined strategies for achieving mutually agreed upon objectives. For a variety of reasons which we will attempt to spell out in this paper, we have begun the process of developing and applying more explicit strategies to the research and development process. These strategies are neither rigid nor lightly held. *Some* notions of what we are about and why are clearly necessary; not to have them is to default a major responsibility. In this paper we try to spell out both the general outlines of the strategies we are pursuing and the procedures by which we hope to continually modify the specific substance implicit in those strategies and the actual strategies themselves.

The improvement of American education depends upon the systematic investigation of the process and the necessary conditions for learning, the development of instructional objectives, strategies, and materials based on the knowledge educators and others accumulate about the learning process, and finally on the implementation of those strategies and the use of those materials in instructional settings across the country. We take this as a fundamental article of faith, but it is a faith which has been substantiated over and over again in all fields of human endeavor whether they relate to space, health, poverty, industry or education. To claim,

---

* *Associate Commissioner for Research, United States Office of Education.* Formerly, manager of the Industrial Computer Program and Associate Director, Westinghouse Research Laboratories (1953-66); Member of the Graduate Faculty, Carnegie Institute of Technology (1946-53). Fellow in IEEE, Tau Beta Pi, Sigma Xi, Eta Kappa Nu, Phi Kappa Phi.

** *Director of Program Planning and Development, Bureau of Research, U. S. Office of Education.* Formerly, Research Coordinator and Program Advisor, U. S. Office of Education (1964-65); Instructor, Bowdoin College (1963-64) and Wheelock College (1961). Member, *Harvard Educational Review* (1959-62), and Chairman of the Board (1961-62); member, Editorial Board, *Educational Researcher* (1966).

however, that significant and continuing advances in the process of education depend upon research and development is only the barest of opening statements. A perspective and the setting need first to be sketched in, and then a full exploration of the ramifications of that article of faith needs to be conducted.

SETTING THE PERSPECTIVE

Any consideration of the role of research and development in American education necessarily relates to the nature of the existing "system" through which we have institutionalized education in our society. With legal responsibility for education in this country vested in the states and operational responsibility for schools largely delegated to some 25,000 local educational agencies authorized by the states, the role of the federal government has largely been confined to providing specified categorical financial support.

These different levels of responsibility are complicated by another feature of American education. Not many of the diverse institutions and agencies which serve education in this society are well-coordinated or formally related to one another. When we use the word "system" as applied to American education, we are being generous. What we have is a de facto system which serves the broad needs of the society well, but perhaps not as well as it might if it were generously laced with efficient communication channels designed to make it an integrated, functionally related entity of many parts and many purposes.

From the point of view of the general improvement of education, it makes more sense to talk of the educational system as composed of classes of institutions and agencies. Each class embraces organizations which perform similar functions and which, if there were an organized system, would be expected to fulfill a particular role. Thus, the classes of institutions include the three levels of responsibility for education—local, state and federal. They include professional associations and institutions for training teachers. They include the industries which supply materials and equipment to the schools. They include universities and institutes under whose aegis research on education and learning is performed. The existing "system", in other words, is largely a collection of nearly unrelated sub-systems or institutions representative of sub-systems. This feature is of no small importance in devising strategies for the general improvement of the whole.

A NATION-WIDE NEED FOR EDUCATIONAL RESEARCH AND DEVELOPMENT

The nation-wide nature of the need for educational research and development is becoming increasingly apparent. Schools, districts, state education agencies, private institutions, colleges, and universities all have major needs relating to the improved fulfillment of their instructional responsibilities. While individual institutions and agencies differ, many if not a majority of the problems which confront them are similar. Serious questions of economies of scale have been answered in effect by the relatively small amounts of money which have been devoted to educational research at the local level. We have seen for decades an entirely reasonable response on the part of local and state agencies with respect to the funding of major research and development efforts. While they have no doubt been aware that sophisticated, well-conceived research programs would benefit not only themselves but also many others as well, very few have felt that they themselves could assume the financial and human burden of mounting large-scale research programs. It would make vastly more sense if the actual cost of generating those findings and materials were amortized more proportionately across all the potential beneficiaries.

The teaching of mathematics, for example, is not likely to be much different for similar children in Maine and Arizona. On the other hand, there may be significant differences in instruction in mathematics within a state for children having different socio-economic characteristics, learning styles, or motivational problems. It would be a philanthropic district or state that felt it could mount the requisite research and development projects to serve all the immediate local needs when some other mechanisms could be developed which would distribute the cost more fairly in return for the mutual benefits that would be derived.

THE EMPLOYMENT OF NATIONAL RESOURCES

The resources for conducting educational research and development, though not as limited as some people would have us believe, are in fact unequally distributed across the country. No necessary conclusions with respect to continuing patterns of supporting educational research can be drawn from that fact, but a consideration of it is certainly one of the relevant contextual matters for the development of research and development strategies. The nation-wide character of the need for research and the unequal distribution of the human resources for research reinforce one another. They highlight the breadth of the problem. In other words, so long as human resources are unequally distributed, the direct or implicit coordination of them to serve research and educational needs of high priority will constitute one of the major background considerations in research strategies.

FINANCIAL RESOURCES

Certainly one of the more important matters lending perspective to research and development (R & D) strategies for improving education is the availability of financing. The resources are limited. Money available from all sources for R & D in education has never exceeded one percent of the total annual expenditures on education in the nation as a whole. Estimated expenditures for this fiscal year for all levels of formal education are $48.8 billion.[1] By contrast the funds available at the federal level for educational research and development are somewhere between $200-

---

[1] *Digest of Educational Statistics, 1966*, U. S. Government Printing Office, Washington, D. C., 1966, p. 17.

220 million.[2] A little simple arithmetic reveals that this amount constitutes less than half of one percent of the total annual expenditure on education. We do not by any means take that as "a given" for the future, but it is most assuredly an important element in developing perspective on the problem of research strategies for the present.

THE DISTINCTION BETWEEN "RESEARCH" AND "IMPROVEMENT"

A final element for consideration in this context is our conviction that R & D in education and the change process in education are two very different functions or processes which must, however, be related intimately, sensitively, and integrally to one another. The research and development process produces the substance of improvement. It yields the knowledge about the learning process and the social setting for learning and education, and encourages the refinement of objectives and the development of materials and instructional processes which incorporate that knowledge into improved educational practices.

The *implementation* of those practices in the school systems across the nation—the differential accommodation of different institutions and agencies to the new roles and expectations created by the improvements—however, is a very different kind of problem and requires strategies and tactics commensurate to the task as it is revealed. The differences between the two processes and the unique characteristics of each may very well shape significantly the strategies adopted for one or the other. The functional demands of educational research and development, for example, place certain constraints on the process of implementation. Similarly, the exigencies of the process of implementation may impinge upon the strategies for R & D which may be adopted.

RESEARCH, DEVELOPMENT, AND THE PROCESS OF IMPLEMENTATION

Recent policy-level discussions of educational research and development within agencies responsible for research funds, between such agencies and their constituencies, and within the research community itself, have made it clear that there is far from unanimous agreement on the definition of the terms commonly applied to research and development. For this reason, we believe it would be helpful to establish how we are now using various terms—not to develop for all time a thesaurus as applied to the research process, but rather to clarify our concepts and interpretations.

The research and development process involves all those activities designed to produce knowledge about the learning process (research, for example, designed to improve learning theory or to improve our under-

---

[2] The imprecision in the estimate derives from a number of considerations. The research authorizations of USOE in FY 1967 total $99 million, but $6 million are for training and another $14 million are for construction. The National Science Foundation spends close to $17 million a year on curriculum development, and almost certainly some of the curriculum development efforts of the Office of Economic Opportunity will be used by schools. Similarly, the National Institute of Mental Health and the National Institute of Child Health and Human Development also spend a considerable amount on research related to areas of interest to learning and education. Title III of ESEA, if past percentages hold, could well spend $81 million on development and demonstration activities. Part of the development of strategies for educational R&D is the coordination of these several sources of research and research related funds.

standing of the fundamental chemical, biological, and neurological processes underlying learning). It includes other kinds of activities devoted to the social context of learning (for example, the classroom or school as a social system, or the relationship among non-instructional factors such as motivation of peers, socio-economic status, educational level of the home and the direct instructional interventions of the school such as curriculum, instructional methodology, facilities and so on). It includes studies pertaining to the organization and administration of the instructional enterprise.

Research and development also includes the development of new practices, materials, and processes based on the knowledge newly created in the other kinds of studies. This involves identification of the specific improvement desired and then the systematic engineering of that improvement, using all the information derived from basic research that is relevant.

A third part of the process, closely related to development, *is the demonstration of the feasibility of the new materials, processes, or organizational forms* in other than the hot-house setting of the development laboratory.

Finally, *a fourth element in the R & D process is the systematic dissemination of information relating to all the different stages.* Information about research projects completed and underway is essential to the basic researcher. The educational developer also needs to know the latest findings about learning if he is to be able to incorporate them in his work. Researchers and educators in the schools need to know what the development people are up to. On the other hand, the kinds of problems encountered by those engaged in curriculum or hardware development may suggest research projects to the psychologists and sociologists. School people need to keep aware of new techniques and possibilities under development. Demonstrations need to be publicized, too, and the success or lack thereof provides further information to both researchers and developers. Finally, the existence of the dissemination capability itself needs to be widely publicized to insure that all those having the need can make appropriate use of it.

Applied to any given piece of knowledge or any given improvement in one or a few schools, the R & D process and the implementation of improvement process appear to be identical. The differences between the two processes begin to become visible, however, when the systematic implementation of improvements in the entire educational system is the desired objective. The systematic and continuing introduction of improvements in education through judicious innovation and change based on research requires careful attention to the different roles played by the many independent agencies and institutions in education.

The first attempt, for example, to implement a new curriculum in economics in a secondary school undertaken with the aid of the original project staff responsible for developing it can easily be viewed as the normal demonstration responsibility of the project. But if the scope of responsibility is enlarged to include developing the capability of *any* teaching staff anywhere in the country where a decision to implement that curriculum has been made (that decision assumes, of course, knowledge about the curriculum and a judgment as to its suitability), the problem is clearly larger than an individual project. Attention needs to be paid to the problems of developing mechanisms for the in-service and pre-service training of teachers to use the new curriculum. That effort in turn may point to the particular responsibilities of teacher training institutions across the nation both to assist in the particular effort and to insure, more generally, that pre-service training is undertaken in the light of the almost certain need for continuing education of teaching staff to keep up with new departures in curricular application. Thus we have moved in this one instance very quickly away from the individual school setting to the much larger question of how teacher training institutions—and maybe, therefore, also state teacher certification agencies—are to play their particular and general roles of enhancing the likelihood of the adoption of proven innovation.

The matter can be carried still further. School boards should be apprised of the need to continually re-examine curricular objectives in terms of present and future social needs; as a consequence they can be expected to play a significant part in the networks of differing responsible agencies having unique roles in the process of implementing educational improvements based on and validated by research. The responsibilities of industry in helping to develop materials, in manufacturing, and in selling them similarly need careful attention. Their responsibilities, if any, for training their customers in the use of newly developed materials also need to be considered.

Viewed on a larger scale, then, it would appear that *many of the questions associated with the actual implementation of solid innovations system-wide depend on factors more closely related to the dynamics of social change than to the actual research and development process itself.* This dynamic—whether called administration, the politics of change, or continuing attention to the intricacies of the process of building conviction in and a demand for more effective materials and practices in the schools— is a necessary condition for the implementation of the products of R & D in schools. It constitutes, therefore, an absolutely essential problem for educational R & D strategists.

RESEARCH, DEVELOPMENT, AND DISSEMINATION STRATEGIES
OF THE PAST

In describing the strategies of the past, present and future we have elected to characterize broadly in generalized form the major outlines of attack as pursued until a very few months ago, the kinds of changes which took place and that have placed us in a crucial period of transition, and the sorts of directions we project for the future.

The availability of millions of dollars for educational research and development is a relatively new phenomenon. The recency of this growth and its absolute size give some pause for thought. A review of developments will help disclose the range of options available to us now and in the future.

The first piece of legislation specifically authorizing the United States Office of Education to support research, surveys, and demonstrations in education—the Cooperative Research Act—was passed by the 83rd Congress in 1954. In effect, the Congress said that research in education was important enough that the nation needed legislation to authorize federal support for it. The Act itself, of course, represented a first step in the development of strategies for conducting R & D to improve education. Four years later, in 1958, the Congress included two titles in the National Defense Education Act (NDEA) authorizing research on the uses of new media and on modern foreign languages. These three authorizations turned out to be but a beginning. There are now a total of seven pieces of legislation including authorizations pertaining to vocational education, handicapped children and youth, libraries and information science, and an authorization under P.L. 480, a special foreign currency program based on the distribution of surplus foods.

The passage and funding of federal legislation authorizing research in education was a major departure in and of itself. It was recognition of the conviction that federal support needed to be directed to a problem bearing dimensions larger than those of individual states and calling upon resources, both financial and human, then currently beyond the means of state and local educational agencies.

The initial forays in support of educational research combined the identification of areas of concern and the support of technically excellent proposals submitted in response to a general call. In the very first instance, for example, proposals were requested dealing with mental retardation. As the research programs expanded in dollar size, greater proportions were administered on a nonpriority basis. Areas of importance were identified periodically and interest maintained in those areas, but the guiding principle for the support of research was the technical excellence of proposals rather than the type of research or the substantive area of concern. That principle was viable because in the early days of the research effort it was always possible to fund all the technically excellent proposals without regard to the field of study.

Over the years, substantial amounts of applied research as well as basic research were stimulated and supported. In more recent years the research program has moved into two kinds of activity: curriculum improvement and the establishment of research centers designed to explore programmatically R & D in a defined problem area in education. Even with the addition of these new thrusts the same principle mentioned before was still applicable. The field was young and growing, but it was still possible to support all of the quality proposals submitted.

THE RECENT PAST AND THE PRESENT

In 1965, several groups including staff inside the Office of Education, a Presidential Task Force, and others began to take a hard look at federally supported research in education, then nearly nine years old. The wisdom of earlier strategies was apparent. They had been successful —in part bcause of the availability of dollars, in part because of the generally unsolicited mode of operation—in stimulating the growth of and interest in research and development. The field was growing; the submissions of proposals was increasing rapidly (in fact, at a faster rate than appropriations); the educational community as a whole was beginning to pay attention to the possibilities of research.

IMPORTANT RESEARCH DEVELOPMENTS

Research and Development Centers. The newly acquired visibility of research and development, however, led to concern over some of the apparent deficiencies of the total research effort as it had emerged to that point. First, it became apparent that the individual research projects as a whole—while of acceptable levels of quality individually—did not fit together well enough to be considered coordinated approaches to substantive problems in education. The Research and Development Centers were in part created in response to this need, but it was felt that major chunks of the research effort should be better coordinated and designed to lead to cumulative results.

Second, part of the difficulty in developing highly coordinated cumulative research efforts could be attributed to the inadequacy of the dissemination of information to the educational research community regarding the findings of *completed* research and the nature of *current* research. A strong need was felt, therefore, for the establishment of an effective research dissemination system.

Third, a careful examination of the outcomes of research in terms of service to the schools revealed that in two senses insufficient attention was being paid to the gap between the research stage and implementation. First, the stage of development was not being supported to anything near the degree that it should. Second, very little attention was being directed to the change process whereby improvements could be actually implemented in wide-spread fashion.

Fourth, it was clear that the human resources available for R & D activities would need to be expanded in at least two ways. Training programs to develop new talent would be required. New agencies and institutions previously not eligible for support would need to be tapped.

Amendments to Research Acts. The response to these felt needs took the form of a series of amendments to research legislation, the creation of a series of new program efforts under the aegis of the newly acquired authority, and the passage of a new piece of legislation. The basic piece of research legislation administered by the Office of Education, the

Cooperative Research Act, was amended in 1965 by Title IV of the Elementary and Secondary Education Act (ESEA). The amendments broadened the existing authority—to support research, surveys, and demonstrations in education—to include *dissemination.* The range of eligible institutions was expanded to virtually all kinds of public and private organizations whether profit or non-profit. Authority was included to develop programs designed to train educational research and related personnel, and to upgrade training programs. The Office was authorized to award grants as well as contracts, and the Commissioner was given authority to award funds for the construction and equipping of facilities for research and related purposes.

These amendments vastly extended the range of activities possible under the research program, and made it feasible for the research program to meet directly some of the needs identified in the reviews of the program to that time. In addition, the testimony before the Congressional committees—or the legislative history, as it is called—made it very clear that the broadened authority was to be used to bridge the gap between research and practice and to pay substantially more attention to the problems of implementing the knowledge derived from the research efforts to date and in the future. The broadened responsibilities represented by these additional authorizations have created new demands on the administration of research and at the same time have offered new tools for meeting emergent shortcomings of the research effort.

Training Program. To date, three major new program thrusts have undergone spirited development. A training program designed to expand the corps of educational researchers has been developed. This program provides both program development grants and an array of training mechanisms ranging from institutes of short and long duration through undergraduate and graduate training programs to a small post-doctoral effort.[3]

Educational Research Information Center. The Educational Research Information Center (ERIC) has been established with Central ERIC, 12 clearinghouses, and more to come. ERIC is designed to provide to researchers and practitioners alike an information storage and retrieval mechanism to make available instantly in easily accessible indexed form all the research and related data relevant to a particular problem. *Research in Education,* the monthly publication of the ERIC system, is now in its third issue, and already the usefulness of this effort has begun to prove itself.

Educational Laboratories. The third and largest development in the research program has awakened the interest, excitement, and the enthusiasm of the entire educational community from local schools, state agencies, and teacher training institutions to industry, scholars from the arts and

---

[3] This of course is the area of concern to which David Clark has addressed his attention in "Educational Research and Development: The New Decade," *Implications for Education of Prospective Changes in Society* (Denver, Colorado: Designing Education for the Future, 1967).

sciences, and the lay public. We refer to the National Program of Educational Laboratories. Drawing from resources in regions extending across the nation, new institutions called *educational laboratories* have been created to bridge the gap between research and practice. These institutions were created by representatives of all the many agencies and institutions which play different roles in the implementation process. They are reflections of the conviction that it is not enough to do research; that research must be followed up by development projects which, having established the desired objectives—whether curricular, instructional, organizational, professional, or technical—then move to the development of solutions drawing upon the best that research has to offer. The laboratories have also been charged with the responsibility for active dissemination campaigns based on the successful development projects they and others engage in.

We have encouraged the laboratories to conceive their responsibilities broadly—encompassing much more than merely the distribution of information, although that is a critically important function among many. Clearly, one of the important steps in the diffusion of research-based improvement throughout the educational system is the establishment of demonstrations. First time demonstrations of feasibility will be the direct responsibility of the laboratories; the more widespread diffusion of the successful innovations will depend on the degree to which information about the innovation is distributed to various parts of the systems, the degree to which the innovation recommends itself to professionals, and the degree to which credible demonstrations of the new practice or curriculum are mounted in schools. This last part of the diffusion process—the establishment of real-life (*not* hot-house) demonstrations of the innovation without the intervention of the inventer—represents a place where the labs can work with state education agencies and local school districts to make use of Title III of ESEA. Such demonstration efforts must be coordinated and well-conceived. Laboratories can help only in their areas of competence and program thrust and only by cooperating closely with state education agencies and the local school districts.

The laboratories were conceived in such a way as to involve in their government and their operation the many types of different responsibilities and resources that combine to form the educational system as we know it. The hope is that these new institutions—responsible for their own program development and implementation and knit closely together to form a network—will, as their resources permit, at one and the same time engage in (1) major efforts to develop new materials, practices and organizations using the outcomes of research; and (2) by utilizing the expertise brought to them by the involvement of different agencies and institutions, pursue courses of action which help to hasten the process of improvement once tested innovations are available.

The strategy for these three new program thrusts is straightforward. If there is to be an expansion in research and development, people will need to be trained or recruited from new areas to fill the demand. In order to build structures of knowledge and cumulative improvement, dissemination networks and the material which moves through them will need to be better systematized and improved. Finally, to fill the gap between research and practice, a new autonomous institution drawing institutionally and representationally on many resources in the education system has been created.

Title III of ESEA. In addition to the new authorizations for research and the programs mounted as a result of them, the 89th Congress passed Title III of ESEA. This program, authorizing support for projects submitted by local educational agencies designed to supplement existing school programs or to serve as models for existing school programs, was an innovation in itself. When (former) Commissioner Keppel testified before the House Subcommittee on the Elementary and Secondary bill he told the Congressmen that he viewed Title III and Title IV together. Title IV was to be the means whereby the substance of educational improvement would receive increased impetus and attention; Title III would be the means by which local schools could inaugurate the kind of credible real-life demonstrations which would be convincing to their counterparts and become thereby one of the moving forces for the widespread adoption of tested innovation. Those responsible for Title III estimate that this past fiscal year fully 60 percent of the money went to support projects relating to the functions of development and demonstration. This year the program expects to do at least as well. Most important, for the first time local educational agencies were provided with the funds and the encouragement to experiment with new ideas.

CURRENT DEMANDS AND STRATEGIES FOR THE FUTURE

A thorough consideration of the present status of educational research on the basis of five variables provides important clues to the directions future strategies may well take. Those five variables are discussed briefly in the following paragraphs.

VARIABLES RELATED TO STRATEGIES

The Research Function. The research function has been charged broadly with (1) the basic research responsibilities relating to improving our understanding of the nature of learning and the conditions for it, (2) developing materials, practices, processes, and institutions designed to improve instructional practices, and (3) engaging in a range of activities running from demonstration to dissemination to training, in order to ensure that improvements find their way to implementation in operational settings.

The Financial Demand. The financial demand, represented by the broad responsibilities indicated above, is difficult to estimate with precision, but its dimensions can be sketched. Recent experience accumulated by the National Science Foundation, the Office of Education, and the Office of Economic Opportunity has shown that full-scale multi-media curriculum development can range in cost from $2 to $6 million per course; even this expense is engendered by building curriculum for schools as they are *presently* structured. The costs for similar development for *newly* organized institutions might well be more. In any case, however, it does not take very complicated arithmetic to multiply the above figure by the number of possible course experiences that might be developed for pre-school, elementary, secondary, community college, undergraduate, graduate, and adult education. If one assumes, as we think is reasonable, that such curricula probably ought to be re-developed every five or seven years it is not unreasonable to project an *annual* expenditure of a half billion dollars just for curriculum, hardware and organizational development alone. The research effort to support that kind of development effort will add another $150 to $200 million to that figure annually. The cost of demonstrations must also be added—perhaps as much as three or four hundred million annually. A rough rule of thumb for dissemination activities indicates that approximately 5 to 10 percent of the research effort ought to be spent in that area. We can add conservatively for that purpose another $50 million. The total is slightly more than a billion dollars annually, an amount which—if added to the current estimated expenditures of educational institutions for this fiscal year—would constitute just 2.2 percent of the total. That rate of expenditure for research and development approximates the minimum percentage devoted to R & D today by American industry. It strikes us as reasonable that the education industry, with estimated expenditures of $48.8 billion in fiscal 1967, should devote a similar proportion of effort to research and development in areas relevant to its missions.

   The Dollars Available. The *actual* dollars available for the broad range of activities associated with the research effort have grown dramatically. They are by no means equivalent to the demands briefly sketched above. But major funding for research and related activities is still in its infancy. Significant educational research funding began only in 1957 at a combined USOE/NSF level of $1.7 million and has grown this year to an annual level of $200 to $220 million including USOE research appropriations, the NSF Course Content Improvement Activities, other miscellaneous agency expenditures, and Title III of ESEA (assuming that the 1966 proportion—60 percent—of the Title III, ESEA, activities going to development and demonstration holds for 1967).[4]

---

[4] The actual figures by program and year are as follows:

	USOE Research	NSF Course Content	Title III, ESEA Dev. and Dem.
1954	$	$ 1,725	$ ......
1955	......	35,000	
1956	......	18,000	......
1957	1,020,000	650,140	......
1958	2,300,000	750,310	......
1959	6,716,000	6,180,485	......
1960	10,350,000	6,302,055	......
1961	10,117,750	6,167,740	......
1962	11,770,000	9,389,948	......
1963	14,188,400	12,626,771	......
1964	19,820,000	14,157,650	......
1965	37,703,000	14,889,081	......
1966	100,141,241	16,393,383	45,400,000
1967	99,600,000	17,000,000 (est.)	81,000,000 (est.)

This level of funding, matched with the estimate of the conceivable demand for funds for research and related activities, underscores the critical nature of the allocation of financial resources.

Manpower Resources. The problem of manpower resources is of crucial importance and is not easily resolved. A direct response, although a long-range one, is to train a new corps of professionals having the kinds of skills required to perform the entire range of research functions. There are other possible approaches, however. There already are—in other disciplines and in other kinds of institutions—individuals skilled in the research and development environment, and who could probably be persuaded to turn their attention to the field of education. These considerations were in no small measure part of the strategy behind broadening the list of eligible organizations to participate in R & D. They also played a major role in the very early decision in the administration of research to secure the active involvement and participation of arts and sciences disciplines in educational research, a strategy that has continued until now and will be maintained in the future.

The combination of approaches adopted for the provision of adequate manpower supplies can be expected, then, to have considerable bearing on the possibilities for growth.[5]

Successes of Past and Current Efforts. The successes of educational research and development, the growing visibility of operations in this area, and the increasing conviction that research will in the long run provide the basis for substantive improvements in education have created new demands upon the human and financial resources available to the research enterprise. As soon as the demand out-stripped the resources, something that happened only very recently, the entire picture of support necessarily altered. It has now become necessary to allocate limited resources in the face of demands which exceed those resources.

ADDITIONAL STRATEGIES ADOPTED

The five considerations discussed above have led to the adoption of additional strategies. Broadly speaking those strategies embrace the three principal functions discussed below.

Careful Long-Range Planning. Now that demand has clearly out-stripped the supply of resources, particularly in the financial area, *it is critically important that the allocation of research dollars to various research functions and to particular topics or areas of development be accomplished in a careful and logical manner.* This must be done in ways to ensure that both short-term and long-term interests are met, and to maintain and strengthen the existing political structure of education as it has developed over the years.

---

[5] For more detailed analyses of the manpower problem in research and related activities see Egon Guba and Stanley Elam, editors, *The Training and Nurture of Educational Researchers,* Sixth Annual Phi Delta Kappa Symposium on Educational Research, Phi Delta Kappa, Inc., 1965; J. E. Hopkins, "Scope of the Demand for Educational Research and Research Related Persons," AERA, February, 1967; and David L. Clark, *op. cit.*

The careful long-range planning of those resources is much more likely to produce optimum levels of support for all the different functions and areas for research and development than is a totally non-directive approach embracing the competitive selection of technically excellent but unsolicited proposals for support. Such planning will need to take into consideration the instructional and administrative needs of the different educational levels and the many kinds of agencies, institutions and organizations in the field of education, industry, the professions, and government. Attention will have to be given to the needs of different target populations including the general student, the handicapped, the disadvantaged, and the gifted. This implies, of course, that it will be necessary for us to develop much more effective mechanisms for planning research and related activities in order to ensure that all relevant data are canvassed and that maximum flexibility is built into the planning and administrative policies devolving from that planning. We must be careful, for example, that we continue to pursue the wisdom of earlier efforts in support of research by maintaining a significant portion of the research budget for unsolicited efforts. This is only one element of the larger planning picture, however, although a very important one.

As part of the attempt to improve the data on the basis of which research and other educational planning is now done, the Bureau of Research has recently called for proposals to begin pilot projects we hope will ultimately lead to the establishment of educational policy centers. These centers would, on a continuing basis, conduct the kinds of studies which would enable all of us to have better ideas of the five, ten, twenty, and thirty-year picture for education. How should or might the schools relate to the society? What ought the range of curricular objectives to be? What kinds of sources might exist for financing education? How might schooling be structured in the society in the years to come? What technologies are likely to be available? These centers *will not* be engaged in predicting what the future will be. Instead, they *will try to project the many alternatives* available to us, cost them out, examine the consequences and thus provide much better data to policy planners than are now available. They will provide a new kind of information and analysis looking to the future in a systems-oriented interdisciplinary way, supplementing the improved present-oriented data collection which must also accompany the planning process.[6]

The Outputs of the Research Process. Our concern for the outputs of the research process is pragmatic in part, but it is tied closely to our conception of the mission of the research effort in education in general and of USOE's research program in particular. We have stated our faith that the improvement of education depends in the long run on the systematic prosecution of a well-conceived R & D effort. The improvement of educa-

---

[6] These are, we believe, precisely the kinds of enterprises John Goodlad called for in his paper, "The Educational Program to 1980 and Beyond," *Implications for Education of Prospective Changes in Society, op. cit.,* p. 59. At the time Goodlad's paper was given our planning for this had been underway some nine months.

tion is the fundamental thrust of the mission; that criterion must be the continuing evaluative guide we employ in judging the success of our efforts.

While it is true that the justification for supporting research and related activities in education with public money can only be the eventual and significant betterment of the educational system as a whole, it is also true, happily, that the more we can demonstrate that research has affected school practices in a positive way, the more likely it will be that greater support for the entire research process will be forthcoming. Thus we believe that such objectives are not only good public policy, but good politics as well.

There can be no denying the growth and the strength of the interest in results. The Congress is concerned. The Executive Branch is concerned. Local school people have made their interest felt in a number of ways, particularly in the development of the programs for the educational laboratories.

We believe, however, that a strong and continuing tension exists between the conduct of research designed to increase our knowledge of basic learning processes, for example, and the pursuit of development projects designed to yield specific outcomes for instructional use. The demand for results has raised the appropriate and thoroughly justifiable concern of the academic and scholarly research community that such demands may tend to compromise the long-range efforts which are so badly needed. The continuing tension between short-term and long-term requirements—between today's youngsters and tomorrow's—is real and constitutes one of the continuing nightmares of the research administrator. This problem is the responsibility of the administrator of research, and it must be squarely met. *We believe that it is important that the two functions not be confused, but that they both be served with sophistication and energy.*

The importance of concentrating on the improvement of schools, and the significance of development projects in that effort, signals an increasing attention to such activities as curriculum development and explicit attempts to improve instructional practices. We are increasingly persuaded, for example, that prudent management of the limited resources available at the present time makes it necessary for us to adopt a research strategy that relates applied research projects closely to identified development efforts. We would hasten to add that the preservation of a significant portion of funds for unsolicited proposals will still permit the support of some applied research unrelated to development since good ideas will also be generated independently of development projects or research planning groups and should be supported on their own merits.

We anticipate, then, still further increase in attention to development kinds of tasks designed to produce substantial, measurable, and cumulative improvements in the nation's schools.

Continued Expansion of Research and Related Activities. There is no question in our minds, as all the preceding analysis should clearly indicate, that *research and related activities must continue to expand in rapid but judicious ways.* By directing our attention to the development of coordinated strategies for the support of research with the implication that greater attention will be paid to the *outcomes* of the research effort, we believe that constituencies in support of educational research will grow and the dollars available for the function will increase to what we believe are the regular minimal levels we suggested earlier.

IMPLICATIONS FOR STATE AND LOCAL EDUCATION AGENCIES

The possibilities and potentialities of participation by state and local education agencies in the research and implementation processes are exciting, if not tremendous. The consequences of this view of two different processes integrally tied with one another place weighty responsibilities on those agencies responsible for administering schools. We view these responsibilities in several dimensions.

THE EDUCATIONAL LABORATORIES

The involvement of state and local educational agencies in the laboratories is intensive and direct. By establishing, as a criterion for funding, that state and local agencies be meaningfully represented in the governing and advisory bodies to these new institutions, the Office of Education intended to underscore the fact that *only local school officials can actually implement change.* Bridging the gap between research and practice relates to the research continuum. It also intersects with the direct administrative processes of school and educational systems and is thus subject to all the vicissitudes of the political processes of change in any major social institution. Schools cannot do the job of improvement alone; neither can university researchers or creative experts in development. Nor is the transmission process a one way channel. Schools must define their needs, on the one hand, before development or research can help them; on the other, schools must exercise the most careful judgment before adopting or adapting an innovation produced and demonstrated for them. We think that in building the laboratories we have adopted a sensible strategy, but it will be in the results that its wisdom will be vindicated or invalidated.

ERIC AND OTHER FORMS OF INFORMATION DISSEMINATION

Pointing out the importance of making full use of ERIC and other forms of information dissemination may on its face seem slightly simple-minded. We believe that calling attention to such information networks, however, has implications far beyond simply establishing an awareness on the part of practitioners of what is going on.

First, we would ask whether it makes sense to keep abreast of research and related information without having specially trained personnel who are in a position to work with what they find there to improve the activities in which they are engaged. In other words, preparing school systems for an awareness of research has many implications for the future course of events for those systems beyond the simple receipt of information.

Secondly, information networks are only as good as the usefulness of the data and analyses transmitted through them. Users have a real responsibility for communicating criticisms of the way the material is disseminated including, for example, possible improvements and corrections of indexing which may be discovered. Most important of all, however, is the kind of feedback which must be transmitted to the disseminators regarding the substance of the data. Is it at all useful? Are useful problems being attacked? Are there better objectives to be served in various development activities? Are the research programs affecting the thinking of educational professionals of all kinds at all levels? This we need to know, whether in the context of ERIC, the laboratories, or research planning, and we need to have this kind of information from researchers and practitioners alike.

TITLE III

A third major area of activity full of implications for state and local education agencies is Title III of ESEA. This Title gives state and local education agencies the opportunity to develop coordinated plans for the development of exemplary school programs based on research, based on the development efforts of the laboratories and other organizations, and designed to serve as the models for regular school programs. There is sufficient research evidence on the process of the diffusion of innovation and improvement to convince us that two or three demonstrations for a state are not going to do the job. What is needed is a fully coordinated plan of carefully planned exemplary activities of different kinds, calculated to integrate well with existing school efforts, and in the aggregate providing opportunities for educators of all kinds and all levels to witness a range of new practices. In addition, the *exemplary programs should constantly change as earlier ones become more widely adopted.* This opportunity places special responsibilities on state and local officials to keep abreast of new developments in research, materials, and practices, to evaluate them on the basis of their own experience or the experience of others, and to stimulate the development of model programs which pass muster and would, therefore, be worth implementing more widely. This is no easy job or light responsibility. It is the essence of the school man's task. *The degree to which the system as a whole improves as a result of the exercise of this responsibility is the ultimate measure of the success or failure of the entire research effort.*

IN SUMMARY

In this paper we have sketched out the two parts of the change process: research and development, on the one hand, and implementation, on the other. We have suggested that the principal purpose of the research effort ought to be viewed as the improvement of education in the schools. We have indicated the national need for research, and the importance of drawing on national resources to meet that need. We have described the discrepancy between the potential size of the need in dollar terms and the actual fiscal resources available. We have suggested that these conditions lead us to adopt, in effect, multiple strategies for R & D. These include: (1) better planning of the research effort; (2) more attention to the training of research and related personnel; (3) the establishment of new institutions—the laboratories—and new programs—Title III—to greatly increase the opportunities and responsibilities of local school officials in the research and implementation process; (4) the continuation of significant proportions of unsolicited research and development funds; and (5) increased attention to development efforts designed to yield better materials, equipment, and instructional practices for the schools. All of these strategies will, we hope, lead to increased understanding of the ultimate impact of the research effort, help to bring about substantial increases in the amount of support committed to research and development in education, and will provide the foundation for the continuing improvement and self-renewal of our educational system.

*   *   *

SUPPLEMENTARY STATEMENT
ROBERT L. BAKER*

There is no lack of agreement that the solution to most educational problems depends on the systematic execution of well conceived research and development. What is at issue is the design of strategies for the allocation of finances and resources with maximum pay-off in the classroom. Until quite recently there was no reason to expect that such a pay-off was a possibility or that anyone should assume such a responsibility. Until 1957 so little of the nation's resources was invested in educational research that it was almost fruitless to be concerned about development or implementation. Improvement in educational practice was based largely on the pragmatics of running a school.

It was not until 1962 that the big "D" was recognized as a partner in the R and D enterprise, and not until 1966 that we finally realized that the development of products for improving educational practice had something to do with the schools. The research and development centers of 1962 and the regional educational laboratories of 1966 were preceded only by the efforts of the Cooperative Research Branch of the Office of Education and the National Science Foundation course content improvement projects. In other words, when we talk about translating research into practice and closing the gap between the "ivory tower" and the "little red schoolhouse", we are talking about only the last decade. We should not be too surprised, then, that there is so little empirical foundation for our educational practices.

Prior to 1957 there were, of course, many agencies, institutions and people interested in and actively involved in educational research, develop-

* *Project Director, Southwest Regional Laboratory for Educational Research, Tempe, Arizona.* Formerly, Director, Bureau of Educational Research and Field Services; Head, Department of Educational Psychology; and Coordinator and Professor of Educational Psychology, Arizona State University. Member, Editorial Board, *Journal of Educational Measurement.* Author of numerous articles in professional journals.

ment and dissemination; and there were a number of significant contributions. However, these efforts were diluted by mixed motives and frail financing.

SOME BASIC CONSIDERATIONS

Lest I be accused of suggesting that the creation of institutions external to the "establishment" will afford a panacea, I should like to amplify what I consider the most important observations developed by Bright and Gideonse. In describing the present educational scene they point to several rather compelling "realities": (1) the legal and operational responsibilities for education are split and vested in two distinct political units; (2) the efforts of the various and diverse agencies involved in education are not coordinated; (3) when viewed as a whole the educational "system" is a collection of unrelated parts; (4) a dearth of money has been invested in educational research at the local level; (5) an unequal distribution of resources exists, both dollar and human resources; and (6) there is a general unavailability of trained personnel and technological resources.

In the face of these realities it is impossible to expect an integrated effort. Any semblance of integration must be attributed to the efforts of a handful of dedicated educators; and even the integration of these efforts is perhaps as much a function of chance as of design. Those who deal with the "educational system" at different levels (whether local, state or national) become painfully aware that, in effect, *what we have is not a system, but rather a collection of sub-systems.* This makes it not only possible but quite probable that, for example, a pre-service teacher training institution might provide a program whose objectives are 180 degrees counter to the in-service public school expectations and demands. Engineers concerned with systems often refer to the "interface problem". This problem occurs when sub-systems have conflicting or incompatible functions and objectives. In the above example, the correction of the problem cannot be achieved merely by developing better interface procedures or communication techniques. Interface and communication are important only when two agencies have frequent and important interactions.

It seems to me that Bright and Gideonse are suggesting three things: (1) significant educational progress could be made if the discrete agencies comprising our total "educational system" were to function more like a system; (2) research efforts should be integrated and systematized, and provisions made for massive support for finding solutions to critical educational problems; and (3) the various governmental agencies can play an important role in helping the sub-systems become an integrated system.

The major question is: What set of operations and procedures can be used to put the above suggestions in motion? Some argue that the safer route is to "muddle through", allowing change to occur as a function of the interpretations and implications of new knowledge. In response to criticisms of the looseness of this position, proponents counter with the notion that massive, "integrated" support for change often tends to be uni-directional and blind to useful alternatives which may have as great if not a greater payoff.

It is unrealistic to assume that educational practices will change markedly as a function of "new knowledge". To be sure, knowledge feeds action, but for one thing we too often assume that knowledge in its raw state can be adequately applied by the user or consumer to his own problems, and to ignore the problem of translating it. Data displayed in research journals and technical reports necessarily conform to the professional level represented by the authors. To expect other groups to "consume" the literature is unrealistic. In the absence of an integrated system the pertinent research literature has been substantially ignored by many, while others who are searching furtively for help have made gross extrapolations to the educational scene with remarkably little success.

The knowledge "gap" will not be closed, nor will the "system" become integrated through the magic of any one or several mechanisms. To date, our "alternative" efforts have involved a useful but inadequate array of activities. We have analyzed the obstacles to effective educational practices in terms of a weak knowledge base, the absence of an adequate change agent, lack of an empirically founded curriculum, and complacency resulting from the guaranteed existence of public schools. The sequel to this phase of activities has been the establishment of many schematic models—none of which offers specific procedural cues for the conduct of our behavior. We have modeled the nature of change and the organization for change. We have variously described the change agent. We have even schematized the anthropology of change in educational practice.

The approach education has been using is a reflection of an instiutional perspective. This approach has been largely ineffective. The main reason is because it presumes people and agency roles to be inviolate. If this were the case, an effective linking or change agent to bring an "interrelatedness" to the sub-systems would be demanded. Presumably, the agent's task would be to search for the functional interdependence, the sharing of goals, and the development of common value structures among the sub-systems.

What has been assumed here is that the sub-systems are indeed functionally interdependent and share the same goals. This is a questionable assumption. For example, a professional college of education many times has less direct contact with public school personnel than other agencies, such as textbook companies. Moreover, the college has goals and values that are quite distinct and apart from those shared by the schools. This has led to a sort of well-rehearsed set of parallel play activities—each is interested in what the other is doing but each is so engrossed in its own task orientation that they are unable to work effectively together. As one writer on the subject put it, ". . . the educational research and training community and the field of educational practice are a couple of crudely defined sub-systems that are non-overlapping and have discrepant values and interests."

FUNCTIONS TO BE PERFORMED

Perhaps a more beneficial way to approach the problem of educational improvement is first to specify the functions that must be performed. Certainly, as one reads the Bright-Gideonse paper there are a number of implied functions which need to be operationally specified. Performance of these functions should insure that efforts at the basic level of research are organized and converge on significant educational problems. The ultimate criterion, of course, is some kind of improvement in the classroom. By first outlining the functions to be performed we should be better able to determine what kinds of teams of people or teams of agencies are required and where we can get the manpower to handle these functions. This has to be accomplished independently of institutional considerations. Only when there is some operational agreement by the "educational community" that the functions have utility and are placed in the proper perspective can we begin to consider where and how existing institutions can make the greatest contribution, and what new institutions need to be created.

We need a generalizable outline of the functions necessary to initiate a sequence of activities and products that starts with basic investigations of the conditions affecting learning and ends in a phase in which schools adopt the improved products and teachers are trained to use them. Implicit in the outline of functions is the notion that the era is past when stand-alone, individual efforts were sufficient to insure the effectiveness of a massive and integrated attack on our educational problems. Scientific and technological information is being generated at such a high rate that individual mastery has become an impossibility. To maximize the utility of new knowledge we must turn to a group approach, defining accurately the individual specializations and organizing our activities across or over individuals.[1]

I do not suggest any dramatic innovations. As a matter of fact, I shall use the language popular in today's educational market place. Underlying this structure is the assumption that *the success of any system is its ability to apply the procedures of the self-corrective mechanism.* Through continuous evaluation—the revision cycling, procedures and approaches are modified and the product successively approximated. In other words, we should generate an empirical foundation and, if the data indicate that the product structure is inadequate, we should change it.

This first approximation of the functional structure consists of the following functions around which activities are organized.

RESEARCH IN THE LABORATORY

Within various institutions there are experiments being conducted which relate to the formulation of theories and the identification of principles. The theoretical and empirical results of basic research have a wide variety of applications even though they have been generated in a fairly

<hr>

[1] J. C. R. Licklider, "A Crux in Scientific and Technical Communication," *American Psychologist,* December, 1966, pp. 1044-51.

sterile laboratory environment, using subjects not necessarily representative of any school population, and sometimes not even human. As a matter of fact, without this function to feed on, all subsequent functions would become terribly undernourished. The activities will range from the identification of variables and delineation of theoretical constructs to the systematic manipulation of variables located in the applied but artificial setting. This, in large part, constitutes the nucleus of our knowledge base.

RESEARCH IN THE NATURAL SETTING

This function involves the conduct of research that brings to bear the theoretical formulations and empirical results on educational practice. Emphasis is placed on close observation and analysis of ongoing educational programs in order to better relate the critical variables to the natural educational context. This function is distinguished from laboratory research in that the variables identified are studied in a natural setting and the researcher must become intimately involved with the school. Another distinction is that the school no longer may play a passive role in the research activity. It is distinguished from developmental activities in that the preparation of educational products is done only to provide an experimental vehicle for the study of the specific variables or strategies.

Critical to this function is the experimental analysis of the variables identified in the laboratory as they interact with the noisy educational environment. It is this function which they should help identify and develop the essential ingredients of an education technology.

EDUCATIONAL DEVELOPMENT

In defining this set of functions I will lean heavily on the experiences to date of the Southwest Regional Laboratory for Educational Research and Development. SWRL has given considerable attention to procedures and methods. These have been and will be continuously refined, using the trial-evaluation procedures suggested by the self-corrective mechanism.

As described by Schultz:[2] "Educational development is user-oriented rather than knowledge oriented. It is conducted in pursuit of a finished product of maximum utility. The product is not ordinarily restricted to a fixed physical entity; each 'product' is embedded in a technological and social context which determines in large part its usefulness." To be sure, research activities are an integral part of this function. But, the emphasis is on "application". In the main, developers "feed on" the knowledge produced in the research laboratories. However, there is a respectability about this kind of applied research which negates the equation made by one writer between the developer and the parasite.

Development activities are unique, too, in that they necessitate a functional relationship between individuals and groups of individuals. Development is so specialized and at the same time so diffused that the work of one becomes the work of all. Generalizing a bit from some

---

2 R. E. Schultz, "Developing the 'D' in Educational R and D," *Theory into Practice*, April, 1967 (Prepublication copy).

comments made by Licklider, the discovery or invention and application of heuristic methods requires more than the simple additive power afforded by computers, information clearinghouses, research laboratories, and the like. Solution of problems and development of courses of action that involve "closely interwoven heuristic and algorithmic threads" necessitates operational interdependence between and among the researchers, inventors, developers and installers.

Educational development activities may be organized around six functions. The development of the methods and materials flow sequentially through the first four. The two additional elements provide coordinate functions to the development of methods and materials, *per se*.

Instructional Design. The purpose of this function is to translate available theory and empirical data into instructional specifications and to prepare prototype materials and methods which reflect these specifications. This is the first stage in "closing the gap" between research and practice. These activities concurrently draw upon and feed into a simultaneous program of research focusing upon curriculum content and instructional material.

Test-of-Prototype. The prototype product inevitably includes built-in assumptions about the real world, which may or may not hold. Before proceeding with further development, it is desirable to obtain an empirical check on these implicit assumptions. No assumption is made that if the product accomplishes its objectives under artificial or simulated conditions it will likewise do so under real-world conditions. However, there are typically many "bugs" to be worked out, and until these have been eliminated, there is little chance it will perform as desired under more complicated conditions.

Production. This involves converting the prototype instruction into a form suitable for real-world testing. This includes both an "assembly line" element and a research element. Research will have to be conducted on such things as the appropriate "cosmetics" of the product and how best to introduce motivational devices to make the product more attractive to pupils and teachers alike. This is not to be confused with the old saw, "ninety percent of the sales is in the packaging."

Quality Verification. This involves the successive trial-revision cycles required to bring a product to an acceptable level of performance under complex real-world conditions. Quality verification activities typically involve a succession of corrective cycles to identify and eliminate defects until the product adequately satisfies current user needs.

This is not a demonstration function, although it may sometimes serve the role quite adequately. The central purpose of placing the product in a wide variety of user locations is to better specify the "engineering" requirements of the product as they relate to various tolerance limits and the like. Although some school practitioners and researchers might view it as a demonstration, the quality verifiers are only interested in product performance and the development of effective user specifications.

Instructional Technology. The function of instructional technology is to apply the latest developments in modern technology to increase the efficiency of educational development and practice. Activities here relate to all the functions. Whether attempting to analyze a word list for the purpose of defining sequencing rules in preparing a reading program or of developing an information feedback system to increase the teachers' monitoring efficiency, instructional technology is involved.

Staff Training. An educational product cannot reasonably be considered apart from the professional staff who will be involved in using it, yet this has been the common professional practice. A number of questions are of research and development interest for staff training. For example, what form should instructions to school personnel take if the objectives relate to specific professional behavior rather than general teacher education? Or, what instructional system is appropriate if one views the education of teachers as continuous rather than as a dichotomy between pre-service and in-service?

IMPLEMENTATION

This function constitutes a discrete set of activities. However, implementation in an educational context is an inherent aspect of the end product which has been developed. Implementation concerns cannot be delayed until the end of a development phase, as is frequently the case. Rather, each product developed should, from its inception, be influenced by implementation requirements. These requirements are in large measure determined through the verification and research activities conducted during the development phase. By verifying the quality of the products in a variety of educational settings the resulting user manuals should include most of the critical specifications. Even if the manual seems to be complete, the implementers must have the technological skills necessary to determine what each new location must do to meet the specifications. This runs counter to some notions that the implementation of a well researched educational product involves only the services of a well-dressed huckster. Granted, this is the marketing phase, but as any successful merchandiser or marketing expert will tell you, "There is a lot more to putting one of those things together than the directions tell you."

The activities and elements of the implementation function involve the complex problems of interface between educational development and adoption. I have tentatively identified four elements or functions around which fairly homogeneous activities are organized.

Dissemination. The dissemination function stands between two subsystems. Activities here include the translation of the product specifications, from design through quality verification, into the language and operations of the practitioner. Personnel must have the wherewithal to establish effective demonstrations. They must also enjoy the professional confidence of the user. Whether they are document producers or field specialists, their job is to develop comprehensible methods for "getting the word out".

They also have the responsibility for helping potential users to determine what modifications they must make to accommodate the new product.

Installation. It is one thing to "purchase" a complex machine; it is quite another thing to install it. As it sits on the floor, or as it is demonstrated by the disseminator, it looks so straight forward. But who would guess that meeting the installation specifications of the product would be so complex? Activities related to this function will involve analysis of the peculiar characteristics of the user to determine what must be done to maximize the success of the new product. In addition to the product requirements, such considerations as how adoption of a new product will influence related already existing programs and what involvement the community should have would be important here.

Evaluation. The activities related to this function involve the collection, organization and analysis of data necessary to make a decision on the adoption of a product or the modifications required for a more effective performance of a product. The evaluation function differs from quality verification in that there is greater emphasis placed on criteria not directly related to the product's objectives. In addition to measures of student performance, criteria involving such things as attitudes, cost benefits, logistics and total curricular continuity would be of importance. Although the central focus remains on learner behavior, decisions on adoption require data related to many aspects of the instructional setting.

Program Review. This function is critical. Judgments are made and decisions are handed down with respect to adoption and revision. It is necessary that this function be supplied with sufficient and interpretable data. Although distinctly an administrative function, activities here should constitute respectable input for the product development stages, especially as the evaluation data become amalgamated with the educational beliefs, attitudes and motivations of the decision maker.

IN SUMMARY

The importance of defining the functions in the R and D enterprise is not that it constitutes a "breakthrough", or even that it is definitive. Rather, it provides a more systematic way of looking at what must be done without the confounding of institutional goals, traditions and politics. There is no denying the eventual legitimacy of such questions as what role the university should play, or how Titles III and IV of ESEA might best relate to the functions to be performed. However, before specifying the activities and assignments of responsibility, the structure of the system must be architected and the mechanisms for providing the necessary integration of functions must be designed.

The set of strategies that Bright and Gideonse suggest has an inviting openness about it. At the same time, for some, a disturbing message is implied. It is open because the opportunity is provided for input to any function by any institution. It is not a closed shop! There is more than enough work to go around. However, due to the urgency of the problem, limited resources available, and the historic lack of coordination, a more systematic approach to the assignment of priorities and allocation of funds must be developed. Even here, though, their strategies are not suggestive of a closed shop.

The portentous message is related to the reality that, irrespective of social-political conflicts and institutional traditions, there are definable functions that must be performed in a more systematic way. The message is disturbing only for those who cannot or will not modify their institutional behavior sufficiently to take part in a massive and integrated approach to the solution of persisting educational problems and the designing of education for the future.

CHAPTER 6

Power Structures and Educational Change

RALPH B. KIMBROUGH*

The activities of the eight-state project, *Designing Education for the Future,* have emphasized societal changes and their implications for education. In this aspect of the project the basic consideration involves the process of purposeful educational change. The purpose of this paper is to explain the role and importance of power structures in the process of planned change. Much has been said and written in recent years concerning how community power structures influence educational policy. The focus of this paper is not on how educators are influenced by power wielders, but rather on how those interested in improving education can influence power structures in making purposeful change.

Since most of the power structure research has involved local government, much of this paper directs attention to implications of local political structures for state agents of change. In a paper prepared for the second project publication,† Professor R. L. Johns emphasized the need to develop strong state departments of education in interaction with strong local educational agencies. The enhancement of power for planned change among state agencies need not be at the expense of political power in local governments. In fact, it may be the result of having strong local agencies. Educators must recognize at the outset that leadership for educational change involves political leadership.

SCHOOLS ARE POLITICAL

In past years many educators were enamored with the idea that education should not be in politics. To discuss a superintendent of schools as "a politician" or to refer to a school system as "political" conjured up images of cigar smoking, pot bellied politicians and selfish businessmen. Teachers often blamed the failure of a pet school improvement project on the premise that "it got mixed up in politics". Until recently many educators were content to believe that the reform model school government assured the nonpolitical reality of schools. That is, it was assumed that the nonpartisan election of a school board and the appointment of the professionally educated superintendent "removed the schools from politics". Persons in

* *Professor of Educational Administration, Chairman of the Department of Educational Administration* and *Director of the Institute for Educational Leadership, College of Education, University of Florida.* Has directed numerous studies of community power structure in local school districts. Author of *Political Power and Educational Decision-Making (1964);* Co-author of *Community Leadership for Public Education* (1953), and of *Philosophic Theory and Practice in Educational Administration* (1966).

† See "State Organization and Responsibilities for Education", chapter 14 in *Implications for Education of Prospective Changes in Society* (Denver, Colorado: Designing Education for the Future: An Eight-State Project, January, 1967).

public administration made similar assumptions about the city manager model.[1] Yet, through what evidence can one support the nonpolitical nature of schools? Were not the schools born of, and continued through, the tooth and claw politics of state legislatures? Is the often convulsive process of governing local schools nonpolitical?

The term "politics" need not—and should not—be viewed as confined to narrow conceptions of shady deals, unscrupulous patronage activity, or other forms of unprofessional conduct. Instead of viewing politics as something unsavory or disreputable, it should be perceived as a necessary procedure for making decisions in a democracy.

The studies of community power structure have demonstrated that education is—and indeed ought to be—in politics. For example, these studies demonstrate that many professional educators and lay boards of education do not have sufficient power to legitimize (make generally acceptable) major policy changes for schools. Educators are confronted with the fact that leaders other than schoolmen in the political system of the state and local school district may hold greater power to legitimize ideas than does the professional group. Consequently, educators must grapple with leaders in the political system for the legitimization and adoption of educational change just like other leaders who desire to influence community direction. Those who attempt to make major policy changes usually receive object lessons in the exercise of political power. When educators actively seek the legitimization and subsequent adoption of changes in the educational policies or the scope of educational activities, they are engaged in politics. Promoting the passage of a bond referendum, for example, is a political activity. It seems reasonable to expect that *educational leaders interested in changing the schools should become good politicians.* The rise of teacher militancy may be indicative that school adminstrators, in the eyes of teachers, have not been very good politicians.

WHAT IS A POWER STRUCTURE?

Variations in popular usage of the term "power structure" probably complicate my task in this paper. *Power structure refers to a description of the relative distribution of social power in decision making among the interacting persons and groups of a political unit,* such as a city, special school district, or state. In attempting to approximate an empirical description of this complex phenomenon, the researcher must obtain answers to several questions. Let us assume that the task is to describe the power structure of a city of 20,000 population. We must discover and describe within a given period of time those decisions that are significant in determining the basic socioeconomic, governmental policy of the city. Then we must attempt to answer many questions such as: Who were the persons that provided leadership in these decisions and what was their relative influence? How did these men interact in accumulating power in the decisions? What were their power resources and how did they use

---

[1] Gladys M. Kammerer, et al., *City Managers in Politics* (Gainesville: University of Florida Press, 1962).

these resources effectively to influence public policies? What was the process by which power was applied by individuals and groups? Why were leaders interested in promoting certain decisions? The object of study is to obtain enough understanding of the dynamics of power in decision making in the city to make reasonably accurate generalizations that will describe the nature of power structure.

The term "power system" communicates better the political reality than "power structure". Structure has a static connotation which emphasizes relationships between relatively stable parts, whereas the term "system" reflects the dynamics of interaction between the parts of a living system. Thus, *we can define the power relationships for any political unit as a political system or power system with interacting subsystems.* For example, we can conceive of the power relationships and dynamics of the state as a political system. The national system is a suprasystem of the state system. Local governmental units (that is, cities, counties, special school districts, etc.) are subsystems of the state political system.

POWER SYSTEMS DIFFER

Prior to the 1950's many scholars believed that one major type of political system—namely, pluralism—was characteristic of American communities. Research about community power structure demonstrated that there are numerous kinds of political systems. In fact, this may well be one of the significant contributions of the research. Officials of state as well as of local education agencies may find that change strategies that are successful for some political systems are ineffective for others because the power structures are different.

The differences in power systems are a result of variation in conceptual elements. Without making any claims for definitiveness, some of these elements will be discussed.

In *most* political systems there are influentials (persons who exercise considerable influence) who accumulate a disproportionate share of power to legitimize ideas and practices in the system. Some writers suggest two categories of influentials: the key influentials and top influentials.[2] Rapidly changing suburban districts and areas that are experiencing civil disorder constitute examples of communities in which the influentials may not be stably manifest. Further differentiation and diffusion of leadership role and power behavior are found in the power system. For instance, many leaders function to maintain the system. Formal and informal groups or subsystems permeate the system. Some of these groups are used by leaders and influentials for the cumulative or collective use of power. All subsystems are convenient vehicles for communication and propaganda in the system. The day-to-day maintenance of these subsystems is tended by organizational leaders, politicians, and selected influentials. Some lawyers, for instance, serve as the "hired guns" for influentials and groups in the system. *Certain beliefs about community living are espoused by influentials and*

---

[2] William H. Form and Delbert C. Miller, *Industry, Labor and Community* (New York: Harper and Brothers, 1960).

other leaders. These beliefs influence the normative perceptions of community influentials and citizens concerning the kind of community and the kind of school system desired. The interaction of the above elements in decision making results in the legitimization of procedural norms for guiding the exercise of power in the system. Citizen participation is an element that must be considered by educators; it varies greatly in different systems. In all power systems there are latent centers of political power that are seldom active and their participation in politics is sporadic. The size of this element complicates attempts to predict system behavior in decision making.

TYPES OF COMMUNITY POWER STRUCTURES

Variations in these elements or in their arrangement in the political structure will produce different political systems. For instance, if the influentials of a system are in different power groups and there is little overlap of leader activity in different decisions, a form of pluralism is suggested. If the influentials are usually arranged in a singular group in the exercise of power in decisions, a form of monopolistic system probably exists. Obviously the kind of a system one finds is affected by such elements as patterns of citizen participation, degree of consensus about civic liberalism and conservatism, and the relative power of formal and informal groups. There are at least four types of community power structures. These are discussed briefly in the following paragraphs.

Monopolistic Power Structure. The monopolistic power structure refers to several forms of monolithic elite systems. It exists where a group of influentials exercise a dominant—but not necessarily complete—influence over public policies. This singular structure may be formal, informal, or both; furthermore, it may be tied in with several different satellite subsystems or "crowds". These men seldom rule without some opposition. The opposition may arise sporadically on one issue from latent sources of political power in the system. Generally speaking, opposition by the same group (or groups) will not survive more than two successive elections. General citizen participation in policies is relatively ineffective.

The Multigroup Noncompetitive Structure. This structure is often prevalent in rural districts with several small villages or towns. Each of these villages or towns has a power structure. The influentials of these different structures do not interact as a singular group in "running" the school district. Political action for change involves co-opting the support of influentials of the different areas. There is general consensus among the influentials and other leaders in the district about the nature of community living. In one community studied by the author, for example, there was general consensus among leaders in favor of conservative civic beliefs. Competition was restricted to the awarding of contracts, fees, and the like. This system is representative of the closed social system in which general public policy has a high degree of equilibrium.

The Competitive Elite Structure. The competitive structure is usually characterized by regime conflicts. Power struggles often occur between groups and coalitions of influentials when a basic question such as "What kind of a town should ours be?" is asked. A high percentage of the community leaders participate in decisions in two or more issue areas. For instance, at least 40 percent or more of the same leaders who are engaged in a decision about planning and zoning will likely be involved in decisions in other areas, such as education, health, and economic issues. This is an elite structure because many citizens are not effectively involved in decisions.

Pluralistic Power Structures. In a pluralism several fragmented power groups are involved in decisions. The influentials of these groups tend to be specialized with respect to their participation in decisions. That is, few of the influentials who provide leadership in the field of education are involved in other areas of political activity, such as urban renewal, public health, and street improvements. Numerous organized interest groups are effective centers of power in public policy. The citizens are effectively involved in decisions of the political unit; usually much of the involvement is through membership in organized interest groups. Pluralism is more consistent with democratic ideals than the other typologies discussed previously.

Numerous variations are found within each of the power structure typologies discussed. For instance, the monopolistic structure may be run by one man or a group of influentials. It may be a loose coalition of influentials or a rather tightly knit group. The structure may be formal or informal, conservative or liberal. There may be widespread use of coercion or extensive use of persuasion as a means of controlling decisions. The influentials may be made up of politicians at the head of a machine (political), consist largely of a group of businessmen (economic), involve such other persons as schoolmen and professionals (specialist), or include any combination of these categories. Other illustrations of variations in monopolistic structures as discovered in local school districts could be given. The point of the discussion is that many variations in power structures are found within the major typologies discussed.

Agger and associates have used two factors in delineating four types of community power structures: (a) the convergence or divergence of the political leadership in ideology; (b) the distribution of political power (that is, broad or narrow) among the citizens.[3] For example, a divergent ideology among influentials and a narrow distribution of power produce the competitive elite typology described earlier. A narrow power distribution and convergent ideology produce what the authors refer to as a "consensual elite". A competitive mass structure is produced where there is broad power distribution and divergent ideology. Convergent ideology and broad participation produce a consensual mass structure.

OPENNESS AND CLOSEDNESS OF SYSTEMS

From general systems theory we may borrow additional concepts

---

[3] Robert E. Agger, Daniel Goldrich, and Bert Swanson, *The Rulers and the Ruled* (New York: John Wiley and Sons, Inc., 1964).

to describe the differences among the power systems of local school districts. All political systems have a boundary. In local school districts these boundaries are evident in such statements as "our town" and "our schools". Many leaders and citizens within the boundary interact with each other more frequently and easier than they interact with leaders and citizens outside the boundary. All political systems seek to survive in their environment. Educators who have sought to consolidate schools and school districts or enforce change in local practice should be well aware of this system tendency. The system expends much energy in boundary maintenance. For example, some local schools will expend much energy in hiding deficiencies in order to look good to accreditation officials.

The state department leader may find that local political systems have characteristics of closedness and openness. Some theorists make much of the point that all human systems are open systems and that there is no such thing as a closed social system. Yet, one could likewise state that absolutely open systems do not exist. Such a system would become so loaded with conflicting inputs that it would cease to survive as a political system. Consequently, as Hearn[4] and Chin[5] observe, the social system may be conceptualized as having characteristics of closedness or openness.

System closedness maximizes activity in reaction to inputs so as to maintain the system direction toward equilibrium—that is, toward what is sometimes referred to as a state of *static* equilibrium. Examples of systems having a high degree of closedness might be rural town and village school systems that are losing population or are barely maintaining a certain level of population. In many such school districts there is much inbreeding of "locals" as governmental officials, administrators, teachers, and manager-owners in the economic system. Kinship ties may be an important power resource in the community. Reaction to inputs so as to maintain the system in its original state is maximized in such school districts. We can predict that the system will exert much energy in boundary maintenance and that it is better characterized by its closedness (resistance) than by its openness to change.

Certain suburban school districts or districts with rapidly changing population characteristics are illustrative of system openness. Studies of community power structure have demonstrated that system openness and a redistribution of political power are facilitated in districts having a large influx in population whose basic political concepts differ from those of the indigenous population majority. The tendency toward a steady state is maximized in school systems having openness. Such a district will tend to react to inputs by a shift in its activity or a modification in goals, that is, to seek *dynamic* equilibrium by making needed changes.

Perhaps the most vivid illustration of closedness and openness of political systems in recent years has been in the matter of racial desegre-

[4] Gordon Hearn, *Theory Building in Social Work* (Toronto: University of Toronto Press, 1958).
[5] Robert Chin, "The Utility of Systems Models and Developmental Models for Practitioners," in Warren Bennis, Kenneth Benne, and Robert Chin (eds.) *The Planning of Change* (New York: Holt, Rinehart and Winston, 1961).

gation. In the first place the states have demonstrated different degrees of closedness and openness to integration. The variation in the change among the districts within any given state is very great. Closedness in some districts resulted in the abolition of the public schools rather than in change. In highly publicized cases the federal government had to make an input strong enough to crush the system before the symbol of acceptance became reality. Yet, many school systems that had a policy of segregation prior to the 1954 decision shifted activity with a resultant change in goals without strong federal inputs.

STUDIES OF STATE POWER SYSTEMS

In the preceding discussion I have been using the results of studies of local government as a basis for generalizing about political systems. This is relevant to the purpose of this paper because the leaders in state education agencies must deal with local political systems in the process of change. Nevertheless, the question arises with regard to the relevance of the material about local power systems for guidance in describing state politics. For example, is there evidence to support the existence of a monopolistic system in state government? Do the state systems have different typologies of power structures?

Numerous persons have discussed the need for studies of state power structure with the depth accomplished in studies of community power structure. This is a very difficult undertaking. From the investigations made, it appears that state power structures, like local power structures, form different typologies. For example, Masters and associates have studied how educational decisions were made in the states of Illinois, Missouri, and Michigan.[6] They concluded that educational decisions were made within a clearly identifiable power structure. Furthermore, the power structures of the states studied were different. The power structures of Missouri and Illinois were relatively stable and clearly defined, whereas power in Michigan tended to be fragmented with less stability. Starkey reported a recent study in which he concluded that state educational decisions in Texas were made through a clearly identifiable power structure.[7]

In studies of local power structure one obtains data which have implications for the exercise of power at the state level. I believe that it is safe to hypothesize that state power structures within given periods of time may approximate the typologies discussed for local communities; however, there is greater likelihood that the state power structures will be competitive or pluralistic in nature rather than monopolistic. It is obvious that some states are less competitive than others.

The forced reapportionment of state legislatures by the one-man -one vote decision of the Supreme Court may result in a redistribution of the power structure of many states. Consequently, until the process of

---

[6] Nicholas A. Masters, Robert Salisbury, and Thomas Eliot, *State Politics and the Public Schools* (New York: Alfred A. Knopf, 1964).
[7] Albert E. Starkey, "State Level Educational Decision-Making in Texas" (Doctoral dissertation, University of Texas, Austin, Texas, 1966).

power realignment, if indeed there is one, has run its course, the power structures of many states may not be stabilized.

TYPOLOGY OF POWER AND OPENNESS TO EDUCATIONAL CHANGE

The question arises as to whether there is a relationship between degrees of system openness and closedness and the power structure typology. A definitive answer to this question is not yet available. A pertinent related question for consideration is: Can educators influence desirable educational changes with less input of political energy in a pluralistic power structure than would be necessitated in a monopolistic power structure? For instance, will the adoption of a multimillion dollar tax increase for education require less political power in a pluralism than in a monopolistic power structure? This question should also be asked another way: Will the influentials of a monopolistic power structure of a local school district be less open to suggested educational changes from the state department of education than those in a competitive elite or pluralistic structure?

I believe that the monopolistic and the multigroup noncompetitive power structures tend to be associated with system closedness. I am also hypothesizing a relationship between system openness and competitive elite and pluralistic power structures. In attempting to test these propositions we must exercise our usual patience of not expecting miraculously high correlations. I recognize immediately that in some case studies the evidence would not support the relationships hypothesized. For example, in our power studies at the University of Florida we have found monopolistic power structures in some fairly progressive school districts. In their studies of the multicentered political system of New York City, Sayre and Kaufman concluded that the structure was inherently conservative toward innovation.[8] Obviously the influentials of a monopolistic power structure may have progressive attitudes (open-mindedness) toward innovation. If so, they surely can assist greatly in speeding up guided innovation.

However, let us examine the other side of the coin. What is the effect if the influentials are opposed to an educational change? Educators could utilize factual evidence to try to persuade the influentials to change their attitudes. Suppose after the use of persuasion the influentials are still firmly opposed to the change. How does the educator proceed? The answer is obvious. In order to make the desired change, enough energy (power) must be put into the system to redistribute—or at least threaten redistribution of—power in the system. This requires a great amount of political power. Is the political system open if a single interacting cluster of men have enough power to sanction educational change? The mere exercise of their power, even if it were to bring about change, effectively closes the system to some viewpoints about change.

We must recognize Rokeach's point that closedness may be associated with liberals as well as with conservatives.[9] Therefore, we might well

[8] Wallace S. Sayre and Herbert Kaufman, *Governing New York City* (New York: Russell Sage Foundation, 1960).

[9] Milton Rokeach, *The Open and Closed Mind* (New York: Basic Books, Inc., 1960).

lament rather than rejoice over our dreams to have a monopolistic power structure for either liberalism or conservatism. The reality of either dream is hardly defensible unless one favors a dictatorship.

LEADERSHIP BEHAVIOR AND THE PROCESS OF MAKING DECISIONS

Through the interaction of influentials with each other and with other leaders and politically active citizens, important channels of communication crystallize. For instance, the differentiation of leadership roles as a part of this crystallization results in the so-called "establishment" of the legislature or of the local school district. However, due to the unpopularity of politics among teachers, many educators have not participated effectively in the activities through which this crystallization is shaped. The interaction of those persons who are most active in the political process results in the formation of some perceptions of great significance in the process of educational change.

DEVELOPMENT OF NORMATIVE PERCEPTIONS

Many influentials in the power system have strong beliefs about the function of government in the system in such areas as finance, economics, the nature of education, and the nature of society. These beliefs influence their personal inputs into the system. The almost constant interaction results in the determination of one or more normative perceptions about "the kind of community (or state) we want." If the influentials are in general agreement or have enough power to handle pockets of disagreement in the system, there is a form of monopolistic control over normative perceptions. Those with the most power in the system will have the most say about perceived reality. If subsystems of disagreement over normative perceptions occur among the influentials, the system may become competitive.

If we look at the process in a monopolistic system, there are no crucial differences between the normative perceptions held by the influentials who are the intellectual leaders in the system. For instance, these men literally "brainwash" each other on the basis of the assumption that the schools they have are the best in the state. In fact, through their control over mass media in the community they may also brainwash large segments of the citizenry. Influentials in school districts which have pitifully poor schools will convincingly comment, "We have wonderful schools; in fact, George Mahoney (a prominent state official) says, 'We have the best schools in the state.'" Thus, these men, in addition to convincing each other, are getting powerful reinforcement for their ideas from men outside the system. Think for a moment how this complicates the problem of state and local supervisors in bringing about change in the schools of such a district.

PROCEDURAL NORMS IN THE SYSTEM

I will turn now in my discussion to another significant element of power systems, namely, the procedural norms for decision making in the system. Through the activities that occur in the decision making process,

*certain ideas crystallize about how a man should use his political power
to influence the structure.* Accepted in the system is a set of perceived
rules of the game for exercising power in the system. For example, in
one school district the influentials felt that a project should be discussed
informally before it was promoted through official channels. The procedural
norms vary among the districts of a state and probably among the states
themselves. A violation of the procedural norms could result in the exercise
of sanctions against the "culprit" and—if he continues—will result in
powerlessness for him in the system.

As emphasized earlier, the systems of different states and communities
have different sets of procedural norms for the making of decisions. Consequently, the *kind of input to produce change will be reacted to on the
basis of the extent to which it violates the set of procedural norms.* In
the past the educational literature has been rather general with regard to
the kind of procedural input required to produce educational change in
a political system. For example, we have endlessly referred to idealized
concepts of democratic procedures. As a result, the *practicing school
administrator has not had much assistance from the college and university
professors in tailoring political strategies to the different kinds of political
systems which he attempts to influence.*

In promoting school improvement projects, school leaders have not
always used effective political strategies. In many cases of public school
referenda there has been no formally prescribed strategy. Many school
elections are lost because the educators had no well-defined strategy or
because the strategy used ignored the unique nature of the political system
in which it was used.

IMPLICATIONS OF POWER STRUCTURE FOR PLANNED CHANGE

Research about power structure has implications for the process of
change because political action is usually involved when changes in educational policies and significant changes in the scope of educational activities
are involved. One cannot discuss the "strengthening" of the state education
agency as though it operates in a political vacuum. Strengthening the state
department of education as an agency for change obviously involves attention to its effectiveness in the political process. I believe we can obtain
some insights that will help to improve our effectiveness from our studies
of professionals in the exercise of political power.

The state education agency (department of education) may be conceptualized as a subsystem of the state political power system. Likewise,
the local school district is a subsystem of the local political system. Thus,
the state department and local schools are interacting subsystems within
two interacting political power systems. To influence significant decisions
at either the state or local school level involves influencing political systems.
Therefore, my initial focus in discussing implications of power structure
for the change process will be on the process of influencing changes through
political systems without reference to whether they are local or state systems.

If we are serious about improving (changing) education, we must face the proposition that the educational leaders will have to obtain and exercise a greater share of the political power than they have enjoyed in the past. This is not to imply that educators will go-it-alone. This would be futile. We have always had prominent lay leaders who have exercised their power for good schools. We want to expand participation of citizens in school improvement projects. This cannot be done without well-organized professional leaders who give most of their time and effort to ways and means of improving education. The public has a right to expect leadership for change from state department and local school personnel.

What have we learned from our studies of political power that will be of assistance in building stronger leadership for educational change? There are no simple answers to such a complex question. In the following sections I have given a few of my own thoughts concerning implications with the hope that by doing so readers will be motivated to complete the answers to the question.

ESTABLISHING EDUCATIONAL GOALS

I was reminded recently that not all groups who invite speakers to talk about the process of educational change are seriously interested in changing education. When one such group was asked about the changes they would like to make in their state, there was an embarrassing period of silence followed by some rather insignificant suggestions. *Political action must be based upon commitment to attainable legislative goals.* The degree to which well-defined educational goals for change are established will affect the accumulation and exercise of political power in a group.

It is very difficult to generate political power without goals which are generally accepted by the group that attempts to exercise influence. *Every great movement in education has been based upon some purposeful goal that captivated the minds of those who led the movement.* Lack of commitment to clear cut goals and purposes has retarded the building of political power for educational improvement projects.

A recurring tragedy in attempting to generate political power for educational change is the continuous reenactment of the Tower of Babel scene among educational leaders. When we talk of educational goals or even of means for attaining them we speak with many tongues. Thus, we split into different little intellectual camps. In these little intellectual camp sites there are numerous people who struggle to become the intellectual generals. The resulting confusion of purposes and objectives creates an excellent medium for innovation hucksters. Unfortunately, the innovator does not need to develop his product before it is sold to the relatively easy market. All that he needs is some foundation money, a good publicity program, and some modern sounding terminology.

State departments of education need to furnish aggressive leadership and coordinative services in the planning of long range goals for education in the states. Much energy should be expanded in developing general agreement on a defensible conceptual design and, finally, on personal and group commitment to realistic legislative and local school district goals. Have the state departments been providing such leadership? My general impression from visiting in numerous states is that state education agencies have stressed administrative management leadership more than developmental leadership. Clark found that in Illinois there was no group with responsibility for clarifying educational goals.[10]

State planning proceeds more on an individual, personal basis than on an organized basis. Sometimes state leaders try to mold the many requests arising from local interests into one so-called program. The result is a pie-in-the-sky legislative program which is unrealistic even to the teachers who are asked—often as an afterthought—to give personal commitment to it.

Serious attention to development will require the creation of leadership positions somewhat detached from the mire of administrative routine. A way must be found for the leaders of state agencies interacting with leaders of local school districts to develop goals for which major elements of the profession have a politically active commitment. In their study of state politics, Stephen K. Bailey and associates found that this function needed intellectual leadership.[11]

KNOWLEDGE OF POWER SYSTEMS

Successful political activity involves knowledge about political systems. I might suggest at the outset that educators (even local school superintendents) are not noted for their knowledge of community power structure. Longstreth has reported a study of representatives of different sectors of communities and the degree to which they were able to identify leaders in the power structure of local government.[12] Shown below are the different sectors and the accuracy with which representatives of these sectors predicted who wielded the most power in local government. The following data are based on power studies in thirteen different school districts.

Sector	Position of Person Most Frequently Used for Sector	Percent Accuracy
1. News media	Newspaper editors and publishers	83
2. Banking and finance	Bank president of large bank	80
3. Health	Physicians	76
4. Business	Owner of a large business	75
5. Chamber of Commerce	President or executive director	73
6. Law	Outstanding lawyer in community	71
7. Women	Women active in social activities	70

[10] John F. Clark, "The Illinois School Problems Commission: A Case Study" (Doctoral dissertation: University of Chicago, 1965).

[11] Stephen K. Bailey, et al., *Schoolmen and Politics* (Syracuse: Syracuse University Press, 1962).

[12] James Longstreth, "Guide for Administrators—Knowing Who's Who in 'Power Structure' Can Pay Dividends," *The American School Board Journal*, August, 1966. The percent accuracy column was added by the writer of this paper.

8. General government	Old line politician	69
9. County commission	Member of county commission	65
10. Religion	Ministers of largest churches	64
11. Partisan politics	Executive secretaries two parties	62
12. Farm	County agents, farmers, ranchers	59
13. Labor	Well-known union leader	58
14. Education	School superintendent	57
15. Negro	Recognized leader in Negro ghetto	45

These data indicate that school superintendents were more isolated from the general political power system of local government than leaders of other major sectors. It is significant, for example, that the accuracy of superintendents was considerably below that of other professionals such as physicians, lawyers, and ministers; only the Negro leader's scores were more indicative of an isolation from the general political system of the communities.

RESEARCH TECHNIQUES FOR STUDYING POWER STRUCTURE

School personnel often ask how they can identify and describe the nature of a community power structure. One method developed by Hunter and used widely is often referred to as the reputational technique.[13] In this method, selected persons at the center of civic activity in the system under study are asked to name leaders of prominence in business, government, civic organizations, wealth, and social life. For instance, persons from areas such as the following may be asked to provide the lists: League of Women Voters, Chamber of Commerce, newspaper, community council, government. The lists obtained are then pared to manageable size by submitting them to a panel of competent judges who select the most prominent persons from the lists. Extensive interviews are conducted with these prominent persons, and with others named as prominent in decision making by these persons, in order to obtain data to use in describing the nature of power in the system.

Another method used in the study of power is the decision analysis technique developed in a study by Dahl.[14] Several areas of political decision making activity are selected (for example, party nominations, urban redevelopment, public education) for intensive study. Persons representative of each issue area are asked to identify the most important decisions made in their area within recent years. Data about these decisions are obtained through the study of various kinds of documentary evidence (for example, newspapers, public documents, board minutes), direct observation of decisional activity, and interviews with persons involved in political activity.

Some researchers who have compared the results of the reputational and decision analysis techniques have concluded that both approaches have strengths and that the most complete description of a power system can

---

13 Floyd Hunter, *Community Power Structure* (Chapel Hill: University of North Carolina Press, 1953).
14 Robert A. Dahl, *Who Governs?* (New Haven: Yale University Press, 1961).

be obtained through a combination of the methods rather than by the exclusive use of one.

How the Educational Leader Can Study the Power System

Neither of these techniques for studying power structure through research may be of much value to the educational leader who is, himself, a part of the political system that he wants to understand. For example, there might be a question as to whether one who is enmeshed in a system could obtain the same cooperation or exercise the detachment that a university professor could realize in interviews designed to provide the basis for describing the nature of power in the system. Consequently, the educational practitioner might use appropriate outside agents to give him a detached view of power and his particular function in the system. However, he must also employ his own effective way of describing the structure in addition to the studies by outside authorities. Some of our outstanding leaders in education have excelled in understanding power structure. I will now provide some suggestions as to practical ways through which the practitioner can describe the political system.

The initial suggestion is a matter of personal perception. The mythical town meeting concept of democracy is so implanted in the minds of some educators that they refuse to accept the idea that a structured power system exists. The educator must assume that such a system exists and that it may have numerous forms. Fundamentally, he needs to view people as unequal in power. As Warner has commented, "All men are equal, but some are more equal than others."[15] The practitioner needs also to view the system as manifesting both formal and informal structures. In the past we have missed the mark by observing only the formal structure for decision making. Power may be like an iceberg in which only a small portion of the structure is visible.

The practitioner must open his eyes to the possibility that the nature of the power system with which he is dealing is not like some popular textbooks have described it. He can describe the system for himself by active observation of decision making in the system and by seeking the observations of others about the system. What have been the significant political, economic, and social decisions within recent years? What decisions currently being made seem to have the greatest importance in the system? Who are the persons in the system who have had and are presently exerting the greatest influence in these decisions? How do these influentials and other leaders work together or in competition? What are the major formal and informal subsystems in the system? What is the level of citizen participation (that is, broad, narrow, etc.) in these decisions and how is this participation manifest? Are the beliefs of the influentials and other leaders and citizens characteristically liberal, moderate, conservative? What are the critical norms in the system concerning how a leader should use his power to influence the system? What are the latent sources of power

---

[15] W. Lloyd Warner, *Democracy in Jonesville* (New York: Harper and Brothers, 1949), p. 294.

(such as, executives and workers of absentee owned corporations, teachers) that could become active in the structure? Leaders in different sectors of community living in the system, such as those listed earlier in this section, have tried to answer these questions. Some of them will share this information if the school leaders will seek it.

In addition to direct observations and the use of observations of others, the practitioner will find documentary evidence useful. For instance, it is sometimes important to know who among the influentials have business ties with one another, with members of the board of education, city council, and other public boards and agencies. These can be noted from certain published materials. I have talked with some influentials who made it a regular practice to clip information about people and events from newspapers. Yet, I believe that the documentary evidence is of secondary significance to the constant probing interaction with leaders in different sectors of living in the system.

The school leader who wants to learn about power in the system must become politically active in that system. Many "big men" in power structures are fully politicized men. That is, they make it their business to become good politicians. Leaders for change in education must be good enough politicians to get other good politicians committed to educational improvement. I am suggesting that the educational leader who attempts to influence the system must become as fully politicized as possible. He needs to break out of the narrow isolation of school influence and participate in the larger structure. By full activity in the general political system he "learns the ropes" of the system. One sure way of learning about the system is to become involved in influencing it. Educators are not noted for their aggressive participation in politics. They have been told repeatedly by state legislators to "leave the politics to us." I, for one, do not enjoy the consequences of this.

Assessing Professional Resources for Political Influence

Influencing a political system enough to change educational policies requires much input of political energy. In some systems this energy must be in the form of sheer political power. Who is going to generate enough political thrust to intercept the attention of influentials? Is this not one of the responsibilities of teachers? Obviously, educators have a responsibility to use collectively their power resources to influence the system with regard to educational change and improvement.

Power within a system can be conceptualized as an effective use of resources. Some of the resources that give people power are wealth or control over wealth, control over votes, social status, friendship ties, kinship ties, public position, leadership ability, intellectual leadership, and position in the informal power structure. What resources does the educator control that may be used to influence the system? If the leaders of teachers work at building solidarity, teachers can control a sizable share of votes in the system which could prove critical in close elections. Educators control some powerful public positions. The superintendency (state or local) is a powerful position if it is used effectively. Educators should marshall intellectual leadership. Creative ideas for school improvement constitute a power resource. From new research and idea development the educational profession should be able to use intellectual leadership as a resource.

Leaders in education have the task of using every resource as effectively as possible in creating a better climate for change and improvement in the schools. This must start by working toward the solidary, collective use of power resources under the control of professional educators. Some of the process may be like building a political machine within the profession itself so that power in the profession may be used collectively to support school improvement. All of us have observed short periods in which teachers worked together in state legislation and accomplished much and other times in which educational change failed when educators splintered into conflicting groups.

The collectivization of resources for use in improving education need not result in the monolithic control within the profession. It will no doubt curtail irresponsibility among educational leaders. The profession can protect freedom within the professional ranks and still present a united front for change.

Using Power Inputs from Outside the System

The power resources used in a particular system are not restricted to that system. Remember that these sysems—local, state and national—are interacting. There are constant inputs of power among these systems and subsystems. We tend to think that these inputs are only from the federal level downward. This is not true. Local politicians can noticeably influence the national system. For example, a group of influentials in a city may want a federally subsidized highway changed. Through their ties with congressional and other national leaders they exert pressure upon professional planners to change construction and are often successful.

There is a constant flow of inputs among these interacting systems. This means that educators at any system level are not entirely restricted to the collectivization of resources in their immediate political system, nor is the opposition to educational improvement so restricted. Educators at any given level of the social system (local, state or national) may arrange for the input of resources from outside the systems. The use of sanctions by the NEA is an example of the use of resources controlled by a profession. Many local leaders welcomed the "arranged" inputs of federal courts to help legitimize racial desegregation in local school districts.

Under the present organization, *educators need to develop political strength at all system levels.* Local school districts need a strong, supportive state department of education in order to influence change. The state department also needs strong local school leadership in dealing with the state political establishment. Attempts on the part of educational leaders to ignore leaders in other systems in channeling cross-system inputs may well jeopardize educational improvement projects. It is not entirely a matter of whether inputs are or are not made across system boundaries. The matter of system reaction to these inputs and whether they are seen as legitimate inputs will be very significant in making planned change in a system. For this reason educators must keep the channels of communication clear between the systems so that one system does not become arbitrary with the other. Feedback is very important in the control of inputs between systems.

The implications for the state department of education are clear. *State leaders must be effective (strong) enough to motivate and assist local educators to bring about changes.* Unless this is done the local school leaders who serve "closed" political systems may be largely ineffective in initiating needed innovations. The local educational leaders are often unable to gather together enough power to influence changes that are needed in order to prevent the sacrifice of children. In these instances the power of the state must be brought to bear upon the structure.

The implications for local school leaders are just as clear as are those for state leaders. *Local leaders need to "stand and be counted" when political strength is needed by leaders in the state education agency.* This has not always been true in the past. In fact, the coordinated and effective exercise of power by both state and local leaders has left much to be desired. Many local superintendents, for example, spend much time resisting the use of state inputs of power.

Educators should freely use the exchange of inputs between the state, local and federal systems to influence educational change. In fact, this could also be used to counteract questionable practices at any level, including the federal level itself.

POLITICAL STRATEGIES FOR EDUCATIONAL CHANGE

Changing educational policies involves the use of political strategies to influence different kinds of political systems for the attainment of specific educational goals or the improvement of the political system. The strategies employed will depend upon a number of conditions, such as the nature of the improvement project sought, the extent of power resources held by teachers, the kind of political system that must be influenced, and the power inputs from outside the system that will provide support or opposition. When we turn to the matter of the implications of the strategy used, there is obvious lack of experimental research. Until adequate funds and resources are available for needed research, we must use the observations and experience of the past combined with status studies of power in order to discuss the matter of strategies for change.

Educators can influence political systems. These are not static structures. They are constantly reacting and adapting to inputs from within and from outside the system. Systems that experience a massive input— such as a large federal installation, or a very large factory—sometimes undergo extensive redistributions of power. For example, studies of fast growing districts in Florida have shown that a population increase of a different characteristic from the indigenous population majority will likely produce political convulsion and change in the power structure. Producing changes in the policy and scope of educational practice within a political system involves the development of strategies which will encourage power resource inputs of the right kind and quantity.

This process can be reasonably justified from two perspectives. First, the process of education is carried out within a political system. Changes in educational policies are often desirable; therefore, strategies need to be tailored specifically to accomplish immediate policy changes in the existing system. Second, educators must assume more responsibility than they have in the past for improving the system itself.

Certain political techniques have been emphasized in the various strategies used to legitimize specific ideas for educational change within the existing political system. For example, some educators have spent a lifetime emphasizing the use of citizens committees for making educational change. Other educators emphasize the public relations approach. The grass-roots approach to passing bond issues is very popular. Yet, *the modern change agent will not depend entirely on one political technique.* He will use a combination of various techniques, depending upon his political assessment of the system at the time.

The fallacy of using one particular approach for all situations can be easily demonstrated. Exclusive use of the grass-roots technique is often based on the assumption that the political system is a loosely structured, democratic pluralism. Also it is often assumed that the educators and their boards are the primary legitimizers of educational policy. Thus, the exclusive use of the technique may ignore the possibility that in a monopolistic power structure certain influentials may have greater power to legitimize ideas than a group of propagandizing educators and school board members. The influentials in a system which is characterized by closedness may have more power to legitimize ideas for educational change than the school board, state department personnel, or professional educators. As a result, the propaganda effort through a strategy tied exclusively to one technique may fail more often than it succeeds.

TECHNIQUES EMPHASIZING PERSUASION

Educators can make effective use of techniques based on persuasion. As suggested above, the use of such procedures as public relations and grass-roots approaches is based almost exclusively upon massive persuasion through the input of information about the need for change. Emphasis is placed upon the communication of information through mass media, through personal inputs to organized interest groups via a bureau of speakers, and other means.

In politics, personal commitment is valued highly. Judging from my own studies, the personal leadership of school superintendents with influentials in the political system has not been adequately achieved. In a recent study I made it a point to ask influentials in the political system how often the superintendent of schools talked with them about school problems. These men said that it had been years since this had happened. Many of these influentials are reasonable men who are responsive to suggestions for school improvement.

The leaders in the state department of education and other designated persons should make specific plans to discuss education personally with as many influentials in the power system as possible—remembering always that many of the influentials are not members of the state legislature. This should be based on a calculated political strategy. One objective, of course, is to enlist as many of these men as possible in using their power in support of specific projects.

Another objective in the techniques of persuasion is to broaden, and possibly change, the attitudes and beliefs of these leaders about education. Some of these men have never taken the time to think seriously about the problems of education. Frank conversations on a personal basis will also result in a better understanding of the beliefs and attitudes of influentials. These men probably have ideas that need to be considered by those who have the immediate responsibility for schools.

TECHNIQUES EMPHASIZING INVOLVEMENT

Educators have also emphasized techniques to change involvement patterns. The citizens' committee approach is based upon the idea of bringing about a change in the patterns of leader involvement in decision making. Inherent in the approach is the concept that an involved and informed group of influentials will redistribute set patterns for decision making in the system. The purpose is to expand the formal leadership for legitimizing ideas for educational change in the system. The board of education often is viewed by citizens as a special interest, reference group. This feeling may cause some citizens to be suspicious of board proposals; therefore, a committee of prominent citizens can be formed to help legitimize ideas for change. Also, a mixed committee of citizens and professionals has been used. The idea of the "mixed" committee is to improve communication between professional and lay leaders.

As emphasized earlier, the formation and use of citizens' committees will be affected by the kind of power system we wish to influence. A citizens' committee that excludes influentials in the political system is a revolutionary course that may or may not succeed. The educator, in fact, must decide whether an evolutionary or revolutionary tactic has the best chance of success. Knowledge of the power structure is essential in using citizens' committees.

The cooperative survey represents another technique to change patterns of involvement of leaders in educational decision making. We must recognize, of course, that the citizens' committee and survey techniques emphasize persuasion. It is hoped that these men who are involved in the study of education will become as convinced as educators that there is a need for specific changes.

Such techniques as the citizens committee and the cooperative school survey emphasize changes in involvement of leaders and influentials of the political system in educational decision making. There has also been a great emphasis in the literature in educational administration on the democratic involvement of masses of citizens in educational decision making. One central political idea seems to be that involved interaction on a massive scale will convince many citizens that they should support educational change. The latent centers of power in the community will be brought to bear on the political system. Another more subtle idea is that massive involvement will produce a continual redistribution of power in the system thereby preventing the crystallization of power into anything like a monopolistic system.

STRATEGIES INVOLVE THE USE OF POLITICAL POWER

Each educational improvement project initiated by those interested in education should be promoted by a well-thought-through political strategy. The strategy may well encompass many political techniques, including some of those traditionally used by educators (such as surveys, citizens' committees, consultants, public polls). Obviously the strategy should always be planned specifically to win in the particular political system in which it is employed. As the strategy unfolds in political action, care should be taken to exercise flexibility and to effect changes in strategy emphases in the light of political feedback and the actions of other politicians. Any strategy that is employed should involve effective leadership from the teaching profession.

Decision making in the political arena involves the use of social power. In an earlier section of this paper the importance of the collectivization of power resources was emphasized. We need to work to moderate those conditions which prevent the unified use of power by the profession for school improvement. In the final analysis change cannot be facilitated by a concept of powerlessness. Even the acts of persuasion are facilitated by the perception of those being persuaded that educators have some power and will use it as necessary. Teachers may telescope a number of resources into a power base of sufficient magnitude to fix the attention of other elements of the political systems upon the importance of educational improvement.

The teachers should use their influence to encourage other power groups to utilize their power for the support of educational improvement projects. An example would be the use of latent centers of power in the political system. Monopolistic systems, for example, will have numerous latent centers of power that could become involved in supporting educational decisions. In one system the power of several absentee owned corporations was co-opted by educators to overcome rigidity to change in the structure.

The effective use of political power means that some educational leaders must become fully politicized men. Some of these men will be consultants to other educational leaders in the use of political power to achieve educational goals and others will be operating educational leaders sophisticated in the use of political power. These men will find ways to interact informally with state, national, and community influentials when decisions affecting education are made. I am not speaking of a petty or ruthless kind of political leadership. These politicized men will be the influentials of the educational subsystem who interact as peers with other elements of the power system. They will have the power to interact effectively—and even bargain effectively—with other individuals in the establishment and attainment of desirable educational goals.

POLITICAL SERVICES TO LOCAL SCHOOL SYSTEMS

The state education agency should provide developmental political services to local school districts. This function involves both the development of goals and the development of political strategies to achieve these goals.

For example, the state department of education should establish leadership services to assist local school districts in designing effective political strategies for political campaigns. If a school district desires to revise its objectives or to promote a bond referendum, it should be able to obtain expert services from the state department in designing a tailor-made strategy for the district. Such services might include expert assistance in political systems analysis, polling techniques, preparation of materials, and political techniques and strategies. Professional associations may also assist in the provision of these services.

IMPROVING THE POWER SYSTEM

There are limits to how much educators can improve schooling unless attention and power are focused upon improving the political power system in which the schools function. School administrators and teachers function in many communities marked by closedness to change and the threatening watchful eye of extremist groups. Unless the political systems of some school districts are changed, we are unrealistic in expecting schoolmen in those districts to be innovators. *The school organization as an interacting subsystem in the larger political system tends to mirror elements of the larger system.* Consequently, one should expect schoolmen in political systems characterized by openness to be more adaptive to educational change than schoolmen of systems exhibiting closedness. It follows, therefore, that to attempt to change the nature of education exclusive of attention to changing the political power systems is unwise and is likely to be fruitless.

One of the great domestic challenges that studies of community power structure provide is the need to improve the climate for decision making in political systems. It is indeed shocking to find so many systems in which only a small number of citizens are effectively involved in making policy. The citizens of many school districts do not feel that they can influence "city hall," and perceive that public officials are unresponsive to their needs. In many schools the teachers attempt to teach ideals of democracy to pupils who are daily denied equal opportunity and whose parents seldom, if ever, participate in decisions, except to vote once every two years or so. *The very future of democratic society depends upon developing democratic power structures that cope successfully with the changing environment.* Leaders in the field of education have a special responsibility in cooperation with leaders in other institutional sectors to work toward improving state and local political systems.

Teachers should assume a responsibility for political leadership beyond that associated directly with educational improvement. How can teachers assist in changing monopolistic systems that exhibit closedness to change into competitive or pluralistic systems that are open to the emergence of new influentials? How can educators influence the normative perceptions of the influentials in a power system? Is it possible to increase the participation of latent power forces in political decision making? How can general citizen participation in the operation of the structure be increased?

Leaders in state agencies in interaction with leaders in local school districts should consider the political systems in which schools operate as being in different stages of development. For example, in describing different types of political regimes, Agger, Goldrich, and Swanson used the terms "underdeveloped democracy", "oligarchy", "guided democracy", and "developed democracy".[16] Educators in a state may well begin to use expressions such as these to describe the extent to which a democratic regime and a power structure characterized by openness or closedness exist in different school districts. By working with leaders in the general political structure of the state, much can be done to develop and improve the political systems in which local school boards operate. *It is important, therefore, for educators to become better agents of good government.* Teachers should be encouraged to provide leadership with other sectors of society in the interest of good government.

* * *

SUPPLEMENTARY STATEMENT

PATRICK D. LYNCH*

Change in school organization is a widely discussed topic at the present time. If we look at a school system and the likelihood of change within it, we must look first at the actor whose intervention may make it possible for change to take place. In his study of New York schools Brickell found that only in systems where administrators sponsor change do any important changes occur. The purpose of this paper is to explore various change strategies appropriate for the superintendent—on the basis of the application of research on community power structure—to the policies of the administrator. These strategies are, in effect, hypotheses, some of which are dependent on further research for valid support.

* *Project Director, Educational Service Center, Albuquerque, New Mexico.* Formerly, Director of NIMH Administrator Training Program, University of New Mexico (1964-66); Assistant Professor and Associate Professor of Educational Administration, University of New Mexico (1960-). Author of *Inter-Institutional Model for In-Service Training and Changes in School Systems;* Co-editor of *Continuing Education of School Administrators.*

16 *Op. cit.,* p. 83 (see footnote 3).

A superintendent of schools is responsible for the management system of a school district, upon which the technical system is dependent. The management system mediates and controls the organization; the technical system carries out the tasks or produces the "product".[1] One of the supporting resources which the management system provides for the technical—or teaching—system of the schools is that of "procurement". The superintendent is responsible for procuring the financial and other support in the community which makes it possible to employ the necessary professional and non-professional personnel.

The procurement process has become increasingly complicated as school support patterns have changed. State financial support constitutes an increasingly larger part of the school revenues but raising the local effort is becoming much more difficult in many states because property taxes are already high. Federal funds are providing a larger share of school finances, but the most recent legislation has tended to be of the kind that requires districts to formulate requests and proposals. These proposals must state objectives, include evaluation procedures, and provide rigorous accountability of funds which may be authorized for limited periods of time. Even though a certain amount of federal dollars are earmarked for each state, each district must now prepare a proposal and explain why it should receive a share of the funds.

THE COMMUNITY POWER CONTEXT

In viewing the community which supports the schools and which receives their product, we are looking at a social system which has a certain kind of power structure. This power structure is identifiable by means of a number of approaches, and is classifiable by Kimbrough's scheme into one of several categories depending upon the extent and kind of citizen participation in the structure.

In order to predict the amount of change the superintendent of any district can sponsor one must, first of all, be able to assess his effectiveness in obtaining or procuring resources. If he effects change in a system, he may or may not be successful in obtaining more local resources depending upon the community's assessment of those changes. Parents look at the children and make judgments about the new math, the new linguistics or the new social studies. Power holders get reactions from some of the parents, teachers, administrators, or board members who hold linkages to them, and may make judgments about the superintendent's worth in the community on the basis of various criteria. However, the superintendent may be judged largely in terms of how he personally relates to members of the power structure or their representatives.

Resistance to raising more local resources for school support may be increasing; certainly, local resistance to more bonding for school buildings

---

[1] Talcott Parsons, "Some Ingredients of a General Theory of Formal Organization," in *Administrative Theory in Education*, Andrew Halpin, ed. (Midwest Administration Center, University of Chicago, 1958).

is increasing across the nation.† The power holders participate vigorously in the community's decision to raise or to keep constant the local effort for schools as delegated to the school system under state statute.

If the new superintendent of a local school system is able early in his administration to obtain a grant for a project from a source which had hitherto been untapped or to take some similar step, he may be in a position to build power resources in his own organization that will allow him to facilitate change. By obtaining "new" resources he can first of all impress the locals with his procurement ability. We note from the report by Vidich and Bensman[2] that such communities are resistive to increasing their own financial efforts for almost any kind of public function. Small town power holders prefer outside money brought in to improve their situation. If we classify communities according to Kimbrough's power structure model, we would probably find that most of those communities with wider participation in the power structure are apt to provide a higher level of local effort for education as well as other public functions than many other types. The less competition for power, the more closed the system and the more resistance there is to any input, according to Kimbrough.

If we speculate about the more closed communities we would hypothesize that such communities are like the one described by Vidich and Bensman. We could speculate further that the more closed the community and the more monopolistic the power system, the less the local effort that is feasible, and the more necessary outside input becomes for the school system if it is to change in any way. If the community is relatively "closed" according to Kimbrough's terminology, and has experienced little change or has had few inputs, it is probably resistive to upping the "ante" for the schools for any purpose. So the superintendent who wishes to change the schools in such a community must try to bring in resources from all available outside sources including federal funds. Certain communities have, of course, even been resistive to allowing their schools to apply for federal funds. Such a stand is consonant with very conservative ideology, but even in these communities persuasive new superintendents have been able to convince the board to allow for some "flirting" with federal dollars. If a school board has not previously allowed its superintendent to apply for federal funds but permits a new superintendent to do so, it probably can be construed that this school system is ready for some "unfreezing". If the board continues to resist the attraction of federal funds, then it is not yet ready to countenance change.

THE SUPERINTENDENT'S CHOICES

We could further hypothesize that the superintendent in such a closed

---

† The State of New Mexico seems to constitute an exception to this trend inasmuch as its state support constitutes 75 to 80 percent of all school revenue, federal money constitutes roughly another 10 to 15 percent and local support provides the remainder. In New Mexico the federal share has increased with the impact of ESEA, while local support has increased slightly and the state proportion has decreased slightly in the past two years.

[2] Arthur J. Vidich and Joseph Bensman, *Small Town and Mass Society* (Anchor Books, Garden City, New York, 1960).

community would be faced with more "locals" or "place-bound" and fewer "career-bound" teachers, to use Carlson's typology.[3] Procuring outside resources, then, becomes necessary for the superintendent in order that he may be able to hire outsiders or career-bound types who are more loyal to the profession than to the locality, and more amenable to the superintendent's ideas about changing the school organization. The locals are probably less likely to feel loyalty to a career-bound, change-oriented superintendent, than to a man they feel will stay around and accept local norms of the school and community.

The superintendent who comes to the closed monopolistic community has two choices to make with respect to his career. He can proceed slowly in accordance with local norms, bringing about little change of consequence, or he can try to improve the schools—and his career situation —by changing his organization. In the first case he will probably wish to remain in the community longer than if he tries the second possibility. He will probably have to leave after two or three years if he attempts any significant change.

The superintendent who moves into a more open community where power is shared more widely and the social structure is more pluralistic will probably be expected to apply for outside resources because the citizens are used to competition between groups—some of whom look far and wide for as many inputs as possible to give them leverage in the community.

In the closed community the superintendent will probably have the option to procure "soft money" from Title III, MDTA or other sources, depending upon whether he wishes to change his organization significantly and/or whether he wants to move or "stay put". In the community with a pluralistic structure he must play the game as the community is used to playing it.

It might be hypothesized at this point that the closed, monopolistic community does not look for a career-bound superintendent except at rare times when some unusual threat to the power structure is posed. After a short honeymoon with the change agent the board lets him go and begins to look for a person less disposed to change, probably someone from the local ranks. Carlson describes such patterns effectively. The closed community with monopolistic structure might well have a succession of local superintendents, not change oriented, with lengthy tenure interspersed with change agents who last only briefly. My remarks are based on the assumption that the local school board is either part of or conditioned to the desires of the power structure.

In the more open community, the change agent may have a greater chance of lasting beyond a short honeymoon, but we might also find that superintendents in such communities succeed each other regularly in five or six year intervals, the occupants being largely career bound types who

---

[3] Richard O. Carlson, *Executive Succession and Organizational Change* (Midwest Administration Center, University of Chicago, 1962).

move on because the excitement and challenges for them appear greater elsewhere.

Communities which are in the process of change present some interesting and difficult choices to the superintendent. According to John Walden,[4] the superintendent whose board is in a turnover stage is likely to have to move. The antecedents to board turnover are interesting to speculate upon but as the districts which Walden studied are located in Southern California, one can surmise that these districts largely are those with high inputs of all kinds. Hence they may be experiencing an opening up of the power structure to more complex power groupings. As this happens, the incumbent superintendent is probably vulnerable. But more important is the question of whether districts are also ready for the change agent as they turn over their boards and turn out their superintendents. Our hypothesis is that they are ready.

The superintendent who considers it important to change his organization is in a much more difficult position than the superintendent who wishes to preserve the system and settle down for a long tenure. He must first of all have the acquiescence or mandate of his board to change the system. He must, if he is to stay long enough to effect the change, satisfy his community—and its power holders. Finally, he must build linkages outside the community—to the state capitol, to Washington, to the foundations perhaps, to the distant headquarters of the local industry, as well as to his professional organizations. He must build and maintain such linkages if he is to secure outside support for his ideas. But he must tend those outside linkages while keeping the local power system satisfied that he is devoting adequate time to the superintendency. He can never expect to have the satisfaction of finding an adequate local formula, and then settling down to relative comfort.

If we were to study community perceptions of the superintendent, we might find that the more "open" the community and the more competitive its power structure, the higher toleration and higher esteem it would have for the career-bound, and possibly the lower esteem it would have for the place-bound. The latter type might be observed in the open community as one who is identified with an older power crowd and who is less professionally competent. In closed communities with a monopolistic power grouping, we might find that the perception of the superintendent who leaves after two or three years is less favorable than of the one who settles down, accepts and reflects local norms, and who is less disposed to change.

The place-bound superintendent is probably less disposed to seek "soft" money partly because he does not wish to change the structure and partly because it is a kind of game which requires high professional skills that he does not possess. He may not want to bring in his own team, because he accepts the local norms as reflected by the school staff. The place-bound superintendent must continue to exert most of his efforts in

---

4 John C. Walden, "School Board Changes and Superintendent Turnover", *Administrator's Notebook* (Midwest Administration Center, University of Chicago, Vol. 25, No. 5, January, 1967).

seeking what is so often called "hard" money to maintain the system in its steady state. This of course is no easy task, faced as the superintendent is with steadily rising costs to maintain the system as it is. If the place-bound superintendent does seek special federal money, it will probably be used more for maintenance objectives than for change-oriented objectives.

Convincing the local board and community that they must exert more financial effort for the schools becomes quite difficult for the place-bound superintendent, unless he can show that the extra effort is required just to maintain the system at its present state of performance. For the career-bound superintendent this kind of system maintenance behavior would be tantamount to operating at the frustration level. The community with a closed structure would not be as willing to listen to arguments for increased financial effort based upon changes in the school organization or increased school outputs. Further, their perception of the place-bound superintendent is that he would be overstepping the bounds of his role.

Staff Relations and Types of Resources

We have so far been discussing procurement activities and succession patterns by superintendents in various types of communities as Kimbrough classifies them. A very interesting study in Oregon by Zeigler[5] allows us to hypothesize further about high school staffs in various types of communities. If we sort communities as to size and look at patterns of conservatism-liberalism in ideology and education, we can see some implications for the superintendent in relating to the community and its power structure.

We see that teachers in small towns are more conservative politically than their community but they are probably more educationally progressive. Teachers, further, are more concerned about sanctions within the educational system than from the community at large, which might suggest that they know their communities well enough to trust them, or they are naive enough to think that sanctions really originate from within rather than from without. According to the study, high school teachers are not politically active and only teachers with long tenure are active in their professional organization.

The superintendent can see in his staff the kind of ideology found in his community. Usually there is apparently a good "fit" of teacher to community. The superintendent can depend upon his staff to move somewhat professionally, as they are probably apt to be more change oriented, educationally, than the community. But the teachers are not activists. They have long been rewarded for being politically inactive. Hence, the superintendent must learn on his own about the power structure and how it works. Teachers will blame or reward him for success or failures of the school organization. They will not pin the blame on outside forces. So his activity in seeking outside sources of support will seem

---

⁵ Harmon Zeigler, *The Political World of the High School Teacher* (Center for the Advanced Study of Educational Administration, University of Oregon, 1966).

mysterious to them and may not appear to the staff to be too necessary or beneficial.

COMMUNITY AWARENESS OF LINKAGES

If we turn to the community's perception of the need for outside resources, we are faced with some paradoxes. The conservative community may demand new, outside support as the price for innovation in the schools, but such a community may not contain the skills to obtain the resources, because it is not easy to make the necessary plans to share in the newer federal programs. A hallmark of every new federal program is its insistence upon planning goals.

Residents in small communities in New Mexico studied by fellows in a National Institute of Mental Health (NIMH) supported administrator-training program exhibited accurate knowledge of the local power structure but little awareness of the linkage between local power structures and those at an area-wide or state-wide level. In discussing critical incidents from an historical perspective, community members attributed blame to local cleavages for uncompleted projects or the failure to procure outside resources for the communities. In the smaller and more insular communities the local power holders had fewer outside linkages and were less knowledgeable about the "real" reasons why local projects had failed to materialize. The communities that had more success in completing projects had more complex power groupings, and the members of the power groups had more access to higher level power holders in the state. The superintendent of the community with the most complex structure was also the most risky in his association with certain power holders, was most mobile, and most career-bound.

IN CONCLUSION

The programs of the New Frontier and of the Great Society have presented opportunities to school systems but at the same time have created competing organizations which are involved in the task of training young people and adults. The opportunities to schools and their communities can be used to best advantage if these systems are ready to change themselves and have the kind of personnel available to plan for the application and use of such resources. The superintendent—as a community leader—has to provide much of the impetus and vision in communities to pull together planning resources and to identify goals which will change the school, as well as its community. Many communities simply do not have available the trained manpower to plan applications for projects available from the federal government. Not all superintendents have the skills or vision to perform such tasks but, even given such skills and vision, the community structure may not allow a superintendent to perform as change agent. It is the task of the superintendent to judge first, whether the community has given or will give him the mandate to change its schools, and second, whether he can pull together the forces to change either the schools or the community.

CHAPTER 7

Some Political Problems Involved in Educational Planning

NICHOLAS A. MASTERS*

The term "plan" is defined as a "method of carrying out a design". A design suggests a particular pattern and some degree of achieved order and harmony. If these definitions are applied to the American educational system, it is fairly obvious that we do not have anything resembling a plan —nor do we have anything that suggests a particular pattern or some degree of achieved order and harmony. However, it is very common in educational circles today to hear people talk of the need for planning and effecting needed changes in education. Almost all critics emphasize the fact that our tremendous commitment to education now has to be given a more definite direction (or directions). All point to the vast numbers of people involved and—in view of the vastness and the amount of resources that have to be allocated to meet the commitment—that this should be done on a much more systematic basis than ever before. And, finally, all stress the imperative necessity for establishing and maintaining an educational structure that not only will provide for the technological and vocational needs of our society, but also will provide avenues for upward mobility at least for the majority of our population.

Both educators and laymen point to certain salient facts in order to demonstrate the need for more systematic planning and for national policies with respect to education. James B. Conant, for example, in his controversial book *Shaping Educational Policy* noted that, in the majority of states, educational policies—similar to public works programs on the national level—were sanctioned through the dictates of pork barrel politics. In state after state, Conant said, legislators tended to represent educational constituencies—often even specific institutions—and to bargain solely for the promotion of these interests. This has led, in his view, to unhealthy competition and costly duplication of services. Conant concluded that, although the results of such excessive pluralism had not always been detrimental to the system, the nation could no longer—given the nature of its commitment, particularly in the higher education field—continue to

* *Professor of Political Science, The Pennsylvania State University*. Formerly, Research Associate for James B. Conant, Study of the Education of the American Teachers; Associate Professor of Political Science, Washington University; Assistant Professor of Political Science, Wayne State University; Project Director, OEO Decision-Making Study (Penn State) 1966-67; and Research Consultant, Joint Committee on the Organization of the Congress (since 1965). Publications include: (Co-author with Thomas H. Eliot), *State Politics and the Public Schools;* (Articles) "House Committee Assignments" in Nelson Polsby (ed.), *New Perspective on the House of Representatives;* "Organized Labor as a Base of Support for the Democratic Party," *Law and Contemporary Problems*.

follow such an irrational basis for making decisions. In brief, he said, the states and the national government are going to have to devise a much more rational allocation of resources.

The way out of this dilemma, Conant suggested, is (1) each state should develop a master plan, particularly for the higher educational system, that will provide for the optimum use for all current institutions and which will, as a basic purpose, eliminate costly duplications of both programs and institutional research; and (2) an interstate compact should be created—and one has been created—in order to provide a basis for the exchange of information among the states and, thus, facilitate the development of a nation-wide policy with respect to education.

Today, every state in the nation has some form of plan that it is attempting to implement. The California system—which has run into rather severe financial strains as a result of a change in policy of the current governor—has the oldest operational plan. Pennsylvania has just completed a two-year study and has laid down an elaborate blueprint for the state's higher educational system in terms of institutions, program development and boards of control. Many of the issues raised in the Pennsylvania report are quite controversial, and it has yet to be adopted by the powers that be. Somewhat similar studies and proposals are being implemented or discussed in almost all of the remaining states. Over 25 states, for example, have coordinating councils which are designed to provide some kind of budgetary planning and unification of their respective state higher educational system.

Before we get into the politics of planning and the pressures involved in the formulation of guidelines for future political action on the part of school administrators at all levels, it might be well to review or to highlight some of the major policy changes that will have profound implications for long-range planning. These may be divided into the following categories: (1) the changing and expanding role of the federal government, (2) developments at the state level, and (3) changing patterns at the metropolitan level.

CHANGING AND EXPANDING ROLE OF THE FEDERAL GOVERNMENT IN EDUCATION

The Joint Committee on the Organization of the Congress recently recommended that both the House and the Senate create separate committees to deal with the educational activities of the federal government. This recommendation was justified, in the eyes of the Committee, on the grounds that "the activities of the federal government dealing with the varied aspects of education and research related to educational institutions [have] undergone a remarkable expansion in recent decades." The Joint Committee further pointed out "that some 42 federal departments, agencies and bureaus administer funds aimed at educational programs and activities." The Bureau of the Budget has estimated that the obligational authority of such funds for the fiscal year 1966 was approximately

$9.7 billion. It could hardly have been foreseen in 1946, when the Education and Labor Committees were combined in one unit, that the involvement of the government in this area of public policy would assume such gigantic proportions.

At a conference on vocational education in Columbus, Ohio, a short time ago, I noted that the recent growth in the variety and scope of federal programs affecting just state educational agencies is still largely unrecognized, even by generally informed observers. I pointed out there that, between fiscal year 1961 and fiscal year 1966, the total financing for state administered programs nearly quadrupled. The 1966 figure was $2,995,-976,521, an increase of approximately $2.5 billion.

These figures really do not reflect the nature of development at the federal level. Actually, the federal government has entered a period when it has specific educational goals that it is attempting to achieve or implement, either through the existing educational structures or through the creation of new educational, organizational entities. The new programs extend far beyond the earlier federal educational commitments in which the three largest federal programs were surplus property, school lunches and special milk—which are obviously only indirectly related to educational goals. The new programs include such basic educational components as programs for books and materials, student support, teaching equipment and provisions for training personnel. At the recent conference on vocational education, I noted that:

> . . . among them are the higher educational facilities' construction program, activities under Sections 211 and 214 of the Appalachian Regional Development Act, the 1963 Vocational Education Enactment, the arts and humanities teaching equipment program and the equipment grants programs under Title VI of the Higher Education Act of 1965, the student loan programs under that Act and under the National Vocational Student Loan Insurance Act and Titles I and II of the Elementary and Secondary Education Act (ESEA) of 1965.

The table on page 146 provides a summary of all of the appropriations being proposed in the 1968 budget by the Office of Education. Between fiscal year 1966 and fiscal year 1968, as noted, there has been an increase of almost $2 billion in the appropriations for the Office of Education.

The burgeoning activities of the Office of Education have not been greeted with wild enthusiasm, however, by school administrators. At a recent conference of the nation's administrators in Atlantic City, a number of them vigorously criticized the U. S. Office of Education for imposing its policies and its views upon the administration of schools at the local level. John B. Davis, Jr., Superintendent of the Minneapolis school system, summarized their complaints by saying that the superintendents throughout the nation are "vexed, irritated and exercised over the aid they fought to get". One complaint was that the practice of providing aid on a categorical basis is said to infringe upon the local autonomy of the schools in order to achieve certain broad national goals, such as educating the children of the poor or training new scientists. The school administrators indicated that they preferred to have the money without any strings attached because

OFFICE OF EDUCATION, DEPARTMENT OF HEALTH, EDUCATION AND WELFARE,
APPROPRIATIONS

(Congressional Budget Submission, 1968)

	FY 1966	FY 1967	FY 1968
Elementary and Secondary Educational Activities	$1,308,097,000	$1,464,610,000	$1,707,000,000
School Assistance in Federally Affected Areas	438,078,000	439,137,000	439,137,000
National Teacher Corps	9,500,000	20,000,000	36,000,000
Higher Educational Activities	980,784,000	1,177,251,000	1,175,194,000
Expansion and Improvement of Vocational Education	235,691,000	268,016,000	289,900,000
Libraries and Community Services....	76,300,000	146,950,000	165,950,000
Educational Improvement for the Handicapped	28,300,000	37,900,000	53,400,000
Research and Training	94,550,000	91,050,000	99,900,000
Educational Research and Training (Special Foreign Currency Program)	1,000,000	1,000,000	4,600,000
Salaries and Expenses	27,384,000	32,836,000	40,253,000
Civil Rights Educational Activities....	8,000,000	8,028,000	30,000,000
Arts and Humanities Educational Activities	1,000,000	1,000,000	1,000,000
Colleges of Agriculture and the Mechanic Arts	2,550,000	2,550,000	2,550,000
Promotion of Vocational Education, Act February 23, 1917	7,161,455	7,161,455	7,161,455
Student Loan Insurance Fund	550,000	3,200,000	......
Higher Education Loan Fund	110,000,000	200,659,000	2,625,000
Total	$3,328,945,455	$3,901,348,455	$5,054,670,455

the needs of the local school systems differ widely among the fifty states. Denver's superintendent, Kenneth E. Oberholtzer, in a panel discussion, argued strenuously for some form of tax sharing, perhaps similar to that proposed by Walter Heller a few years ago. In partial response to this development, the Office of Education has indicated that it intends to decentralize a number of its functions by the creation of certain regional offices which will be able to make certain allocations based upon local needs. The school administrators were also apprehensive of this development, noting that, in their opinion, it would just be the imposition of another level of authority. Moreover, they said that the nine offices probably would not have any power to act without Washington approval.

Another complaint was termed the so-called "paper blizzard". Massachusetts Education Commission Owen Kiernan stated that federal aid "produced cumbersome paper work, delays, standards below those of the states, arbitrary funding and cut-off dates, and the attitude of 'spend it, we can improve the program next year'."

Other criticisms included the by-passing of the states under such programs as the National Teacher Corps and supplementary education centers which tend to ignore state administrative agencies; the difficulty in getting Congress to appropriate money until the last minute which often makes advance planning very difficult; failure to provide money for planning or to offset the schools' costs when they attempt to take on additional programs such as helping poor children; lack of federal coordination, saying especially that the Office of Education duplicates the work being performed under the anti-poverty programs; and, finally, a general failure on the part of the Office of Education to consult broadly enough among the superintendents about new federal education programs.

The nature of these complaints points to one of the important dimensions of the politics of educational planning and design. Suffice it to say at this juncture, however, that, if the major criticism of the Office of Education is related to the idea of categorical aid—that you really cannot have national goals, that the local school systems should preserve their autonomy and make their own plans and have the over-riding authority to make decisions —then all of the other criticisms of the Office of Education are irrelevant.

Still another development at the federal level needs some notation. Under the Economic Opportunity Act of 1964, as amended, community action agencies have been created at the local level which—as part of their purpose—have the administration and development, in relationship to the school system, of educational programs designed specifically to assist the poor.

The community action agency (CAA) represents a significant departure in educational organization in several respects. It cannot help but have very important implications for designing educational programs in the future. First, the majority of the community action agencies are private, non-profit corporations which grew out of the work of volunteer organizations such as settlement houses, the United Fund and similar organizations. Secondly, these are entirely at the local level; although, initially, the governor's office had some kind of veto power over the creation of the specific agencies, all of them had precious little to do with state poverty programs generally, the governor's office or state departments of education. Third, it has been a principal purpose in the creation of this kind of new decision making entity to provide the opportunity for those who are affected—namely the poor—to be represented in decisions about programs designed to affect them. Finally, these agencies are designed not only to reflect national goals—however broad or however specific in terms of the alleviation of poverty—but also to be instruments to circumvent local biases and resistance, particularly in the educational field. Whether or not these agencies have been successful is, of course, another question.

It might be useful to look at some examples of community action agencies to see what has actually happened there and what implications such developments have for the future in designing educational goals. The CAA in Corpus Christi, Texas, is known as the Community Committee on Youth, Education and Job Opportunities, Inc. (CCYEJO). Based upon a survey of seven existing community action programs scattered throughout the United States, the most impressive example of close community action agency cooperation with a local school district can be found in Corpus Christi. The CAA there was originally formulated by education officials in cooperation with welfare agencies. The CAA, in effect, adopted programs proposed originally through the school system. Without question, the school system is the dominant delegate agency and the school component programs provide the core for most of the other CAA activities. The school superintendent, himself, is one of the major decision makers on the CCYEJO board. In fact, all CCYEJO programs are operated through delegate agencies, thus making it very difficult to separate the school and CAA initiative in the educational components of the program.

The relationship between the new CAA and the school system in Trenton, New Jersey has been a very close one and one of mutual cooperation. The Trenton CAA has had a strong and effective role in establishing programs through the public schools—in particular in helping to shape such programs under Title I of ESEA as head start and other related educational programs. Even in relatively rural areas of Missouri and Kentucky, which have been the subject of intensive study and investigation, it was found that head start and adult education have been the most effective and popular of all CAA programs.

At least a tentative conclusion can be drawn from this experience: that certain programs can be developed, administered and carried out effectively, even though their introduction came through a decision making structure that was outside the traditional educational establishment.

I cite these developments on the federal level merely to indicate some of the major (and for lack of a better term) concerns that must be involved in educational planning.

Another development taking place at the federal level, and to some extent at the state level also, can be identified as the planning-programming-budgeting-system (PPBS) development. The PPBS has what I believe to be profound implications for education should it be implemented. Every effort is being made today to make the entire federal budget conform to such a system.

The PPBS would consist of four basic elements. The first, and obviously most difficult part of the development of PPBS, is the definition in concrete terms of program objectives. Every program, it is assumed, has an output; that is to say, every program has something that it is designed to accomplish within a given period of time. In order to make sound budgetary system decisions, it is necessary to compare the output with what is being paid for the output—briefly, to compare output with costs. To do this, Budget Director Schultz has pointed out, "We need to be quite specific about program objectives."[1]

A second major element, and one very difficult in the field of education, is that, in order to determine whether or not objectives are being met or goals are being realized within a given time span, it will be necessary to develop very precise indicators that will tell how well or how poorly a

[1] Joint Committee on the Organization of the Congress *Hearings,* pp. 12 and 1779.

program is meeting its objectives. These are noted in the trade as simply "measures of effectiveness". As I indicated, this is extremely difficult in the field of education where, of course, the objectives are quite complex and sometimes—since they are primarily for social or psychological purposes—defy precise measurement of effectiveness. But, it is not entirely beyond the ability of federal administrators to define certain objectives even in these complex fields. A manpower training program, for example, which, of course, has an important educational component, may be evaluated in terms of the number of people who are actually employed after receiving the training.

A third and crucial part of the process, according to Budget Director Schultz, is "The development and comparison of alternative ways of doing the job."[2] This means that every program of the federal government will need to be examined every year in terms of its costs, in terms of its objectives, and in terms of its outputs. Such re-examination may reveal that some programs are enduring even though their original purpose is no longer being served. Under this system, for example, the agricultural educational programs carried on in our high schools for years at elaborate costs would have been drastically altered or perhaps even eliminated, I am sure. I say this because the nature of our society has changed rather drastically since the inception of these programs. Alternative ways of doing things might have brought about improvements at a much earlier date or could have resulted in the elimination of certain aspects or components of that program.

According to Budget Director Schultz, adoption of the program approach is not very far in the future. In fact, in the federal budget document submitted this year, a number of analyses of various types of programs are included, although there is little being done with respect to educational programs thus far. The President has ordered all department Secretaries —and, in turn, they have ordered all of their subordinates—to start preparing detailed statements about the objectives and goals of the various programs under their jurisdiction. Obviously, this means that, if the decision making machinery within the federal government is capable of evaluating programs, we might, as a result, have a much more clear-cut definition of what is the federal policy in education.

Professor Lawrence K. Pettit and I have stated,

Educators, who have complained justifiably that the many education-related programs of non-education agencies are not in fact "aid", but are contractual arrangements that often violate institutional and state priorities in education, ought to seize this opportunity to bring the full force of their consultative powers to bear on the government's evaluation of programs that affect the educational system. Regardless of the form or nature of such an evaluation, the structure of educational policy making at the federal level is undergoing a change and system-related evaluations of educational programs may be commonplace in the future.[3]

We have further pointed out that PPBS marks the passing within a policy system

---

² *Ibid.*, p .1780.
³ "Some Changing Patterns in Educational Policy Making," *Educational Administration Quarterly*, April 1966, p. 86.

. . . from the symbolic to the qualitative stage; once broad, symbolic objectives appear to have been achieved, attention is focused on potential objectives greater in number but less inclusive in scope. This transition from the amorphous to the particular tends to reduce consensus—thus the probability that conflict over objectives will increase. The normative environment changes commensurately. Once society accepts the notion of federal aid to education in the abstract, policy questions become more discrete and the search for norm consensus leads to many paths.[4]

These imminent changes in the federal budgetary procedure unquestionably will have a profound impact also on the Congress in the way it evaluates what is being done. If the Reorganization Act of 1967 is examined carefully, it will be noted that it has, as one of its major purposes, the strengthening of Congressional capacity to evaluate existing or on-going federal programs. In the deliberations and hearings before the Joint Committee on the Organization of the Congress and in the debate on the floor of the United States Senate and House of Representatives, it has been brought out many times that Congress does not have adequate resources at its command to evaluate critically programs that it has enacted in the past.

In planning for education in the future, it will be necessary to be alert to the following types of Congressional activities:

1. A more sophisticated and detailed review of the budget, both by the permanent standing committees which authorize the expenditure of funds and the Appropriations Committees of both Houses. This will include not only improvements in the budget document itself, but additional hearings and the earmarking of specific staff members on each committee who will have as their purpose detailed analyses of various components of the programs coming under the jurisdiction of that committee. *Education is a key area for the improvement of legislative review or oversight.*

2. Under the terms of the Reorganization Act, the General Accounting Office (GAO), an instrumentality of the Congress, has been given authority to create a new organizational entity within itself that will be primarily concerned with program evaluation. Traditionally, of course, the GAO has been the federal government's principal auditor. It seldom, if ever, has gotten into the objectives of a program or the Congressional intent of a program, but, rather, has seen whether or not the expenditure of monies was done in accordance with government regulations. This is not so any longer. Congress intends to expand vastly the activities of the GAO, particularly in the federal grant-in-aid area.

All of these developments indicate the need for administrators to be intensely familiar with the content of what is going on at the federal level. This will be necessary, as previously mentioned, so as to bring their full consultative powers upon the development and alteration of existing and new federal programs in education, because there is no question that the federal role will continue to be a vital one, even if it is only a junior partner.

---

[4] *Ibid.,* p. 87.

I would recommend, therefore, that in the future school administrators through their professional associations, both at the state and national level, create divisions that are concerned specifically with analyzing the new developments that are taking place at the federal level. I envision that at first only a small staff will be needed, since program budgeting is only in the primitive stages and the GAO has yet to conduct its first cost-effectiveness study. But the politics of the situation will require superintendents, through whatever organizational vehicles they find most effective, to keep themselves in close, continuous contact not only with the participants in the decision making at the federal level, but with the *precise* nature of the developments taking place.

SOME CHANGING PATTERNS AT THE STATE AND LOCAL LEVEL

It seems unnecessary at this juncture to go into elaborate detail about the increasing financial commitments of state governments in the field of education over the past decade. In every state, educational facilities at all levels have been expanded, enrollments have increased at an almost incredible rate and, of course, more and more money has been appropriated. Everyone knows this to be the case. *The important consideration is what political developments have taken shape and what assessments of the political situation are imperative in order to shape and design educational policy for the future.*

First and foremost, there is no question that in every state there is increasing concern among various elements of the state power structure (if it may be called that) or significant groups within the configuration of a state's political system, over the magnitude of state expenditures. There is substantial political evidence in every state that a growing number of people are becoming concerned that the extent of educational commitment may be outstripping the capacity at the state level to finance it. Perhaps even more importantly, the degree of educational commitment seems to be greater than our willingness to finance it—especially if it involves substantial alterations and changes in the tax structure. In a number of states, we have begun to see direct evidence of this development. California, of course, is the most notable. There the governor has publicly announced his intention—and I think the budget document itself reflects that intention—to reduce substantially the appropriation requests at the University of California and the state colleges. The tremendous problem that California faces in educating a large and rapidly growing population with limited contributions by private institutions should be apparent.

But California is not the only state where substantial political forces are beginning to raise serious questions about the extent and nature of the educational commitment. Texas, North Carolina, Illinois and Connecticut have taken direct action to curb or to control more effectively the flow of finances into educational institutions. In these states, councils of one kind or another have been formed to coordinate all of the various requests made from institutions of higher learning for funds for both operational and capital expenditures. Thus far, the independent institutions in a majority of the states have prevented these coordinating councils from becoming very powerful, or from having a great deal of veto power over their specific requests. How much longer they will be able to by-pass or significantly influence these councils or new organizational entities is difficult to say.

Further evidence of the increasing concern over the extent of state expenditures, as well as over the fear of federal control, can be found in the rapid creation of the interstate compact for education (the Education Commission of the States). Largely through the impetus of Dr. James B. Conant and, later, former Governor Terry Sanford of North Carolina, the "Compact" was created as an instrumentality for the exchange of information. However, it must be said, politically speaking, that the institutions of higher learning are suspicious of this compact, because they view it as an instrument of their respective state governors to be used against their requests for increased appropriations. In short, they have felt that most of the studies would be biased in favor of a political position already taken by the governor in terms of requests for appropriations at that particular moment in time.

Finally, a development at the state level that is just beginning to take shape is a substantial change in and alteration of the role of state departments of education. This has been and will continue to be very difficult because the state departments have been hampered by the fear that they may interfere with local autonomy, coupled with a desire to exercise some statewide leadership. Also, I do not think there is much doubt that these departments have been overly oriented to the views of a special interest, namely the state affiliates of the National Education Association.

In designing education for the future, I look for the following political developments to take shape at the state level:

1. A substantial change in the nature of the staff of state departments of education. I think they will cease to employ primarily former superintendents from small- and medium-size school districts as their basic staff personnel. I look rather to the staffing to include urban sociologists, budgetary experts, psychologists and social workers, in order to develop a well-rounded staff that can evaluate all phases of educational programs.

2. I look for state departments of education to develop a budgetary division and to make at least an attempt to deal more directly with the governor and the state legislature in the preparation and execution of the budget of the state in all phases of education. Whether or not state governors will accept their respective state educational agencies as their budgetary arm or instrument in the field of education is yet to be seen. There is little or no question that they can no longer rely on certain specialized interests to have the predominant influence in shaping educational policy at any level.

3. Finally, at the state level I see an increasing trend toward the use

of specialized task forces for specialized problems, particularly as they affect urban areas. State educational agencies may take the lead in dealing with educational problems that cut across jurisdictional lines, so to speak; that is, they may involve a number of agencies at the metropolitan level. In short, I think that state departments of education will take the lead in showing the interrelatedness of various kinds of educational problems with the urban problems that have traditionally been classified as non-educational, such as health, juvenile delinquency or specialized types of housing and urban renewal programs. In fact, all urban programs today have an educational dimension as a basic component.

There will be, and there has been already, considerable resistance on the part of metropolitan authorities against the intervention of state authorities in their jurisdiction. They have expressed a strong desire to get direct federal aid and then to be left entirely to their own devices to solve their own problems. (By officials or authorities I mean the mayor, the superintendent of schools, the various department heads within a city, etc.) During February 1967, mayors and state officials testified before the Intergovernmental Relations Subcommittee of the Senate Committee on Government Operations. In this testimony the mayors indicated they wanted a direct return to the city of tax monies, whereas state authorities argued that, if there was going to be something like the Heller Plan implemented in terms of a tax-sharing system, it should operate through the state authorities.

Despite the complexity of metropolitan problems and the rigidities of many state constitutions, I think *educational leaders should take the initiative in looking for state-wide solutions to their problems.* Moreover, it may be necessary to venture out from the protective shield of the bureaucracy and confront lay leaders and politicians through appropriate means including publicity programs. "Risk-taking" may have to become an accepted administrative practice for educators. The notion that rural-dominated legislatures have been hostile and impossible for metropolitan areas to deal with is largely an outmoded concept. School superintendents, in particular, should show a greater desire for—and should demand—greater leadership on the part of state authorities in educational decision making. But these developments have yet to take place because of various political obstacles and jealousies that I will discuss briefly in the concluding section of this paper.

CONCLUDING OBSERVATIONS AND RECOMMENDATIONS

First, it is essential that school personnel—and especially educational administrators—understand some of the social and psychological aspects involved in planning for any major change in our society. The politics of planning—where there are a number of on-going institutions that are highly bureaucratized—will inevitably involve the expression of aims and values. *In order to design educational programs for the future, it will be necessary to become very explicit about goals.* The plan will have to have not only explicit guidelines, but specific ways for implementing the aims or desires that it encompasses. We might as well face the fact that, under normal circumstances, most people do not make their goals explicit.

It is usually possible to get widespread agreement on expanding whatever services are currently being provided in order to meet the needs of population growth. But disputes come when the discussion centers on what kinds of and which new services are going to be provided, as well as on what segment of the bureaucracy is going to administer them. Disputes come over questions of how much of the resources are going to be allocated for new purposes and programs. Moreover, serious conflicts arise as to who is going to determine these allocations. For example, on the metropolitan level, questions arise as to whether or not the central city school system is going to be the focal point for vocational instruction to serve certain segments of the population. To do this, resources may not permit anything but elimination of the comprehensive nature of, for instance, the secondary school system in certain areas. Expression of such values may bring about direct and serious conflict with the various types of civil rights groups which would contend that using the central city school system for primarily vocational instruction relegates Negroes, in particular, into a second-class system and perpetuates their unequal status in our society. On the other hand, it may be totally unrealistic economically to have elaborate college preparatory facilities available in certain parts of our metropolitan areas.

Therefore, it is crucial today for educational leaders to start expressing explicity what their objectives and goals are for the future. I have already indicated that I think *one explicit objective of superintendents should be a substantial strengthening of the instruments of educational leadership at the state level.* This has been resisted in large part by school superintendents at the local level over the years, and I believe the effect has been disastrous. I recommend that each state hold a broadly representative conference primarily to assess the future role of the state agency for education with an eye toward strengthening, in particular, its capacity to coordinate local, state and federal programs and to assist the governor and the legislature in the preparation of plans for legislation related to education, including the educational budget.

A second major area of concern to superintendents is the need to determine the exact nature of the design and plans for education in terms of their execution. A plan, if it is to be executed, obviously involves certain types of delegations of authority which may take a variety of forms. It would be useful at this juncture to examine those forms.

First, there is what might be called the voluntary approach. This has great symbolic value in our society because the theory of the voluntary approach is that one can preserve all of the benefits of a pluralistic structure, including autonomous decision making power, and reap all of the benefits of a centralized system or plan. The voluntary approach is based upon the fundamental assumption that if they are provided with objective information, people will make rational decisions and cease to be competitive, particularly by the avoidance of duplication of effort. This, unquestionably, is a dubious assumption, particularly in the field of education. More information may, in fact, intensify competition by arousing a desire to have that service provided in that locale. Or, competition may be intensified simply on the grounds of professional pride—wanting to have the institution that is the most comprehensive and providing the widest possible range of services.

Another type of arrangement would be the creation of an agency that actually has the formal, legal authority to allocate resources or to execute the guidelines of a plan. This is a very difficult thing for educators to do at any level, primarily because they are devotees of pluralism; they are committed to local or institutional autonomy. The roots of these feelings run deep within the educational community; even universities pride themselves on the degree of their internal decentralization. When such agencies have been created in the states in order to develop or implement various types of plans, they have been met with a great deal of resistance by educators.

Essentially what I am saying is that—regardless of whether a voluntary approach is used or whether new agencies are created that will have the "muscle" to implement certain plans, or whether or not educators are willing to sacrifice some of the pluralistic elements of the current educational system—*educators must decide whether they are going to have institutional autonomy or institutionalized planning for the purposes of executing specific programs.* The "conventional wisdom" associated with public schools and other aspects of education may—indeed must—be redeployed to adapt to planning needs at any level. Are educators prepared to plan on a nation-wide or a state-wide basis for vocational instruction, for remedial reading, for the preparation of teachers? The federal government, as I have indicated, has made a basic decision in the budgeting field which will involve explicit statements of objectives as they relate to educational programs. The decision that confronts people today, politically, is whether or not, in designing educational programs for the future, administrators and faculty alike are going to cling to the old and well-worn symbols of institutional or local autonomy. If they decide that, in a new era, greater centralized planning is necessary, they are going to have to raise very specific questions about the over-all educational function as it applies to each institution; that is, *in each state the question must be raised to the effect that, if the educational system were performing at an optimum level, what would it or what should it be doing?*

Finally, I conclude with an illustration of the dilemmas of planning. In this instance, it involves the Detroit National Bank. A few years ago, the vice president of the bank indicated that the executive committee of the board had approved the objective of constructing a new bank building in downtown Detroit that would, first of all, be an entirely self-contained unit; they did not want any outside rentals, etc., involved in the bank building. Second, it would meet the bank's needs within the community for at least the next quarter century. They carefully studied the population and economic projections of the Detroit Edison Company and hired several distinguished university economists to assist them in making economic projections about the Detroit area. Then they went to a well-known architect and gave him all of the various parameters (including where they wanted the trust division and what its relationship with the small loan division would be, etc.). The architect came out with an elaborate plan for an approximately 50-story building. The only difficulties with the plan were: (1) it had three underground garages, two of which would have been empty for the first five years and one of which would have been empty for the first 15 years; (2) it was a 50-story building of which 25 stories would be empty for five years and 15 stories would be empty for 15 years; and (3) the edifice to be constructed, in order to meet and contain all of the objectives laid down by the bank board, was impossible to build on the geological foundation available in that part of the state. What they had to do was go back to the drawing board and be a little more "realistic". They tried to design a building that would be functional for at least the next five to ten years in terms of a design that would provide for expansion on the basis of projected needs. In brief, it should be apparent that we cannot leave practical considerations out of the planning process. But even if we must curb our implementation to fit reality, progress usually demands that we have the *grand design* first.

*　　*　　*

The Politics of Planning and Change

JACK M. CAMPBELL*

One of the easiest ways for a political candidate for public office to brush up his "good guy" image is to declare that if elected he will take some public activity "*out* of politics". As any amateur semantist knows, the word "politics", expressed with an appropriate sneer, is one of those all-purpose clubs that orators can use to knock down anything from military action to free schools. It also happens that political activity— with or without the sneer—is the heart of our democratic system where the interplay of political interests determines what happens to whom and when. Politics means public involvement. *It is only through participation in some form of political activity that proposals regarding such matters as proposed changes in our public schools—or other aspects of education— can be defined, debated and tested.* Those who wince at the association of education and politics may be in the same position as the fellow who said he could cut his car's operation and maintenance expenses by eliminating the engine.

Eliot has described politics as involving the making of governmental

* *Director, Institute for State Programming, University of North Carolina.* Attorney-at-law; member of Advisory Board for American Council on Education Study of Higher Education; Governor of New Mexico, 1962-66.

decisions "and the effort . . . to gain or keep the power to make those decisions."[1]

To talk about educational planning and change presumes expectation of political action and the ability and willingness to use political influence to translate public need into public policy. If educational planning is to have any meaning at all, it must be concerned with organization, finances, programs, personnel, buildings and cooperative federal-state-local relationships—none of which will ever get off the drawing boards without some kind of interaction by the individuals and groups—public and private— who struggle to exercise power in the political arena.

Francis Keppel, former U. S. Commissioner of Education, told delegates to the National Congress of Parents and Teachers at their 1963 convention, "The making of national educational policy is not a spectator sport."

COMMUNICATION IS THE KEY

This brings me to a particular point that I would like to make in this discussion of the politics of planning and change: *The key to effective political action is effective communications.* The educator had better establish some pertinent dialogue with the key members of the political process—the politician, lobbyist and layman—immediately.

The public officials and business leaders who play prominent roles in determining the direction of government at the state level need to know why education is a first-class investment from a cold-blooded financial point of view. They need to be shown in straightforward terms that schools are economic as well as cultural assets, paying dividends for the main street businessman, as well as for the youngster who receives an effective, contemporary education.

I am convinced that, without this kind of candid personal exchange of viewpoints and interests with political and lay leaders—all the lofty planning, research and programs our education experts can devise will have little effect on the desired disposition of public finances and on faith in our public school system.

I have been pleased to see the progress the states have made in this direction in the last few years. Dr. Masters has mentioned the interstate compact which established last year the Education Commission of the States. This voluntary association—proposed by Dr. James B. Conant, and made a reality through the political acumen and effort of former Governor Terry Sanford of North Carolina—already has enlisted 38 member states wishing to encourage closer relationships between governors, legislators, professional educators and lay citizens. The Commission provides a nationwide meeting ground for political and educational leaders to sit down as equals and talk about ways to improve each state's contributions to better education. It offers a forum for the development of

---

[1] Thomas H. Eliot, "Towards an Understanding of Public Politics," *The American Political Review*, LIII, No. 4 (December, 1959), p. 1035.

public policy alternatives in education; a clearinghouse for up-to-date information on which states can draw to meet their educational problems. It is making national studies of problems shared by many of its member states.

Each member state has seven commissioners, including the governor, four top educators selected by the governor, and two legislators appointed by the state legislature. The full commission meets annually to set broad policy. A Steering Committee of eight governors, eight legislators and sixteen other commissioners meets quarterly to carry out these recommendations and review proposals for new policy. An Executive Committee chosen from the Steering Committee may confer between steering committee meetings. Permanent headquarters for the Commission have been established in Denver. This organization should be of great benefit to the public officials and educators of the eight states involved in this project, Designing Education for the Future, as well as to others.

The commissioners include university presidents, school superintendents, junior college presidents, state education board members, PTA officials, state education superintendents and commissioners, private school officials and college trustees.

Although educators expressed some fears at first that the Commission would duplicate activities of other organizations and be a tool of narrow political interests, most of them who have ventured into the interstate sessions have been pleased and excited by the enlightened concern they have discovered there. The association with state officials on a national basis has given them a new perspective on the political-education picture and a growing hope that this kind of communication can be strengthened and expanded.

Present commission studies deal with financing elementary and secondary education, community-centered post high school education, vocational and technical education, higher education, special problems of urban schools, techniques to secure communications and understanding among all groups and individuals involved in the education process, and the organization of school districts. The purpose of these studies is not to propose uniform school systems nationwide, but to show how educational problems are being met in different areas of the country so that the executive and legislative branches of state government, local officials and both lay and professional groups in education may have access to the experience of the entire country and share in the formation of new public policy in education.

Other significant meetings of educators, industrialists, and politicians have been sponsored in recent years by such groups as the Institute of Humanistic Studies, Aspen, Colorado; the California Industry-Education Council, and the California Civic Seminar. Regional conferences concerned with higher education have been conducted by the New England Board of Higher Education, the Western Interstate Commission for Higher Education and the Southern Regional Education Board, with profitable results for all the states concerned.

FORMAL EDUCATIONAL-POLITICAL RELATIONSHIPS

All branches of state government are involved in one way or another in the formation of educational policy at the state and local level, even though little has been done in most states to set up long-range goals for their schools.

Most state boards of education, at their inception, had a largely ex-officio membership, which usually included the governor, the attorney general, and the state superintendent of public instruction. In the general evolution of state boards during this century, board members came to be appointed by the governor or to be elected by the people. The board members in more than half the states are now chosen by the governor (often with the approval of the senate) with the remaining states about equally split between those where the board members are elected by the people and those where membership is acquired in other ways.

Although state boards may be considered as a kind of special government, they have not been taken out of the general state governmental operation in any sense. The state legislature is still the "big board" and may establish special agencies related to education, may charge state boards and state education commissioners with specific functions, may alter the educational machinery and change the functions. Budgets recommended by the governor may affect legislative action in various ways also. The governor, of course, has the power of veto of educational bills as he does with any other legislation.

The men and women who hold these elected positions of executive and legislative power deserve the fullest cooperation from state and local educational leaders in their search for candid and current information about school policy and programs in their particular states and in comparison with other states. As the authors of a recent book have noted:

> Difficult as it is for some educators to realize, we are convinced that the future of education will not be determined by need alone. It will be determined by schoolmen and their friends who are able and willing to use political influence to translate the need into public policy.[2]

INFORMAL EDUCATIONAL-POLITICAL RELATIONSHIPS

The central question of effective political activity is power. Who really makes the decisions? Who influences whom? As Kimbrough (Ch. 6) and others have pointed out, power is often wielded by informal structures of power elites—the social decision makers. These people often are unaffected by the usual appeals of public relations, citizen committees or formal lobbying of state officials. The public relations approach, using extensive information programs and all forms of public media, play an important role in any educational operation. Voters need to be informed of educational needs and issues and to be motivated to do something about them. The use of citizen committees to ignite group dynamics and involve professional and community leaders can be most helpful. However, it is

---

[2] Roald F. Campbell, Luvern L. Cunningham and Roderick F. McPhee, *The Organization and Control of American Schools* (Columbus, Ohio: Charles E. Merrill Books Inc., 1965), p. 339.

often found in local situations, and sometimes on the state level, that an informal group of power-holders may have more influence than public officials and committees in making changes or initiating programs for public institutions. Local social power and decision making resides in a few, seldom-publicized leaders, largely drawn from the industrial, commercial and financial interests of the area.

Communication between these informal leaders usually has been established over a period of years by friendship, family, business and political interest ties. It is up to the educational leadership to know who these people are and how to reach them to discuss long-range plans and proposed changes and what they will mean to the progress and improvement of the concerned community or state. The favorable interest of such an informal, influential group can mean a great deal to the political success of any educational program. Men of power—contrary to popular images —are not all selfish, evil men by any means. Many of them are likely to be openminded about well-substantiated facts presented in support of quality educational proposals. Therefore, one vital responsibility of every educational leader is to collect adequate and honest background facts and statistics about problems and progress and see that they are made available to influential leaders in the school district or state. Failure to initiate educational policies without factual support, or with sloppily collected or analyzed facts, is almost certain to doom any attempts to obtain the assistance of influential leaders.

Private organizations or special interests—in addition to informal power structures—can exert strong influence on political decision making regarding education. It is often the politician or public official who deals with these conflicting interests, suggests compromises and generally acts as the bargaining agent. Legislators and private citizens often depend on the clash of opinion by special interests favoring and opposing a particular program to help them in understanding the issues involved.

When there is conflict between educational interests and other special interests, it is often up to the executive public official to act as the broker to work out a compromise or to tip the political scales in favor of one side or the other.

Such an experience occurred during my first administration as Governor of New Mexico. A public letter from twelve business and agricultural associations was sent to me and to the members of the 1964 legislature recommending a four million dollar reduction in my total executive budget, cutting sharply into my proposed appropriations for public schools and higher education. In my reply, also public, I defended the educational requests as sound investments in New Mexico's economic future. In the ensuing battle I was able to persuade a majority of the legislators to my point of view regarding the significance of public education for our state's progress. An interesting development in this philosophical and fiscal dispute: The spokesman for the special interests had predicted a four to seven million dollar deficit by the 1965-66 fiscal year if the executive budget was approved; instead of a deficit, however, the state ended the

1966 fiscal year with a $20 million surplus—the largest in New Mexico's history.

Special interest or lobby associations serve a necessary and important role in our representative system of government. Friendly or unfriendly, their political power and usefulness should not be overlooked or under-estimated, especially with regard to taxation legislation.

THE NEW PUBLIC

Finally, the schools must look to the larger public for approval of their organization, values, resources and program. And as recent political elections have indicated, there is a new crowd out there with whom we must talk. Peter Drucker, a noted management consultant, has outlined in his writings the political, economic and social revolution that is taking place in this country as a result of the population explosion and the emergence of the new center of political gravity in the young, affluent, professional, technical and managerial middle class. Drucker predicts that the focus of domestic politics will shift to two new areas: the metropolis and the school.[3]

He points out that in 1960, when the late President Kennedy was elected, the average American was about thirty-three years old. By next year the average will be twenty-five or lower, and this age drop of eight years in the span of eight years will be the greatest in American history—probably making this the youngest country in the Free World by 1970. The center of political power will lie with a generation that knows of the Great Depression and World War II only out of history books, or what their parents or grandparents told them.

They will not be apathetic politically. The Goldwater and Bobby Kennedy movements and the civil rights revolution have demonstrated that these young people are an outspoken contrast to the silent generation of the 1950's. Economically secure, but not large property holders, they will care little about the burning economic issues of the first two-thirds of this century, but they will be concerned about education for themselves and their children, which will have a direct impact on their security, opportunities and place in society.

Drucker says this is the group which will determine the direction and the character of American politics for the next generation. They will be the products of our educational and financial affluence. They will have the buying power and the voting power in the suburbs, the cities and the nation. With high incomes and overall job security, they will hardly be in the traditional liberal groups. Yet they will not fit the traditional image of the conservative. The "conservative" and "liberal" labels will have little meaning in their thinking about public issues. These people will be concerned basically with what Drucker calls non-economic interests—with the quality of life—rather than with the division of the economic product. It will take more than emotional appeals—even from educational professionals—to influence their vote or win their support for financial requests.

[3] Peter F. Drucker, "American Directions: A Forecast," *Harpers Magazine*, February, 1965.

The fact that something has always been done in a certain way will make little impression on them, since they will have grown up in an environment of change and innovation, ranging from the new math to the new morality. They will be the children of television—the first generation to have been exposed to television since their earliest recollections. Their most intense allegiances will be to personalities, rather than to parties; to immediate issues, rather than to long-term theories. They will have more leisure time than now and there will be a variety of encouragements to invest some of that time in educational opportunities, with stimulation from their employers and the government.

It is inevitable that this new power group will affect the informal power structures of communities and states, the type of public official to be elected to executive and legislative offices, the outlook of special interest groups to varying degrees, and their attitude toward education and other institutions and services.

IN SUMMARY

In a speech to the National Legislative Conference at Portland, Oregon, in 1965, Terry Sanford, director of the Study of American States, said:

> The only way to assure creativity in education is to make certain that every governor is involved in the problems of education; that every state legislature is informed and alert to the potential of new programs; that there is a constant flow of ideas between the political forces which must support education and the educators who must transform new funds into real achievements.

I believe that political action is intrinsically involved in public education—whether it progresses or regresses—and that effective political action starts with effective communications. In communicating with unorganized power groups, public officials, special interest leaders or the new voting public, educators must advance beyond generalities of "education is a good thing" to specifics of what better schools mean in economic terms to the state and community and to the individual citizen who is paying the bills.

The new Education Commission of the States appears to be a move in the right direction in bringing governors, legislators, professional educators and lay citizens together, not only to exchange views candidly but to make recommendations on a national scale to be applied locally in accordance with the specific needs of each state. Local social power and decision making often resides in a few, seldom-publicized leaders, largely drawn from the industrial, commercial and financial interests of the area. It is up to the educational leadership to know who these people are and how to reach them to discuss long-range plans and proposed changes and their economic meaning for the community and state. Special interest groups can exert strong influence on state executive and legislative officials regarding educational proposals. The larger public to which the schools must look for approval of changes will soon be dominated by a young, affluent educated middle class. By the end of this decade the center of political power will be found in a generation that knows of the Great Depression and World War II only out of books and which will be attracted primarily to non-economic interests, such as the quality of education.

CHAPTER 8

Planning and Effecting Needed Changes in Individual Schools

DON E. GLINES*

Across the nation, schools are preparing—or are attempting to prepare —to make sweeping improvements. The seeds of dissatisfaction with present efforts are being sown on the basis of a strong conviction that something better must be created for the future. Inventive educators, joined by visionary social and behavioral scientists, are accepting the challenge. The great problem is to replace the obsolete programs, procedures, and buildings currently in use with a dramatically new concept in education: *"If schools are to be significantly better, they must be significantly different."*[1]

The most important consideration for any group contemplating improvements in a school or school system is to accept a sincere commitment to this philosophy, and to the significant changes (improvements) it implies. Without such a belief, most improvement efforts will be unsuccessful—they will not reach measures of substantive quality or quantity. Envisioning a new kind of education requires a new kind of educator in terms of orientation and perspectives.

Changing a school involves the adoption by staff members of personal convictions that are not commonly held among present administrators and teachers. Even with new attitudes and new philosophies, how can individuals and groups plan and effect needed changes in education? The purpose of this paper is to suggest strategies for achieving improvements in individual schools. There is no prescription to be provided but there are common threads or guides. Blaine Worthen has summarized the situation well:

> The field of education has no real mechanism for planned change . . . many skillful innovators are unable to tell others how they achieve results . . . however, the mechanism must include staff involvement, evaluation, and provision for continued innovation.[2]

THE FOCUS OF CHANGE

A most important consideration relating to change is that *the focus must be on the individual student and teacher and on individualized instruction;* the intent is to provide a better education for *all* boys and girls.

* *Consultant for Educational Innovation, University City (Missouri) School District.* Formerly teacher and administrator in public and private schools in California, Oregon, Spain, Taiwan, Haiti, and Arizona. Consultant for numerous national, state, and local groups in education. Publications include articles in *Phi Delta Kappan, Research Quarterly,* and *Physical Educator.*

[1] A favorite expression of Dr. Marion Donaldson, Superintendent, Amphitheater Public Schools, Tucson, Arizona.

[2] Blaine Worthen, "The Innovation Dilemma," *Newsletter on Strategies for Educational Change,* Ohio State University (December 1966), p. 1.

To focus on the individual, four systems in a school must change. Part of the challenge to successful improvement is to analyze these systems—not to criticize the people operating them. In introducing innovation (change) it is very difficult to change people, *per se,* but *people must change if the system is to change.* When personal efforts are attacked, the educator—as well as any other person—is likely to become resistant. Considerable success—and positive receptivity to change proposals—tends to be achieved when it can be shown that the systems in which educators operate need to be altered. The flexible personality is then in a position to adjust and adapt.

The four general systems—teaching strategies, curricula, organizations, and facilities—must be changed together. Obviously each system cannot continuously receive the full attention of everyone concerned; but the processes of improvement must be interrelated so that growth in one area is accompanied by improvements in the others. In each system, there are several (probably seven to ten) needed changes; a school planning to improve its entire program significantly must embark on 30 to 40 major revisions to its systems.

Unless those involved in making decisions about effecting needed changes in a school are ready to visualize the immense scope of the task, attempts at revision usually will not effect much improvement. Thus, planning and implementing new programs in a school will probably require —in addition to a different attitude and philosophy—the implementation of some 30 to 40 improvements. Before suggesting the possible steps to accomplish this task, examples of revisions in the four systems will be given. More detailed presentations of these are found in previous statements by the author.[3, 4]

TEACHING STRATEGIES

The first system includes the topics of learning theories, instructional theories, and learning climate. Educators and social scientists are finding better ways to conduct the interaction and communication that must take place between teachers and students. The instructor's role must become that of listener and motivator rather than of spoon-feeder and lecturer. The tools of technology and the instructional strategies will determine whether the teacher is dispensable or indispensable on a given day. Teachers must learn to diagnose and prescribe. Action alternatives will lead to individualized instruction.

CURRICULA

Hilda Taba summarized the need to change curricula when she indicated that "the principles of scope and depth of curriculum organization are contradictory and, therefore, the problem of curriculum organization is to replace the current concept of coverage with the concept of appropriate sampling."[5]

[3] Don E. Glines, "A New Kind of School," paper delivered at the Professional Day Conference, Kansas City, Missouri, Public Schools, February 25, 1966.
[4] Don E. Glines, "Why and How of Daily Variable Scheduling," paper delivered at the Georgetown Conference, Washington, D. C., August 1, 1966.
[5] Hilda Taba, "Learning by Discovery," *Elementary School Journal* (March 1963), pp. 308-316.

Personalized curricula are being developed as part of the concept of continuous progress and self-pacing. Teachers must develop most materials for individual students rather than for groups of 25 or 30. The total curricular experiences should be interrelated—and designed around themes such as *man's quest for values.* New curricular materials should emphasize inquiry, discovery and process. *A major focus must be that of development of critical thinking and self-direction.*

ORGANIZATION

Flexible scheduling, team teaching, flexible grouping, nongradedness and new techniques of student evaluation require flexible organization. Schools must adopt types of daily variable scheduling and team arrangements which provide for transactions among professionals. *The most important responsibilities of teachers are to plan and conduct meaningful learning experiences and to understand children.* This means that teachers will be expected to teach 10 to 20 hours a week rather than 25 or 30; teacher aides will help to make this possible. Students will be working independently most of the time, with 40 to 50 percent of their day or week eventually so structured that they must make choices of how best to use their time. *Students must learn to make decisions; they must learn to accept freedom and responsibility.*

FACILITIES

Imagination and money are needed to change facilities; fortunately much can be done with creative imagination. The Educational Facilities Laboratory is leading the way in showing school people new architectural designs. Those fortunate enough to build a new facility can create a wonderful, open, flexible kind of environment that lends itself to new teaching strategies, new curricula, and new organizational concepts that are being devised. In the new schools no permanent interior walls should be built. In the old structures, educators must eliminate as many as possible of the permanent walls. Tremendous learning resource centers, holding 30 to 50 percent of the student body, will replace the obsolete, crackerbox libraries which exist in most schools today.

REVIEW

Administrators, realizing that these four systems within a school must change, need to plan accordingly. Everyone must keep foremost the concept that the only justification for upsetting a school is the real focus: the student.

GUIDELINES FOR PLANNING AND EFFECTING IMPROVEMENT

Once a decision is reached that the school must be improved—and that to do so, massive changes in the attitudes and systems of the school are needed—the next consideration is to implement action for achieving the desired results. Having been personally involved in a number of districts attempting to innovate, the author has identified 10 broad steps which have been of immense value in each situation. No claim is made that these are original or exhaustive, nor that they necessarily guarantee success.

They are suggested as guidelines for changing the attitudes and future directions of a school—for changing the four systems, and for step-by-step implementation of each of the 30 to 40 specific changes necessary in a school. They are presented here in a logical order for implementation, and in a general context relating to the process of changing all the components in a school. One common element existing in all the guidelines is the necessity to communicate; *successful change in a school demands constant interaction among members of the school staff.*

DEVELOP COMMITTED LEADERSHIP

The first and foremost factor in planning and effecting neeeded changes in a school is that of developing creative and committed leadership. The school reflects its principal (he will attempt to develop the kind of program he wants) as well as the climate of the school system. Most schools are rather dull, unimaginative, conventional 1930 kinds of institutions because most principals in America today are products of obsolescent educational training and traditional experiences. Most are afraid to venture very far off the time-worn path.

Fortunately a new breed of school administrators is being developed. Sometimes they are relatively silent; sometimes they are rather noisy—but always they function in the role of a change agent, innovator, advocate; they are on the move; they realize that their schools mirror them. They seek promising new opportunities and the challenge of exciting educational developments. Rogers states,

> Innovators are venturesome individuals. . . . They are generally young. . . . They are cosmopolite, even breaking considerable geographical distance barriers to form groups. . . . They spread new ideas as their gospel. . . . They are likely to be viewed as deviants by their peers. . . . They are in step with a different drummer than their peers. . . . They march to different music.[6]

Administrators of this new type envision their primary responsibility as the achievement of needed change—not for the sake of change, but in an effort to effect improvements. They realize they are able to block or to promote change in their schools; they are willing to gamble on their ability to lead in accomplishing change without a great deal of trauma in the community.

Further testimony of the impact of the school leader on change is found in statements by Ralph Purdy. Participating in a traveling seminar which visited successful implementation projects involving innovational concepts, he became convinced that the administrator is the key leader in a planned program of change which produces noteworthy improvements. Purdy further stated that innovation, *per se,* seems to be the by-product of an individual's unquenchable thirst for a better way of life—for an improved way of performing and achieving in those areas of his major interests and delegated responsibilities.[7]

---

[6] Everett Rogers, "What Are Innovators Like?", *Change Process in the Public Schools,* Center for Advanced Study of Educational Administration (Eugene: University of Oregon, 1965), pp. 55-61.
[7] Ralph Purdy, "Genesis of Innovation," paper for Conference on Educational Leadership, Columbus, Ohio, October 7, 1965.

The Michigan Cooperative Project in Educational Development reports similar findings.[8] A significant correlation was found between the amount of staff inventiveness—as measured by the mean number of new practices developed by each teacher—and the staff's perception of the principal's support for innovative teaching. The authors further related that findings indicate that an indirect role of the principal is the development of a climate that encourages the entire staff to support innovation.

Certainly *there has to be a supportive climate from the central office, the school board and in the school community.* Significant change is difficult, if not impossible, without such a climate, but as one visits the new and exciting schools in America—those trying to break the shackles of convention—one cannot help but be convinced that the schools which are moving forward are the schools piloted by innovative principals. They recognize they alone cannot effect change, and have surrounded themselves with a core of bona fide innovators—as distinguished from "band wagon" enthusiasts—from among the administrative and teacher ranks. Schools which are successful in change have a committed inner group who are recognized by the principal as "change agents".

CRITICALLY REVIEW THE LITERATURE

The second step in planning and effecting needed change is to review carefully the literature. This may sound like a wornout phrase from a graduate course, but it has become an essential step in innovation. There are two types of materials now available: One deals with the basic concepts; the other is a growing body of knowledge related to implementing the concepts. Current administrators seem to be reading about innovations, but few are aware of and involved in serious consideration of the process of change. Most teachers and many administrators are almost illiterate in their awareness of these latter materials.

Until the past few years, there were few studies and little had been written about the change process. Ideas were developed and implemented pretty much by trial and error. There are still no final "answers", but indications of success and failure are beginning to emerge.

One of the best summaries to date is *Innovation Research and Theory,* by Harbans Bhola.[9] The author's taxonomy of change categorizes five topics: (1) philosophic considerations; (2) content of innovations; (3) nature of inventors, innovators and adopters; (4) process and tactics of diffusion; and (5 measurement and evaluation. A second important pamphlet, previously cited (footnote 6) is *Change Process in the Public Schools,* which attempts to increase the understanding of and skills for carrying out planned change. Richard Carlson's *Adoption of Educational Innovations* and Keith Goldhammer's *The Jackson County Story* are other important documents available from the same center at Oregon. Everett

---

[8] Robert Fox, Charles Jung, and Ronald Lippett, "Report on the Cooperative Project on Educational Development (COPED)" (Ann Arbor: University of Michigan, 1965).

[9] Harbans Bhola, *Innovation Research and Theory,* School of Education, Ohio State University, Columbus, Ohio, 1965.

Rogers[10] has produced an excellent bibliography on the diffusion of innovations. Most references cited are available from the Diffusion Documents Center at Michigan State University. Ralph Kimbrough[11] has discussed the problems of change as related to the community power system. James Wilson[12] discusses the incentive system as it applies to change, as does Jack Gibb.[13] The identification of roles, linkage processes, facilitating agents, and resistances in the flow of information spread and sources of innovation are summarized in an article by Havelock and Benne.[14] J. Lloyd Trump[15] has available papers on "Changed Roles for Teachers and Principals" and "Problems Faced in Organizing a School Differently."

A number of newly-funded projects are currently underway to help determine strategies for bringing about change. The Cooperative Project in Educational Development (a three-year effort in areas of Chicago, Detroit, Philadelphia, New York, and Boston), coordinated by the National Training Laboratories, is attempting to compare five different planned strategies. The recently-funded Institute for the Study of Educational Change at the University of Indiana, the Designing Education for the Future project and the Institute for the Development of Educational Activities (I/D/E/A/), are other examples of concerted attempts to find ways to improve the knowledge and the dissemination of methods of changing education.

The foregoing summary of a few of the many writings on the processes of change in education has been included as part of the second step in planning change, since no one yet has developed a satisfactory model (or models) which can be followed to ensure success. However, no school administrator should consider making major plans for effecting improvement in his or her school or school system without having studied most of the available literature. The publications contain suggestions considered to be essential for the planner. Many pitfalls in changing individual schools will be avoided if the facts, concepts and hypotheses presented by the authors are carefully followed.

EVOLVE A PHILOSOPHY

The new leaders in education have a commitment to a reoriented philosophy. They see schools, learning and students in a new light. They believe that improvement must come rapidly. They know that the goals of American education have not even been approximated in most schools.

Thus, the third step is to develop a philosophy which is consistent

10 Everett Rogers, "Bibliography on the Diffusion of Innovations," Department of Communication, Michigan State University, East Lansing, Michigan, 1966.

11 Ralph Kimbrough, "Community Power Systems and Strategies for Educational Change," paper presented at the Conference for Planned Curriculum Innovation, July 8, 1966.

12 James Wilson, "Innovation in Organization—Notes Toward a Theory," Department of Government, Cambridge, Mass.: Harvard University, unpublished, undated, mimeographed paper.

13 Jack Gibb, "Fear and Facade," *Science and Human Affairs* (Palo Alto, Calif.: Science and Behavior Books, Inc., 1965).

14 Ronald Havelock and Kenneth Benne, "An Exploratory Study of Knowledge Utilization," Center for Research on Utilization of Scientific Knowledge, Ann Arbor, Michigan: University of Michigan, unpublished, undated, mimeographed paper.

15 J. Lloyd Trump, Associate Secretary, National Association of Secondary School Principals, Washington, D. C., unpublished, undated, mimeographed material.

with modern concepts about education in a rapidly changing society. What does the staff really believe? Can they teach more effectively if they plan together? Is the most important function of schools to aid students to become responsible, perceiving, self-directing, self-educating individuals who are capable of making decisions and value judgments? How do they react to Russell's[16] statement: "Our greater need is no longer to learn how to do things, how to perform, how to act; it is rather to learn how to think, how to judge, how to balance, how to perceive"? Are self-image, intrinsic motivation, and student goals more important than teacher goals? What conditions affect the child's desire and ability to learn? How are concepts of inquiry, discovery, and memory related to teaching?

The staff must resolve such issues before internal and meaningful acceptance of the need for change will occur. They must have the courage and conviction that there is much promise in appropriate changes that are designed to lead to something educationally very much better. They should read such publications as *Prospective Changes in Society by 1980*[17] and *Implications for Education of Prospective Changes in Society.*[18] They must agree that there is something basic in the constant seeking for a better way of doing. They must find professional success and personal satisfaction in needed innovation—a satisfaction that will result from seeing boys and girls become excited about their school experiences. Without developing such a philosophy, further planning and implementation attempts will be futile.

CREATE DISSATISFACTION WITH THE INAPPROPRIATE

Keeping in mind the need for staff involvement in all ten steps, the next task in change is to create a dissatisfaction among the faculty, students, and parents with concepts and practices that are no longer appropriate. There must be a recognition that educators can and should do a better job. The schools of America probably reach no more than 50 percent of the students in any significantly positive way. Nationally, the dropout rate indicates that, unless major improvements are effected, nearly one-third of the students will never finish high school; another one-third can be classified as the in-school dropouts (they finish school and get a diploma, but they are not excited about their formal educational experiences); and the remaining one-third will go on to college. Of these, many have not been adequately challenged.

One of the most shocking needs for change in our educational system emerges from a study of unemployment statistics. John Donovan[19] points out that young people, 14 to 24 years of age, account for only 18 percent of the labor force—yet constitute 37 percent of the unemployed—and

---

[16] James Russell, *Change and Challenge in American Education* (Boston, Mass.: Houghton Mifflin Co., 1965), p. 47.
[17] *Prospective Changes in Society by 1980*, Designing Education for the Future: An Eight-State Project, Denver, 1966.
[18] *Implications for Education of Prospective Changes in Society*, Designing Education for the Future: An Eight-State Project, Denver, 1967.
[19] John Donovan, "Implications of Manpower Training for American Education," *Phi Delta Kappan* (April 1965), pp. 366-367.

that a recent U. S. Department of Labor study reveals that, if the nation were to hold to its present course in the fields of education and training, it could anticipate having some thirty-two million adults in the labor force by 1975 who have not finished high school.

Not only do the labor market statistics shock one into a stern analysis of the educational program, but also so does the matter of college dropouts. Recent studies[20] indicate that approximately 50 to 60 percent of those students who enter four-year college degree programs fail to complete them. The problem seems to be twofold. Many of the entering students arrive ill-prepared for the programs they must face. The other portion of the problem is that colleges and universities are probably less likely to make any significant improvement in their educational programs during the next few years than the public schools.

The impact of challenging new concepts on actual classroom practice, with some exceptions, has been disappointing at all levels. To overcome the inertia in the schools and colleges the staff must become dissatisfied with the present situation and must seriously seek an opportunity to change that dissatisfaction into satisfaction. Instead of maintaining an attitude of "I am a good teacher (or administrator) and am satisfied", educators must develop an attitude which says, "I am a good teacher (or administrator) but I am looking for ways to become a better teacher (or administrator)".

OVERCOME THE BARRIERS

As a new era of dissatisfaction develops in the schools, the barriers to improvement will become more obvious. The informal and formal power structures in a community will take on new significance. The nature of the communication between school leaders and teachers, and between school and community leaders often becomes a critical factor in determining whether innovative school projects become acceptable. There has been much discussion as to whether superintendents, college professors, state departments, boards of education, parents, teachers, or principals are the major barriers to change. Obviously, all of these must accept some of the blame. Many superintendents fail to provide improvement leadership; many boards of education understand very little about the needs of society or about the teaching and learning process; many teachers are not willing to try new techniques. Many state departments of education have entrenched the *status quo;* they have not been effective leaders for the development of exciting, innovative programs. Many colleges of education involved in teacher training do not understand the need to change their methods; comparatively few college professors have been involved in innovative programs in public schools. No school in America has really moved forward significantly without dynamic, innovative leadership provided by a competent and dynamic principal.

Studies of time lag are illustrative of the barriers facing education.

[20] J. Spencer Carlson and Kenneth Wegner, "College Dropouts," *Phi Delta Kappan* (March 1965), pp. 325-326.

Rogers[21] has indicated that 2.5 percent of the schools are innovators; 13.5 percent are early adopters; 34.0 percent follow somewhat later; 34.0 follow much later; and 16 percent are notorious laggards. Unfortunately, it may take 50 years for the laggard school district to eventually adopt an idea begun by one of the innovative schools.

The interviewing of teachers remains a barrier to improvement. Too much stress is still placed on their knowledge of content and not enough placed on point of view, on understanding of the learning process and on personality structure. Virgil Blanke[22] has pointed out that to overcome barriers to change, once teachers are employed, group cohesion is necessary. Teachers must be open and frank with each other. Included in the group must be those with deviant ideas. Behavioral scientists should be part of change teams—persons who are perceptive enough to see through blockades in values and to bring the "idea" people, the needlers, and the implementers into heterogenious discussion groups. People often will not listen when core values are attacked; but they will listen to ideas relating to learning experiences for boys and girls.

Perhaps the best summaries of some of the educational barriers are those by J. Lloyd Trump[23] and Eugene Howard.[24] Among the impediments to progress are the following traditional concepts: (1) the optimum size class for *all* educational purposes is 25 to 30 students; (2) one teacher alone should be responsible for classroom instruction in a subject or grade; (3) the best ways for students to learn are by reading and listening to the voice of the physically present teacher in a self-sufficient classroom; (4) a subject is learned best if the student is in a classroom 200 minutes per week; (5) a seven-period day is better than a six-period day or vice versa; (6) teaching will be most satisfactory if teachers have one free period a day for preparation; (7) all elements of pupil learning organized by the school should be under the direct supervision of a teacher with 18 semester-hour credits in education and 18 hours in a subject field; and (8) the quality of learning is measured primarily by the number of books in the library in proportion to the school enrollment and scores on traditional tests. Although educators now can overcome most of these barriers in the educational setting, only a few schools have actually attempted to create the new kind of learning laboratory.

ARRANGE FOR MODELS

If a school is going to overcome some of the barriers to change, it must develop models or examples of new programs. The importance of developing models for change is supported in a statement by Vice President Humphrey,[25] "the tragedy is that the magnificent effort to discover knowledge is not accompanied by a similar effort to make sure that the knowledge

---

[21] *Op. cit.,* pp. 56-57.
[22] Virgil Blanke, "The Diffusion of Educational Innovations: A Continuing Frustration," Columbus, Ohio: College of Education, Ohio State University, unpublished, undated, mimeographed paper.
[23] J. Lloyd Trump, "Changed Roles for Teachers and Principals," unpublished, undated, mimeographed paper.
[24] Eugene Howard, "Individualizing Instruction: A Challenge for the Future," *Cook County Educational Digest* (January 1964).
[25] Hubert H. Humphrey, *Congressional Record* (March 8, 1962), p. 3396.

is effectively and promptly communicated." However, regardless of the quality of the models that are accepted or of the developments that occur in a particular school, care must be taken to see that the outlook is kept flexible. There is always a danger that new ideas, new systems of teaching, or beliefs about particular programs in education can be held on to so firmly and so long that minds become closed to future developments.

There are a number of suggestions for a school attempting to develop models for change. Some teachers seem to be most easily influenced by what might be called the *rational model*. In other words, they may become oriented toward the concept of change by reading some of the excellent literature and research now available about the teaching-learning process. Other teachers are led to new ideas through the *sales model*. Here the outstanding speaker who enthusiastically "sells" notions about ways to improve schools can influence many staff members to take another look at what they are doing. A third model can be called the *demonstration method*. Some teachers are best influenced by visiting schools and actually seeing the concept in operation. The fourth model might be termed the *money model*. Some staff members may not be sure that the program is what they really want, but if money is available, they are willing to try the idea. All four models are essential in terms of changing a school, because different teachers react in different ways.

Another useful approach to the preparation of models is to take a close look at the success agricultural experts have had in bringing about change. The county extension agent has played a major role here. Broadening the base of the school outlook and involving teachers in educational activities outside the walls of the school provides tremendous opportunity for the development of new ideas. Schools can cooperate with and obtain services and ideas from a university or an area center specifically established to focus on the change process. The regional educational laboratories are certainly a step in this direction.

CONSIDER THE BUDGET

It is true that most significant innovation is going to require additional money. This is one reason foundations, such as Ford and Kettering, have become involved in helping to finance the introduction of educational inventions and innovations. In-service sessions to train teachers to teach differently; the development or purchase of new curricular materials; teaching individuals to use flexible scheduling and other organizational concepts; building new facilities or remodeling existing "egg crates"; and many other pertinent steps, will result in increased costs. Most schools will need money to completely revamp and expland their library resource center facility. To automate a school with dial-access carrels and to provide computer-assisted instruction and educational television will be costly, as will travel and consultants.

Fortunately, the initial stages of many educational innovations can be undertaken without substantial additional funds, although there may have to be some change in budget allocations. In fact, many schools and school districts, through the initiative and creativity of administrators and teachers, have found ways to reorient and modernize important aspects of their school program without significantly greater expenditures. However, truly substantive improvement can usually be accomplished more effectively and more rapidly when additional funds are made available. Many desirable programs cannot be implemented under present financial arrangements.

Before the final budget is formulated in any district, innovative proposals should be carefully considered. For example, perhaps instead of contracting four teachers for the fifth and sixth grades, three excellent teachers can be hired; and, with the money available for the salary of the fourth teacher, three aides could be employed. Three teachers and three aides in four adjoining classrooms—with appropriate help and encouragement from the administration and other teachers—could institute many exciting new programs. This group can involve itself in daily flexible scheduling, team teaching, large and small group instruction, independent study, continuous progress, new curricula and inquiry techniques. It could remove the walls between rooms—both physically and mentally—with minor costs.

SELECT AN ALTERNATIVE

The first step in planning and then selecting alternatives is a careful diagnosis of the needs of the school. A number of different diagnostic tools should be utilized such as judgments of faculty, parent, student and consultant groups. Following the diagnosis, guides and steps for improvement must be outlined. These must include several choices.

One of the alternatives available would be to attempt to *change the entire school*. Here almost every teacher and student would be placed in a new type of school setting. The decision would be to gamble on the possibility of taking the entire staff and community along at the same time.

The second method open is what the writer chooses to call *"the 30-40-30 method."* On almost any school faculty about 30 percent of the teachers are enthusiastic about some of the innovations in education. About 40 percent of the members are still rather skeptical—they ride the fence, are willing to try if convinced, but probably would not make changes on their own initiative. There are about 30 percent who are strongly against any change from the present conventional school. Under the 30-40-30 plan, the administrator can encourage 30 percent to set up an organization designed to innovate and implement the needed improvements, and make an effort to influence the 40 percent sitting on the fence to cooperate. Perhaps the attitude of the "antis" cannot be changed significantly, if at all, the first year.

A third method available is to select *one project* for attention. Two first-grade teachers or two secondary English teachers might be interested in moving into a new type of organization with remodeled facilities, new curricula, new organization, and varied teaching strategies. This can be called a pilot study and observed by the other teachers.

174 *Effecting Changes in Education*

A fourth choice open is the *no-project method*. The first year no tangible steps are taken except to plant seeds and begin to structure the organization to produce ideas that, in the coming year, will enable some new programs to function.

In choosing the alternative to be followed in an individual school, the time sequence must be considered. If the program calls for a comprehensive change in one to three years, the entire program change or 30-40-30 method must be used. If the plan provides for a five or ten-year program, then the one-project or no-project methods might be better. Most innovators are reluctant to accept alternatives three and four. Their attitude is that since there is urgent need for improvement, as the evidence indicates, we cannot wait until the present third grade students are in junior high before the third grade program improves. It must take place while these students are still in that particular year of school. In determining strategy, the general impression now is that it usually takes two to ten years to achieve truly substantial improvement in every classroom, with seven or eight years the time span for most schools.

The alternative structure will be further influenced by whether the building has been newly constructed or is an older structure that has been used for some time. If it is a new school, built for a reoriented program, and if the staff is hired from this viewpoint, certainly the 100 percent method should be employed. With an older school, the chances for success are probably greater with the 30-40-30 method, although much depends on the courage and ability of the administrator and the readiness of the teachers and community.

Once the method to be used has been selected, the principal should attempt to involve as many staff members as possible in the change process. Teachers undertaking new approaches need to have recognition and praise. They need to be part of various team structures which have as members needlers, dreamers and implementers. The needlers are necessary to get people off center; the dreamers are essential, for once the needlers have brought home their points, the dreamers need to come up with creative ideas which will help the implementers get new programs adopted. The use of a sociogram is a good device for structuring teams. The innovative teachers should be led by an administrator who purposely seeks to break some of the outmoded traditions which still exist in American education.

PROVIDE ONGOING EVALUATION

Are the attempts to change American education having a significant impact? Are boys and girls receiving better education in the schools where change in teaching strategies, curricula, organizations and facilities have taken place? The comment is often made that innovators are not evaluators. This usually has been true in the past. Subjectively, those who have become deeply and successfully involved in innovation are convinced that the new kinds of programs being developed are better than conventional approaches. Objectively, evidence is being collected which further validates this opinion. The Kettering Foundation, for example, is financing research projects that attempt to identify successful innovations, and then to disseminate the findings to other schools. Informal studies have found that in successful, innovative schools, attendance percentages have increased, discipline problems have decreased, library circulation has increased, and student scores on achievement tests have been at least as good if not better than those scores from traditional programs.

As schools move into new programs, provisions must be developed for prompt adoption of better ideas. Built into the organization should be a constant search for improvement. It is essential that plans be made to establish research projects relating to existing and proposed adoptions. Objective evaluation must be available as new ideas are disseminated. In the meantime, subjective opinions can hold great weight for direction. Student, staff and parent questionnaires are means of judging tentative success. The quality and quantity of applicants applying for jobs in a particular school can help to indicate views by teachers. Evaluations by the many visitors to innovative schools add outside observations.

Not only must new evaluation programs be established for the schools themselves, but also new methods of evaluating individual students. The old Carnegie unit, 275 minutes a week, class rank, and A, B, C, D, F report cards are obsolete. Goals of schools are to develop decision-making, responsible, self-directing, perceptive, value-judging individuals. What present measurements do schools use to determine success in these areas? If continuous progress and individualized instruction are desired, how can schools continue to evaluate student progress only in comparison with that made by classmates, or the knowledge of one student in relation to the knowledge of another?

A new era is about to descend upon schools in terms of measurement. Ongoing evaluation of new programs, student progress and readiness for college will all find dramatic new techniques in the next ten years. In the meantime, schools must seek to do the best possible job with the existing tools, and to explain the inadequacies to the community so that it will be ready and willing to accept better techniques.

INTERPRET DEVELOPMENTS AND PLAN FURTHER IMPROVEMENTS

As a school makes decisions to implement changes, the community, teachers and students must be convinced that the change is desirable. Ideas should be implemented, modified and improved as rapidly as possible. Evaluation must take place. If the program appears to be successful, further efforts must be made to interpret the results to everyone concerned. If the innovation does not seem valid, it should be replaced. There is nothing wrong with admission of a failure, especially if the effort was a sincere attempt to improve education.

Educators have talked about public relations for years. If we are to deviate significantly from the type of school attended by children in most communities today, the problem of communication takes on new dimensions. Most schools have not utilized all the opportunities available to them.

Probably *the greatest single omission is that of deep involvement of students in planning, implementing and evaluating the change process.*

Present schools are liberal if they allow students to participate in 10 percent of the decisions concerning their education; they should be involved on a more nearly 50-50 relationship. This does not mean that students should have a 50 percent control of the school; it does indicate that students must help plan and select programs. If they understand why their school is changing, and how these improvements will benefit them as individuals and their society as a whole, they usually become tremendous ambassadors in the community. If students are members of idea teams, curriculum teams, communication teams, and evaluation teams, and frequently meet with teachers and administrators to discuss the process of improving the school, education can take a great stride forward. No parent is influenced more quickly than to have his first-year child come home bubbling about what happened in school that day and anxious to get up early the next morning to be there before classes begin.

Parents will accept change if they are helped to understand a relationship between change, their welfare and that of their children. Parent evaluation groups should have ideas discussed with them. A sympathetic parent group can alert the administrator to emerging problems. The present typical PTA organization in many districts does not enhance community understanding of change; thus a different parent organization is needed as an addition to or replacement of the PTA.

Superintendents and school boards often refuse or fail to make simple adjustments that can enhance the possibility of successful innovation. Attendance boundaries provide one small example. Most educators insist that if Sally lives on the west side of her street, she must attend School X, while Janie, who lives on the east side of the same street, must attend School Y. The point here is that Sally should be allowed to attend the kind of school in the community where chances for success each day are most apparent.

In the process of planning and implementing new programs, administrators must provide time for teachers to really think and communicate. The concept is not idle philosophy. Boards can provide substitute teachers where necessary, but by restructuring the school and using more flexibility in scheduling, many teachers can be released without substitutes. If teachers are going to plan new programs, they must have time to think and create. Giving teachers time to dream is one of the best supportive steps that can be taken to implement and sell new programs.

When new ideas are developed, a thorough, and different, in-service program must be provided. Many changes in schools have failed simply because continuous evaluation was not planned to insure the successful implementation of a new program. Telling teachers to "be creative and do anything you want" usually does not work. They need assistance as well as encouragement. Conventional methods of deployment of available staff usually hinder rather than aid the adoption of a model.

Getting involved with experimental college programs and private or federally funded efforts to improve education usually enhances the possibility of success. Constant communication about the conviction that schools must improve, attendance at conferences, both within and without the district and other appropriate methods help. Recognition and acceptance of a working relationship with both the informal and formal power structures in the school and community sometimes make the difference between a successful or an unsuccessful invention, innovation or adoption.

Much could be done to speed up the acceptance of improvement if state departments of education would adopt the fostering of inventions as one of their major tasks. Their influence on legislators and on the lay public could be tremendous. However, few state departments—or local school systems—have thus committed themselves; as a result, individual schools must usually include a plan which will enable them to gain permission to stray from the accepted procedures. For example, schools employing optional class attendance must usually try to find ways to "get around" the state department and state legislative regulations, instead of having their cooperation in a cooperative venture. Hopefully, the Eight-State Project will help to make state departments positive, influential advocates for, and interpreters of, needed improvements.

SUMMARY AND IMPLICATIONS FOR THE FUTURE

This paper has been an attempt to portray some of the essential considerations for any school that is planning significant improvement. As a method of summarizing results of attempted change, as witnessed in schools throughout the United States, reference is made to parts of a report by the Systems Development Corporation of Santa Monica.[26] Observers found that new programs are often helped financially by grants; most of the innovative schools were either new or were undergoing rapid growth. The developmental patterns varied widely and depended upon the leadership; there was evidence of strong, positive, dynamic leadership. The stress toward more flexibility was justified as allowing greater attention to individual needs. A formal structure for change was not visible in the school systems studied, but it was felt that one could be built if the roles played by various institutions were clarified.

No school in America has yet accomplished the goals envisioned by forward-looking educators. A few schools have adopted a number of the needed reforms, but not one has combined all the possible improvements. Further, no one knows exactly how to proceed successfully to change schools. There is no tried and true formula; a method that has been successful in one school has often not proven adequate in others. Scientific methods, as opposed to trial-and-error, are needed, but at this point of development only suggested steps or guidelines can be offered.

Individual schools must become more than 50 percent effective. The evolving educational philosophy demands significant improvement; creating

---

[26] Don Bushnell, *et al.*, *Proceedings of the Conference on the Implementation of Educational Innovations*, Systems Development Corporation, Santa Monica, California, 1964.

better schools means 30 to 40 changes in the systems of teaching strategies, curricula, organizations and facilities. To accomplish these tasks, 10 guidelines are offered as aids to planning and effecting improvement: (1) develop committed leadership, (2) critically review the literature, (3) evolve a philosophy, (4) create a dissatisfaction with the inappropriate, (5) overcome the barriers, (6) arrange for models, (7) consider the budget, (8) select an alternative, (9) provide ongoing evaluation, and (10) interpret developments and plan further improvements.

Planning and effecting needed changes in individual schools is difficult at any time; to plan and effect improvement to the extent suggested by this paper may seem to some an insurmountable task. The timid at this point will shy away, but schools must change; there is a growing commitment to the improvement and the personalization of programs for all boys and girls. Educators who are "in step with a different drummer" must rise to the challenge. Leaders in the Eight-State Project area should join with others throughout the world to dramatically increase the vision of, and the search for, significantly better schools.

*   *   *

SUPPLEMENTARY STATEMENT

BERNARD V. REZABEK*

Change is an inevitable phenomenon of nature and of society. Planned change occurs when human forces are organized to regulate certain occurrences during a defined period of time.

The concern of those responsible for education is that change in society can be anticipated with sufficient accuracy to plan related changes in formal institutions of learning. Planning change in education for the future, at best, is an attempt to project impressions and needs into the decades ahead for which many cues have been given. The projections for the eight-state area are being made for the next fifteen years; the purpose has been clearly indicated: to plan improvements that should be made during that period.

The purpose of this paper is to recognize certain changes (as viewed by experts from selected segments of American society) and relate these prospective changes to educational needs, and specifically, to give consideration to planning improvements in a functional school unit—the attendance unit, consisting of a building principal, his staff, and the teachers and students assigned to that school on a full-time or part-time basis.

It should be observed that those responsible for planning needed changes in an individual school hold a partnership with school children, parents, and community agencies, on the one hand, and with the lay board and governing agency at the line and staff level, on the other. An outgrowth

* *Assistant Dean, Undergraduate Teacher Education, College of Education, University of Wyoming.* Formerly, Associate Professor, University of Wichita, Kansas (1953-59); and Associate Director, NCATE, Washington, D. C. (1964-65). Has had public school experience in Arizona and Oklahoma.

of the need for federal funds to finance new programs has resulted in some evident shift of authority in line-and-staff administration from the building principal to a central-office administrator assigned or employed to prepare projects and direct innovation on a district-wide basis. At the same time, some teachers in the individual schools may be selected, oriented and directed to participate in action research apart from the routine schedule of a given school. It is hoped that improvement can be accomplished at the level of action classified by Chin (Ch. 3) as "communication and influence patterns".

A much-voiced caution is that, once implemented, a new program should be permitted to run its course and be evaluated before competing innovations are interjected. For the majority of school administrators in the local school, the choice is not as much one of innovation as one of selection and utilization of the appropriate strategy for change.

The building principal stands at a point in his school where he must move within an arc of 180 degrees. Educational planning and subsequent decisions require action to achieve an agreed upon goal with related advances to either flank; in rare cases there may be need for a temporary retreat. The strategic steps for improvement in an individual school embody several realms; however, the three which can be directed by a principal may be called: (1) targets—or the objectives of learning to be reached in an environment over the next decade; (2) organization—or the deployment of resources, agencies, facilities, priorities, personnel, and schedule to influence both change and economy; and (3) procedure—or the application of professional ideas, methods, and techniques generally viewed as the special tools assigned to those concerned with responsibilities for formal education.

TARGETS

Pointing for targets ahead is predicated on a belief that their sequential, or parallel, attainment will accomplish a needed end—or at least an appropriate means to a distant end. This contention emphasizes that change must have both purpose and direction, and depends on certain assumptions.

Richard Shetler[1] has summarized important trends in the world of 1967 which relate to goals for 1980. He defines them as: (1) world urbanization; (2) industrial automation; and (3) information technological revolution.

Within these aspects there is continued reference to people—increased populations, congregating in small areas, being relieved largely of manual labor and granted more leisure time, but seeking an interdependence with other people. This growing complexity of improved human relations appears as a chief target for change in the future. A second target growing out of increasing population and urbanization involves the technical ability of all people to comprehend and manage a variety of systems in daily

---

[1] Richard L. Shetler, "Major Problems of Society in 1980" in *Prospective Changes in Society by 1980* (Denver, Colo.: July 1966), p. 261.

living. A more frustrating set of targets are those technical accomplishments leading to production, distribution and operation of an economy which minimizes the opportunity for full-time employment.

Gordon Swanson's analysis[2] of the shift in occupational structure from natural resources development to human resources training and retraining points up at least five avenues for goal formulation in local schools:

1. Specific attention must be given to economic education as part of the general education curriculum. Basic knowledge of national goals and of contemporary work values should precede any attempt at specialization or occupational counseling;

2. Local priorities for special programs must be appraised in relation to state and national demands. Supplementary funds should be viewed as an incentive for improvement rather than an excuse for change;

3. Community agencies and employers should be asked both to plan and to supervise certain technical aspects of vocational programs for which a school district cannot assume full responsibility. It is apparent that an expansion of diversified occupations and work-study represents this trend;

4. Guidelines for local school districts for retraining should be adapted from national goals and extended through post-high school, evening school, part-time programs or other media of manpower retread design;

5. Some type of "culture appreciation" experience must be devised as part of the regular program and of post-high school occupational retraining. With emphasis on improved human relations and a promise of more leisure time for 1980, individual schools should assess possibilities for constructive expression, or lead a community in this development.

ORGANIZATION

The internal organization of an individual school, without the restriction of legal guidelines or the direction of district policy, could be either effective or inhibiting. Even the design for instruction must mesh with elements of the emerging local-state-national picture in response to educational needs or to effect educational change. The proposal that educational planners understand and use the power in political systems, as outlined by Kimbrough (Ch. 6), suggests certain serious limitations upon change—such as, fiscal resources and extended educational services. At the same time, these two areas of need offer a focus for immediate planning.

Assuming that the priorities for education objectives are to be increased in the federal budget by 1980 as Lecht suggests (Ch. 1), state and local school systems and schools must resolve the dilemma posed if state-local government spending for education is projected to diminish from 36 percent of total budgets in 1964 to 29 percent in 1975. Lecht's further indication that a 30 percent gap is seen between state-local resources and projected aspirations of the society of 1975, leaves administrators of local schools at least two alternatives: they must reach beyond state-local govern-

---

[2] Gordon I. Swanson, "Education for the World of Work" in *Implications for Education of Prospective Changes in Society* (Denver, Colo.: January 1967), pp. 98 ff.

ment sources to obtain resources for bridging the gap; or they may effect changes in local organization and instruction in light of reorganized targets for education.

The provision of extended services involves decisions to justify the need or extent of pre-primary experiences and the need, extent and rationale for post-secondary education of both a terminal and preparatory nature, not to mention the obligation for manpower retraining. Four guidelines are presented relative to these needed changes:

1. The scope of the program must be visualized as needed for an individual school but provided in an urban, multi-district, country or regional area with maximum effect. Area schools, junior colleges and opportunity schools are examples of extended organization;

2. Facilities for needed change must be modified, leased or shared if budget priorities are not available for new construction. Reported population in rural, small school districts of the eight-state area will compound the effort for "expanded" facilities and demand a stronger appeal for quality improvement. Alternatives may be seen in cooperating districts, residence schools, busing of students or the leasing of appropriate facilities related to innovations for vocational, technical or personal services.

3. Staff in-service growth and retaining is prerequisite and co-requisite as part of any reorganization for educational change. As noted earlier in this paper, a building principal can expect to obtain the cooperation of local district specialists in effecting innovations;

4. Non-professional education personnel in the status of para-professionals, auxiliary services, public services or technical consultants may be employed to assist instruction under direct supervision of certificated teachers. Business, industry and the vocations can expect to be utilized in the work-study programs of terminal and post-secondary program.

PROCEDURE

There have been repeated inferences in the eight-state conferences that change in educational procedures is needed to assure better schools. Another premise might be that change results in differences, but only the evaluation of these differences can support the value judgments about improvement. Glines provided a comprehensive list of steps to be employed for planning change in four systems of a school. Teacher strategies and curricula can be considered together along with supervision, as a system comprising the "instructional" obligation of an individual school.

The changing role of a school principal has been described by Eye and Netzer[3] under the four components of process—controlling, initiating, appraising and implementing. One premise derived for this project is that the responsibility of an individual school is primarily for the *realization* of appropriate new trends in instruction to be understood, planned, adopted, tested and evaluated before wholesale adoption. At this point there should

---

[3] Glen G. Eye and Lanore A. Netzer, *Supervision of Instruction*. Harper and Row, Publisher, New York, 1965, p. 400.

be a strong caution that suggested models should be appraised and modified before existing programs are abandoned or alternatives considered. It would be ironical if an untested model became the master that determined the changes to be made.

Appropriate procedures can be summarized as follows:

1. The school principal must accept the shift to central-office specialists for innovation and planning of new programs.

2. He must plan procedures of communication with members of his staff in policy formation or program implementation.

3. He must provide opportunity for expression of each staff member within his school and channels beyond his school.

4. As public schools assume more responsibility for observation and student teaching in preparation of teachers, a principal and his staff must plan procedures for the complete process from orientation to follow-up in partnership with the designated teacher education council on college and university campuses.

5. Individual school staff should recognize the need for a clearing house group (including the Congress of Parents and Teachers) to interpret change and its success for public understanding, endorsement and support.

CHAPTER 9

Planning and Effecting Needed Changes in Local School Systems

RODERICK F. MCPHEE*

To paraphrase a recent popular song, change is a many-splendored thing. Change seems to be the theme for countless conferences, conventions, books, articles and speeches. While I occasionally detect among some of my colleagues a wistful yearning for some future day when "stability" replaces "innovation" as the key to quality education—or to grantsmanship —I do not see that happening in the near future.

As one who has admittedly found it relatively simple to give speeches on change—preferably at some distance from my place of work—and considerably more difficult to write meaningfully for publication about change, these two tasks are miniscule when compared with the actual "doing" of planned change. Moreover, they are also infinitely less fun.

GENERAL CONCEPTS REGARDING CHANGE

Nearly everyone is enthused about change these days, and with excellent reasons. The two previous publications of this project give overwhelming evidence concerning the kind of society we have ahead of us and the implications for the schools. However, I have observed over the years that *our individual enthusiasm for a specific change is usually inversely proportional to how much we ourselves must change.* We desire it greatly, in and for others. *We praise changes for others, but seldom value changes for ourselves.* Thus, we have representatives from universities urging (for good reasons) many substantive organizational changes for the public schools, but seldom attempting to lead in a reorganization of the institution or department they represent. We have superintendents urging changes in programs of teacher education, but not re-examining the opportunities and responsibilities of the public schools with respect to student teaching. I could extend the list of examples—as could each of you—but I suspect the point is clear. As John Gardner put it in a slightly different but related manner in his marvelous book, *Self-Renewal,* we usually reserve our affection for innovators long dead.

At least I hope the point is clear, because I am going to be discussing planning improvements in local school systems. Stripped of excess exhortation and verbiage, basically this means changing what the teacher does.

* *Superintendent of Schools, Glencoe, Illinois.* Formerly, Assistant Professor, Harvard Graduate School of Education and Director, Advanced Administrative Institute, Harvard; Assistant Executive Secretary, AASA; staff member, White House Conference on Education (1955). Co-author of *The Organization and Control of American Schools.*

Thus I am also in the enviable position of encouraging changes which essentially must be done by others. But I realize fully that the administration must lead in creating and maintaining a favorable climate for change and in encouraging and facilitating needed changes.

I am impressed with the wealth of material that is available on change. Moreover, when I examined your second project publication,[1] it became clear that the general implications for education of prospective changes in our society have been superbly handled by many authors. The usual conflict between projecting *what will be* (probably) and describing *what ought to be* is well illustrated throughout this book. From my present vantage point I think I will cast my lot with the realistic views explicitly expressed particularly by Goodlad (chapter 3), Brickell and Goldhammer (chapter 13), and Cunningham (chapter 11)*. In brief, I accept their thesis that change in our schools will come slowly, even reluctantly, and at a very uneven rate.

RESISTANCE TO CHANGE

I do not think resistance to change is *necessarily* bad. Some institutional inertia is necessary to prevent the bandwagon tendency from creating chaos by stimulating too many shifts in our schools as new claims are made for untested programs. The great difficulty, of course, comes when the organization becomes so committed to stability that it resists all efforts at change. The improvements in our schools will come only if we pay organizational attention to both continuity and change, for both are crucial. At times it seems to me that a cult of innovation for the sake of change is present in American education, making it difficult to hold to the position that conservatism in some matters may be the wise course. I believe that in our efforts at improvement we must lean strongly in the direction of needed change, but I do not believe we should accept the thesis of some that if we are not innovating frantically we are not progressing. Nor do I think that we need to accept the collective guilt feelings I notice permeating our profession when we do not have a different answer each month to the question "What's new?" After all, many of the old ways are worthwhile and defensible—but not all of them.

A look at the educational changes over the past few decades would not impress one with the significance of many of them. The impression of massive change sweeping the educational world is conveyed by our journals, and by our annual reports, but these aim largely at surface features. Generally, our reports to the public emphasize the new gadgets or tools or groupings we are using, rather than the changes in how the student learns, what he knows or how he acts on this knowledge.

Anyone who doubts the institutional inertia in our schools needs only visit a dozen of the schools which reputedly have new organizational

[1] *Implications for Education of Prospective Changes in Society.* (Denver, Colorado: Designing Education for the Future, January, 1967).
* These and all other similar references in this chapter are to authors and chapters in the second project publication cited in footnote 1.

patterns, such as nongrading or team teaching, to discover that the changes are usually more publicized than real. There may be outward signs of innovation, but there seldom seems to be any major change in what is happening between teacher and student, as Goodlad pointed out in his statement in the previous report (chapter 3).

Let us consider some of the factors involved in the relative inability of public schools to adapt rapidly to changing times. The following findings of a congressional sub-committee were recently printed in *Nation's Schools*:

1. Less than 1 percent of the annual expenditure for education is devoted to research and development.

2. An innovation in medicine is adopted universally in about two years.

3. It takes thirty years before an innovation in education has widespread adoption, and it requires ten to fifteen years for even the first 3 percent of the schools to make significant change.

Carlson has suggested three basic reasons for the slow rate of change in public schools.[2] He cites the absence of a change agent, a weak knowledge base, and what he calls "domestication" of the public schools. To these I would add the failure of administrators and teachers to accept the inevitability of change and the failure to comprehend the accelerating rate of change.

Perhaps one of the most crucial barriers—one which is not mentioned by Carlson and is ignored by many other students of change—is the realization that behavioral changes by staff members can by no means be assessed on a rational basis alone. The emotional upheaval which is involved in any significant change is too often ignored by those who write about the change process. *Most improvement involves changes in what the teacher must know and must do.* This clearly attacks individual vested interests in the psychological sense and we should anticipate the high levels of anxiety which are normal.

One writer who has confronted this aspect of individual resistance directly is Herbert A. Thelen.[3] He suggests that in-service training must be carefully structured and must take into consideration the awareness of individual resistance. Without such awareness, we often settle in the schools for superficial indications of change which disappear over time. Any one who has observed the behavior of an automobile driver after he sees a serious accident will know precisely what I mean. He will be exceedingly cautious for the next few miles, but will very quickly revert to his original patterns. So it is with teachers and administrators.

There are other reasonably clear reasons for resistance to change. One of these is the commitment of most present leaders to the *status quo*.

[2] Richard O. Carlson, "Barriers to Change in Public Schools," in Richard O. Carlson, *et al.*, *Change Processes in the Public Schools* (University of Oregon, Center for the Advanced Study of Educational Administration, Eugene, Oregon, 1965), pp. 4-8.
[3] Herbert A. Thelen, "Developing the School through Faculty Self-Training," *Dynamics of Groups at Work* (Chicago: University of Chicago Press, 1954), pp. 70-92.

It will be interesting to see what happens when the advocates of the new math today become the defenders of what will be the old math in a few years. *The momentum of the past is often more compelling than the unknown promise of change.*

SOURCES OF CHANGE

There are at least two major categories of change in education. One is the natural shift which occurs when personnel changes, either in the teaching or administrative staff. We have tended to regard this as an evolutionary process, and therefore have too often paid little attention to it as a specific strategy for change. I shall say more about this later. This paper will be primarily concerned with change which may not originally be initiated by school personnel, but is deliberately designed, is purposefully directed, and is implemented by them. I am going to follow the example provided by Robert Chin in his paper in this publication and avoid attempting to define change. Suffice it to say that I shall focus my comments on *educational improvement* rather than speaking only of *educational change.* Clearly, of course, *there can be no improvement without change of some kind, although there certainly can be change without improvement.*

The problem is to discover what needs improvement on a priority basis and then to allocate resources—time, money and people—in ways to be suggested later. Since priorities usually must be related directly to purposes, and since purposes frequently remain at a level of generalization that defies rigorous analysis—much less evaluation—this is an exceedingly crucial and difficult task. In his companion paper Melvin Barnes has dealt carefully with this issue. On close examination it becomes painfully clear how wasteful have been many of the efforts to change our schools with no clear priorities in mind.

One possible reason for the difficulty we find in agreeing upon priorities—in addition to the overriding factor of the awesome complexity of education—is the large number of groups which have a direct impact on the local school district. Pellegrin[4] has identified ten sources of educational innovation, and it is clear that these individuals, groups or organizations often have conflicting views with respect to a number of things including priorities. The ten he identifies are: (1) the classroom teacher; (2) the administrator (principal and superintendent); (3) the school board; (4) the lay public; (5) the state departments of education; (6) education faculties in colleges and universities; (7) professional associations; (8) the United States Office of Education and other federal government agencies; (9) textbook publishers; and (10) scientists, technical specialists, and other experts.

Pellegrin is impressed—and indeed one cannot fail to be impressed—by the fact that the greatest stimuli to changes in education originate in

---

[4] Roland J. Pellegrin, "An Analysis of Sources and Processes of Innovation in Education" (University of Oregon, Center for the Advanced Study of Educational Administration, Eugene, Oregon, 1966), pp. 6-14.

sources *external* to the field.[5] Many, if not most of the recent improvements in public schools have come about because of demands from the greater society rather than because of pressures generated within a local school district or a state. Indeed, the systems analyst tells us that the major impetus for change in most organizations comes from the outside. Clearly the emphasis on pre-school education, modern foreign languages, new mathematics, and most other recent major changes have not been initiated by local schools. They have been adopted, with local modifications, but the initiation came primarily from outside.

Nevertheless, we should consider the roles to be played by some of the sources identified by Pellegrin. Only the first two can be considered as internal, but the crucial nature of the teacher and the administrator should be emphasized.

THE TEACHER

As a source of innovation the classroom teacher seldom plays a major role. In most cases the influence of a given teacher does not range far beyond his classroom, and very rarely does it reach beyond his own school. The organizational structure of our schools makes it difficult for this to be otherwise.

The teacher generally must confine his efforts at improvement to his own classroom practices. He does not have the time (or usually the energy) to disseminate his influence much beyond this. Coffee hour conversations and faculty meetings do provide some opportunity to exchange views on promising practices, but this is generally unsystematic.

It may well be that the changing role of the teacher will bring teachers more directly into what Cunningham (Chapter 11) has called the allocation-decision team. If such participation deals substantially with the welfare of children, then improvement may in a sense become institutionalized. However, if such decisions are concerned primarily with teacher welfare, then this may sharply reduce the influence of teachers on educational improvement by creating institutional barriers to change. Strong unions in fields other than education have seldom sought changes other than those relating to welfare and working conditions.

At this time, however, it appears that teachers are more likely to be acted-upon than to be actors in the beginning of the improvement process. The impact of militant teacher organizations is yet to be seen.

THE ADMINISTRATOR

There can be no doubt about the fact that the key element in planning and effecting improvement in local school districts is the administration. The superintendent is the crucial figure on a district basis, and the principal plays a somewhat similar role in the school building.

The importance of the superintendent is clearly derived from the power—real or perceived—of his position. The power to allocate resources, in terms of people, money, or time, carries with it the ability to encourage—

---

[5] *Ibid.*, p. 15.

or to stifle—and this is the essence of seeking improvement—or of maintaining the *status quo*. The superintendent has more authority than anyone else at the local level in making these decisions, and thus he is the key figure.

It is in part through the process of allocation of resources that the administration creates the climate of expectation of change. While such an organizational climate will vary somewhat from building to building, the overall tone is essentially determined by the central staff, and ultimately by the superintendent. If he is dissatisfied with things as they are and is interested in innovation and experimentation, his staff will know it and will tend to react accordingly. On the other hand, if he prefers a static situation, the staff will also be aware of this and changes will be few in number and in scope. At a time when it is unfashionable to openly oppose change, his staff members will also be conscious of the possible gap between his public statements on innovation and his allocation decisions at budget time. In this respect actions clearly speak more loudly than words.

At the building level the principal plays a similar role in creating a climate that nurtures or discourages change. Although he may not have the authority of the central administration when resources are being distributed, he can do much within the building to provide or deny the kind of help needed to launch any new venture. Demeter summarized the situation well when he concluded, "Building principals are key figures in the process. Where they are both aware of and sympathetic to an innovation, it tends to prosper. Where they are ignorant of its existence, or apathetic if not hostile, it tends to remain outside the blood stream of the school."[6] This is the essence of the conclusion reached by Brickell in his well known study of change in the state of New York.

THE BOARD OF EDUCATION

Boards play an important role in the process of change, largely through their influence and, indeed, control of the distribution of resources. However, they seldom exert much leadership in specific program changes, for this is essentially the responsibility of the professionals.

The major contribution of school boards is the initial provision of resources to do the jobs which are agreed upon as necessary. In short, once the educational programs are decided upon, the school board should lead the fight for the money. Much of the literature on school boards suggests that too often they impede any changes because of cost. No doubt this will continue to be the case with many boards. However, with the increasingly competitive nature of American schooling some of these traditional stances may be altered. This will happen, of course, only to the extent that community values shift accordingly.

THE LAY PUBLIC

Who can say what the role of the public is? There are so many sub-publics that perhaps the question is meaningless. All I can say for certain

---

[6] Lee H. Demeter, *Accelerating the Local Use of Improved Educational Practices in School Systems*, Ed.D. Thesis, Teachers College, Columbia University (1951), p. 23.

as a superintendent is that every change we make in our school program will delight some people and outrage others. This is about as close to a universal rule as I can come.

I have the feeling that those of us in education make the serious mistake of assuming that most of the public is nearly as interested in the schools as we are. Except at times of crisis this is not so. There is a group of people who are continuously active in school matters in most communities, but this tends to be a relatively small group.

Probably the most useful function of the public is to be certain that the members of the school board are highly qualified and competent people. If they are, the schools may (note that I said *may, not* necessarily *will*) progress and improve. When the board is ineffective, however, it is doubtful whether the schools will move forward.

STATE DEPARTMENTS OF EDUCATION

To this point the state departments of education have played a modest role in effecting improvement in most local districts. They have enforced minimum standards, administered regulations, distributed funds and performed other service functions. However, with few exceptions, the furnishing of stimulation and direction by state department personnel is more of a hope than a reality. In many states these personnel are too few in number and are too overburdened with other duties to exert much leadership. Recent staff additions for federal programs, plus the influence of money from Title V of the Elementary and Secondary Education Act to strengthen state departments may possibly shift this picture significantly.

I believe that, until now, the great shortcoming in state departments of education has been that long range planning was largely overlooked. This project is the essence of the type of activity which should be carried on continuously by the states, either singly or in concert. Should such an activity become an ongoing project for one or more state departments it could provide significant data and impetus for improvement in local districts. Fortunately the significance of this project is spreading far beyond the borders of the eight state departments whose vision made this possible. Planning is a crucial problem, for most of our educational development and expansion usually takes place in a near vacuum. For example, Medsker (chapter 7) speaks of the future development of community colleges, and Passow (chapter 5) mentions the downward extension of schooling in the years ahead. Neither raises the question as to where to find the teachers for these new institutions. Currently the burgeoning community colleges are beginning to recruit staff members from present high school faculties, who in turn are reaching into the junior high school for replacements. There apparently is no agency in our society prepared to take a long-range look at the source of competent faculties for these new institutions. As education now involves more people than any other field in America, it seems clear that someone should study the manpower problems on a long term basis.

State departments of education might also assist in speeding improvement by developing state aid formulas which would reward extra effort, once the minimum standards had been met. Unless the states do this, the funds for the truly exceptional programs will come from the local level or from Washington. Since it is the so-called lighthouse districts that receive the publicity, I believe the state is missing the boat in not having some involvement, and receiving some recognition, for these outstanding programs.

EDUCATION FACULTIES IN COLLEGES AND UNIVERSITIES

It appears doubtful whether college and university faculties in education have had much direct influence on school practice. As teachers of teachers they would appear to have a strategic position to influence future developments in the schools, but I do not see much evidence that they have used their leverage well.

There are some significant exceptions, of course, but I will not attempt to name them here. Each generation produces a few giants, but the overall performance record has not been impressive.

PROFESSIONAL ASSOCIATIONS

The impact of most professional associations on local practice has been negligible. Indeed, since control of these associations is usually in the hands of well established, frequently older members of the profession, it would be surprising if they were not relatively conservative when new developments are proposed.

Even if the associations were in the forefront of new movements, their influence on local school districts would be so diffuse as to be difficult to assess. Nevertheless, their conventions and other activities do serve to acquaint members with new practices, and their literature often tells how someone is doing something that seems promising. The only problem is that most of this literature describes only the successes and ignores the failures.

THE UNITED STATES OFFICE OF EDUCATION AND OTHER FEDERAL AGENCIES

Until recently the U.S.O.E. had no discernible effect on local school districts. Today, however, it is clearly the most influential force on the education scene. I would ascribe two distinct reasons for this extremely rapid shift in status. First is the clearcut influence of the relatively great sums of money which it dispenses, and second is the correspondingly great improvement in the caliber of much of its professional staff.

Some of the most able and imaginative talent in American education is now working for the Office of Education—partly because that is where the money is and partly because that is where much of the action is. These two—money and action—usually go together and they can perhaps generate some enthusiasm for change which will have a lasting impact. The Title III funds to spur innovation are undoubtedly stimulating many changes, most of which could be called improvements.

The influence of the National Science Foundation, the Office of Economic Opportunity, and other federal agencies may also be profound over a period of time.

TEXTBOOK PUBLISHERS

In past years publishers were instrumental as curriculum builders, because of the influence of the textbook on teacher planning. The increasing fight for a share of the rapidly expanding educational market may spread this dependency somewhat, due in part to the increasing use of a variety of instructional materials rather than dependence on a single text.

At the moment we are witnessing an amazing number of corporate acquisitions or mergers, as the giants in American industry are becoming aware that education is second in spending only to national defense in the public sector. At present about forty billion dollars is spent on education. Thus, for reasons not wholly altruistic, we see the major technological firms acquiring publishing houses, undoubtedly with the hope of getting a piece of the action. The IBM purchase of Science Research Associates, the R.C.A. purchase of Random House, the Time, Inc. and General Electric creation of General Learning Corporation, and most recently the Bell and Howell purchase of Charles E. Merrill Company are among the potentially significant recent developments.

The impact of these companies is yet to be determined. There is little doubt, however, that education will receive the "hard sell" for whatever products are created. At the moment educators are partially protected because there is no clear market mechanism for education, with each district operating as a separate unit.

CATEGORIES OF CHANGE

Many of the authors in *Implications for Education of Prospective Changes in Society* dealt with the kinds of changes we should anticipate. I suggest that the prospective changes may be categorized in three major areas: changes in content; changes in organization for instruction; and changes in instructional materials or technology.

I do not think that these three categories of change can necessarily be dealt with through the same processes, for they involve considerably different dimensions of teacher behavior. The area of content essentially involves what the teachers know about a given subject. With regard to mathematics, it has been relatively possible to re-educate mathematics teachers to the new terminology and, hopefully, to some of the new concepts. This was also true in physics. It is not nearly so easy, as many curriculum study groups are discovering, to do the same thing in the social sciences or in English. Unless the teachers can master the new subject matter or instructional approach, change will be non-effective.

The organizational changes, such as team teaching or non-grading, involve inter-personal relations between teachers at a level which heretofore have been lacking. The performance before peers, which is required by team teaching, has apparently been a major obstacle for many individuals. Undoubtedly, one desirable aspect of teaching for many people is that they will relate essentially to younger persons whose evaluative reactions have little or no effect. The demands of team teaching undoubtedly involve behavioral changes and psychological adjustments of a large nature.

The impact of technology is still undetermined, and it will undoubtedly be some time before sophisticated programs catch up with appealing hardware. We have heard a great deal about the technological revolution in education but as Dean H. Thomas James at Stanford has commented, there has probably never been a revolution about which so much has been said and so little has been seen. As Goldhammer said so well (chapter 13), no one has really determined what to do with the machines after the socially acceptable investment has been made. At one point, the developers of curriculum and the hardware people flirted with the inane idea of developing what was called "teacher proof" materials. Nothing is teacher proof and I am sure that the most rapid way to sabotage any technological advance would be to propagate any such nonsense.

To this point I have perhaps sounded somewhat negative, but I do this only because I believe that my present assignment forces me to be realistic. My school system is far more open and receptive to change than most others of which I know, and my staff has shown great willingness to experiment, explore and to invest time and energy in new efforts to improve instruction. Even then, major change comes slowly and, to the revolutionary, at a rather frustrating pace.

IMPLEMENTING CHANGE IN SCHOOL DISTRICTS

Fortunately in this paper I do not have to deal with urban and metropolitan areas, but I still must consider (or at least dispose of) the disparities present in the remaining 20,000 or so districts which qualify as suburban or rural. A reasonably large percentage of the schools in these eight states are suburban or rural, and most people are aware of the great disparities with regard to level of support, calibre of faculty and administration, community expectations, and so forth. The best that I can do is acknowledge these great differences but there will be insufficient time to discuss them. Moreover I believe the suggestions I make should generally be universally applicable for those local systems concerned with improvement.

PLANNING FOR CHANGE

Perhaps the most serious inadequacy at the local district level is the absence of any assigned responsibility for long-range planning. The first requirement in grappling with change is to understand the forces of change and to gain an appreciation of the kinds of technological and social developments affecting the schools.

School districts seldom have any organizational mechanisms for forecasting which provide a sound base of preparation for future developments. John Gardner has suggested the creation of a "Department of Continuous Improvement." Most school planning is restricted to an occasional population study, or a short term budget projection. There is a clear lack of a "sensing mechanism" to anticipate the future. We make no provision for systematic planning, and we must therefore reach many of our decisions in a hurry, and with less information than we should have available.

Clearly an effort of the type exemplified by this project is needed at the local level, as well as at the state and national level. Someone in the system needs the time and the administrative support to anticipate the future. If that old standby of senior class mottoes is right, "The future belongs to those who prepare for it," then we may not deserve the future, for most of us do little by way of preparation.

I would suggest that a major responsibility of school administrators is to ensure that the system has a capability to gather and analyze information on those forces which may affect it—and others—profoundly. Careful attention should be paid to the *timing* of forecast changes ("When will they come?") and the *rate* at which they will materialize (How great will be their impact?).[7]

Much has been written in recent years about the inadequate sums spent by school systems on research and development. My list of priorities would begin with the assigning of responsibility for predicting future needs and opportunities. If it is not budgetarily possible to add a position for forecasting, there are possible organizational structures to attempt to reach the same goal. The creation of a curriculum council, for example, can be utilized in this way. We have created such an organization composed of teachers and administrators in Glencoe and have asked the members to take the long view in assessing our educational program. In the past several years we have added a number of programs, such as foreign languages in the elementary school, creative dramatics, and others, but nothing has been removed from the curriculum. Thus the school day simply becomes more frenetic. Through the council's use of task force groups we hope to get a look at precisely where we now are and where we hope to be several years hence.

Whether it be a staff position, or a council, or whatever, the tasks are nevertheless quite clear. Needed is a series of steps in an overall planning process which will help administrators and school boards to make sounder decisions with respect to the allocation of resources. Such steps should include:

Anticipating the future needs and pressures

Locating and defining change requirements

Evaluating alternatives to achieve various objectives

Evaluating alternatives with respect to task achievement and cost

Determination of priorities

Allocation of resources

Evaluation and review

---

[7] Patrick H. Irwin and Frank W. Langham, Jr., "The Change Seekers," *Harvard Business Review*, January-February 1966, pp. 81-92.

STAFFING FOR CHANGE

Earlier in this paper I mentioned two major categories of change, one which was evolutionary in the sense that there were some natural shifts with new teachers and administrators, and the second category was directed or purposeful improvement. I suggest that the turnover in personnel provides an excellent opportunity for recruiting staff members who will assist in the process of improvement. This can be accomplished by seeking teachers who are young, who come from a variety of teacher preparation institutions, and who are cosmopolitan in outlook. It is quite apparent that teacher preparation has improved considerably in recent years, and the strategic placement of well-prepared, enthusiastic teachers can be helpful.[8] Clearly, however, the system must be receptive and the climate encouraging for such people.

WORKING WITH THE INCUMBENT STAFF

Students of change have written much about the possible interventions which can be utilized within an organization to induce improvement.[9] One practical difficulty is that the type of change sought will clearly affect the strategy to be employed, yet such differences are seldom considered. To return to the three categories of change mentioned earlier (content, organization for instruction, and technology), it is apparent that these should not be considered in the same manner. The problems of bringing teachers up-to-date in a given field of knowledge are quite different from the problems involved in moving a faculty into team teaching. One clearly requires the acquisition of new knowledge, while the other involves different relationships with fellow teachers. Time prevents my treating these different problems more fully, but I do want to emphasize that all suggestions for change strategies are not equally applicable to all kinds of desired improvements.

The changes in content in recent years have involved intensive in-service efforts to attempt to bring teachers up-to-date in such areas as mathematics and some of the sciences. If the linguists prevail in the current struggle in the field of English, most of our present teachers will need to be retaught. It is becoming apparent that in many subject fields teachers will need to be re-educated two or three times during their professional careers if the present rate of change continues. Somehow the concept that a college degree signals the end of learning for many teachers must be eliminated. I am not sure that we can do this if we continue to treat teaching as a ten-month occupation. Some form of summer programs, operated by local school systems, must be used both to improve the induction of new teachers into the profession and to permit the constant up-dating of the present staff with respect to content and new instructional materials.

Since not every district can afford to provide programs each summer

[8] Howard Baumgarten, *et al.*, *Guidelines for Staffing—A Study of Ways to Facilitate Constructive Change in California School Districts* (Sacramento, Calif.: Arthur D. Little, Inc., 1966), p. 31.
[9] For an interesting analysis of some promising interventions see Matthew B. Miles, "Planned Change and Organizational Health: Figure and Ground," in R. O. Carlson, *et. al., op. cit.,* pp. 27-32

in all fields, this would appear to be one clear avenue for inter-district cooperation. For example, it would be reasonable for one system to concentrate its resources on mathematics, another on science, another on English, and so forth, with the appropriate staff members from each system attending the program of his interest, rather than to have each system spread its resources too thinly by attempting to do too much.

One of the clear necessities of any program of change is to get the involvement of those who will be affected. The objective of the administrator is to get people involved and committed. To do this, of course, demands that change be planned far enough in advance so that those affected will have sufficient lead time to understand the change and accept the need for it, and also to understand and accept what it will mean to them.

TRAVEL

One useful device for stimulating improvement is the effective use of travel. Some of this is simply making provision for teachers, principals and superintendents to participate in out-of-town educational meetings. This exposure to new and different thoughts can be a very wise investment, if one is interested in change.

In addition to participation in educational meetings, the support of travel itself as an educational experience needs to be utilized far more thoroughly than has been done up to the present. With the mobility in our current society we cannot afford teachers who tend to be provincial in their own experiences and outlook. We have attempted this for years in Glencoe by providing a $500 subsidy for foreign travel for teachers who have been in the system for three years. This is a relatively inexpensive method of encouraging visits to foreign lands and these travels may have an important impact on the future instructional effectiveness of the teachers who participate.

Travel within a district can also serve a very useful purpose. It can enable beginning teachers to observe the most effective teachers within the system and also enable experienced teachers to acquaint themselves with other instructional practices. Even in a small system, like Glencoe, we find that principals and faculty in one building tend to know far less about what is happening in other buildings than is desirable. This year we have inaugurated a rotation of principals, for one day each month. The principals involved simply exchange buildings on a mutually convenient day and report to the other building for the day. Since they do not want to become involved in the paperwork left by their compatriots they have spent most of these days visiting classrooms in the other buildings. In addition to their observations of the variations in educational programs despite a general system-wide curriculum, they have become dramatically aware of how little time they have been spending in classrooms in their own buildings. If nothing else happens, I believe that this awareness and their subsequent efforts to get out of their own offices more often will have been well worth the effort.

OTHER POSSIBILITIES

Another way at least to begin the softening up process with respect to improvement is to ask the question "why" far more often than is usually done. It is sometimes amazing to discover what apparently inane questions do with respect to eliciting self-analysis on the part of others. For example, if some form of non-grading is useful in the primary grades, why must it suddenly stop when the children reach grade four? Goodlad (chapter 3) pointed out some practices which may prevail simply because no one has stopped to ask "why?".

In the beginning of this paper I mentioned that improvement means changing what the teacher does. A major aspect of that, of course, is *how he does what he does.* The evidence to date is quite clear that our attempts to change teacher behavior through supervision, observation or rating scales or what have you have been almost useless. On the horizon, however, is a technological development which may change this. The video tape recorder which will enable a teacher to view and analyze his own performance may give us the tool for a real breakthrough. These are now becoming economically feasible for a school system. If a teacher could watch himself, and the reactions of his students, with a portion of the analytical interest of Vince Lombardi watching the performance of the Green Bay Packers, we might yet achieve professional status. This development offers more promise for the improvement of teaching than anything in the past century, in my judgment. I hope we are wise enough to use it well.

IN SUMMARY

Progress in education comes slowly and on a broken front. Despite the claims of recent years, schools are not very different from what they were many years ago at the truly important place in education—that place where the teacher and the student confront one another.

The climate for change is essentially set by the superintendent. Certainly a necessary ingredient for successful change in school systems is simply for the school administrator to set aside for himself the time for the thoughtful analysis necessary to prepare for innovation. Cunningham (chapter 11) pointed out that the needed reflections cannot be made in the intense surroundings of the work-a-day world of the superintendent. It is clear that there is a kind of "Gresham's law" in administration; *routine drives out creative thinking.* At present we do not know how to beat this, for the "setting aside time for thinking" idea invariably gives way to the accumulated pressures of demands which cannot wait. Nevertheless it is a fine idea. Perhaps it works for others better than for us.

Whether we administrators have the time, however, is perhaps less crucial than our awareness that we have the responsibility to set the tone. Our actions speak loudly, and they reveal whether or not we are truly seeking improvement.

Possibly the overriding factor to consider in planned change is that it cannot be done inexpensively. Improvements will clearly require expenditures of money or time or personnel, or a combination of these. To assume otherwise is to overlook the realities of people and organizations.

Unfortunately, many school systems seem to do this. Without adequate preparation of staff, or without proper materials, they attempt to move into new programs. I am reminded of a comment of Frederick the Great who, watching the efforts of the Emperor Joseph II of Austria to modernize his empire, reportedly remarked that the trouble with him was that he always took the second step before he took the first. This is a familiar error in our schools.

We should recall, during the frustrations experienced in times like the present, that the effort to reform education is not a one-shot affair. Whatever efforts are made should be carried on continuously and in appropriate relationship for we know that most of what we do can stand improvement. As Oliver Wendell Holmes once remarked, "I find the great thing in this life is not where we stand, but in what direction we are moving." While we have a very long way to go, I am convinced that our direction is—and must continue to be—forward.

*   *   *

SUPPLEMENTARY STATEMENT

THEODORE E. ALBERS*

McPhee has carefully considered various kinds of resistance to change, identified and discussed numerous sources of change, and dealt with the problem of implementing change in school districts. This report suggests several bases on which teachers and administrators may be helped to reorient themselves to the need for change, to changes that are now underway, and to the exciting changes in education that are promised in the days ahead. These bases are of such a nature that they are self-renewing—that is, they provide for continuing reorientation to changing conditions. Hopefully, such reorientation will help lay the groundwork for achieving the changes that are needed in the learning situation.

SOME BASES FOR PROMOTING DESIRABLE CHANGE

As McPhee points out, there is a wealth of material on change and change is a popular topic at conferences, conventions and workshops. However, we will make a serious mistake if we assume that *most* teachers and administrators are aware of much of the material and discussion or that they are psychologically attuned to the need for change. In fact, the opposite is more probably the case. At a recent series of meetings—involving more than 250 staff members of nine elementary, junior and senior high schools—we found a serious lack of knowledge about recent educational innovations. There was disturbing evidence of apathy, also.

* *Assistant Superintendent of Schools, Mesa County Valley School District No. 51, Grand Junction, Colorado.* Formerly, Field Administrator, University of Colorado Extension Division; and Director, Division of Research and Statistics, Colorado State Department of Education.

Unfortunately, most school systems are not disposed or geared to counteract the various resistances to change. We spend so much time and effort keeping the system operating that we pay too little attention to how to improve it. Ordinarily, no one is assigned, or has accepted, the responsibility of planning for change, except on an extra-duty basis. Few systems budget enough to evaluate properly what they have—let alone what they should have—and most have been reluctant to fight as hard for the new devices that relate to learning as they have for those that will improve budgeting and accounting or will ease the building maintenance problems. In addition, they have been slow to capitalize on the strengths of cooperative effort.

Perhaps some of the following suggestions are worthy of consideration as ways in which to help foster needed changes in education.

Providing for a Full-Time District Change Agent

To keep everybody's business from becoming nobody's business, school districts of sufficient size should establish one or more staff positions, the function of which would be to help to plan, promote and implement desirable change. This need is recognized by Carlson who states that "the problem of establishing a viable change advocacy function among the many levels in our system of education is one of extreme importance and one for which we should recruit our best minds."[1]

While the need for this function to be served is found at all levels—federal, state and local—the crucial point is in the local school system where the changes must be felt by—and be beneficial to—students. Unfortunately, this is where there has been the most difficulty in getting the need for the function accepted.

Organizationally, the change agent's position should be placed immediately under that of the superintendent of schools and no other operational responsibilities should be given to the position. The person assigned this position must believe in change (improvement) and must be able to work with others in a manner that will promote good relations and encourage confidence in his work. He must be familiar with the realities of present public school circumstances and also be knowledgeable about current innovative practices and technological advances which may be applicable to education.

The change agent should have freedom to travel extensively outside the district—to visit schools which have outstanding innovative programs—and within the district—to interpret and assist with new programs and exchange ideas with staff members. He can play a major role both in building attitudes favorable toward change and in helping teachers keep informed.

Building Favorable Attitudes and Helping Teachers Keep Informed

If teachers are to utilize new equipment, materials and procedures,

---

[1] Richard O. Carlson, "Barriers to Change in Public Schools," in *Change Processes in the Public Schools* (Eugene, Oregon: Center for the Advanced Study of Educational Administration, 1965), p. 5.

they must not only know about their existence but also be favorably disposed toward using them. Many things can be done to help build a favorable attitude toward change and to aid teachers in keeping informed. Because there are so many possibilities, the real danger is that we may leave all of them to chance. To avoid this, I suggest that school systems organize some of these measures into a definitely planned and scheduled program of activity.

In setting the tone and creating a favorable attitude, the role of the administration is of paramount importance. First, the superintendent and other major administrative heads must live the part they need to play. Not only must they express in their manner a positive attitude toward needed changes, but also they must convey a spirit of enthusiasm toward the prospects for educational improvement and toward the suggestions which teachers put forward. No constructive idea should be considered unworthy of trial until it has been given fair evaluation. Perhaps it is even more important that the administrative attitude find expression in as many tangible—and intangible—ways as possible. Lip service alone is self-defeating.

Setting the tone and building a favorable attitude should begin with the recruitment of teachers. The recruiting brochure should give appropriate information about the school system's interest in innovation and improvement. If there is a rather definite indication that the prospective employee is looking for a rut to follow or is frightened by change, it may be wise to avoid him unless there are important compensating factors.

The provision for frequent interaction among staff members—both within and among schools of the system as well as with the staffs of other progressive systems—is important. Engelmann, in his systemic dynamic social theory, cites frequency of interaction as the fundamental variable in social and psychological organization.[2] Provisions for interaction should include the widespread involvement of staff members and should be planned to provide ample time for every important activity. The experience, whether formal or informal, should be conducted in a scheduled and orderly fashion and should encourage active involvement in the work to be done, rather than merely superficial participation which can be more harmful than helpful. The latter may take the time of the staff member without the compensation of commitment to a successful project. Over-involvement of any one person or group should be guarded against.

The inadequate and haphazardly serviced and used professional library of the past is not sufficient to meet today's needs. Instead, a comprehensive instructional materials center, serving both student and teacher needs, must be established at both the district and school levels. The district center should service the centers at the individual schools and also provide for the needs of the central office staff. Each center

[2] For a discussion of the importance of interaction, and its frequency, in relationship to changing attitudes, see Hugo O. Engelmann, *Essays in Social Theory and Social Organization* (Dubuque: Wm. C. Brown Book Company, 1966), pp. 53, 75.

should cater particularly to the professional needs of the teachers and should include the receipt and cataloging of the various publications which report new developments in education. The area should also house the various items of newer media equipment which the system can afford to provide, and space must be available for teachers to utilize both the publications and the equipment as they prepare for the management of learning situations. The fact should be kept in mind that one of the best ways to encourage teacher use of materials and equipment is to be able to provide what is wanted at the time of the request.

One or more people in the central office staff should be designated to abstract the contents of publications which either suggest interesting new ideas or which may have special meaning for particular parts of the educational program. The abstracts should be circulated to staff members and should identify the specific publications involved so that teachers may follow up for more detail. Information on equipment newly acquired must be publicized similarly. A periodically revised guide to the content of the teachers' section of the materials center and to uses which teachers may make of it should be available to all staff members.

The change agent—if there is one—or the instructional department staff in consultation with various teacher committees, should plan special programs for orienting teachers to new developments considered to be particularly important and suitable for possible implementation in the district. These programs should constitute a special part of the overall in-service educational program of the district.

IN-SERVICE EDUCATION—A SUGGESTED COOPERATIVE PLAN

Most school districts have a variety of in-service education activities. I do not wish to dispute the fact that these are of benefit to educational programs and make some contribution to desirable change. My thesis, however, is that, in general, these efforts are inclined to be piecemeal and hodge-podge and that in-service education—properly planned—could become a far greater force for the improvement of education. The great need is for a cooperative program that would make available to the school staff, in an efficient and coordinated manner, the combined resources of colleges and universities, state departments of education, regional educational laboratories, and the public schools. In the process, a sensible tie-in could be developed between pre-service and in-service education of teachers. Let us consider further what such a plan might have to offer.

The public schools have need for a variety of in-service educational activities, many of which they can provide themselves. No one can question the desirability and reasonableness of a school faculty working together for the improvement of its educational program.[3] In fact, there is no substitute for this kind of activity if it is well planned and conducted and does not attempt more than the faculty can handle. There are also very appropriate in-service activities which a school district can plan and

---

[3] John I. Goodlad, "Beyond Survival for the Elementary Principal," *National Elementary Principal,* Vol. XLVI, No. 1 (September, 1966), p. 14.

conduct with little, if any, outside assistance. Examples include the strengthening of articulation of course work among the various levels, the improvement of report card design and procedure, and the proper administration of tests and the utilization of their results.

However, when it comes to such matters as major curriculum content revision in the various subject matter areas or the introduction of a special program for the emotionally handicapped, most districts will need the assistance of experts from other agencies and institutions. My suggestion is that this assistance will be better given if the agencies which furnish it have an opportunity to coordinate the use of their resources in the light of the needs of all the districts in a particular area or state.

There are many advantages of a coordinated state-wide in-service education plan for teachers, some of which are related both to the efficient use of area or state-wide resources and to the quality of assistance that might be given to school systems. For one thing, such a plan would encourage colleges and universities to coordinate their extension course offerings, and thus eliminate duplication of travel expense and staff time. Properly planned, this could have the more important result of permitting institutions to focus their efforts on areas where they have greater strengths, thus giving higher quality assistance to the school districts served. It could also have the advantage of assisting in the identification of major educational improvement needs since people with different points of view would need to reach some agreement on what is of paramount importance. The special needs of individual districts could continue to be served through such special arrangements as the districts are able to provide.

Perhaps the greatest advantage of such a plan, in terms of fostering desirable educational change, would be the possibilities it might have for the appropriate conduct of educational research and development activities and experimentation with innovations. This does not imply that districts cannot profitably enter into desirable private arrangements with universities and regional educational laboratories, but it does indicate that a general cooperative plan would tend to encourage coordination and continuity in research and development and the avoidance of piecemeal and duplicative effort.

In addition, such a plan would make possible greater coordination between pre-service and in-service education of teachers by furnishing a formal structure to relate the two programs, provide a more meaningful relationship between state certification and re-certification requirements and institutional programs and teacher-in-service needs—and help to minimize the problems school districts often face in administering professional growth plans.

A SUGGESTED STAFF EXCHANGE PROGRAM

McPhee discussed the value of travel as well as attendance at out-of-town meetings and rotation of principals. I would like to suggest another aspect of this topic for serious consideration: that of a formally-planned nationwide staff exchange program. While the general idea of staff exchange is not new and has been utilized in exchanges between countries, I have in mind a plan specifically oriented to the study of recognized innovative programs.

If, for example, the non-graded program at use in Melbourne High School in Florida[4] has broken the shackles of lockstep grades in such a successful way that it deserves to be introduced elsewhere, why cannot the principal of a new high school—soon to be constructed in a district such as Grand Junction—spend an academic year at Melbourne in exchange for one of Melbourne's staff members? While the staff member is getting on-the-spot experience in Florida, the Melbourne staff member could be orienting the teachers and administrators in Grand Junction to the new program. Each could assist in the on-going work at the other's school.

Such a program could be coordinated by the United States Office of Education (USOE) in cooperation with state departments of education. School systems of the various states should indicate their interests and, insofar as feasible, these could be matched up by the USOE working through the states. Final negotiations, however, would be between the school systems involved. Of course, it is very probable that many school systems may desire such an experience to the extent that they will be willing to make their own arrangements.

I believe it is reasonable to suggest that the USOE's cooperation in the program could extend to the provisions of grants to support desirable exchanges. Such might be a wiser use of money than a grant to a system wishing to develop a new program already in use elsewhere without the provision for extensive staff visitation study. While most Title III proposals already funded and applicable in this context probably contain provisions for staff visitation, I suspect that few, if any, provide for an exchange for an academic year. Yet a visit of nine months should have proportionately far greater advantage than one of a week's duration.

While there is no question that such arrangements can be—and undoubtedly have been—worked out cooperatively by interested parties, a properly planned and coordinated program would be necessary if widespread use of the practice were to be achieved.

IN SUMMARY

Changes in the public schools are necessary to meet the challenges of a new age. In seeking changes, attention must be directed to the teachers and administrators, who are the ones who must change if our present practices are to be improved.

While change is a popular topic today, most teachers and administrators are insensitive to the need for change and are unaware of much that is new in education. In addition, most school systems are not geared to counteract effectively the various resistances to change.

---

[4] B. Frank Brown, "The Nongraded School," in *The Revolution in the Schools* (New York: Harcourt, Brace and World, Inc., 1964), pp. 100-114.

Desirable bases for change are self-renewing in that they provide for continuing reorientation to new conditions. Those which are suggested are: (1) providing for a full-time school district change agent, (2) building attitudes favorable to change and helping teachers keep informed, (3) a cooperative plan of in-service education, and (4) a staff exchange program.

A full-time school district change agent functions as a planner, promoter, and implementer of desirable change, thus assuring that these activities are not neglected by the system. Building appropriate attitudes and helping teachers keep informed should encourage teachers to use new equipment, materials and procedures. A cooperative plan of in-service education is intended to provide in-service activities of a high quality, encourage innovative practices, and prevent a piecemeal, hodge-podge approach. A nationwide staff exchange program will provide an efficient way to disseminate information about exemplary innovative programs.

CHAPTER 10

Planning and Effecting Needed Changes in Urban and Metropolitan Areas

MELVIN W. BARNES*

As a superintendent of a school system in which it is my daily responsibility to observe the great distance between *where we are* and *where we would like to go,* I am reminded of the necessity for viewing progress in all its earthy reality—to descend frequently from flights of imagination to an inspection of the hitch that ties the engine to the train. Therefore, I am inclined to follow the lead of the systems analyst—to review the entire scope of the urban school operation, and to define as sharply as possible the problems that must be overcome if progress is to be made; then to attempt to select the most effective methods at hand to attack each problem. Accordingly I shall proceed by discussing some major obstacles to progress and suggesting some procedures that might help to remove or to minimize them.

OBSTACLE ONE: VESTIGIAL VALUE SYSTEMS

Anyone who has helped teachers to define instructional goals in behavioral terms is impressed by two facts: (1) teachers often have difficulty in sensing the universal value framework into which their particular segment of instruction fits; and (2) most teachers have serious difficulty in defining the precise pupil behavior they believe their instruction should help to bring about. How does this relate to the subject of change? *Enlightened change can only occur when the objectives on which the proposed change is predicated are consistent with the value system of the person whose behavior is altered by that change.* To effect some changes in behavior in teachers is, in itself, not difficult. In fact, we have seen great swings in practice from complete preoccupation with the "needs" of children to an equally misguided emphasis on subject matter. Some change, therefore, is possible in the absence of defensible controlling value systems. The lesson to be learned is that *the quality of change—not change itself—should be the concern of the profession.* Herein lies one of the greatest problems and challenges of public school systems interested in effecting change.

Kenneth Boulding comments on "equilibrium systems" and specifically on "control systems" that maintain an equilibrium somewhat as a thermostat

* Superintendent of Schools, Portland, Oregon. Formerly, Superintendent of Schools, Oklahoma City, Oklahoma (1957-61); Assistant Superintendent and Deputy Superintendent of Schools, Oklahoma City (1950-57); Director of University Extension, University of California, San Diego (1946-50).

controls the temperature of a room at given levels. He points out that economists employ this principle to "counteract the random and perverse processes which operate on the economy", and that any such control system must have "equilibrating feedback" which enables it to detect and interpret the information about outside disturbances that threaten the equilibrium of the system and to set in motion processes to counteract deviations.[1]

The key to developing adequate "equilibrating feedback" is in determining precisely where a system should be at a given point in time; in other words, it is a projection of well-defined goals. But here, at its inception, is where the process usually fails. Lack of appropriate values, or perhaps of a sense of commitment to values, is the greatest weakness of administrators. Without a sense of values, projections of vital and significant goals are impossible, and equilibrating is reduced to vascillating.

WAYS TO MINIMIZE OBSTACLES

The processing of helping to develop or improve value systems is a joint responsibility of higher education and public school systems. This process begins in the homes and schools, may be sharpened in teacher education, and continues throughout the professional life of the teacher and administrator. What do we mean by a value system? Teachers and administrators need to understand clearly, and be committed to, the goals of education—the scope of social and personal development that society requires of each individual—and to know how their personal and professional acts are expected to influence this development. They need to value these goals sufficiently that they will bend every effort to see them realized. They need practice in designing their own approaches to meeting these goals so that, through the process of creating their own means to achieve ends, they better understand the ends they work for. Teachers so educated will welcome innovation that is consistent with logical and defensible values and will reject that which is not. All evidence indicates that neither teachers nor administrators have had enough experience in relating practices to values.

OBSTACLE TWO: INSTITUTIONALIZATION

Institutions were undoubtedly created by man partly to foster his own security. I, for one, am no foe of security as a broad human goal or as a personal one. Nonetheless, the very qualities of an institution that help to make people secure also tend to mitigate against change. But we live in an age when change is increasingly accepted as a condition of progress. Not only has the organization of urban school systems become institutionalized, but professional practices have also become deeply rooted in tradition. High school students are still graded on a five-point scale; teachers still meet 150 students or more a day; subject-matter lines are still sharply drawn; similar curricular fare is still presented for students of widely

[1] Kenneth E. Boulding, "Expecting the Unexpected: the Uncertain Future of Knowledge and Technology", Chapter 12 in *Prospective Changes in Society by 1980.* (Denver, Colo.: Designing Education for the Future: An Eight-State Project, 1966).

varying interests and abilities. These practices have been discredited, yet they persist. They are part of the established order.

It would be well for the profession to ponder its own inability to move itself quickly toward practices more consistent with the findings of research and the thinking of its leaders. Why, for example, do most school systems maintain inflexible college preparatory standards after the clear demonstration of their needlessness in the Eight Year Study?[2] Why, after the painstaking experimentation made by Wrinkle[3] in the 1930's, do we continue to use sterile systems of marking instead of evaluation systems based on goals of instruction? There are other significant questions of this kind that might be asked; but the concern here is to call attention to an important difference between urban school systems—which have depended for their wisdom and direction on external sources, and industry—which incorporates its research, planning and development into its own organizational framework, and thus achieves a much closer unity of thought and action.

This is an interesting and instructive contrast, for industry formerly was almost as institutionalized as school systems. Competition in the marketplace forced industry to incorporate the Research and Development (R and D) function, which gives it a head as well as a body. It now has the capacity to think and to change as well as to act. All school systems need to develop the same capabilities.

WAYS TO MINIMIZE OBSTACLES

Any assault on institutionalization must recognize the practical difficulties in attempting to change the value systems of thousands of teachers and administrators. Incorporated in many of the present value systems is the conviction that what is now being done is right—or at least is not wrong. The institutional character of a large system provides teachers with all sorts of reinforcement for these convictions—from colleagues, from supervisors and principals, from parents, and even from the children themselves. Thus, practice is often flagrantly at odds with enlightened and visionary thinking.

These remarks are offered in support of the concept that many changes must be effected by more subtle means than a frontal attack on existing values and practices. All school systems should develop, within themselves, the capacity and appropriate procedures for planning and testing experimental programs that should demonstrate the increased efficacy of new methods. *Values may be expected to change as new methods are tried and promising results are experienced.* Adoption of this policy will require R and D expenditures comparable to those in business and industry. Creating R and D capabilities within a system—instead of relying on research and experimentation carried out by external agencies—could constitute an important and much needed "system break" that should lead

---

[2] Wilford M. Aikin, The Story of the Eight-Year Study (New York: Harper & Bros., 1942).
[3] William L. Wrinkle, *Improving Marking and Reporting* (New York: Holt, Rinehart & Co., 1947).

to other changes. If the experience of the past thirty years suggests anything, it is that *most research conducted outside the realities and value systems of particular institutions is not likely to change these institutions.* Government agencies would do well to ponder the implications of this concept as they consider expansion of R and D grants to colleges and universities and increased investments in regional research centers.

The controlled experimental approach must be supplemented by carefully conceived and designed field studies, following criteria such as those outlined by Guba in a paper on "Methodological Strategies for Educational Change."[4] Urban school systems must acquire the capability for planning and conducting many of these studies themselves, sometimes with the assistance of competent consultants, in order to assure their consistency with local objectives. When this is done, these systems and their schools will take on a self-renewing character that could—over a period of time—rid them of the static concepts and programs that now inhibit progress.

OBSTACLE THREE: LARGE AND HETEROGENEOUS POPULATIONS

Although size of urban systems exerts an influence on all other factors that mitigate against change, and might therefore be questioned as an obstacle to be singled out, it does create a series of special problems that might best be considered under this heading. These include organization, communication, and logistics—which, in turn, affect efficiency, sense of purpose, and morale. One is led to wonder whether these problems can be solved in a large school system; yet the example of industry once more suggests that they can. Many large corporations have encountered the problem of size and have dealt with it effectively. Where this has been done, size, in many cases, has been found to provide some advantages, and is not necessarily a detriment. Obviously, the ability of large organizations to mobilize and apply talent to the solution of problems greatly exceeds that of small organizations. But without effective means of identifying and coordinating this talent, big organizations can be as impotent as small ones.

Size also creates problems of communication that inhibit change. Communication difficulties in urban systems have increasingly cast administrators and boards of education in the role of management, and teachers in the role of labor. The alienation of interests reflected here constitutes a serious threat to constructive change in urban districts. *Administrators cannot hope to innovate without the cooperation of teachers any more than teachers can innovate without the support of administrators.* The importance of mutual trust, respect, and full cooperation between teachers and administrators cannot be too strongly underscored. Perhaps school systems—as well as industry—can produce adaptive and coordinated systems to foster creative inter-group collaboration.[5]

---

[4] Egan Guba is Director, National Institute for Study of Educational Change, Bloomington, Indiana.

[5] Warren G. Bennis, "The Coming Death of Bureaucracy", *Think*, Nov.-Dec., 1966, pp. 30-35.

There are several vehicles available for urban school systems for over-coming the obstacle of size. The most obvious is decentralization. Decentralization has been tried by a number of major school systems with positive results. To be most effective, decentralization should carry a degree of fiscal autonomy. Decentralized leadership that must rely entirely on controlled financial allocations from the parent district is less likely to develop initiative than leaders that are able to enlist local support.

As urban school systems contemplate their problems—especially their limited (and limiting) boundaries, the departure of leadership to suburbs, and the growing problems of race and poverty—they must examine practical means of changing the boundaries to include suburbia as well as the urban core. The only condition under which most suburban systems will consider a reorganization that would include the urban districts is when they are guaranteed a degree of fiscal and managerial autonomy.

It is time to engage administrators and boards of education actively in an examination of possible forms of reorganization that would simultaneously establish or improve decentralization of urban systems and include suburban systems. This is urgent business that will require diligent attention and effort; it must involve state legislators who will need to shape the laws required to make it possible. This issue will be discussed further in the last section of this chapter.

The obstacle of size can also be attacked through improved communication. The computer is, of course, a powerful tool for communication, and many experiments are under way to make it an even more effective tool for this purpose. Its capabilities even now far outstrip our ability to use them. One thing that is important is a study of the communication needs of urban school systems and the ways of utilizing computers in helping to meet those needs. Such a study might consider computer uses to improve communication between the business and education divisions; principals and supervisors; school boards and administrators; the administration and the community; special education services and classroom teachers; vocational and general education; and pupils, teachers and parents. The Portland Public Schools are presently experimenting with a system of communication that would coordinate all information collected by special education personnel to improve its accessibility to classroom teachers and workers in the various services. Studies have revealed that problems of communication have been blocking effective teamwork among special services and between teachers and special services personnel. A system for the storage, retrieval and reporting of data in natural language form is being developed.

Such studies and experiments are time-consuming, and demand highly skilled personnel who are in short supply. The face of change is not smooth and benign; it is wrinkled, pained, and sweaty.

Another device for improving communications is the conference or negotiating committees now in use in settling salary and teacher welfare questions in urban systems. These committees afford the administration an opportunity to help the teaching staff to educate itself on problems of school management. The strategy here is to provide members of the committee with adequate time for thorough study of the problems facing the school board and superintendent, and to inform the teaching staff fully about all evidence presented, subjects considered, and conclusions reached. To date, however, negotiating committees have found few effective techniques for enlisting the genuine participation of the teachers they represent. If the time to speak is when people are listening, then the period when salaries are under negotiation should offer the most favorable opportunity to help the teaching staff to understand all aspects of the situation.

OBSTACLE FOUR: ISOLATIONISM

Logically, no public agency should be as closely attuned to life as public school systems, for their objective is to prepare young people to live happily and productively in their own society. Yet the physical arrangements, organization and instructional programs of most school systems work to perpetuate for children a world of enforced values and artificial tasks.

The most important changes that will be made in education in the next decade will be those that bring the curriculum of the school into juxtaposition with life so that students see education as meaningful and important to themselves. This problem must be solved if problems of race and poverty are to be resolved. The schools can only motivate the children of the underprivileged through greater appeal to personal values and natural learning interests.

Throughout the short history of American education, colleges and universities have with increasing effectiveness fostered the concept—not only through the public school curriculum, but through their own—that public school education should consist of ever more specialized study leading toward scholarship in a subject matter field. The four basic subjects of the present day public school curriculum—language arts, social studies, science and mathematics—are shaped and molded, almost from the first grade, to serve the needs and requirements of the student who will some day emerge as a scholar in one of these fields.

It is time this influence is brought into perspective in the public school curriculum—not that the contribution of fields of scholarly study should be forsaken, but that they should no longer be permitted to dominate the curriculum and make it so convenient and honorable for teachers to make many children learn what they so rightly perceive as irrelevant to their lives and needs.

This is not the death rattle of the progressive educator; it is the fresh, strong cry of a new breed who view the primary job of the public schools as turning out self-valuing, reliant individuals who are able to elevate the economic and social functioning of this democracy. Rigor, in their view, is not devising ever more exacting academic hurdles, but rather the designing of curricula and programs that assure attainment of important personal and social objectives. They seem to sense that the schools have moved too far from life and that we must capture the interests and imagination of the young if we are to enlist and develop their minds.

Isolationism takes other forms, among which might be mentioned the absence of effective coordination of urban school systems with other agencies of government. This is a weakness that paralyzes progress, since there is hardly an important social problem that could not be solved more readily through cooperative action. The most obvious illustration is the racial problem where housing, employment and education are the three keys required to open the lock; too often only one key is turned at a time.

Still another form of isolationism is the lack of coordination and identity of purpose between school systems and related educational agencies and institutions. Perhaps the most evident examples are the weak ties between school systems and teacher preparing institutions, and between school systems and state departments of education.

WAYS TO MINIMIZE OBSTACLES

Even as this is written the walls of isolationism are under seige. National curriculum groups are pooling the thinking of people representing public schools, colleges, and industry and other lay interests to insure that objectives truly represent current social, scientific and economic concerns. Urban school systems are making wide use of lay advisory committees in designing guides for vocational and other curricula. Stimulated by federal programs, school systems are working directly with other agencies of government in attempting to solve problems of race and poverty. Even school systems and teacher education schools are beginning to cooperate on intern programs, clinical professorships, and other joint appointments, and on cooperative in-service education arrangements.

An urban school system that wants to work at strengthening its ties with the outside world might well consider employing professional liaison officers who would devote part or full time to the coordination of efforts of the system with those of other public and private agencies whose objectives are shared by the school system. Such liaison personnel should work cooperatively with the city planning commission, the park and recreation bureau, the public housing authority, the juvenile court and other appropriate agencies and groups. Agencies that independently spend millions of dollars on programs that overlap in purpose are missing a great bet by failing to share their concerns, their information, and their resources. A new day of metropolitan collaborative effort appears to be dawning now that the model cities legislation is beginning to take hold. An inspirational model for planning is the new city of Litchfield Park, Arizona.

There still seems to be a considerable pessimism about the likelihood that quality of leadership and guidance from the state level will match the critical needs of urban and metropolitan school districts. But this is exactly where state governments can be most effective.

As state departments of education build in strength, it may be expected that their concern with regulatory functions will diminish. With a reduction of emphasis on regulation, a major shift of attention may be expected: to identifying problems, to providing vehicles for their solution, to representing the interests of local districts in state legislatures—in short, to providing leadership and planning for the improvement of all aspects of education.

In the administration of federal funds and programs, for example, the principle of employing liaison personnel could be effective. Just as the clinical professor has one foot in the school system and the other on a campus and is paid by two institutions, so might a liaison officer between the state department of education and metropolitan schools unite the interest and further the objectives of both agencies.

State legislatures establish and provide for the operation of school systems. More complete information is needed to aid decision making. Legislative committees need better means of assembling and analyzing information and of getting a balanced view of citizens' concerns regarding public education. Collaboration between state departments of education and urban school systems could result in vastly improved information for legislators.

Even stranger than the somewhat alienated relationship of large school systems and state departments of education is the failure of school systems and universities to work cooperatively and effectively to improve teacher education, in-service education and educational research. Many promising cooperative programs are being developed in in-service education (Atlanta, Miami, San Diego, Portland, and others); the introduction in many urban systems of intern programs, clinical professor programs and programs of jointly-supervised practice teaching is beginning to reveal the value of cooperation in producing teachers who are more adequately prepared to meet the needs of students in society today. These vigorous pilot programs may be expected to bring about a more universal acceptance of their value through the results they achieve.

In the area of research, it is suggested that the involvement of university research personnel or consultants and co-workers in solving operational problems of urban systems would serve two important purposes. First, it would re-direct much research talent from laboratory to field enterprises, which is almost essential in social research where laboratory conditions cannot hope to account for the mass of variables encountered in the situations the research is attempting to consider. Second, it would focus more resources on the problems that are meaningful and urgent in the schools, and for which solutions are not forthcoming due largely to shortages of competent personnel and funds.

OBSTACLE FIVE: PUBLIC APATHY

The American public has traditionally looked with pride on its system of universal education. The increasing value placed on education is reflected in the extension of compulsory school attendance and the expansion of school programs in many areas including the mentally and physically handicapped, adult education and community colleges. On the other hand, expansion of expenditures seems, at least temporarily, to have encountered new resistance thresholds in many school systems. There is evidence of considerable public apathy toward school tax levies and appropriations—which, needless to say, are the lifeblood of public education in America.

Some possible reasons for this may be advanced. First, there has been too little demonstrable improvement in the quality and performance of public school teachers. To administrators who have suffered through 20 years of teacher shortage the reason is basically clear: staffs assembled can be no better than the overall quality of teachers available during that period. Since the public is so close to the teacher, there is little chance that the uneven quality of instruction has escaped the public consciousness; and it weighs heavily in every consideration of requests for levies for higher salaries.

A second reason that may underly public apathy is the remarkable similarity of the school programs to those the public experienced in an earlier and less costly era. Despite occasional (and often transitory) experiments, and despite some significant advances in objectives and methods in science and mathematics, the same subjects taught, the same general approaches to teaching, and the same disregard for individual differences found thirty years ago are the rule, not the exception, in most large (and small) school systems today. Is it possible that the public rejects the notion that teaching that has changed so little should require larger proportions of their incomes?

A third possible reason for resistance to local taxes is frustration with federal taxes and programs over which the public has little or no control. The only remaining level of government where people can control taxes is the local level where property taxes are often disproportionately heavy. It is only natural that many people who cannot escape federal and state tax mechanisms will regulate local taxes in an attempt to ease their burdens.

A fourth reason for resistance to local taxes may well be a reaction to federally inspired programs of racial mixing which, however meritorious they may be in the minds of persons seeking solutions to racial problems, incur the disfavor of large segments of urban voters.

A fifth, and very important cause of declining public interest in school support, is the absence of effective methods of involving the citizens of large urban school systems in the direction of school affairs. In fact, aside from the board of education itself, and occasional advisory committees, there is virtually no way for citizens to maintain close and effective participation in school matters.

There are several approaches to enlisting public interest in the schools. In the long run, the *soundest approach is through the improvement of educational services,* for the public will respond and support programs of demonstrated efficacy. But this path to public favor is arduous. Large urban staffs are not moved very far very fast. Greatly increased expenditures should be made for in-service education; and closer relationships between school systems and teacher education schools should be relentlessly pursued in the interest of improving teacher education.

Citizens respond to invitations to consider the aims of school programs. We should see an increase in the number of lay advisory committees working with school administrators and school boards on major problems, including that of determining the most effective ways of committing resources for schools. According to a recent Gallup poll, the possibilities for engaging the public in school planning are promising. It appears that the citizens are at least as ready as school administrators to accept change and that they have an unerring capacity to pick out the important possibilities for change.

At present, Gallup is conducting a study of school board members to ascertain their attitudes toward educational innovation. This survey is to be followed by one of teachers and school administrators. The purpose is to find out what specific changes they would support in their own educational systems.

Enlisting the help of influential people in a community is recommended by such students of school administration as Kimbrough (chapter 6), who sees members of the "power structure" as especially important in shaping community attitudes toward the schools.

In searching for effective ways of recruiting public interest in the schools, one should not overlook the link between education and economic productivity. This relationship is attracting increasing attention in business as well as in educational circles, and is a concept which may be used to encourage community leaders to examine ways of making the schools a more effective force in advancing the economic welfare of the community. Coupled with this is the idea that improved programs of education and city environments attract citizens of high ability together with the industries such people manage. Concepts like these are appealing both to conservative and liberal community leaders, and provide an entree for consideration of a wide range of problems facing urban school systems.

If the link between community, citizens and the public schools is to be strong, however, school boards and administrators must plan for the systematic involvement in school affairs not only of prominent members of a community, but also of the rank-and-file members whose children they mostly serve. There is, in fact, a danger that if the community power structure is too heavily relied upon, the eyes of the board and chief administrator may be somewhat diverted from instructional improvement—

which is the most potent influence in shaping community sentiment for school support.

Ways of achieving broader participation are allied to matters of organization. Decentralized control and a degree of fiscal autonomy stimulate citizen participation. In these days of big government, people will embrace any defensible system that returns to them some measure of direction over their individual destinies. Psychologically, the time is ripe for this type of change in all realms and levels of government, including urban and suburban school systems.

OBSTACLE SIX: ABSENCE OF CRITERIA FOR MEASURING PROGRESS

Measurement of meaningful change in education is in a bad way. Despite the wealth of talent that is to be found in the field of tests and measurement, experimentation is virtually hamstrung by the absence of good criteria for measuring educational change.

This dilemma—which perhaps more than any other single factor retards the progress of education—is traceable to the origins and development of educational measurement in this country. Almost from the beginning of the movement there has been a preoccupation with normative testing which basically assumes common curricula, like instruction, and similar characteristics of groups of students tested. Obviously these conditions have never been met: but tests have been designed, administered and interpreted as though they had been. The fact is that the degree of relevance of most standardized tests to the curriculum content, grade placement of subject matter, and student characteristics of any given urban system or metropolitan area is sufficiently askew to render such tests useless as tools of scientific inquiry. Applying statistical tests of significance to measures of educational change on the basis of such grossly invalid measures is absurd.

Great obstacles, such as the following, face anyone attempting to resolve this problem: (1) goals and objectives of instruction are undergoing constant revision, necessitating continuing review of criteria measures and all the painstaking work required to make them reliable and valid; (2) a large segment of important objectives falls in the higher cognitive domain as well as in the affective domain, and observable behaviors that reflect attainment of these objectives are illusive, if not downright ephemeral; and (3) the profession has not yet produced practitioners who are able to define their objectives precisely and in behavioral terms and to teach with exact reference to those objectives; until this is done the slippage in any measuring device based on the teacher's objectives will be somewhat proportionate to the lack of consistency between objectives and methods.

WAYS TO MINIMIZE OBSTACLES

Some urban school systems have already moved to local testing norms which yield a higher degree of reliability of measurement than national norms. This alone enhances their ability to measure educational change, though the tests themselves represent only limited measures of the total instructional program—usually skills and information. *Greater validity is achieved where local tests are devised which are based on the objectives of local courses of instruction.*

A promising movement which urban districts can help to foster is the use of testing organizations such as Educational Testing Service (ETS) to help in designing tests for measuring local programs. Such a procedure combines the values of local curriculum knowledge with the technical test-making skills of professionals in measurement. Major test companies may be expected to resist this movement since it threatens their economic structure; but it will be necessary for them to alter the character of their services as more enlightened measurement practices are employed by school systems.

Colleges can make an important contribution to improved measurement through greater emphasis in teacher education on designing and carrying out instructional experiences based on behavioral objectives. This should also be emphasized by school systems in the in-service education of teachers. Unquestionably the new regional educational laboratories should be able to reinforce and assist local school systems in producing more relevant measures of productivity.

OBSTACLE SEVEN: ARCHAIC SCHOOL FINANCE PROGRAMS

Urban school systems have for years been handicapped by state finance programs based on unrealistic measures of educational need and of local effort. It should be recognized that many present programs have done much to raise the level of expenditure and quality of education in rural and suburban areas. But it is increasingly apparent that the provisions were incomplete; that they failed to recognize important factors which invalidate the idea that rough measures of school tax equality produce equality of educational opportunity. Especially harmful to cities (and to some other areas) was the failure of these formulas to recognize the heavy property tax load in these areas for purposes other than schools; the costs of compensatory education; concentration of special education services required, especially in cities; the lower income of city residents than of suburban residents (who often benefit greatly from equalization formulas); the tendency of assessors to undervalue rural property; and the failure to recognize the substantial funds received in lieu of taxes by some other units of government.

The chairman of the Portland school board sums up the problem as follows:

> Everywhere the real property tax—supplemented by state funds—is the chief means of raising local revenue, both for cities and school districts. The core city spends less per child on education than do the suburbs because it must spend more per capita on the burdens incident to dense population and upon extra layers of government. Taxpayers in the core pay higher total real property taxes. Inhabitants of the core have lower average incomes than inhabitants in the suburbs and a good many more expensive social problems. For these reasons state legislatures give to the central

cities substantially less money per child than the suburbs in basic school support.[6]

The longer states delay the reform of finance programs, the more critical will become the city problems of cultural deprivation, racial tension, and erosion of school staffs and physical plants. The problem of the city is not the problem of the suburb. To offer education that is suited to city requirements requires greater adaptation of curricula, more intensive and differentiated in-service education, greater expenditures to renew the too-often neglected physical plant, and more research and experimentation aimed at solving the educational problems created by race and poverty. Some obstacles to change are certain university school finance experts who cling to outmoded theories and often influence the thinking of school administrators and state legislators; state legislators, who are often more interested in the local impact of finance formulas than in matters of equity, and who find it next to impossible to evaluate complex equalization formulas; improper legislative apportionment, which has often permitted rural domination and anti-city legislation; and emotion and self-interest, which prevent objective, cooperative analysis of the issues.

WAYS TO MINIMIZE OBSTACLES

Although this problem has been the subject of great debate and legislative study over at least two decades, the only apparent solution is intensified effort to identify all of the relevant facts and issues and to work toward more equitable solutions. School finance experts in the universities need to re-evaluate their positions (many are currently doing so), a process which could be aided by closer communication with city school administrators and school board members. Urban school systems, for their part, need to discard their mantles of righteous indignation and produce facts and constructive amendments to finance theory that are both sound and politically palatable. State departments of education can establish study committees to prepare recommendations for governors and legislators.

It has been helpful that the dilemma of the cities has received dramatic publicity in such publications as *Slums and Suburbs*[7] and that anxiety over racial violence has produced in the public a more receptive attitude toward city problems. Strategy for change often waits upon the natural evolvement of conditions favorable to change, and conditions are now much more favorable to change in state finance formulas. The rising power of teacher organizations is augmenting the pressure for more adequate state aid for the schools.

State legislators are traditionally oriented to conservation of taxes as a principle in deciding levels of state support, and are increasingly interested in using state funds for property tax relief rather than for stimulating local expenditures to improve school quality. Significant improvements in the state support in many states await better and more thorough studies and a basic change of attitude among legislators. Enough is now known to

---

[6] John J. Beatty, Jr. in an address to the City Club of Portland (January 14, 1966).
[7] James B. Conant, *Slums and Suburbs* (New York: McGraw-Hill, 1961).

make it possible in every state to develop and justify: more adequate and realistic measures of educational need; equitable measures of local ability and effort; and an incentive plan that will encourage local effort and initiative in local support (rather than depress it) and thus to assure more adequate support for schools.

OBSTACLE EIGHT: UNCOORDINATED GOVERNMENT

The school district is a local unit of government—legally a quasi-corporation—established in most states for the local administration and operation of schools in its area. In the long run, the destiny of the school district is tied closely to the destiny of other local governmental units. The city and the suburb also share a common destiny in many respects. Havighurst says, "The future of the suburbs depends upon the central city and the city depends on the suburbs."[8]

Integrative, collaborative action in metropolitan government, however, lags for want of organizational order and collaboration. All around us local governmental machinery is creaking under new responsibilities it was never designed to meet. Existing local governments are proving incapable of local execution of national policy—even as massive funds and new programs become available.

Recently the Committee for Economic Development (CED) issued a report which made the point that "Overlapping layers of local government —municipalities and townships within counties and independent school districts and special districts within them—form a crazy quilt of jurisdiction." CED drew a profile of the city of Fridley in the Minneapolis-St. Paul complex showing the confused pattern that can confront the citizen. This city holds elections (apart from federal and state offices) for nine separate superimposed governments including fourteen independent school districts and two sewer districts, as well as for hospital, soil conservation, county officials, airport, and the Metropolitan Mosquito Control District.[9]

To contemplate such a tangled web is to provide a basis for understanding why citizen interest in local government is generally so low that fewer than 30 percent of American voters take part in city, county and school elections. Faced with the colossal complexity of this confusing complex, many voters see no point in trying to participate.

The conventional wisdom of school administrators and school boards is also inadequate for constructive governmental interaction. School men are disposed to overlook the municipalities while municipal officials tend to stick to their own official knitting.

In our professional associations we have largely ignored our civic responsibilities. For example, the statement of goals and activities of the American Association of School Administrators entitled "A Plan of Action

---

[8] Robert J. Havighurst, *Education in Metropolitan Areas* (Boston, Mass.: Allyn & Bacon, 1966), p. 133.

[9] *Modernizing Local Government* (Washington, D. C.: Committee for Economic Development, July, 1966).

for the Next Five Years, 1966-1970," acknowledges AASA's relationships
with NEA, ASCD, NSBA, the Council of Chief State School Officers and
others but does not mention such organizations and associations as the
City Manager's Association and the Mayor's League. On the other hand—
over a five-year period—the American Mayors' League has not mentioned
schools at recent annual meetings. In this regard Roscoe Martin says:

> It would seem a difficult feat to avoid the mention of public education . . .
> but the mayors managed it: they passed by the schools as dexterously as
> the schoolmen pass by the cities in their professional conclaves. The same
> story may be told of the International City Managers' Association which
> . . . never takes up the public school as a municipal problem.[10]

A study of education in the San Francisco Bay area by Dean T. L.
Reller revealed that schools are not only withdrawn from other governmental units but also from other school districts. Reller says, "The most
striking fact regarding . . . public education in the Bay area is that it is
in no way consciously associated with the metropolitan area." He noted
that there was no desire to create such associations. Citing a survey of
school administrators, he reported:

> A selected group of school administrators were asked whether there were
> any educational problems which they believed indicated the desirability of
> a metropolitan-wide approach. They were unanimous . . . there were no
> problems . . . which required a metropolitan probe. They did not see
> the development of a metropolitan organization for education as being
> relevant to their own problems.[11]

Even in metropolitan areas where cooperative study councils have
long been in existence, these have led to little more than a sharing of
information—leaving each individual district to attack its own problems
independently.

WAYS TO MINIMIZE OBSTACLES

The winds of change are blowing. The Department of Housing and
Urban Development (HUD), with substantial resources, is making an end
run around the traditional roadblocks to planning. Today school superintendents frequently are on the phone with mayors concerning the model
cities program and are using planning funds from HUD for studies of
associated governments.

It seems safe—and encouraging—to say that constraining attitudes
will rapidly soften. We can expect intensified and prolonged attention to
be given to matters involving integration of government and of decentralization of school authority as reorganized districts are contemplated. New
models of organization should be sought and studied. State departments
of education should provide leadership and services for metropolitan area
studies and cooperative efforts.

Legislative doors to joint efforts can be opened. In one state, early
in 1967, fifteen pieces of legislation had been introduced to deal with the

---

[10] Roscoe C. Martin, *Government and the Suburban School* (Syracuse University Press, 1962), p. 67.
[11] Theodore L. Reller, *Problems of Public Education in the San Francisco Bay Area* (University
of California, Berkeley, Institute of Governmental Studies, 1963), p. 1.

problems of governmental overlap in local areas, because, as the secretary of state said, "At the moment governmental units may not legally hold conversations with one another."

Educators should cooperate in their states to facilitate needed legal changes in the governmental organization. Careful study and serious cooperative effort will be required to assure progress, but the climate is favorable. We can expect the efforts at times to be halting and clumsy. Good ideas will not work every time or in all situations. Local creativity will be especially important.

Some Models for Metropolitan Planning

Educators are receptive to prototypes and models as guides for trying out promising ideas. In metropolitan planning some interesting examples can be found.

One is the recently-formed metropolitan school district of Nashville and Davidson County, Tennessee. In July, 1964, the two public school systems of Nashville and Davidson County became a single system to serve 90,000 students. This action followed a survey and report conducted by Francis Cornell and a cadre of consultants under his direction. Not only did the plan propose merger of the two systems, but it also made numerous long-range recommendations of the sort that can only be realized under an organization and administration with the capability of implementing them.

The records of the studies, the enactment of permissive legislation, and the work of a transitional board under the chairmanship of Henry N. Hill—which led to the creation of the metropolitan district—make instructive and exciting reading. Under a metropolitan board and a metropolitan director of schools the new system is moving forward. It is bringing about a reorganization in administration, instruction, operation, maintenance, transportation and other services.[12]

It might be noted that certain objectives of metropolitan planning and financing can be achieved through such a consolidation, but that objectives of local control and citizen interest must rely on the invention of effective forms of decentralization within such metropolitan districts.

An imaginative plan for a mixed pattern of educational government to operate schools in a broad metropolitan area was recently developed by Luvern L. Cunningham and a consultant team for the school boards of Louisville and Jefferson County, Kentucky. The Cunningham study offers a plan for two-level educational government. At the top is a Metropolitan Education District to raise funds and insure quality education. The second layer contains several smaller semi-independent school districts of 10,000 to 20,000 enrollment, each with its own superintendent, staff, and board. The major taxing power and planning responsibility would reside in the metropolitan district level but the smaller districts would have the authority to organize and administer their school and to vote taxes to enrich them.[13]

---

12 "New Directions for Schools Under Metropolitan Government." Mimeo. Feb. 4, 1966.
13 "Report on the Merger Issue," Luvern L. Cunningham, et al. Louisville, 1966.

Reller's proposals for educational organization in the Bay Area make challenging reading, especially when related to the Nashville and Louisville plans.[14]

Whether city and school government should actually be integrated is an old issue that is almost certain to come in for increasingly lively debate. Buried in the question are such considerations as fiscal theory, educational quality and partisan school boards. These questions will continue to be argued in innumerable forums for a long time to come. There is, however, no rational argument against neighboring working relations between cities and schools. Metropolitan living depends on cooperative skill which the schools profess to be developing in the rising generation. Moreover, new national goals of education—"to keep democracy working", "to deal constructively with psychological tension" and "to make urban life rewarding" —impose on us a responsibility to widen the circles of dialogue and community action. This should be the first order of business.

SOME OBSERVATIONS ON LONG-RANGE PLANNING

Planning, research and development lie at the heart of the change process. Earlier comments in this paper reflect the author's belief that R and D capabilities must be organic with large city school systems and require a commitment similar to that which business and industry accord these activities. Educational research, like research in industry, must serve directly the objectives of the institutions using it.

Suggestions to equate percentage allocations for R and D in education to those in industry are probably ill considered because the character of organizations, functions, and personnel are not comparable. What, then, should be the criterion for commitment?

This is a question that every city superintendent and board of education must answer in terms of their own goals as well as their own fiscal and personnel resources. Millions of dollars have been spent uselessly on evaluation of federal programs because evaluation was an afterthought— not a part of the original planning. Any experienced evaluator knows that planning, execution and evaluation cannot be treated as separate entities. Successful evaluation can only take place where goals and procedures are so clearly set forth and faithfully followed that results can be replicated.

The point to be made, however, is that success in planning, developing and evaluating educational programs should be demonstrated in ever increasing increments by internal organizations entrusted with this function. As the worth of these functions is proved, greater responsibilities should be given until planning and development reach their full potential in the improvement of instruction and administration. This, I suppose, is to caution against plunging heavily into R and D functions without first testing the quality of work done by those to whom the functions are assigned.

Up to this point I have discussed only the matter of developing a

---

[14] *Op. cit.*, pp. 27-33.

staff R and D function in a city school system. It would be well now to note that *planning and development can be no better than the conceptualization of what is to be planned and developed,* and this is a function both of the school staff and the community.

Big thinking is in the air—in business, in industry, in government, and even in religion; and herein lies an opening for public school boards and officials interested in greater lay participation in school planning. Problems of race, housing, maintaining a separate parochial school system, transportation, air pollution, automation, finance and taxation, and the phenomenon of space exploration have challenged the public imagination and produced a new forum of free thinking in public planning. Into this arena the public schools should project themselves without restraint, for within it exist unprecedented opportunities for interacting with community leaders, for creating understanding of the goals and requirements of the school system, and for cooperative planning to further common interests in community improvement.

But the conceptualization of what is to be planned and developed will remain primarily a function of the school board and chief administrator, and *the value of the planning that is done cannot transcend the quality of thought and vision of these school leaders.*

This leads to a final consideration: how to find time for the reflection and unharried deliberation that planning requires amid the overwhelming distractions and responsibilities of operating an urban school system.

I would like to suggest that finding a means of freeing planning talent from executive responsibilities is an urgent necessity if long-range planning is to get beyond the talking stage. There is a level of planning between th "big idea" and the level of detailed planning that requires extended analytical attention, and the time given to this level of planning often determines the quality and worth of an entire endeavor.

* * *

Some Basic Strategies and Procedures

BENJAMIN E. CARMICHAEL*

NOTE: The commitment to prepare this paper was made while the writer was the superintendent of schools of Chattanooga, Tennessee. Since that time he has become director of the Appalachia Educational Laboratory, one of a system of regional institutions established under ESEA with the broad mandate to accomplish change. However, this paper is written primarily from the point of view of a superintendent of schools. In the final analysis, the superintendent is the person who must provide the leadership for accomplishing change. He should be the theorist at times, but always he must be the practitioner. Failure to recognize this important role of the superintendent may well be responsible for the attrition that so often is the end result of suggested change.

* *Director, Appalachia Educational Laboratory, Charleston, West Virginia.* Formerly, superintendent of schools, Chattanooga, Tennessee (1960-66); director of research and professor of school administration, George Peabody College; elementary and high school principal and assistant superintendent in charge of instruction, Marlboro County, South Carolina; and teacher, Oak Ridge, Tennessee.

OBSERVATIONS ON CHANGE AND CHANGE PROCESSES

Change in education is bound to occur. Obviously *the direction of change is most important;* the needs already identified in urban and metropolitan school systems are sufficient to make imperative the giving of directional guidance to inevitable change.

However, many of the strategies and procedures suggested are not clear. Some do not seem to be basic. Not enough thought has been evidenced concerning the unintended and not always recognized consequences of the intended change. Finally, too much is often made of the attributes of change—and too little of the actual accomplishers of change.

We hear much of *resistance to change.* We learn that resistance to change is always "entrenched," "massive," "fixed," and on and on, but is always powerful. This concept constitutes a *bogeyman.* I was brainwashed to fear him before I took my first teaching assignment. He has been out there somewhere in the shadows for these eighteen years. It appears that with every pronouncement, with every description, with every proposed stratagem, he becomes more formidable. But is he *really* there? Is it not possible that our mistaken image of him may be skewing our thinking of strategy to effect change? It would seem that the continued obsession with "resistance to change" tends to constitute a denial of the nature of man and his social order—to deny that human behavior tends to be rational.

But man is rational, or at least has the potential of being rational. He behaves in a way he believes will insure reasonable security. It seems, then, that our direct means of effecting change would be to build a base of security and confidence upon which to structure change and innovation.

Receptiveness to change on the part of the teachers and patrons with whom I have worked has often been greater than my staff and I could provide leadership for. Certain ideas and suggested practices have been acceptable to a degree that we were embarrassed because we could not provide adequate rationale, the know-how, assistance and preparation needed for adequate implementation.

Over the years I have failed in some valiant efforts to effect change; I have succeeded in others. In retrospect, I know that I have failed at times because the idea was not entirely defensible or because my performance was poor. I succeeded when the concept was sound and my performance adequate. This experience leads me to the generalization that *educational change can be accomplished when the suggested change is needed and the need is understood.* I think the implication is strong that elaborate strategies sometimes fail because the basic idea is unsound or because a clear forceful presentation is impossible within the elaborately designed strategy.

In the final analysis, at the root of every strategy is a person or a small group. *People* effect change. Every change that affects human relationships comes about through the efforts of people. Sooner or later, the most involved of strategies for change in education get to the root of the matter and the leaders appear. My question is a simple one: Why not start with people? Let's build a strong intellectual leadership in education. With strong leaders, change in education is possible and will proceed smoothly. The basic strategy for change is *leadership* and leadership is provided by competent people.

The leadership must be armed with ideas which stem from knowledge. We have areas where achievement is solid and quality and excellence are the rule. These areas do not go unnoticed. Quality and excellence in education beget change and adaptation to needs. It is self-renewing.

We should look to this strong base to beget the sound concepts and guidelines for educational change and innovation. The basic strategy needed is to develop a sound idea upon the base of quality and excellence, develop the leaders to recognize and utilize these sound ideas, and arm them with the personal knowledge and skills necessary to interpret the soundness and logic of the concept to others.

The process inevitably comes back to the soundness of the idea and the way it is presented. However, we face the pressures to accelerate change and under this pressure we are tempted to take the "short-cut" offered by those who see the effecting of change as a process in itself utterly divorced from the change to be effected. If the idea is sound and the information convincing, then the change comes about.

We hear much today about "the establishment." Supposedly "the establishment" resists change. In education "the establishment" includes those who ostensibly have some stake in keeping things as they are. Education is said to be "over-institutionalized"—meaning that the organization has become more important than the people in it. To the extent that this is true it is regrettable—partly because it presents a barrier to change. Change comes about because people make it come about. If the institution becomes stronger than the people in it, then people are prevented from bringing about change.

There is a parallel here with religion. Religion is a positive force so long as people, in the name of religion, lead men to truth. Religion ceases to be a constructive force when its people become less important than the particular religion they profess—when they obey the laws of the church but forget the teachings, and when they take more pride in being members of a church than in aiding the church in its never-ending search for basic truth.

Education, too, is a positive force so long as people in the name of education search for truth. Here the truth is to be found in developing, demonstrating, and implementing better ways to assure achievement of the goal of education—an adequately educated citizenry. To the extent that education defends itself against attack by pulling together in mutual protection of present practices—to that extent, education is in error. It cannot allow itself the luxury of becoming institutionalized if for that luxury it pays the price of stifling leadership.

Some would say that institutionalization is necessary because the schools must fight a political battle; that they must fight force with force. It is true that education must fight an unfriendly force with a force of its own—but that force need not be the development of an institution that resists change.

Education is potentially good. Properly conducted, it can be a force that is irresistable. But it must be properly presented and it must use as its evidence all the quality and excellence of which it is capable. Its essential role is the development of people. As we demonstrate that education can develop people that demonstrate excellence of achievement, we demonstrate quality of education. Quality education is a powerful force —far more powerful than the machinations of local, state or national groups concerned primarily with narrow and institutionalized interests.

It would be comforting to say at this point that the leadership for quality education is in place—that we have but to hand over the reins and all will be well. Of course, this is not true. We have too few educational leaders who can be called educational statesmen. Too many measure their status by their position in the pecking order—the power hierarchy. The educational statesman wields great power for the cause of education; too many educational leaders spend their time maintaining *status quo*. The educational statesman contributes to change and the development of quality education; too many leaders are content to deepen the entrenchment of education.

Kimbrough suggests that the rising teacher militancy of today may be the result of school administrators being poor politicians. My conclusion is that the rising teacher militancy is a rebellion against a negation of leadership by the superintendent.

Many educators seem to have lost their faith in democracy. The essence of democracy is the right of the individual to be heard. It is from this cauldron that leadership emerges. As leadership emerges, ideas come forth—the people listen, adapt, enlarge, adopt and utilize. This is the democratic process—the constant search for leadership, then the constant evaluating, checking, and balancing before the decision is made. But always the way must be open for new leadership to emerge.

Some educational leadership, in its obeisance to the institutional concept, has tended to short-circuit this process. Too often it has paid a steep price for a temporary truce; it has knuckled down to the political structure. It has formed an unholy alliance and it is partly this unholy alliance that stimulates teachers to be militant.

PROPOSED STRATEGIES FOR CHANGE IN EDUCATION

A strategy is designed to achieve a goal. In this case the goal is clear. We wish to effect changes in education. The need is obvious. Change is needed to update our practices and methods to include all we have painfully learned about teaching and learning. Change is needed because education must look to the future—to find ways to serve the accelerating needs of the country more effectively. We must learn to grapple with the ever accelerating accretion of knowledge to the end that education is for the present and the emerging future—not for some period in the receding past.

The strategy we need is one that removes the artificial barriers that interrupt the simple equation: strong leader, sound idea, adequate information convincingly presented.

The strategy must take into account the fact that change does not occur in a vacuum; a single change usually initiates a host of related changes. A single change may be effective for a short time but its effect is too often lost if it is not a part of an orderly and continuing process of change. A strategy for change which concentrates on removing the artificial barriers to change *that educators themselves have erected* does offer promise for establishing the machinery for orderly and continuing change. There are four parts of this strategy.

Establishing a secure base for educational change; a profession of education based upon proficiency in pedagogy. The basis of a profession is its competence in performance. Without this assured competence, other aspects of professionalism—self-regulation of membership, requirements for admission, etc.—are but window-dressing.

To bring about change in education we must first increase our knowledge of the teaching-learning process and develop the skills to translate this knowledge into effective action. The profession of education must assume the control of its own destiny; educators must develop the pedagogy of training and preparation of teachers and the development of professional leaders to direct the utilization of these processes and competencies.

Competence in the science and art of teaching means the ability to diagnose a need, prescribe and administer a remedy with as much accuracy and reliability as does the doctor or the engineer. It means that we must know teaching materials, content and sequence of learning skills, that we know the evaluation tools necessary for diagnosis. This degree of competence does not exist in education. Education is suffering; it is static. The base of the profession must be firmly established in knowledgeable pedagogy.

The profession of education must become independent. It must declare its independence from the public in appropriate respects. It must stop the kind of "handholding" relationship with which it buys temporary peace from the war of criticism. This is a controversial point. It is my belief that the educational profession can put itself in better position to effect change in education and that the public will accept and support needed change more readily if a clear line is drawn between the responsibilities of the profession and those of laymen.

It is difficult to distinguish in many local communities who appoints a new principal to a school—the superintendent or the editor of the local newspaper. It is difficult to determine who appoints a new school board member—the citizens, educators or vested interest groups. It is difficult to say who proposes the curriculum in a local school—laymen or educators. When a crisis comes, responsibilities often have been so entangled that virtually no one knows where we faltered or why.

The point is simply this: the profession should take the very clear position that it will concern itself primarily with the development of proposals for substantive education—practices, procedures, content, resources needed, etc. It should be left entirely to the public to accept or reject the proposals and be prepared to exercise the subsequent rsponsibilities required. The profession in turn should be prepared to accept or reject the conditions under which it will render the professional services of teaching.

Some may interpret this as a proposal to sever essential relationships that must prevail between parents and teachers for the education of children or at the administrative level for gaining proper representation and consideration of education in the public services for the community. This is not intended; it would be argued that such relationships should— and would—be strengthened. There is no relationship quite so wholesome as that which exists between the parent and the physician of his child. I employ an architect to design a house along the general guidelines of size, spacial relationships, and costs that I give him. He is clear and exact in advising me as to what I can and cannot do with regard to structural strains, building codes, etc. In either case—physician or architect —I trust him. I may disagree with either of them from time to time, but when his professional knowledge is on the line and is pitted against my lay opinion, I respect him, and I listen to him.

Unity must be established in the ranks of the educators. The first two strategies indicate the compelling need to perfect stronger unity in the ranks of educators. Unity does not exist at present, and there are no encouraging signs that it is going to emerge from current trends. Educators are dividing themselves into two groups—teachers' unions and professional associations. Then professional associations are subdividing into classroom teachers and school administrators. Both classroom teacher groups and teacher unions are aimed at the exclusion of school administrators and the seizure of power for classroom teachers. Neither group holds much power; the image being created of the profession is damaging; professionalization, independence, and unity cannot be achieved; and no reliable strategy for change can be mounted.

The breach in professional unity begins at the level of superintendency; some widening of it occurs at each operational level below; and the division becomes a gorge by the time it reaches the level of the teacher. The quality and philosophy of leadership can influence the degree of separation, but they cannot close the gap. The proper structure of relationships has not been provided.

The damaging role in practice has been the alignment of the superintendent with the board of education and other groups and with individuals who are power and politically oriented. Too often he has represented them as a negotiator who is negotiating with teachers for their professional services. Communications have been so difficult and school administrative structure and operation so poorly understood that whether this was an intentional mode of operation or not, it has generally been perceived that way by teachers.

School administrators issue profound statements about their interests in education and about the strong positions they take in behalf of teachers. And generally their statements are true. But the fact remains: teachers do not perceive them that way. Thus they are left in the middle.

The progression of the strategy toward unity in the profession requires the development of a profession based on pedagogy; a declaration of independence of the profession; and finally an operational structure, professional and legal, void of obvious pitfalls for misunderstanding and professional alienations. In the professional organization, a structure should be established which will provide opportunities for all personnel to participate in decision making and at the same time maintain a system of checks and balances which will insure that no division of teachers, administrators, or other group, has dominance over the other. One professional association for all educators is implied. Subgroupings should be departments of the association. Decision making should result from compromises emerging from the check-and-balance system. Something on the order of the structure for the national government would be proposed, perhaps, even to the establishment of a superior judging body to render decisions relative to adherence to established goals and objectives.

Membership in the professional association is autonomous; under a board of education, we work in an official, legal structure. But I know of no professional association which has desegregated its membership before the board of education desegregated the school system. Relative to the point under discussion—professional unity—I am of the opinion that the official structure of positions, responsibilities, relationships, etc., has greatly influenced the operation of the professional association and indirectly been responsible for the growing disunity. If this is true, how do we work our way out of it?

Boards of education, in theory at least, seek to select the most qualified educator who can be found to serve in the position of the superintendency. He is selected to be a spokesman for education; he is selected to represent educational personnel; and he is selected for his ability to lead and co-ordinate the efforts of educational personnel in rendering educational services. Some boards of education permit much freedom and grant considerable leeway in the performance of this role. But is it understood and performed sufficiently to prevent the breakdown? Experience would indicate that it is not. The suspicion is strong. The misunderstanding is great.

At this juncture in the development of administrative and legal structure for public schools, I would propose that the profession should have the responsibility for the selection of the superintendent. He is their representative; he is supposed to represent their profession; and he is supposed to be the spokesman for education. With the superintendent serving in this relationship, the board of education and school personnel would be operating under contractual relationships. The board, however, would exercise the same authority toward the superintendent (to the profession) as it does under the present structure.

Some will argue that this arrangement could not work because, educators would select the most popular representative; the emphasis would always be on salaries; or the most militant representative would be selected. The profession, however, would be standing on its merits; the board of education would weigh decisions in terms of what it was getting for its money; and it would be speaking to the profession directly. There would be no middleman to be maligned, mistrusted, and held solely accountable for the quality of the proposals recommended to the board of education and implemented. The profession would have to work in unity to prepare its recommendations on education; it would have to stand in unity to receive the pronouncements and judgments of the public. The public would demand change, even as it is demanding it now; the profession would have to propose and implement change and be judged on the merits of its performance.

Altering the approach to curriculum change. Curriculum change and innovations in teaching in American education are moving at the speed of Fulton's steamboat in a space age. New ideas and knowledge are being produced at an accelerating rate, but implementation is laborious, tedious, and slow. I would propose that we junk the obsolete vehicle currently in use and adopt a new model.

We have been indoctrinated with the grass roots approach to curriculum change: start with the teachers, get involvement, build and design from the ground up. We have tried to carry total communities with us through this development stage. For most major changes, however, the task is too large; the involvement is too cumbersome; more professional knowledge is needed; more research is required; and better communications are necessary. Sufficient time has elapsed and sufficient experience has accumulated without implementing effective change through this approach, to tell us that we need a change in the procedure. We have a recent example which should suggest a new model.

One of the most significant changes introduced in education in the past fifty years has been implemented in the last few years. We have seen an almost universal implantation of the new math and science curriculums in the schools. As Superintendent Barnes points out, vocational education has not been introduced successfully and sufficiently into the public schools during forty years of urgent endeavor. Yet new math and science were introduced as replacements for well-established courses of study. What was different about the development and introduction of the new math and science?

I would suggest that the chief differences were that: (1) a new theory was advanced for the organization of content and instruction in accordance with proven principles of teaching and learning (pedagogy); (2) a program to implement the theory was formulated and tested under controlled conditions; and (3) the program was prepared complete with justifications, materials, and instructional methods, for introduction to teachers and subsequently into the classroom. We had some deep-seated insecurities to overcome. There was reluctance on the part of many to change from the old to the new. But we did it. We had a more viable strategy for change. We were not expected to progress unit-by-unit, teacher-by-teacher, and construct and revise our theory in the process. For emphasis on the process, suppose that the attempt had been made using the conventional method.

I do not intend to imply that the new math and science were introduced without committing mistakes or that they are being taught perfectly now. But it is safe to say that they are being taught as well as the courses they replaced. Somewhat aside, one other point should be made with regard to this innovation. With the introduction of the new math and science, the sharpest thrust was made in the initiation of that fearsome "progressive education" that has been made in thirty years of discouraging efforts. The academic scientists and mathematicians made the breakthrough. I would contend that no other program of instruction or approach to instruction has embodied as many of the concepts and principles of progressive education as has these programs.

A theory for effecting a breakthrough and effecting change in education is of tremendous importance. Most needed changes in education cannot be effected by slightly altering that which is already operative. Controlled testing is needed, and finally proposed changes should be prepared for ready, reliable implementation. Schools of the urban and metropolitan areas are best equipped to adopt this approach.

It is of not much help, however, merely to suggest that we need a better theory. Some would say that we have dreamed too much already. But as an example of what I mean, I will offer a proposal for a major alteration of the high school curriculum through a practical use of televised instruction. We begin with the realization that televised instruction, for the most part, has been limited to teaching established courses in a conventional way, except that the instruction has been transmitted via television. Secondly, in order to project the theory, we recognize that the large city high school is proliferated with courses. We boast of 75 or 80 courses in what we often call the *good* high school. And then we realize that we expect the high school youngster to acquire high school training by taking 16 to 20 of these courses based upon the familiar Carnegie unit. The theory for breaking through this maze of courses through more effective utilization of televised instruction is proposed as follows:

1. Reorganize the total high school curriculum into some five or six major threads or strands of learning—math, science, social studies, language, the arts, etc.— with no course delineations; eliminate duplications, capitalize upon closely related content such as American history and American literature, etc.

2. Employ at least one master teacher for each major area of instruction at a salary of 20 to 30 thousand dollars to teach the strands in one continuous sequence, emphasizing major concepts and principles in each area.

3. Transmit the instruction into TV receiving rooms where students view it with only a monitor present and select and maintain their level and sequence of instruction from the multiple levels of transmissions.

4. Use the regular classroom teacher to provide individualized instruction, direct independent study, etc., from guides and materials that follow and supplement the televised instruction, permitting every child to advance at his individual rate of learning.

This proposal, of course, would be suggested for use with the approach discussed above for effecting educational change in curriculum—design, test and revise, and package for ease and reliability in implantation.

CONCLUSIONS AND IMPLICATIONS

Conclusions concerning the points advanced in this paper for effecting educational change, can be brief and precise. The implications, while they may be generally applicable to all levels and segments of education, rural and urban, bear some special significance for large city school systems.

The emphasis has been placed on *strong leadership, sound ideas,* and *convincing information and presentations.* Strategy is designed to be implemented through educators to meet the challenge issued by Secretary Gardner that

> ... educators ... become not only teachers of their students but teachers of the nation in the new philosophy of learning and living in an ever changing world (and) ... that they ... convince the American people, once and for all, of the truth of Toynbee's (statement) that "civilization is a movement and not a condition, a voyage and not a harbor."[1]

He notes that teachers will have to be the first to learn to live with change and be the earliest converts to the ideal of lifetime learning.

The public is prone to express a great deal of blind faith in education; to some it seems to have become a panacea. It remains the duty of educators to give it inherent power and force for change. This is more imperative than ever before in the history of American education. For as John Stuart Mill said, "No great improvements in the lot of mankind are possible, until a great change takes place in the fundamental constitution of their modes of thought."

I have recommended a strong independent role for the educational profession in the process of effecting change. This would apply to the individual teacher and to the profession as a whole. The urgency is to stop shifting pieces (as a defender in chess) and start attacking the king—the heart of the matter. We should strive to be classified among Rogers'[2] innovators—pioneers, lighthouses, advance scouts, progressists, non-parochials, experimentals, the cultural *avante-garde.* We need not fear the taking of a position of independence in education if we are sound in our proficiency in the art and science of teaching. For as a parent stated in speaking to a school faculty on "The Teacher and the Public,"

---

[1] John W. Gardner, "Impact of Change on Education," *NEA Journal,* November 1959, p. 51.
[2] Everett M. Rogers, "What Are Innovators Like?" *Theory Into Practice,* 2:252-256, 1963.

The old expression that "School PR begins in the classroom" is no joke! As a matter of fact, it ends in the classroom, too. It *begins* in the classroom because even the best public relations program cannot offset the effects of a poor teaching program, or the impact of a group of frustrated or dissatisfied parents. It ends in the classroom because the end result of any school effort, including public relations, should be: Improved educational opportunities for children.[3]

And with regard to the individual leader—the superintendent—Neal Gross[4] provides a good answer. The superintendent runs the schools, reports Gross, if he has the courage of his convictions. His success is in direct relationship to the "role" as perceived by the superintendent. If he feels subordinate to the citizenry or power structure, he is. If he leads (regardless of the power structure), he leads. Ninety-five percent of the decision making potential is in his hands; how much he exercises is up to him.

Special implications for the implementation of the strategy advocated in this paper arise from the conditions and needs prevalent in large city school systems. The lowest of the disadvantaged are found in the large cities of the nation. The most affluent are there too. Each must be served by the public schools. Each may be found in the same school; large majorities of either may be found in separate schools. The severely deprived require many forms of compensatory education. Speech and language development are critical. Vast programs of remedial instruction are needed. Learning for many has developed in an uneven pattern. Fully 50 percent of the children in one of these schools rarely attend the same school for a full school year. Social and personal problems are severe. Self-image is poor. School attendance is irregular. Pre-school programs are essential. Lower class values are often in great conflict with the middle class values usually held by teachers. No school situation in America is demanding greater proficiency in the art and science of teaching, and many proposed programs to meet these needs are being derailed because of a lack of it.

Schools of large cities generally are of sufficient size to make extraordinary uses of team teaching, nongraded instruction, and to introduce other forms and patterns of flexibility. Large city school systems are staffed with personnel who can implement these ideas.

Greatest needs are developing in large city school systems for the independent role of the profession and for the development of unity in it. A greater readiness has developed. A better system of communications can be maintained; defined, formal relationships are more prevalent; and professional associations (or unions) are stronger, better organized, and less subject to domination by administrators. For the conduct and implementation of research, large urban school systems are best equipped with the major resources required. They are already making a significant contribution in this field. By some change in the models for effecting change and the adoption of commitments for new directions, large city school systems can provide ideal testing centers for the strategy proposed in this paper.

---

[3] Beverly B. Stackig, "The Teacher and the Public," unpublished speech delivered to the Jackson Road Elementary School faculty, Montgomery County, Maryland, April 4, 1966.
[4] Neal Gross, *Who Runs Our Schools* (New York: John Wiley & Sons, Inc., 1958).

Role of the Superintendent and
Board of Education

ROBERT H. JOHNSON, JR.*

Any treatment of procedures and strategies of change in urban and metropolitan areas in this country requires careful consideration of the role of the superintendents and boards of education involved. The problems found in these areas are a direct outgrowth of the new stance of people and of their concerns, and create many new problems and hazards for metropolitan superintendents and boards.

LEADERSHIP IN PLANNING

The city and suburban areas of 1980 will find themselves in a state of hopelessness as far as effective educational improvements are concerned, unless educational leadership assumes a more influential position in the city and suburban arrangement. As we study the emerging shape of the nation, it becomes apparent that the educational leader will need to be prepared to face realistically the question: Am I ready for the challenge which this situation seems to present to American democracy, and more importantly, to my own leadership capabilities? The economic, political, defense and other developments, which symbolize world affairs and spill problems upon the city in an ever growing magnitude, require educational leadership to involve itself in metropolitan concerns and with planning groups dealing with problems such as transportation system programming and air and water pollution. The superintendent must recognize and understand his role in these important areas. He must:

> . . . recognize that his job is political by nature. The size of the district in which he serves may determine the amount of political activity in which he will engage, but every superintendent will be involved—be it called political activity or just "knowing the right people".
> The superintendent understands how his political world is related to other political and public agencies. The world of politics is not contained in a specific area or composed of a special group, but takes on many complicated dimensions.[1]

This will require participation on the part of the superintendent to a far greater degree in these matters than has occurred in the past. He may delegate certain of these opportunities for participation to appropriate members of his staff. However, he must assume certain responsibilities himself if his leadership function is to be recognized and accepted among the leaders of power groups in the city-suburban setting. The superintendent must always recognize that his job, in part, is political by nature.

Leo F. Schnore[2] suggests that neither city nor suburb is a homogeneous

* *Professor of Education and Director of the School Planning Center, University of Montana.* Formerly, Superintendent of Schools, Jefferson County, Colorado; also visiting professor of education at University of Colorado, Colorado State College, and Johns Hopkins University. Author of *The School Board and Public Relations,* and of *Rx for Team Teaching* (in press).

[1] Steven T. Pellican, "The Emerging Role of the Superintendent of Schools" (Greeley, Colorado: Colorado State College, 1960), Mimeographed.
[2] Leo F. Schnore, "Urban Structure and Suburban Selectivity," *Demography,* I (1964), pp. 164-176.

area; in fact, he points out that each is internally diverse. Individual neighborhoods, especially within the central city, are so arranged that some social scientists have charged that we are creating tens of thousands of modern economic ghettos. Crime in the cities, delinquency in the suburbs, increasing traffic fatalities, growing mental disease problems, and competition and conflict in society are but a few of the by-products of our city and suburban society that lay a heavy hand upon the potential of the schools in those areas.

The emerging role of the superintendent requires that he understand how his political world is related to other political and public agencies. Awareness of other agencies of the city and of the suburban areas and involvement by boards of education and superintendents in some of the basic issues, is becoming a requirement for educational leadership in our time.

In too many instances, the role of the superintendent is seemingly that of maintaining a most precarious balance above the pool of problems that lies below. The oppressive pall that permeates the core city seems to offer as by-products a collection of educational workers who appear to be drawn away from their central purpose and function amidst the pattern of confusion that seems to prevail in some cities and suburban areas. For any educator or city board member to assume that a role other than one of deep involvement in city and suburban concerns is to deny the long-standing requirement for actual participation in all matters relating to education.

The establishment of constructive relations between the superintendent of schools and board of education and the major power structures give them an opportunity to play an essential part in the development of a new strategy in American cities and metropolitan areas. It also places additional requirements upon them beyond that of creating the opportunity for improvement of overall planning and strategy.

Since the board of education usually represents the people, members of the board should report to the citizens frequently on their stewardship. The superintendent of schools should be the articulate spokesman of the board of education in all matters relating to educational policy. He should commit himself to a plan that will ensure the best communication arrangement possible in relation to education throughout the complex structure of the major city-suburban groups. Total involvement of the community representatives of the power structure in the educational problems of the changing city and suburban situation is of highest priority. This involvement takes on many faces and key professional personnel throughout the school system must render assistance.

ROLE OF THE STATE DEPARTMENT OF INSTITUTIONS OF HIGHER LEARNING

Much has been written in the past few decades about the failure of the state department of education and institutions of higher learning to work effectively and cooperatively with school districts in metropolitan areas. With the increase of federal involvement in education and with a disproportionate share of federal funds going to the cities and suburban centers, the need for a plan for effective cooperation becomes painfully clear. There must be an interest and willingness on the part of the leaders representing the three bodies cooperatively to ensure a better system of education.

A few attempts have been made to establish cooperative councils involving representatives of these groups over the past several years but rarely have they been successful. Historically, they have operated for a period of time—then faded from view—often to be followed by a similar body, usually with the same result. There must evolve within the next few years a strategy of planning for education that will make it necessary for the city and suburban educators to look beyond their usual set of current preoccupations. The colleges and universities must go far beyond their traditional roles in teacher training if adequate cooperation is attained. They will be required to serve as living laboratories; to become places where innovations proposed for elementary and secondary schools can become tested theories and provide results that are available to the city and suburban educators as well as to others.

Further, the colleges and universities must play an ever-expanding role in the involvement of the intellectual power of their staffs in the mainstream of city and suburban problems. To remain aloof from these matters of great importance will be to deny the purpose of education and place the college and university leadership in the same tenuous role as that of the superintendent who chooses to remain aloof from his problems. There must be a sweeping reorganization of the relationships of colleges and universities to the schools, as well as in their philosophy. The role of the state department can and should be extended since it is in a unique position to effect liaison between the colleges and universities and the schools.

One of the weaknesses in the involvement of the state department is found in the formal structure of the state educational machinery. James B. Conant points out that: "This structure possesses a serious problem in some states, especially in those in which the chief state school officer is an elected official, and/or in those in which there is no responsible lay board."[3]

FEDERAL INVOLVEMENT IN URBAN AND SUBURBAN MATTERS

The growing involvement in urban and suburban school matters points up a basic condition that must be dealt with if the outcome is to be a successful relationship. The problems are generally blamed on bureaucratic interference from those who bring outside expertise into the city and suburbs with little awareness of local conditions. A sort of *"carpet bagger from Washington"* theory has sprung up, suggesting a loss of sensitivity during the attempt to implement these federal programs. However, an apparent lack of empathy also has developed among many

---

[3] James Bryant Conant, *Shaping Educational Policy* (New York: McGraw-Hill Book Company, 1964), p. 37.

educators as a result of deep fear and suspicion of grant assistance, along with the accompanying fear of federal control over local affairs. A rigid parochial approach to local administration—an unwillingness to look at the real problems facing the federal, state and local educational authorities— tends to build a wall between these groups that can easily frustrate the sincere efforts of the participating bodies.

The "easier-to-oppose-than-support" theory is taking its toll among some local administrative groups. Certainly, much can be said for the value of federal intervention when conditions are not dealt with adequately at the local or state level. There are many who take the position with Hanson that:

> Federal funds for education will increase because the federal government collects the lion's share of the taxes, but the next step must be general federal aid, paid directly to the state with no strings attached. This is the only efficient course, because states and local school districts and individual institutions of higher learning will always have a better knowledge of their needs than far-away Washington.[4]

Some will argue with his thesis that:

> The USOE may soon be free from the stigma of "federal control" that has retarded it for a century.
>
> This freedom is possible because states are getting stronger in the field of education and no longer feel so threatened by the Office.
>
> Fear of federal control by the Office (USOE) will disappear if the Office can phase out its role as a "moneybags" and remote spawning ground for rules and regulations.[5]

It should be obvious that cooperation between federal, state and local bodies is necessary if local and state governments are to remain effective in the years ahead. Maintaining a system of checks and balances in the metropolitan areas is no longer sufficient without deeper involvement of all appropriate groups. Superintendents, boards of education, colleges and universities, and state departments of education cannot afford to remain aloof from these problem areas.

The need for systematic cooperation stands foremost among all problems of metropolitan educational planning. A procedural system has no defensible strategy unless it includes and requires this cooperative arrangement as the cornerstone of a sound system for educational change. The superintendents and their boards of education must become the rudder and keel for the accurate direction of urban and suburban cooperative educational planning.

THE COMPLEXITY OF THE EDUCATIONAL TASK

Urban and suburban school leaders must have a clear understanding of their roles with regard to the multi-faceted program of offerings that make up the typical school plan in America's highly-populated centers. Urban and suburban leaders must have a unique understanding of the separate and distinct role of each of their programs and how they interrelate.

---

4 Carroll Hanson, "Rise or Fall for USOE?", *Phi Delta Kappan* ILVIII (September, 1966), p. 9.
5 *Ibid.*

Barnes suggests that: "Any assault on institutionalization must recognize the practical difficulties of changing the value systems of thousands of teachers and administrators." He further states that: "Change must be effected by subtler means than by a frontal attack on existing values and practices."

Thus, the educational leader must prepare to meet this need directly or to arrange for outside assistance. Few could quarrel with a plea for intelligent, sophisticated and persuasive planning of appropriate strategies for change, but many will challenge inactivity, neutrality or resistance to such opportunities.

EMERGING PRACTICES AND THEIR IMPLICATIONS FOR PLANNING

The role of city superintendents and boards of education in innovation must be based on the condition and policy stance that supports the theory that active participation requires considerable knowledge in many facets of educational research and experimentation. Thus, a clear concept must be established which enables the educational worker to proceed within the most appropriate framework to accomplish a superior educational plan.

Kelley and Rasey suggest that: "When we get the concept of change into our organism so that we can act as though it was so, we will not try to plan for eternity."[6] As we develop strategies for improvement it is well that we keep this admonition in mind.

At the prseent stage in the strategic development of sound programs for change, it is imperative that the educational leader develop and direct new information campaigns to support appropriate strategy if the educational worker as well as lay citizens are to accept, support and accomplish a new practice.

Gallup points out that innovations can generally be measured in two dimensions: (1) overall acceptance or rejection of the idea; (2) the significance of the important additions of the particular innovation. He states:

> It appears now that parents approve of more needed educational innovations than might be anticipated by any educator. In fact, a greater number of parents favor such innovations than the percentage of their schools carrying them out. As far as the parents are concerned, they are ready for more new practices than the schools are giving them.[7]

The readiness of parents for a new program has great potential for assuring sound support if the plan for change is well directed, and every educational worker is knowledgeable and able to interpret and direct the inclusion of the innovational matter into the mainstream of educational policy and practice.

Since a healthy and supportive attitude is a prerequisite in any community where innovation and change are encouraged, there are many

---

[6] Earl C. Kelley and Marie I. Rasey, *Education and the Nature of Man* (New York: Harper Brothers, 1952), pp. 117-118.

[7] Gallup Poll, "Parents Are Ready", *The Instructor*, LXXVI (October, 1966), p. 154.

important groups that must be kept informed concerning the plans and the strategy for change. The educational leader must be alert to any evidence of a lack of information on the part of any important groups. He must be prepared to set the forces in motion that will increase their understanding.

Kimbrough says, "Educators must recognize at the outset that leadership for educational change involves political leadership." (Ch. 6). There can be little doubt that if change is to occur, educators and boards of education must understand and obtain the cooperation of power structures of the city and suburban area. They must be effective at the highest political level when their views are required on matters relating to the advancement of their communities and the improvement of the general educational position.

One of the most significant emerging issues involving the metropolitan superintendent and his board of education is the establishment of a sound operational procedure with regard to the elements of negotiation. As much as any single issue facing the educational leader, negotiation policy may generate a role which is unfamiliar to the superintendent of schools.

The American Association of School Administrators states:

Concerning the superintendents' specific role in negotiation, two extreme positions are often advocated: (a) that he be completely bypassed and have no place in the negotiative process, and (b) that he be the chief negotiator representing only the board of education in all of its dealings with the staff.

AASA does not believe that either of these positions will contribute to the long-term good of the school district or its educational program.[8]

The superintendent should play a significant role in professional negotiation. He should work closely with both board and staff representatives in an attempt to reach agreement that is in the best interest of the educational program and the community. His position as leader of the staff and executive of the board requires this. The superintendent must utilize his best professional judgment, experience and understanding in the development of appropriate procedures in board of education and staff negotiation.

The chief school officer plays a multi-phased role. On the one hand he is the executive agent of the board of education who must reflect the policy of the board; on the other, he is expected to be the instructional leader for the teaching group. To further complicate this situation, he has a basic moral obligation to the youth that make up the school system. Any repositioning of the superintendent that provides an evasion of any one of these important segments of negotiation places an artificial and handicapping restriction upon him as educational leader.

Should those who would remove the superintendent from the negotiation procedure succeed in this attempt, there is a real possibility that he may also be removed from instructional leadership. It is possible that

---

[8] American Association of School Administrators, "School Administrators View Professional Negotiation", *NEA Journal*, LVI (January, 1967), p. 25.

before the end of the century we may witness such a change in roles in education, that the general superintendent, as he is currently known, will no longer be recognized. If so, is the organized teacher group ready to accept—and can it assume—the responsibilities of providing the instructional leadership needed? This is a central question in this controversy.

The civil rights situation in many metropolitan areas is so critical that it involves important interpretations and decisions by the superintendent and the board of education from day to day. Any position other than one of diligent and forthright treatment of these problems is likely to result in serious consequences for students, staff and the community.

Matthewson observes that: "In the mobilization of social forces against ignorance, cultural diversiveness and emotional slovishness, a rebirth of the spirit of American freedom may occur and our society may be projected into a new era of social processing."[9]

The educational leader who accepts his role and meets his responsibilities in the emerging society understands the necessity for his involvement in these matters. The ultimate purpose of society includes the utilization of education for social and economic improvement.

In Summary

The remainder of this century may well be the most crucial period humanity has ever been required to face. Time becomes increasingly important in man's race to new realms of opportunity—or alternatively to inevitable disaster.

The metropolitan educator and his board face the necessity for, or possibility of, public consideration of almost every condition, belief, issue and fact that relates to any or all aspects of education in his community.

Since education is a chief agency for improving society, planning for change must involve as many elements of the leadership system of the metropolitan area as practicable. A long-range result of the application of this strategy, if wisely implemented, could be a significant gain in new support for the public schools of the cities and suburbs of America.

Boards of education must become knowledgeable in the federal arena if many of the needed improvements are to be effected. A reasonable understanding of federal and state legislation, its purposes and areas of conflict with customary views held in the school system, is essential. When money hinges on compliance, there may be a tendency to accept the money and follow federal guidelines, some of which may not be realistic.

The superintendent, during coming years, will need to demonstrate unusual skill in developing procedures that will ensure that his board of education has adequate information on all matters, including research, and ample time to study and understand every item that becomes a part of any agenda to be dealt with.

---

[9] Robert Henry Matthewson, *A Strategy for American Education* (New York: Harper and Brothers, 1957), p. 266.

Provision of adequate staff support to plan and conduct needed research, write effective position papers, and serve as resource personnel to citizen groups who work on planning projects is essential. The superintendent and his staff must become increasingly involved in school-community relations because the improvement of education requires it. Thus, traditional institutional concepts may have to give way in the face of bold planning and effective execution.

The metropolitan school superintendent has it within his power to provide the leadership necessary to guide the development of strategies designed to result in the development of sound plans and strategies to effect improvements in the central cities and their suburban satellites.

* * *

Role of Non-Educators

BERNARD RUSSELL*

A tacit assumption in the title of this paper is that *there is a role for non-educators in planning and effecting educational change in urban areas.* Few people, in or out of education, would disagree with this assumption. There are many educational areas in which non-educators have played an important, and relatively non-controversial role. They are so much a part of the educational institutional fabric that they are well-nigh indistinguishable. On the other hand, non-educators have been resisted, often, as not having the competence to make a contribution to the education of children and youth.

It is easy to pick out a number of other professions that have contributed to the body of knowledge utilized by the field of education, as well as individual professionals who have contributed as staff or consultants to the growth and change of educational policy and planning. Psychologists and psychiatrists have been used to understand and deal with the problem child as well as to understand and enhance the learning progress of the normal child. The social worker has been utilized in somewhat the same sense as well as to deal with obstacles to learning outside the school. Certainly, economists and budget-makers have become an important adjunct to any school administrator. But all of these groups have been used almost haphazardly, as need for their knowledge arose.

On the other hand, there are two major groups whose contribution in most situations has been negligible. These are the parents of the children being educated and the children and youth themselves. In many communities the parents, through the medium of PTA's, political parties and other mechanisms, have earned a substantial voice in school affairs. However, the parents in the slums of our urban centers—the parents of minority

* *Assistant Director, Model Cities Administration, Department of Housing and Urban Development, Washington, D. C.* Formerly, Director, Office of Juvenile Delinquency and Youth Development, Welfare Administration (1962-67), and Deputy Special Assistant to the Secretary for Juvenile Delinquency (1961-62), Department of Health, Education and Welfare; United Nations Social Welfare Adviser, Ankara, Turkey (1960-61).

group status—have not generally been heard by those setting educational policy.

Nor have the children and youth who receive education been encouraged or permitted to make much contribution. Again, one must ask whether children and youth who are being educated have the competency to participate in planning for education, or whether any significant number of them even desire to do so. Some of the research of the past would indicate that most children and youth have slight interest in participating in the councils of their elders. But the vociferous and sometimes strident voices of youth today would seem to belie this. It is clear that the changing problems of the schools and the rapidly changing society—of which educational institutions are a part—require some rethinking of what those changes are, how they affect the schools, how the schools can respond most constructively, and who is to be involved in shaping and implementing that response.

THE CHANGING SITUATION

Many of the socializing institutions of society are currently in process of change. Given the facts of our changing economy, the rapid and vast population shifts of the past 20 years, and the tremendous technological developments of that period, it would be amazing if we did not see concomitant changes in all of our societal institutions. For example, there have been readily discernible changes in neighborhoods, in families, in the church, and in employment, to say nothing of the schools. Thus, whereas the family was formerly the chief educator of its children up to age five or six, a number of other institutions have become increasingly significant by the age of three. The neighborhood, which used to be a place of comfort and familiarity to children and adults alike, has become barely distinguishable as a "neighborhood" or, at its worst, as a place of danger and fear.

As these changes occur, the schools are faced with a growing array of problems. The character and numbers of the school population have undergone rapid shifts. We are familiar with the flight of the white middle-class to the suburbs, and the influx of minority groups—Negro, Puerto Rican or Spanish-American—to the inner city. These people are, for the most part, poor, unable to compete for jobs demanding high technical skills, and unable to negotiate through the complex bureaucracies that significantly affect their lives in the big city. They have little education themselves, and only a nascent awareness of the relationship of education to progress, or even to survival. The kind of education required by their children, the teaching techniques and the teaching aids all differ considerably from the requirements for the previous school population.

The urban schools have thus had to respond to changing populations with different needs. This response has taken the form of changes in approach and content of traditional education, as well as of the proliferation and intensification of special programs only marginally related to education.

The latter includes special projects in the areas of vocational training and employment, counseling and guidance, family and social welfare, physical and mental health, and intergroup relations.

Response to the basic educational problem has been complicated by the increasing difficulty of getting competent, new staff. Teaching, as a profession, no longer offers the prestige, salaries or working conditions to compete with most other professions. Moreover, transfer from schools with large concentrations of impoverished minority youth is often sought by experienced teachers in systems where fledging teachers must "do time" in ghetto schools before promotion to more attractive, less troublesome areas. This arrangement, it must be noted, is not generally a *formal* system for promotion, but the natural result of market forces; suburban systems and predominantly middle-class schools often pay more. And, facing severe budgetary constraints, city schools rarely can afford compensatory payments to the teachers in the ghettos.

Adequate pay for teachers is but one area in which urban schools face financial difficulties. The expanding population, and the programs and personnel required to meet the special needs of disadvantaged youth have severely strained most school budgets. Most school districts are financed largely through property taxes, but citizens have often been unwilling to vote for greater support through bond issues and tax increases. In many urban areas, the taxable assessed property valuation has decreased; in areas where it has increased, it has rarely kept pace with the increase in school enrollment. Further, cities do not receive state funds that are adequate for their expenditures on the remedial, technical, and more expensive programs required for their changing school populations. Federal support has generally been tied to specific programs, leaving inadequate funds to be applied to ongoing school needs. In summary, urban schools have found themselves with a rapidly growing and fundamentally changing population for which they have grossly inadequate financial means to provide adequate housing or competent teachers, let alone meet the demand for proliferating special quasi- or non-educational projects.

Given this crisis of urban schools in trying to provide even standard school programs, the addition of new programs and new quasi- or non-educational functions is a source of concern. Why, it may be asked, have the schools agreed to take on these functions?

The schools have traditionally been used as the melting pot in "Americanizing" new arrivals, and have been generally successful because they provided a natural, ready access to all youth. More and more, "culturally deprived" minority groups are viewed as needing a whole range of services to put them in the mainstream of urban American life. Again, the schools are being designated as the primary agency of this process, largely because they facilitate easy access to all youth.

Many new functions and responsibilities are being delegated to schools because of a public myth about the knowledgeability of teachers. Not only are teachers presumed to know more about youth and their problems, but also they are presumed to be more effective in dealing with them. Most *teachers,* however, are among the first to point out that their training and primary responsibility are basically educational in nature.

Beyond these factors that promote consolidation of services in the schools, is the rather natural tendency for the schools to actively seek out ways and means to provide services to alleviate some of the most visible and pressing problems which hamper their educational efforts. This has led to school social workers, school psychiatrists, school health services, and so forth. Additionally, it has meant that in several of our large cities, the public schools have been the largest participant in federal antipoverty programs, and have exerted strenuous efforts to gain local control of such programs as Head Start.

ALTERNATIVE APPROACHES

There are two basic approaches to this proliferation of non-educational roles (and, hence, the involvement of non-educators) in the urban school system. The first alternative is to encourage the school to accept these additional roles. The second, not surprisingly, is to encourage other institutions to share the burden.

Those arguing in favor of additional roles for the schools have stressed the schools' immediacy and accessibility to many of the problems and, hence, their presumed ability to devise and implement special programs. Such programs have been shown, however, to tend to spread the thin educational dollar to a point where the regular educational program suffers. Further, *these programs have often been carried out almost autonomously from other established agencies.* The schools have jealously guarded their independence and have, in some instances for example, insisted that school social workers qualify for and hold teaching credentials. Additionally, pilot programs and crash programs may prove dysfunctional to learning by obscuring the basic educational problems. Direct school operation of pre-schools in some systems, for example, may take scarce personnel and material resources away from the regular elementary school program. This is particularly questionable inasmuch as most of the benefits that may accrue in such pre-school programs are not likely to be sustained in the early primary grades when youngsters face "non-enriched" educational fare. Other non-academic functions may further aggravate and strain the schools' resources.

Finally, the new kinds of personnel involved in non-educational programs placed in the schools necessitate new kinds of leadership. High level professionals must be employed and this will require a greater expenditure of school administrative time and a share in the administrative and decision making process itself. Hence, this approach to solving the problems of the urban poor—while probably providing some useful services—has serious drawbacks not the least of which, given current financial difficulties, may be its effect on the regular educational process.

An alternative approach to this proliferation of school roles is one which permits and encourages the development and strengthening of other institutions to *share* the burden of providing special programs, while the schools carry out their primary function of educational development. The rationale for this approach was formulated by Ralph Tyler:

> Only by the fullest utilization of the potential educational efforts of home, church, school, recreational agencies, youth-serving organizations, the library, press, movies, radio, T.V. . . . can this nation meet its educational needs . . . Failure to encourage and to help other institutions to bear part of the responsibility inevitably weakens our total social structure and reduces the effectiveness of our total educational achievement.[1]

This line of thinking, then, necessitates that we delineate the educational responsibilities of the schools and the non-educational but education-related responsibilities of other agencies. Judson Shaplin attempted such a delineation by stating that "the central focus of the school should be upon the development of rationality and upon the learning of the symbolic systems and the communication skills essential to rationality."[2] He pointed out that services and activities to be provided by other agencies would include:

> health information and nutrition, physical education, athletics and recreation, expanding knowledge of the community and its cultural resources, training in skills required for modern living, such as driving a car; training in most aspects of work; treatment of emotional disorders; the training of children not capable of receiving academic instruction; and other activities now frequently included in the school program on a marginal basis.[3]

While one may disagree with one or more of the items included or excluded above, his point is clear. To facilitate long-range improvements in urban education, the schools must be strengthened and should resist *independently* taking on new quasi-educational tasks. The schools, however, must remain related to and supportive of these other, burden-sharing institutions and personnel. *This involvement will undoubtedly take the form of even greater cooperative relationships* with local industry, private agencies, universities, hospitals, and local and state departments of government. Schools can become "all-day" institutions, for example, by providing space while other agencies provide personnel for recreation, adult craft classes, etc. Establishment of pre-school services can be encouraged on the part of local and state agencies for family welfare, child services, etc. In this way, the relationships of the family and the very young child will be strengthened at the same time they both receive services. For older elementary school children, child guidance and child health clinics could be established by the relevant (non-public school) agency—possibly medical schools. School drop-outs or potential drop-outs could be provided jobs in a program jointly worked out by—and utilizing as employers—the

---

[1] Ralph W. Tyler, "Educational Objectives of American Democracy," *The Nation's Children*, Eli Ginzberg (ed.), White House Conference Golden Anniversary, Vol. 2, 1960, pp. 70-72 as quoted in Judson T. Shaplin, "Urban Education in Long-Term Crisis," *Planning For a Nation of Cities*, Sam Bass Warner (ed.) (Cambridge, Mass.: the M.I.T. Press, 1966), p. 255.

[2] Shaplin, *ibid.*, p. 256.

[3] *Ibid.*, p. 256.

schools, industries and city agencies. Additionally, this approach will involve increased use of parents and students as educational resources.

As documented in a growing body of research, it is simply not the case that most parents of deprived urban youth do not value education in general, or education for *their* children in particular.[4] Thus, we may quite safely infer that they have strong feelings about and wish to be involved in the education of their children. The challenge to the school system, however, is to break down those barriers to participation in school affairs that many lower class parents find so formidable, and which sometimes force these parents to go outside the system to make themselves heard. Parents can be encouraged to participate by aggressive reaching-out policies such as those embodied in programs for all-day schools, and the use of parents as subprofessional classroom aides and detached community workers. This participation can yield administrators and teachers valuable personnel, a broader base of support for increased budgetary requests, and increased parental commitment to school policies.

Student involvement—as teachers in the educational process—has been encouraged most recently by Harold Taylor, former president of Sarah Lawrence College. He suggests that older youth can tutor younger children after school and on weekends as well as during regular school hours. This should have the effect of improving the skills and achievement level of both groups of students.

Conferences with parents, teenage representatives of all youth groups, teachers, and agency workers have also been successful in several cities. In some cities, Washington, D. C. among them, youth have set up independent organizations fashioned along the lines of the Office of Economic Opportunity (OEO) Community Action Centers. They employ youth and recruit volunteers to organize, canvas, and engage youth in the planning, advisory and programming phases of various functional areas including education. These are but a few of the types of participation that could result in "locking" students into education, thus preventing the dropping-out, and the loss of interest among those remaining in school.

This approach, as the foregoing examples should have documented, is not one of school unresponsiveness to or isolation from strictly educational problems and programs. All too often, in fact, the schools have independently implemented their programs and maintained a somewhat rigid autonomy from other segments of the community with some disregard to other social values. *What is suggested is a role of cooperation with and encouragement of other agencies, and a more selective participation in non-educational areas.* The problems of our big cities are complex and interwoven and thus require a concerted effort rather than an independent execution of narrowly conceived plans by individual agencies. The schools bring resources control to the community and are basic to a solution to the problems of the city. But they represent only one of the

---

[4] For example, see Richard Bloom, Martin Whiteman, Martin Deutsch, "Race and Social Class as Separate Factors Related to Social Environment," *American Journal of Sociology*, Vol. LXX (January, 1965), pp. 471-476.

major resources and, to be fully effective in carrying out their educational task, the schools must rely heavily on people, organizations and other disciplines.

The mechanism of state and federal aid offers great potential for assisting schools in both their financial crises and their reorganization efforts. Federal programs such as the Model Cities program provide for long-range planning, greater interagency coordination at the local level, and funds that can be used to upgrade the standard educational program, to shore-up other agencies and their service-rendering capability and to experiment and validate new educational arrangements.

Education stands as one of the most crucial and basic needs in society. But it does not stand alone and cannot do the job alone. There are several alternatives that the field of education should consider. My objective has been to sketch out some of the alternatives and possible consequences.

CHAPTER 11

The State Education Agency of the Future:
A Preview

WILLIAM H. ROE*

NOTE: *Let us assume that the reader has mounted a time machine which will move him immediately into the future where he has a chance to look in on a state education agency of 1980. For the purpose of anonymity, we shall call the state "Nova".*

It is difficult to establish a proper frame of reference so far in the future; therefore, certain conditions must be understood: (1) The Nova State Education Agency serves all levels of education and is an integral part of governmental operations; (2) each school district in the state has a minimum population of 10,000 and is capable of providing educational services for all children from kindergarten at least through grade 12; (3) teacher organizations have given up their internecine struggles and established one large professional organization; and (4) the population of the state in 1980 is about four million.†

A BACKWARD GLANCE FROM 1980

Looking back from the 1980 vantage point, it is apparent that the Nova State Education Agency has undergone substantial changes over the years. The struggle to bring about these changes, however, was not easy. Let us trace some of the events that led to the changes and reveal something of the agency's new role.

A most difficult step in the transition was to convince some educational leaders that many long-established organizational "principles" were inadequate for the emerging society. Even to propose changes contrary to these so called "principles" caused grievous conflicts among professional educators. Colleagues, in many cases, violently disagreed. Sometimes friends became foes. And sincere educators, vigorously defending old "principles", were bitter toward the "new thought" advocates whom they believed had "sold education down the river".

* Dean, School of Education, *University of Connecticut.* Chairman, Department of Administration and Higher Education, Michigan State University (1954-65); Assistant Superintendent of Public Instruction, Michigan Department of Public Instruction (1951-54). Publications include: (with Lee M. Thurston) *State School Administration* (1957); *School Business Management* (1961); *Schools Are News* (1960), and *Financing Michigan Schools* (1962).

† The author wishes to give special recognition for the assistance of those who provided advice and suggestions on this project, including: Dr. Samuel Brownell, jointly appointed as Distinguished Professor, University of Connecticut and Yale University; Dr. Ewald Nyquist, Deputy Commissioner, State Department of Education, State of New York; Dr. William Sanders, Commissioner of Education, State of Connecticut; and several members of the staff of the U. S. Office of Education.

This is the sad part of change. The happy part results from the improvements made possible by the changes that have been effected. Certainly the Nova State Education Agency is proving itself to be an organization which not only is adaptable to a changing society, but also is able to stimulate and facilitate educational change where needed.

The reorganized Nova State Education Agency originated from an objective and impartial study by a blue-ribbon "task force" appointed by the state legislature to make a thorough study and to submit a report in 1970. The assignment of this group was "to study the existing State Department of Education to determine if it is the best type of state education agency to serve the needs of a changing society."

The task force concluded that the diffused, uncoordinated system then in existence was woefully inadequate. The findings of the task force—the following ten in particular—had important implications for establishing the character and structure of the present state education agency:

1. Many of the staff services provided by the state department of education unfortunately appear to perpetuate and strengthen inadequate school districts. (The state should not blame shortcomings on inefficient school districts because the state created these districts and is responsible for them.)

2. The present department has the reputation of existing primarily to serve inadequate schools, mostly in small towns and rural areas.

3. City schools, growing suburban schools, colleges and universities are tending to deal with the federal government on their own and obtain little assistance from regular state agencies.

4. Virtually every educational institution and agency in the state—the university, the state colleges, schools for the handicapped, community colleges, local school districts, etc.—goes on its own uncoordinated way, doing what it thinks is best, growing farther apart and further dividing resources and personnel.

5. It is extremely difficult and often impossible for the governor to exercise proper executive direction to solve state-wide problems without responsible educational leadership working closely with him.

6. Crises facing the nation, state and local governmental units cannot command universal and rapid response because education is not a close and integral part of the main governmental structure.

7. There is a lack of unity and responsiveness in dealing with federal programs based on national policy and societal needs.

8. The present structure makes it difficult for various states to get together to solve their own regional-type problems.

9. Coordinated long-range planning is nonexistent.

10. The legislature is too often misinformed about education because its main sources of information are public relations and "lobby oriented" educational representatives rather than official educational consultants.

These were the key points of the 1970 report. As a result of these findings, the legislature passed two major pieces of educational legislation providing that:

1. A task force of educators and laymen is authorized to develop and propose a "model" education agency for the state (including the policy board, executive officer and department staff) which shall be gradually implemented beginning as soon as possible and fully operative by 1980. This task force is encouraged to recommend, in addition, new regional and state-wide structures which can provide

educational training, services and support not possible on a local basis, such as: central television instruction, computer centers, management services, advanced terminal-type vocational-technical education, adult education, and vocational retraining.

2. By 1978 all school districts of the state shall be reorganized so that they may economically and feasibly provide education for all children at least from kindergarten through grade twelve with the minimum supporting services. Only under special emergency situations shall a school district be formed with a total population of fewer than 10,000.

THE STATE BOARD OF EDUCATION

Perhaps the most controversial aspect of the reorganized Nova State Education Agency concerns the power and authority of the state board of education and its relationship to state government—especially to the executive and legislative branches.

Traditionally, education in the state had been a loosely-knit fourth branch of government operating rather independently from the regular legislative, executive and judicial branches. The "principle" accepted by most educators previous to the 70's was that educational government should be separated from the political processes of government—and especially from the partisan political processes.

While almost everyone still agrees that public education should have protection from the vicissitudes of partisan politics, the fallacy underlying the supposed separation of education from political processes became increasingly clear in the critical times of the early 1970's. Common sense and experience clearly indicated that all important educational policies must ultimately be legitimized through the political process. Perhaps even more important—at a time when intensive local, state, and national planning and cooperation of all agencies became essential in an effort to solve the problems brought on by rapid changes in society—it became evident that financial, personnel and other resources of the state were too divided for swift joint action. Insistence upon the complete independence of the education establishment in all matters, therefore, became unreasonable and illogical. The need was for a procedure whereby planning and resources could be coordinated and yet allow education to retain both independence from political parties and protection from the vicissitudes of partisan politics.

The solution was to continue the state board of education and establish it as *the overall coordinating and general policy body for education in the state,* with a minimum of administrative or judiciary authority but with a strong, high-level advisory responsibility to the legislative and executive branches of government relative to the support and coordination of education. The state board's major administrative act would be the recruitment and selection of a highly competent executive officer (chief state education officer). Its major coordinating acts would be to stimulate inter-institutional planning and to review budget requests from public educational institutions and agencies, then submit to the governor and the legislature its recommendations along with pertinent evidence and observations. Its major advisory act would be to provide to the legislative and executive offices broad policy statements which would lend direction to education in the state.

The solution proved to be a happy one for, under this new system, the state board of education soon became the most prestigious and respected board in the state. Its overall stature and method of operation sustains within the department and within the educational institutions a professional non-partisan climate where decisions are made on the basis of research findings and defensible criteria rather than in terms of personal biases or party politics.

The state board consists of twelve members with overlapping terms of seven years. Members are appointed by the governor from a list of the most able lay citizens in the state submitted by representatives of organizations including: the school boards association, the state parent-teacher association and the Nova State Education Association, Professional educators are not eligible for membership on the board. Representatives from these associations join in submitting a list of three names for each vacancy. The governor is then given authority to select and appoint from that list with the concurrence of the legislature. He is also charged with the responsibility of considering geographic, ethnic, social, economic and occupational segments of the state when making appointments to the board.

The Chief State Education Officer

The chief state education officer, now designated as "State Superintendent of Education", is a person selected on the basis of outstanding professional qualifications without regard to his state of origin. He is appointed by the board with the concurrence of the governor and serves at the pleasure of the board. While the salary is negotiable, the understanding is that it shall be at least equal to or above the salary paid the president of the state university and that of the highest paid school district superintendent in the state. In prestige and rank he is recognized as the chief educational officer of the state.

The chief state education officer has sole responsibility for the internal organization of the state department of education and for personnel appointments in accordance with policies of the civil service system, as adapted to meet the needs of an agency that must be staffed with highly competent professional personnel. While the chief state education officer is considered an integral part of the executive office for planning purposes, his relationship with the state board of education gives him the security of overall public support outside the regular governmental structures and protects the state agency from the vicissitudes of partisan politics.

Functions of the State Department of Education

The state department of education has become significantly different in goals and functions as the result of gearing itself to meet the needs of the 1980's.

No longer are its responsibilities limited to elementary and secondary education. Rather, *it has become the one agency of the state which concerns itself with the state's relationships, responsibilities, and interests in all aspects of education*—public and private, and elementary, secondary, higher and adult education.

Figure 1: *Nova State Education Organization*

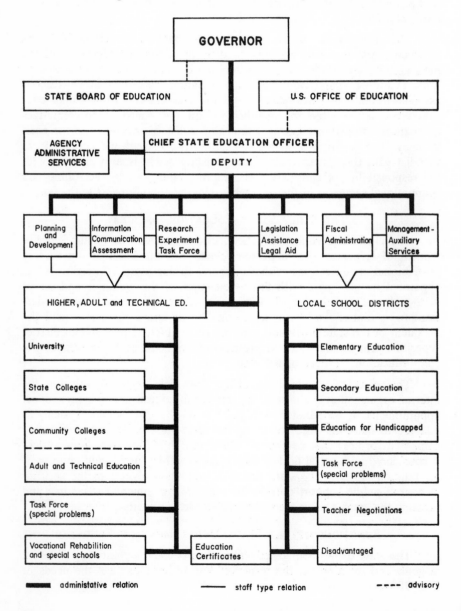

These relationships are not directly administrative and are definitely limited in control. *Each educational institution and agency has its own policy board and administrative officer.* Therefore, the state education agency, through its department of education, performs its functions for all aspects and levels of education in the state in essentially a staff or consultant relationship involving considerations such as the following: (a) areas of service, (b) status information, communication, and assessment, (c) clarification and implementation of legislation, (d) leadership and coordination, and (e) fiscal administration.

AREAS OF SERVICE

Executive. The state department of education has become, for certain purposes, the education section of the executive office of the state. It performs many functions such as: advising, providing reports and research, and working cooperatively with all other segments of the executive branch (such as highways, social welfare, public health, finance, urban affairs and housing) in determining and marshalling state educational resources relating to the multifarious problems of society.

Legislative. While the department of education serves, in effect, as the right arm of the executive for educational planning, it also provides an equally important service to the legislative branch. It supplies staff for legislative committees and its information service bureau is geared to furnish special assistance to legislators. It has set up an office specifically designed as contact for legislators needing data for proposed or pending educational legislation. Finally, it provides in-service education programs for legislators relative to educational developments.

Public. The service to the public is normally performed through the communications office, task forces and advisory committees which provide status and progress reports on all aspects of education.

Auxiliary or Facilitating Services. One of the major activities of the department of education had always been regulation, supervision and control of certain facilitating services performed by the local school districts. These have included a wide variety of management-type activities related to transportation, school lunch, school plant, textbooks, pupil accounting, data processing, budgeting and financial management.

The Nova State Education Agency still considers this a major area of concern, but much of the detail of this work has been eliminated through up-to-date management procedures, data processing and mechanized record keeping. Moreover, the larger school districts now are able to employ adequately-trained personnel to handle their own local operations and supervision. The state agency, therefore, is able to maintain a skeleton staff whose main functions are limited to state-wide in-service activities in establishing up-to-date and tested business management techniques, developing uniform policy and administrative patterns, and programming computers so that contemporary information on these activities is easily available.

Professional. The function of the department has changed radically in relationship to the profession. The local supervisory and specific curricular consultant aspects, normally considered a major function of the department of education, have been virtually eliminated now that most school districts in the state are large enough to have their own supervisors and local in-service education programs. Rather than working with individual schools or single teachers, the department now operates on a state-wide or a regional basis. Leadership is exerted through workshops, conferences, task force assignments, experimental programs and action research. Thus, the character of the staff has changed from a large number of specialists to a highly selected group of perceptive curriculum generalists particularly knowledgeable at the different levels of education.

The state department staff members, operating as perceptive generalists, serve as catalytic agents to stimulate the study of professional and educational problems throughout the state. These staff members also function as inter-communication agents, as rallying agents for the profession, and as general spokesmen for all education within the state.

One of the major services performed for the profession has been teacher certification. However, three changes in the past few years have made the process more of a procedural than a substantive matter. First, determination of initial and limited certification to teach in public schools has been made the responsibility of the preparing institutions. Each preparing institution is responsible for the development of its own quality programs and is approved for teacher training through the accrediting process. Second, following initial certification, teachers are termed "provisional" and are expected to demonstrate good teaching performance for three to five years under cooperative supervision of the preparing institution and of clinical teachers in the local school system. Finally, a teacher certification policy board of twelve people has been created (four representing the teaching profession, four representing the preparing institutions, and four representing local school boards). This board is responsible for developing policies regarding teacher certification in general, but specifically is responsible for establishing criteria and procedures for final certification of teachers as "career teachers" (after three to five years of teaching), including criteria for the administration and grading of the required examinations. A state department professional employee serves as executive secretary for this board with sufficient staff to do all the necessary paperwork.

Under these new procedures, then, the state department of education, acting for the teacher certification policy board, performs the following functions relative to certification: (a) record keeping, (b) administration of certification laws, and (c) coordination of all forces in the field concerned with teacher education.

INFORMATION, COMMUNICATION, AND ASSESSMENT

As the professional arm of the state agency for education, the state department of education has access to all available information on education; is able to render some judgment relative to the assessment of education; and is in a position to communicate with the public, the profession, and the various branches of government about this information.

The statistical information function is easily handled by a network of computers throughout the state. Each school district and institution of higher education has its computers tied in with the state education agency computer center and programmed so that machines can "talk to each other". At any time an up-to-the-minute status report on education can be obtained, and in addition needed information on any one subject is available from one or all institutions at the press of a computer button. The state computer center is part of a fifty-state network of uniformly programmed computers with the central "bank" or "control" in the U. S. Office of Education. National information on education can be obtained as easily and promptly as state information.

The communications office, operated in part as a press office, provides information, statistics, and news service to all segments of the population and to the government.

The assessment office is responsible for school and institutional accreditation and occasionally for specific assessment in areas of concern, doubt or need. It coordinates its activities with those of all independent accrediting agencies in education. Its method of operation and policy are determined by a professional advisory committee representative of major educational institutions and agencies of the state.

The state no longer conducts accreditation studies of its own but accepts the accrediting results of official regional accrediting associations on the basis of state approval for regular schools and colleges. For professional schools and colleges, accrediting approval is automatically granted upon full accreditation by the nationally-recognized professional accrediting association. For example, all teacher training programs are given automatic approval when accredited by the National Council for Accreditation of Teacher Education.

CLARIFICATION AND IMPLEMENTATION OF LEGISLATION

A major activity now performed by the state department of education is assistance with state and federal legislation. Now that the state education agency is looked upon by the state legislature as its major educational resource, the laws are more carefully developed and understood by educators and legislators. At the same time, with an increase in federal concern about education, the need for interpretation of federal legislation is becoming more apparent.

The new legislative and legal office has become an important staff function of the state department. It serves to clarify legislation, develop and codify administrative policy relative to implementation of legislation, and inform school districts, special schools, and institutions of higher education of minimum standards which they should be following. In addition, it operates closely with the attorney general's office when legal questions need to be answered.

Regulatory functions are still performed to assure that constitutional and statutory provisions in regard to education are being followed. However, this activity has become a minor one. Legislation of a regulatory nature normally merely establishes basic minimum levels of education. Now that the institutions themselves have been strengthened, they all maintain standards well above the minimum. As a result, the regulatory functions—formerly so important in state departments of education—have been supplanted by leadership, coordination and cooperative activities.

LEADERSHIP

Creative leadership has become the watchword for the staff of the Nova State Education Agency. Creative leadership is envisioned as a multiplying factor whereby leadership by the agency strengthens and encourages leadership at the various levels of education. The leadership functions of the state education agency may be categorized as follows.

Planning and Development. Not only is it necessary for the state education agency to look ahead at needs in education, but it has to consider the long-range future of society generally and work closely with other local, state and national agencies.

Events have shown clearly that a governmental unit cannot live by itself, and that society's problems transcend city and state boundary lines. It should be apparent, therefore, that planning and development cannot take place in the vacuum of agency administrative authority. There is urgent need for interlocking relationships with many levels of society.

This necessary broad dimension was added when the state education agency's planning and development office was created and charged with establishing formal working relationships with: (a) the state government planning and development commission; (b) regional research laboratories; (c) regional state education agency study and development groups made up of state educational agencies which have formed an interlocking association; (d) The Education Commission of the States; (e) the Study Commission of the National Council of Chief State School Officers; and (f) the U. S. Office of Education and its regional offices.

Planning and development is now realistically tied to all levels of society affecting the education of children. By the same token, with the broad formal relationships established through the planning and development function, the state is making a strong contribution to the development of national educational policy.

Communications. A second major leadership activity is the development of mutual understanding between schools and the public by keeping them constantly informed of the purposes, values, conditions and needs of education in the state, and by the creation of an atmosphere conducive to the improvement of education by establishing rapport among all agents of education and the public.

In-service Education. Here the goal is to encourage all persons in the state engaged in educational work to grow and to create professionally by identifying opportunities for broadening their education and experiences and by providing financial grants for workshops, conferences, seminars, travel, etc.

Coordination. Education within the society of the 1980's cannot be effective unless all levels of education are coordinated and unified as a major force. All members of the state department of education accept as their responsibility the "unified force" theme.

Research and Experimentation. A major area of leadership evidences itself in the encouragement of research, experimentation, model programs, demonstrations and regional projects. The state education agency carefully delineates its efforts by stating that only under special circumstances will it operate or conduct research, except for status and need studies which are an integral part of its central communication system. Rather, agency activity in research concerns itself primarily with identifying research needed in the state, establishing priority for this research, funding research, developing systems for coordinating research, and assisting with the dissemination of research results. Much of the formal research, while funded by or through the state education agency, is placed under the operation and direction of universities and colleges. Many of the regional projects are under the direction of regional laboratories, and experiments and model programs are jointly operated by regional boards composed of representatives of local schools, colleges and universities.

FISCAL ADMINISTRATION OF STATE, FEDERAL AND LOCAL FUNDS

Another essential operation of the state education agency is the administration of state funds. With about 25 percent of financial support coming from the federal government, 50 percent from the state, and only 25 percent from local sources, the state has to serve as the responsible fiscal agent. However, restrictive aspects of the aid programs have been minimized by eliminating line-item aid, most categorical aid programs except in emergency situations, and by establishing the state agency's fiscal office responsibilities as essentially bookkeeping, calculating and auditing *with few administrative controls.* However, proper management and accounting are assured through the auditing process.

Perhaps the most significant contribution of the division is its work with the chief state education officer and the state board of education in reviewing yearly budget requests from various state education institutions and assisting the board to develop a coordinated educational budget for the entire state which can be recommended to the governor and the legislature.

OPERATION OF PROGRAMS AND INSTITUTIONS

The principle has been well established that the state education agency will be diverted from its proper role if it engages in the operation of institutions and programs. Therefore, all programs and institutions formerly under the direct operational control of the state department of education have been phased out of existence or placed under new administrative patterns. The numerous research projects have been distributed mostly to the state university, the state colleges and private institutions; the technical institutes have been made part of the community college system; the special state schools for handicapped have been placed under a separate policy board; the audio-visual and exchange library has been turned over to Central State College along with the television curriculum center; the curriculum materials development and evaluation center has been moved to Western State College; and model teaching and laboratory programs have become the responsibility of selected local school districts with the understanding that the programs are for the benefit of all the schools of the state.

THE PROFESSIONAL STAFF

The professional staff of the state education agency can generally be grouped into four categories: (1) technical specialists, (2) professional education specialists, (3) educator-leaders who are perceptive generalists, and (4) specially designated task force personnel.

The technical specialists are those experts in technical areas such as computers, television, auditing and accounting, statistics and law.

The professional education specialists are employed in areas requiring specialized educational training such as reading, guidance and audio-visual. Such specialists are intentionally limited to a number sufficient only to round out the specialized knowledge of the total staff.

The educational consultants who are perceptive generalists represent the bulk of the state education agency personnel. With school districts large enough to have their own supervision, consultants and in-service education programs, the emphasis at the state level is on broad state-wide leadership exerted through workshops, conferences, experimental programs, task force studies, special emergency programs and research.

Rather than being loaded with subject matter specialists, the new state agency staff consists mostly of perceptive generalists knowledgeable in various substantive areas and levels of education. They are the persons trained in educational administration, curriculum, supervision, research and higher education with a broad liberal arts background. Selected for this role are professional people who are capable of thinking and operating from a total state and national perspective; who are concerned with unity and coordination of programs at all levels; and who are able to exert strong leadership in this direction.

The task force personnel group represents a new concept in state education agency operation. When the new organization was created it was agreed that a rapidly changing society would require numerous special studies and task force assignments in order to provide a basis for understanding many contemporary and future developments and for utilizing this information effectively. It would not be reasonable for the state education agency to maintain sufficient staff to handle all of these various special assignments. Colleges and universities, therefore, have agreed to encourage their faculty members to become available to the state agency for short task force assignments. As a result, red tape has been cut and personnel procedures simplified. Thus, university and college personnel can be—and are—brought in on special assignments for three months, six months, or a year without loss of retirement, tenure or salary benefits.

Thus, in a sense, the state education agency has available for assignment any and all personnel of the colleges and universities of the state. The result is a pool of highly-qualified personnel in research and in all of the various disciplines.

CIVIL SERVICE PROVISIONS

The state has a successful civil service system in operation, but many of the requirements suitable for normal state operation are not appropriate for a state education agency because of the necessity for hiring mostly professional personnel. Therefore, the state agency has been given authority to adapt civil service requirements to employment conditions so that competent educators and other professional personnel can be attracted to state positions.

To ensure that basic principles of civil service are not violated, a special civil service education committee has been formed. This committee works closely with the civil service commission and reviews procedures that might conflict with commission policies. Policies are developed which conform to the spirit of the civil service system, but which allow flexibility in employment and eliminate some of the mechanical procedures. In addition, a salary scale has been adopted for professional staff which conforms to the American Association of University Professors' "category A" rating so that the same caliber of staff can be attracted to the state educational agency as would be attracted to the best universities of the country.

NONPUBLIC SCHOOLS

The Nova State Education Agency long ago clarified the relationships of private and other nonpublic schools with public education. While the nonpublic school cannot be considered a partner of the state, it is highly regarded for its value in adding diversity and competition to the total system of education. Therefore, nonpublic schools are encouraged and protected. They even receive the benefit of services of the state education agency as long as public institutions are not denied services as a result.

The Nova State Education Agency has established the following principle as its guide in regard to nonpublic schools: The inherent freedom of our democracy gives individuals, groups and organizations the right to provide—at their own expense—educational institutions not detrimental to the safety of the state; these institutions must be distinct and independent from the publicly supported and operated state schools, but the state must exercise normal care to ensure safety of life, quality of instruction, legal competency of teachers, and maintenance of an adequate minimum general program of education.

Figure 2: *State Education Agency as Central Cog in the State Education System*
(Leadership, Communication, Coordination, Service)

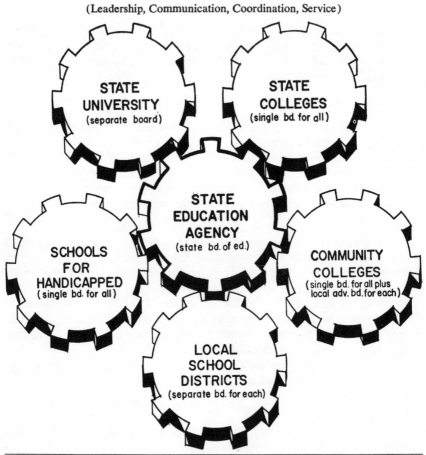

SUMMARY

The state system of education has experienced substantial change since 1970 when a new state education agency was first proposed. Now, in 1980, one can honestly claim that not only is the Nova State Education Agency adaptable to a changing society, but also that it can stimulate and facilitate change in the educational system as needed.

The agency has proved its strength and adaptability over the past few years in the following significant ways:

1.   Education has become a coordinated force within the State of Nova. Local school districts, community colleges, special schools, universi-

ties and colleges work together for the improvement of education. At the same time each institution maintains the integrity of its character through its own policy board.

2. The state education agency has become an integral part of governmental operation in the state. In effect, it serves as a member of the governor's team for education. The governor now is able to marshall the resources of the state quickly to solve emerging problems.

3. The state board of education has protected education and educators, including the chief state education officer and his staff, from the vicissitudes of partisan politics by its prestigious status, its sound policies and procedures and its consideration for the wishes of the people.

4. The organization of the state education agency, with its emphasis on leadership, service and communication, provides flexibility which allows the agency to gear itself quickly to the needs of education.

5. The state education agency has become as concerned about urban education as about rural education and has the resources to help effect improvements.

6. Cooperative planning involving other states has become an integral part of the agency's function so that problems which transcend state boundary lines can be solved.

7. The task force method of studying and recommending solutions to problems has proved to be highly successful. Recent important contributions made by the task force approach are in areas of international education, education of the disadvantaged, teacher negotiations and space age education.

8. Long-range planning on a coordinated local, state and national level has now become a reality.

9. With the phasing-out of the direct operation of programs and the de-emphasis on regulatory responsibilities, the staff of the state education agency now is able to devote its energy to leadership in planning and effecting improvements in education.

10. Now that the state agency works with all levels of education and no longer operates programs, the educational institutions of the state are being utilized to operate programs and services according to their best resources and abilities. For example, the community colleges as comprehensive post-secondary school institutions assume responsibility for much adult and technical education; the university for the formal research programs; Western State College has taken over curriculum materials development and evaluation; and Central State College operates instructional television and audio-visual services and exchange.

11. Undesirable competition and duplication of educational services has been eliminated through the state agency's "unity theme" and the state board of education's emphasis on inter-institutional planning and coordination of budgets.

12. Local school districts are continually being strengthened and sustained. If a smaller school district is not large enough to provide adequate services or instruction by itself, procedures are established so that they may combine resources with nearby school districts.

13. The agency is now able to work more closely with the federal government, particularly the U. S. Office of Education. It is officially designated by the legislature as the state's official contact agency with the federal government in matters related to education.

14. The state legislature has become more enlightened about education and its legislation more responsive to the needs of education as the legislature has accepted the state education agency consultants as part of its own staff.

* * *

SUPPLEMENTARY STATEMENT

WARREN G. HILL*

Dean Roe has provided an excellent model designed to "converge the educational resources of the state on the problems of a changing society." His identification of those resources and problems has been thorough, his analysis of the major responsibilities of central agencies shows great insight; his grouping of services clearly reflects both wide experience in—and study of—state departments of education. It is difficult to find areas of disagreement with most of Roe's suggestions, as the organization and proposed operation of his model generally reflect the best of what we now know. But I will raise certain questions which reflect my earnest belief that much of what we do can be improved and that that improvement will not occur without the best efforts of all of us.

While the prospect of being employed in the Nova State Education Agency would entice almost anyone, there are some questions about the operation that concern this writer. In planning ahead for the best possible agency in each state, it is incumbent on all of us to leave no stones unturned in our efforts to test out various organizational patterns and relationships. The questions which follow are offered in that spirit and might be seen as small "stone-turners".

Is 1980 REALLY JUST AROUND THE CORNER?

No one has to remind a man in middle age how quickly time flies, nor has there been any noticeable cessation of the constant reminders of accelerating change. My concern rests in the possibility that someone could have fed the wrong cards into the time machine which we are asked to mount. The cards included four conditions, only the last of which seems entirely appropriate. The conditions were: (1) the Nova State Education

* *Chief Administrative Officer, Connecticut Commission of Higher Education, Hartford.* **Formerly,** President, Trenton (N. J.) State College; and State Commissioner of Education, Maine.

Agency (hereafter NSEA) serves all levels of education and is an integral part of governmental operation; (2) each school district in the state has a minimum population of 10,000 and is capable of providing education for all children from kindergarten at least through grade 12; (3) teacher organizations have given up their internicine struggles and established one large professional organization; and (4) the population of the state in 1980 is about 4,000,000.

These conditions, or assumptions, are worth examining if they are to undergird the model being recommended. Having dispensed with item (4), items (2) and (3) can be grouped together and dismissed with brief comment. My basic concerns are with item (1).

I would like to believe that all school districts will have a population of 10,000 by 1980 *and that they will be capable of providing education for all children from kindergarten at least through grade 12*, but I do not. I have serious doubts that we are going to be able to rearrange our politics and dollars that fast, and that "capability" will mean "willingness". The burden on the state education agency will depend on how close we can get to perfection by 1980. It is not a long time.

Bringing the entire profession together by 1980 seems equally questionable. The emerging militancy of teachers, the unproductive and often unexamined conflict with the union, and the tenuous position of administrators as "negotiators" become matters for professional and legal determination. The reluctance of those in higher education to accord reasonable status to those who teach in elementary and secondary schools, and other related factors, tend to diminish the possibility of a unified enterprise by 1980. To the extent that it does not happen, the state education agency will have to commit manpower for coordination purposes.

The assumption that is most troublesome is the one that makes the NSEA "an integral part of the government operation." In fact, it is such an agency now—but not in the sense suggested. Noting that, in the 1970's "Insistence upon complete independence of the education establishment became unreasonable", the agency was made for certain purposes "the education section of the executive office", and the chief state school officer "an integral part of the executive office for planning purposes."

Major Concern

This arrangement tends to disregard both political reality and human frailty. The "setting apart" of education was not something dreamed up by educators to make their lives easy; it was arranged by political leadership that placed too great a value on the enterprise to permit it to be subjected to political partisanship. The attractive requirement, ascribed to the model, that education be "allowed to retain both independence from political parties and protection from the vicissitudes of partisan politics" would have little meaning if the relationship with the executive branch were to be implemented as stated. Governors are both the recipients of great pressure and the generators of it. Coordination with a governor's office and among the various constituents of a state's educational enterprise can be obtained without embracing a potentially unproductive relationship.

The appointment of the chief state education officer should be the responsibility of the state education agency. The day the governor has a hand in it, the incumbent becomes, in the public mind, "the governor's man." No board, however highly esteemed, can then protect him from the political pressures that necessarily exist in and around the state's highest office. If it could be assumed that all men, having attained high elected office, would thereafter always choose the right and the beautiful rather than the votes, there would be no problem. A chief state education officer should work tirelessly to provide a governor with any and all information or assistance desired. When major state problems are being attacked, this officer should speedily provide every resource available to him. And when he is asked to approve a new program on the basis of political expediency rather than educational merit, appoint someone whose basic qualification has been his success in delivering votes, or approve a grant where it is not warranted, he should be able to tell the governor it cannot be done. The education agencies will indeed become "prestigious and respected" as they develop and recommend sound public policy—but not by serving as the education section of the executive office.

WHAT PROVISION IS MADE FOR SUSTAINING PUBLIC CONFIDENCE IN EDUCATION?

The NSEA, as presented, is a potential model of efficiency. When buttons are pushed, answers are forthcoming. A communications office is provided. Legislators are assisted and educated. Agency personnel participate in workshops and conferences. Federal money is obtained and utilized effectively. Formal relationships with regional and national agencies are established. Coordination goes on apace.

Major Concern

These are positive and valuable activities and attributes. Thought must be given, however, to the distance which separates an agency, so oriented, from the public that supports it. In this country, we have held out education as the golden key to opportunity for everyone—as a means of cultural, economic and social advancement. We have often urged support for the schools on that basis. Certain recent developments tend to qualify this belief. Among them are:

- Some parents find it most difficult to understand why the schools are demanding such tremendous amounts of work from their children. There does not seem to be time left for normal living or even growing up;

- Many communities provide all of the support requested but still children fail and drop out of school. Not all of these children are low in mental ability and public concern mounts;

- Communications media tend to relate essentially negative items about the schools—probably because they are more "newsworthy". The typical citizen has been getting a fair amount of this in recent years and, because it is published, tends to accept much of it. When the critic happens to be well-known and venerated, accepting what is said—without examination—is that much easier.

An office of *Improvement in Public Service* would provide a means of:

• identifying emerging problems of particular concern to the public;

• bringing together information, knowledge of superior practice, innovative suggestions and concerned officials; and

• answering all requests or appeals, in cooperation with the school system or institution of higher education involved.

CAN A SINGLE AGENCY REALLY COORDINATE THE ENTIRE EDUCATIONAL ENTERPRISE IN A STATE?

The NSEA recommended by Dean Roe might come very close to doing it. It would appear, though, that the chances of bringing the task off completely might depend upon some rather basic agreements that would have to be made early in the game. Coordination is a magnificent concept. No problem exists until an effort is made to coordinate something —then aggreived parties can rise like Phoenix from the ashes. To the extent that these parties can circumvent the coordinating agency, the promise of the endeavor is lost.

Major Concern

The fourth finding of the Nova Task Force, prior to the re-directing of the state education agency, is of interest here:

Virtually every existing educational institution and agency in the state—the university, the state colleges, schools for the handicapped, community colleges, local school districts, etc.—goes its own uncoordinated way, doing what it thinks is best, growing further apart and further dividing resources and personnel.

To remedy this situation, the NSEA—tied rather tightly to the governor's office—is asked to "stimulate inter-institutional planning and to review budget requests from public educational institutions and agencies, then submit to the governor and the legislature its recommendations along with pertinent evidence and observations." It is seen as limited in control— not directly administrative—and performing "its functions for all aspects and levels of education in the state in essentially a staff or consultant relationship . . ." Each agency and institution is to have its own policy-making board and administrative officer.

It is difficult to argue with these concepts, but they tend to place great reliance on universal adoption of the Golden Rule. Unfortunately, not everyone wants to be coordinated. Some see the value in it, but others see central agencies as bureaucratic monstrosities created solely to circumvent their plans for the future. The fact that those plans encompass the mission of every other type of institution in the state, or would utilize effectively every tax dollar, or include every secondary school graduate, has little significance.

Coordination is indeed the most vital role to be played by a central education agency. This fact has been clearly seen by the legislature in the more than thirty states that have created coordinating agencies. Coordination, and the need for it, is also reflected in the emerging regional activities in education and the federal interest therein.

Areas of prior agreement which would complement the model suggested might be:

1. The provision, in the statutes, that certain areas of policy-making would be restricted to the NSEA, e.g., determining what type of new institution of higher education is to be created, where and when.

2. The requirement, in the statutes, that the proposals of any agency for development be submitted to the NSEA before being publicly announced.

3. The governor and legislature would agree to deal solely with the NSEA, subject only to the provision of appeal with the full knowledge of the NSEA.

4. Budget requests not to be reviewed by the state's fiscal officers. These officials can play a significant role in assisting the governor with his suggested distribution of the state's financial resources. Determining the ingredients that go into a total educational system, evaluating them and suggesting any required modification is an appropriate and basic function for a central education agency.

5. Formal, interlocking memberships, as well as meetings between operating agencies and the NSEA would be required.

Coordination is the major function of a central agency such as the one proposed. It has small chance of effectiveness without specified commitments of the kind cited.

Does the Model Have Any Parts Missing?

Dean Roe has indicated a broad range of responsibilities and activities clearly intended to provide anything that a society might demand of an agency established to provide leadership, coordination and service. The "parts" that follow may already be in place, but added visibility for them will do no harm.

Major Concern

There are activities that tend not to happen if they are left as "everyone's business." A central education agency might give appropriate attention to:

Finding and Developing Talent. Talent tends to be a scarce commodity. Considerable effort should be made to locate those who have the talent to go to college and are not getting there, those who are inspired teachers and whose services should be secured for the schools and colleges of the state; and those who can hold responsible positions in the state education system if they are helped to do so.

Backing up the "Perceptive Generalists." If education can be compared to a game, it might be appropriate to say that the playing field is the same, but the players and the rules are changing. The mobility of our people, the concentration of minority groups in our cities, the ineffectiveness of old solutions in new situations—all contribute to a need for new approaches. Beyond the thinkers, there needs to be men who understand and speak the language of the poor, the oppressed and the newly-arrived —of laymen as well as educators. At the state, local and institutional levels, men are needed who are accepted by administrators, teachers, parents and pupils—who may have a lower level of formal preparation in education than normally is required, but whose experience and/or preparation allow them to understand what is needed, and who are dedicated to helping obtain it.

The demise of the subject matter specialist was fore-ordained. His replacement can be a specialist in human affairs.

Asking Questions. If there is money enough involved, or prestige enough, most individuals and agencies tend to "back off" and leave well enough alone. Asking questions can lead to controversy, and inquiries as to who wants that?

No department can be formed for "Asking Questions". If questions are to be asked—the important ones—there must be a climate that permits and encourages such questioning. I can think of nothing more beneficial to a central education agency than the existence of such a climate. It will not exist without a determined effort on the part of the state board of education, the chief state education officer and top-echelon staff members. When it does exist, such things as the following can happen.

• All research will not automatically lead to positive results. Too many times, we allow the same people to design an experiment, carry it out and evaluate it. It would seem that there are few failures. Some questions need to be asked.

• Statutes and regulations will be less sacred. Sometimes years go by before someone questions whether we are admitting the right students to college, whether the task of an elementary teacher is manageable, or whether teachers aides have to have a college degree. Here, too, some questions need to be asked and the central agency is a most propitious place to begin.

• Federally-supported programs will be evaluated in terms of their impact. It is quite possible, for instance, for an institution of higher learning to operate three consecutive summer sessions offering courses in teaching the new math but fail to include any such offering during the academic year for undergraduate students.

There could be other examples, but these may suffice.

Dean Roe's model has few parts missing. If every state in America could be halfway to the level of professional and public service he proposes by 1980, we could rightfully celebrate in the streets!

CHAPTER 12

State Planning for Education

JACK CULBERTSON*

Is it possible that the historians of the twenty-first century will view the current decade as a period when Americans began to use new approaches to planning in a variety of large and complex organizations including educational institutions? Any answer to this question at this point must be speculative and tentative in character; however, a case can be made that an important shift in attitudes toward—and approaches to—problem solving and planning may now be taking place in American society.

The potential shift can be illustrated by contrasting some concepts set forth in a 1962 book by Charles Frankel[1] with those delineated in an article by Max Ways[2] published in early 1967. The first chapter in Frankel's book is entitled "The Politics of Malaise." In this chapter he emphasizes certain themes which were dominant during the 1950's and early 1960's, such as: "the lonely crowd," "the organization man," "the mass society," "the hidden persuaders," and "conformity". "Malaise", in Frankel's view, is associated with a "sense of helplessness and drift" and a lack of what he calls an "inspiriting conception of democracy." Unfocused worries resulting from unclear directions and from ill-defined problems are concomitants of "malaise" as is "moral ennui"—a condition characterized by a lack of meaning, commitment, and purpose in the lives of many citizens. Near the end of his chapter, Frankel postulates that:

> We have lost our assurance about what the facts are, and we have lost something even more fundamental—an assured language in which to speak about the facts, to judge them, and to manage them.[3]

The article by Max Ways presents another side of the picture. Early in his statement he refers to some of the problems of society with which Frankel was concerned. The following passage illustrates the point:

> Specialization of knowledge and work required large and complex organizations; these raised fears that individuality would be attenuated, that an "organization man," blank and malleable, might replace his admirably hard-nosed ancestor. This feared sacrifice of individuality, repugnant on democratic and moral

* Executive Director of The University Council for Educational Administration, Columbus, Ohio. Has taught in elementary and secondary schools and in higher education. Has authored, edited or co-edited a number of books including: Educational Research: New Perspectives; Preparing Administrators: New Perspectives; and The Professorship in Educational Administration. Currently Vice President of American Educational Research Association, member of the Commission on Administrative Technology of the American Association of School Administrators and of the Publications Subcommittee of the AERA. During 1966-67 he has served as a consultant to the Ford Foundation, the W. K. Kellogg Foundation, and the Education Commission of the States.

[1] Charles Frankel, The Democratic Prospect (New York: Harper and Rowe, 1962), pp. 1-9.
[2] Max Ways, "The Road to 1977," Fortune, January, 1967, pp. 93 ff.
[3] Frankel, op. cit., p. 9.

grounds, would not even be compensated for by an augmented sense of social warmth or common purpose. We were moving, obviously, but weren't we adrift?[4]

NEW APPROACHES TO PLANNING

Although Ways clearly recognizes the general problem identified by Frankel, he quickly moves away from it to concentrate upon describing an implied solution. The suggested solution is a "new style of private and public planning, problem solving, and choosing," which, in his view, can provide a missing ingredient and improve the quality of American life. While he admits that there is as yet no universally accepted title for the new style of planning, Ways maintains that the method is subsumed under such concepts as planning-programming-budgeting-systems, operations research, systems analysis, and systems planning. More specifically, he indicates that the following characteristics typify the newer approaches to planning:

(1) a more open and deliberate attention to the selection of ends toward which planned action is directed, and an effort to improve planning by sharpening the definition of ends,

(2) a more systematic advanced comparison of means by criteria derived from the ends selected,

(3) a more candid and effective assessment of results usually including a system of keeping track of progress toward interim goals. Along with this goes a "market-like" sensitivity to changing values and evolving ends,

(4) an effort, often intellectually strenuous, to mobilize science and other specialized knowledge into a flexible framework of information and decision so that specific responsibilities can be assigned to the points of greatest competence,

(5) an emphasis on information, prediction, and persuasion rather than on coercive or authoritarian power, as the main agent of coordinating the separate elements of an effort,

(6) an increased capability of predicting the combined effect of several kinds of simultaneous actions on one another; this can modify policy so as to reduce unwanted consequences or it can generate other lines of action to correct or compensate for such predicted consequences.[5]

Not only does the new planning style represent a significant new social means but, more important, it can—according to Ways—help to generate in the public mind a sense of direction and intelligent choice among competing values. It can, in other words, help to ensure that our evolving capabilities and our evolving values advance compatibly. Contrary to Frankel's view concerning our incapacities to judge and manage facts, Ways believes that in the new method we have a way of organizing facts in a very meaningful fashion as well as a mechanism for mobilizing "specialized and value-free science to work on practical problems."

The new approach to planning is viewed as most appropriate during the current period of unprecedented change when the questions of "What does it all mean?" and "Where is it all headed?" are being persistently raised, often in a disquieting fashion. By bringing to bear the new methods

---

[4] Ways, *op. cit.*, p. 93.
[5] *Ibid.*, p. 95.

on problems of government, Ways argues, science can be democratized. Thus, he enthusiastically endorses the new planning techniques as "the greatest advance in the art of government since the introduction nearly 100 years ago of the civil service based upon competence. The new style, indeed, corrects an old defect of bureaucratic organization, which was at its best when performing routine tasks, at its worst in innovating and generating forward motion."[6] One of his major conclusions is the following: *"The further advance of this new style is the most significant prediction that can be made about the next ten years. By 1977 the new way of dealing with the future will be recognized at home and abroad as a salient American characteristic."*[7]

Whether or not the contrasting views of Frankel and Ways represent only the perspectives of two differing individuals or, in fact, a new watershed in American history cannot yet be foretold. However, it is plainly evident that the concepts underlying the new style of planning are having—and certainly, for the foreseeable future, will continue to have—an increasing influence on many sectors of American life. *One of these sectors is education.* That education is already being influenced by the new emphases on planning is indicated by the title of this project: "Designing Education for the Future."

We would do well initially to understand some of the forces that underlie the trend toward more conscious and systematic planning in education. Therefore, the next section of the paper will seek to describe selected forces underlying the trend. This will be followed by a description of emergent planning techniques, a recommended strategy to advance state educational planning, and a delineation of some implications which stem from the thrust toward planning in education.

WHY THE PRESS TOWARD EDUCATIONAL PLANNING?

What are the major factors that are influencing the trend toward systems planning in educational institutions? The following are judged to be among the most important ones: the increasing value being placed upon quality education and the impact upon citizens and their leaders of the increasingly large investments to achieve quality; the trend toward the use of more systematic planning in state and federal government generally; the large planning capacity of the business community and its growing involvement in education; and the increasingly wide array of tested planning techniques which are now available for use. Each of these factors deserves further delineation.

THE IMPACT OF RAPIDLY INCREASING INVESTMENTS IN EDUCATION

One of the obvious reasons for the increased interest in educational planning stems from the sheer size of investments in education. Not only are large amounts of money being invested currently, but the size of these

---

[6] *Ibid.*, p. 95.
[7] *Ibid.*, p. 94.

amounts continues to grow rapidly. In 1962, for example, expenditures for education were $31,150,000,000. In 1975, according to projections made by Leonard Lecht, our aspirations for educational investments, as measured in dollars required, will be $85,950,000,000.[8] In a period of thirteen years, then, investments in education will be more than doubled. Such an accelerated rate of investment will soon make education the nation's number one industry. As more and more funds are allocated to education, it is understandable that the general concern about allocation decisions will become more intense. As a result of this concern, two questions are being raised explicitly and with greater frequency by thoughtful citizens. First, are we getting our money's worth from current investments in education? Second, do we have the necessary planning and assessment arrangements to ensure that future investments will be productive of the highest quality education possible?

The first question, of course, is one which has been put to educational administrators many times in the past. However, in recent years those responsible for educational legislation as well as elected government executives are also under increasing pressure to seek a satisfactory answer to the question. In large cities, for example, where the competition for the tax dollar is very intense, concern about whether or not optimum value is being obtained from the dollars invested in education is increasingly evident. John Lindsay, Mayor of New York City, is a case in point. Early in his administration he noted that his city was spending considerably more per pupil than were other large cities of similar size; he went on to say that he would be asking for "performance data" when he considers financial support for schools in the future.[9]

Concern at the state level is reflected in a recent statement by Jesse M. Unruh, Speaker of the California Assembly: "In my judgment well-informed legislators, governors and administrators will no longer be content to know, in mere dollar terms, what constitutes the abstract needs of the schools. . . . The politician of today, at least in my state, is unimpressed with continuing requests for more input without some concurrent idea of the schools' output."[10]

The concern among legislators at the federal level of government about wise allocation of resources is evident from statements reported through the mass media. A concrete expression of congressional concern is found in Title I of the Elementary and Secondary Education Act (ESEA) of 1965 which requires that these programs be evaluated at least annually by objective measures. Obviously, the proponents of such measures are concerned about the value obtained from investments and, more specifically, about the relationships between financial inputs and educational outputs.

[8] See Chapter 1, "Strategic Variables in Planning."

[9] Quoted in Ewald Nyquist, "Emergent Functions and Operations of State Education Departments," in *The Emerging Role of Education Departments with Implications for Vocational Education.* Center for Vocational and Technical Education, The Ohio State University (in press).

[10] "State Planning for Tomorrow's Schools," *Newsletter,* National Committee for Public Schools, 1424 Sixteenth Street, Washington, D. C., p. 2.

Another force affecting planning in education is the increasing use of systematic planning methods in federal and state government generally. At the federal level an extremely important symbol of this tendency was President Johnson's decision in 1965 to require the various agencies of government to institute and use the Planning-Programming-Budgeting-System (PPBS). Another evidence of recognition of the significance of this system is found in the text of President Johnson's 1967 budget message to Congress. The following quotation from a section in the budget message indicates the role of PPBS in the federal government:

> Our most comprensive effort to improve the effectiveness of government pro-grams is taking place through the Planning-Programming-Budgeting-System. This System, which was initiated throughout the Executive Branch a little over a year ago, requires all agencies to: make explicit the objectives of their programs and relate them carefully to national needs, set out specific plans of work to attain these objectives, and analyze and compare the probable costs and benefits of these plans against alternate methods of accomplishing the same results.[11]

A few states are beginning to apply PPBS systems to state government planning. Wayne F. McGown, Director of the Bureau of Management of the Department of Administration in Wisconsin, recently described the installation and use of this system in his state.[12] He believes PPBS is essentially an executive tool but argues that it can be applied both to executive and to legislative decision making. He discusses the relationship of the tool to education in general terms as follows: "PPBS provides a bridge between two basic elements fundamental in a democratic society: legislative concern for the purse strings and the necessity in a democracy of a free, yet responsive, system of education. PPBS is one way in which this conflict can be resolved."[13]

Not only is there an expanding interest in state planning among elected and appointed leaders in government but, also, new organizations are being created to encourage and facilitate the application of planning tech-niques to state government. On January 31, 1967, for example, the Carnegie Corporation announced a grant of $385,000 to support an Institute on State Programming for the '70's, to be located at the University of North Carolina. The Institute will seek to bridge relationships between scholarly activities of universities and planning procedures within the political context of state government. Jack Campbell, who recently com-pleted a term as Governor of New Mexico, is heading up the new Institute. Terry Sanford, who developed the Institute idea, made the following observation concerning its relevance to state planning: "The national commitment to land a man on the moon by the 1970's has uncovered an

---

[11] The *New York Times*, Wednesday, February 25, 1967, p. 21.
[12] Wayne F. McGown, "How to Apply Programming-Planning-Budgeting in Your State," National Conference of Legislators, Washington, D. C. (Mimeographed).
[13] *Ibid.*, p. 1.

incredible array of new techniques and devices. The design of a 'guidance system' for state government is one of the central tasks of the Institute."[14]

THE APPLICATION OF THE PLANNING CAPACITIES OF THE BUSINESS COMMUNITY TO EDUCATION

Certainly another factor relating to planning which should not be overlooked is the influence of the business community. This influence stems from the general interest of leaders in the business community in innovation and efficiency in education as well as in the specific planning techniques they have developed and are developing. One example of the general influence can be seen in the recent work of the Committee for Economic Development and, more specifically, its subcommittee on "Efficiency and Innovation in Education." This committee is "reviewing the entire learning-instruction process through the twelfth grade and trying to ascertain ways in which cost-benefit analysis and new teaching techniques can help improve both quality and efficiency in education.[15]

Only one illustration of an industry which is developing specific planning techniques relevant to state educational planning will be offered. In the January issue of Fortune, in an article entitled "Where the Industries of the Seventies Will Come From,"[16] plans by large corporations to apply systems-management techniques to non-defense and non-industrial areas are described. The Lockheed Corporation, for example, is already doing substantial development work, particularly in designing and testing information systems which can and will support planning activities. The Corporation has designed what may become the state of California's ten-year plan for data processing. Such a plan, when operationalized, should support a number of state planning activities, including those associated with education. The relevance and potential impact on education of the growing planning and development capacities of industry is also suggested by the fact that Lockheed, with the aid of a U. S. Office of Education grant of $85,000, is now engaged in development work to speed the transmission of information to secondary schools.

THE AVAILABILITY OF TESTED PLANNING TECHNIQUES

The array of planning procedures and techniques that have been developed and tested in various fields during the last two decades is another factor helping to pave the way toward more effective planning in government generally and in education specifically. There are at least three different but somewhat interrelated planning traditions which have evolved in recent decades and which have implications for educational planners. First, a small group of economists have developed and refined planning procedures which enable them to forecast educational needs and to devise educational plans to advance economic and social development in developing nations. Second, an array of planning techniques is

[14] "A Study of American States" (College Station, Durham, North Carolina, News Release), January 31, 1967, p. 4.
[15] See *Saturday Review*, January 14, 1967, pp. 37 ff.
[16] Lawrence Lessing, "Where the Industries of the Seventies Will Come From," *Fortune*, January, 1967, pp. 97 ff.

found in the technology associated with operations research; a number of the operations research techniques which are available are highly developed ones. Finally, PPBS—which is an outgrowth of operations research—is another planning tradition which encompasses important planning techniques. The array of planning methods available and of techniques which have potential application to education is a very significant factor in the increased interest in planning among educators. In other words, if planning is to be advanced, there must be an appropriate technology to support it. A further significant fact is that specific planning techniques now available can be supported and enhanced by emergent computer technology. The combination makes it possible to cope with large and complex planning problems.

EMERGENT PLANNING TECHNOLOGIES

Very early in the study of administration, planning was identified as a significant process in organizations. Thus, the "P" in Gulick's famous acronym, POSDCORB stood for planning.[17] Various concepts on planning have been elaborated since Gulick's statement and a number of books have been written setting forth theories in planning.[18]

Even though theories of planning have existed for a number of decades, it is only in the last twenty years that precise techniques have been developed to support planning activities. The three somewhat interrelated traditions of operations research, planning-programming-budgeting-system, and educational planning based upon manpower projections encompass most of the techniques developed.

OPERATIONS RESEARCH

Perhaps the most refined and extensive set of planning techniques is associated with operations research (OR). Initiated in Great Britain shortly before the second World War, operations research was applied first to radar problems. During the fifties the movement spread into various countries and was employed in different kinds of governmental and industrial organizations. The first conference on operations research in the United States was held at the Case Institute of Technology in Cleveland in 1951.[19] The various techniques associated with operations research had the greatest immediate impact upon business corporations. By the early 1960's, for example, more than one-third of the 500 largest corporations in the United States were using OR as an aid to planning and decision making.

Ackoff and Rivett, among others, have set forth their views about what they consider to be some of the major characteristics of operations research.[20] One notable characteristic of OR is its special orientation to

---

[17] Luther Gulick and L. Urwick, eds., *Paper on the Science of Administration* (New York: Institute of Public Administration, 1937), p. 13.

[18] For an example, see Preston P. Le Breton and Dale Henning, *Planning Theory* (Englewood Cliffs, N. J.: Prentice Hall, Inc., 1961).

[19] Russell L. Ackoff and Patrick Rivett, *A Manager's Guide to Operations Research* (New York: John Wiley & Sons, Inc., 1963).

[20] *Ibid.*, pp. 1-61.

problem definition. Rather than cutting complex problems "down to size"—which tends to be the pattern of basic researchers—operations researchers seek to look at problems in the large. They do this on the assumption that the activity of any part of an organization may have an important impact on other aspects of the system. The problem of assigning personnel, for example, may be intimately related to in-service training, clique structure, work schedules, and so forth. In the process of defining problems much attention is given to identifying significant interactions between the various sub-units of organizations as well as between the processes which take place in organizations. Because of the encompassing approach of OR and its capacity to deal with large-scale and complex problems, large quantities of information are often required.

A second characteristic of operations research is that it is conducted by a team of specialists. The number and kinds of specialists required depend to some extent on the problem area being considered. However, it is typically assumed that complex problems cannot be understood—nor can their consequences be predicted—by the use of any one discipline or set of scientific concepts. Therefore, economists, urban sociologists, mathematicians, information scientists, computer experts, and a variety of other specialists might participate in defining problems and in designing solutions to them.

A third characteristic of significance is that operations researchers act on the explicit belief that systems cannot be controlled in their original environments. For this reason, they do not entertain the idea of specific experimentation in the classical sense. Rather, the strategy for coping with complex problems is to represent them through mathematical equations. For example, programming techniques involving mathematical equations can be used to resolve a variety of resource allocation problems. A simple illustration of one approach to the use of programming techniques can be found in large-scale menu planning. What menus, for example, will best meet the following criteria: basic nutrient values; a reasonable degree of variety in dishes each day and from day to day; and economic efficiency? By developing measures for each criterion, by assigning mathematical values to the criteria, and by using programming equations, Ronald Gue of the University of Florida has achieved optimal solutions to the menu planning problem within the context of selected hospitals.[21]

In the process of simulating the complexities of reality, it is necessary for operations researchers to use computers and special information-processing techniques. A very important part of the team's work is to determine those aspects of environments which can, and those which cannot, be controlled by responsible agents of the system. Obviously, whatever solutions are developed must be based upon variables which are susceptible to control.

One other characteristic of OR's general methodology is its involvement in the implementation of results. In the words of Ackoff and Rivett:

---

[21] Ronald L. Gue, "Selective Menu Planning by Computer," *Proceedings*, American Society for the Advancement of Food Services Research, October 4, 1965.

. . . The real test of results must come in their application in the real world. For this reason OR workers must translate their results into a set of instructions for management and operating personnel. These instructions should indicate in detail who is to do what, when and how they are to do it. In effect, the researchers must provide a *program* which is similar to the programs prepared for electronic computers. Only with such detailed instructions can assurance be had that the results of the research are being fairly tested.[22]

Because of the concern for implementation, operations researchers must work closely with the managers of organizations in which the techniques are to be applied. This reduces problems of communication and misunderstanding and helps to ensure a fair test of the solutions proposed.

Operations researchers agree that the content of problems varies from organization to organization. However, they maintain that the forms are similar. Ackoff and Rivett have identified eight classes or forms of management problems to which, in their judgment, operations research techniques can be applied in all kinds of organizations.[23] The categories of problems conceptualized by Ackoff and Rivett are: allocation, routing, sequencing, competition, search, inventory, queuing, and replacement. During the last two decades a variety of mathematical equations have been developed for dealing with problems related to the various classes of planning decisions noted by Ackoff and Rivett. One illustration of a technique now becoming increasingly known, which may involve the use of mathematical formula, is PERT (Program Evaluation and Review Technique). This technique, which deals with sequencing and the scheduling of work, has been used in the establishment of a community college, the administration of research projects, and the management of government programs funded by the ESEA. Central to the use of the technique are the processes of breaking tasks down into logical sequences of steps, estimating the time required to perform the various steps, and determining the most efficient sequencing of the steps. A recent publication describes the basic characteristics of PERT and its potential application to a variety of research and development activities in education.[24] Recent work by Stankard and Sisson points to the eventual utility of operations research techniques for improving over-all planning in urban school districts.[25]

PLANNING-PROGRAMMING-BUDGETING SYSTEMS

PPBS may be described as an offshoot of the operations research movement. Operations research techniques, which were being widely used by large industrial concerns in the United States in the early 1960's, began to be adapted about that time to planning decisions within the governmental context. There is some evidence that the full application of mathematical formulae and quantitative measures associated with operations research has been more difficult to achieve within the governmental than in the business context.

---

[22] Ackoff and Rivett, p. 31 (see footnote 19).
[23] *Ibid.*, pp. 34-61.
[24] Desmond Cook, *Program Evaluation and Review Technique: Applications in Education* (Washington, D. C.: U. S. Department of Health, Education and Welfare, 1966).
[25] Martin Stankard, Jr., and Roger L. Sisson, *Operations Research and Improved Planning for an Urban School District: Definitions and a Simulation Model* (Philadelphia: University of Pennsylvania, Technical Memo #11667).

The decision by Robert McNamara in 1961 to apply systems planning to decisions in the Department of Defense may be described as the beginning of the first phase of the PPBS movement. At that time McNamara asked Charles Hitch, who had served as chief economist for the Rand Corporation, to take over the main task of adapting rigorous decision and planning methods to the Defense Department. The success of McNamara and his staff in applying systems analysis to defense planning has been described by Seligman, among others, and needs no detailed treatment here.[26]

The second stage in the development of PPBS involved the spread into agencies of government outside the defense establishment. A landmark in the spreading or diffusion process was President Johnson's press conference on August 25, 1965, when he made the following announcement:

> This morning I have just concluded a breakfast meeting with the Cabinet and with the heads of federal agencies and I am asking each of them to immediately begin to introduce a very new and very revolutionary system of planning and programming and budgeting throughout the vast federal government. . . . This program is designed to achieve three major objectives: it will help us find new ways to do jobs faster, to do jobs better, and to do jobs less expensively. It will ensure a much sounder judgment through more accurate information, pinpointing those things that we ought to do more, spotlighting those things that we ought to do less. It will make our decision making process as up-to-date, I think, as our space-exploring programs.

Bulletin No. 66-3 was issued from the Executive Office of the President to all "Heads of Executive Departments and Establishments" some weeks after the President's press conference.[27] In this bulletin the reasons for instituting PPBS were described and instructions for establishing the system were delineated. The importance of relating programming to budgeting activities was emphasized in the bulletin, and the limitations in existing practice were described as follows:

> Under present practices, however, program revision for decision making has frequently been concentrated within too short a period; objectives of agency programs and activities have too often not been specified with enough clarity and concreteness; accomplishments have not always been specified concretely; alternatives have been insufficiently presented for consideration by top management; in a number of cases the future year costs of present decisions have not been laid out systematically enough; and formalized planning and systems analysis have had too little effect on budget decisions.[28]

Each agency was instructed to develop (1) an analytic capacity which would require permanent specialized staffs to do "in-depth" studies of agency objectives and of various programs to meet these objectives; (2) a multi-year planning and programming process which would ensure the gathering and presenting of data in ways that would aid agency heads and the President in making major decisions; and (3) a budget process which would take program decisions, translate them into more refined

---

[26] Daniel Seligman, "McNamara's Revolution," *Fortune,* July, 1965, pp. 177 ff. For a more comprehensive report see Charles Hitch, *Decision-Making in Defense* (Berkeley, California: University of California Press, 1965).

[27] U. S. Bureau of the Budget: Bulletin 66-3; *Planning-Programming-Budgeting* (October 12, 1965).

[28] *Ibid.,* p. 1.

budget decisions, and provide relevant program and financial data for Presidential and Congressional action.

In more specific terms it is anticipated that PPBS, when properly implemented, will enable each agency to:

(1) Make available to top management more concrete and specific data relevant to broad decisions;

(2) Spell out more concretely the objectives of government programs;

(3) Analyze systematically and present for agency head and Presidential review and decision possible alternative objectives and alternate programs to meet these objectives;

(4) Evaluate thoroughly and compare the benefits and costs of programs;

(5) Produce total rather than partial cost estimates of programs;

(6) Present on a multi-year basis the prospective costs and accomplishments of programs;

(7) Review objectives and conduct program analyses on a continuing, year-round basis, instead of on a crowded schedule to meet budget deadlines.[29]

In achieving objectives such as those just noted, agencies must give precise definition to programs. For this reason, distinctions are made between program categories, program subcategories, and program elements. At the state level, examples of program categories in education might be elementary, secondary or higher education. A program subcategory could be improving science and engineering or improving language training in higher education. Program elements are defined as integrated activities which combine personnel, other services, equipment and facilities. An example would be the number of teachers, the facilities, equipment and related services necessary to ensure the effective teaching of mathematics in the high schools of a given state.

When programs are given precise definition, their costs and benefits can be projected. An illustration of this process is available from recent studies made with regard to projected health programs by staff personnel in the Department of Health, Education, and Welfare. *Business Week,* for example, has described the reasoning underlying decisions about investing in alternative programs to cope with certain types of cancer as follows:

For cervical-uterine cancer, HEW came up with two plans. The most ambitious would cost $155-million and would avert an estimated 44,084 deaths at a cost of $3,520 per person over a five-year period. A scaled-down program would cost $118.1 million and save 34,200 persons at a cost of $3,470 each.

The figures don't stack up as well for colon-rectum cancer. This disease will kill 43,600 people this year. But there is no simple and quick screening test for this type of cancer, and surgery for it has had only limited success. It would therefore cost $7.3-million over five years to save about 710 persons at a cost of $42,941 per death averted.

With this in mind, HEW will place major emphasis on cervical cancer. Its program for colon-rectum cancer will concentrate on grants to find simple mass-screening methods.[30]

One of the cost-benefit studies that is pertinent to state planning in

[29] *Ibid.,* p. 3.
[30] *Business Week,* "Putting a Dollar Sign on Life," January 21, 1967, p. 86.

education was done by Werner Hirsch, an economist.[31] In his study the comparative costs and benefits of community college vs. pre-school education investments were explored. His results led him to question whether the *economic* returns on investments in a universal and publicly supported system of community colleges would be as great as the economic returns on equal amounts invested in pre-school education.

EDUCATIONAL PLANNING BASED UPON MANPOWER REQUIREMENTS

A third planning tradition is associated with the efforts of those who base educational designs upon projected manpower requirements. These efforts have been expressed largely by economists, although in recent years an increasing number of educators with training in economics have participated in this approach. Developing nations have provided the context in which this type of planning has been largely conducted. For example, in the "Mediterranean Regional Project," an endeavor carried out by the Organization for Economic Cooperation and Development, the major focus for planning was scientific and technical education in the countries of Greece, Italy, Portugal, Spain, Turkey and Yugoslavia. Conducted in cooperation with the governments in these various countries, the planning was based upon the "manpower-requirements approach". In this approach an effort was made to foresee "the future occupational structure of the economy and to plan the educational systems so as to provide the requisite numbers of personnel with the qualifications which that structure demands."[32] To foresee the future occupational structure, planners had to make estimates of the following:[33] the number of persons each occupation under consideration would require for any future year or series of years; the number of persons currently in each of the occupations considered; the number of withdrawals from each occupation due to such causes as death, retirement, or movement out of the labor force, for each of the years under consideration; and the number of changes resulting from occupational mobility caused by moves from one occupation to another.

The specific tasks which planners sought to achieve in the various countries were defined after discussions among the National Directors of the Project, members of the Organization for Economic Cooperation and Development, and special consultants. Minimum objectives established were the following:

(a) Estimate for the 15-year period 1960 to 1975 the "required" number of graduates each year from the various levels of the educational system. For levels beyond the primary, these numbers must be broken down by broad subject matter area—at least into graduates of scientific and technical curricula and those of all other curricula, since the content as well as the costs of these two broad divisions of the educational system differ considerably.

(b) Estimate, in the light of (a), the number of teachers required in the several levels of the educational system. As in the case of students, teachers of

31 Werner Hirsch, "New Developments in the Economics of Education" in *Administering the Community College in a Changing World* (Eds.) S. V. Martorana and Pauline Hunter (Buffalo: State University of New York, 1966), pp. 75-87.
32 Herbert Parnes, *Forecasting Educational Needs for Economic and Social Development* (Paris: Organization for Economic Cooperation and Development, 1962), p. 15.
33 *Ibid.*, p. 19.

pure and applied sciences at levels beyond the primary must be differentiated from all others.

(c) Estimate, in the light of (a), the number of additional classrooms, laboratories, school buildings, and the amount of equipment required, and plan the optimum geographical distribution of such educational facilities in the light of anticipated population distribution and the distribution of existing facilities.

(d) Assess the qualitative adequacy of existing educational programmes and make recommendations for needed improvements, including teaching methods and curriculum organization.

(e) Assess the need for new or expanded educational and training programmes outside of the traditional educational structure, such as adult education programmes, apprenticeship-training programmes, on-the-job training, et cetera.

(f) Estimate the total capital and current costs of the expansion and improvement in education implied by the results of (b)-(e).

(g) Establish a "time-table" for achieving the required expansion and improvements over the 15-year period and prepare annual budgets showing total required educational expenditures in absolute figures and as percentages of gross national product.[34]

Economists admit that there is no single universally accepted technique for forecasting occupational requirements. However, there is a variety of techniques which are useful to planners. Specific instructions to planners using the "manpower requirements approach" include the following:

(a) Prepare an "inventory" of manpower for the base year (e.g., 1960) classified by branch of industry and occupation, using an occupational classification system that differentiates as far as possible among occupations requiring different levels of education and, at the highest levels, between "scientific" and "general" education.

(b) Forecast the size of the total labor force for the "target" year (e.g., 1975) and for the intervening period at five-year intervals.

(c) Estimate total employment in each sector and branch for the forecast years.

(d) Within each sector and branch, allocate total employment for the forecast years among the various categories of the occupational classification system. Aggregating the requirements for each occupational category in all sectors and branches gives the total "stock" of manpower required for the forecast years classified by occupational category.

(e) Convert the data on requirements by occupational category into data on requirements by educational qualification. This is necessary because the several broad occupational categories cannot be expected to be homogeneous with respect to required educational qualification.

(f) Estimate the anticipated supply of personnel with each major type of educational qualification for the forecast years on the basis of:

1. present stocks;
2. anticipated outflows from the existing educational system; and
3. losses due to death, retirement, and withdrawal from the labour force.

(g) Compute the change in annual outflow from the various levels and branches of the educational system necessary to create balance in the forecast years between (e) and (f).

(h) Calculate enrollments in each level and branch of the educational system necessary to achieve the required annual outflows.[35]

Clearly, the planning techniques developed and used by economists in

---

[34] *Ibid.*, pp. 10-11.

[35] *Ibid.*, pp. 21-22. For a more technical discussion of planning and projection techniques see Herbert Parnes (Ed.), *Planning Education for Economic and Social Development* (Paris: Organization for Economic Cooperation and Development, 1962).

developing nations have utility in developed nations—especially in relation to vocational education. As a matter of fact, techniques similar to those used by the economists have already been used in planning vocational education programs in this country at both the state and local levels. Leonard Lecht's projections of manpower requirements at the national level certainly have implications for educational planners.[36] The 206 percent increase in the need for electronic and electrical technicians projected for the period 1964-75, the 111 percent projected increase in the need for airplane pilots and navigators, and the 85 percent increase in the need for office workers, certainly have implications for those planning vocational education. The same would be true for Lecht's projected decrease in farm occupations of 22 percent for the 1964-75 period.

LIMITATIONS OF THE NEW PLANNING TECHNIQUES

Even though many new techniques pertinent to educational planning have been developed in the last two decades which have promise for those interested in more effective state planning for education, these techniques do have limitations which need to be recognized. For one thing *they cannot make decisions nor can they replace judgment on the part of decision makers.* Rather, the techniques can aid and support decision makers by providing pertinent data on alternative programs and courses of action. *The decision maker, as a rule, will need to be responsive to values not encompassed by the planning techniques.*

Secondly, since the various techniques involve highly rational procedures *efficiency may tend to be the value which is more forceful in shaping choices.* To be sure the planning techniques of today go beyond those of fifty years ago when the so-called "Cult of Efficiency" in education was rampant, in large part, because these techniques focus both upon costs *and* benefits. However, *since operations research and PPBS emphasize precise measures of outputs, there is a tendency for planners, when using these techniques, to be influenced more by economic measures simply because other measures of values* (e.g., human dignity) *are extremely difficult to achieve.*

Thirdly, *the techniques to be employed require specific measures of output.* In education it is well known that we are only beginning to make progress in achieving precise output measures. In the first place, it is not easy to define educational goals with sufficient precision to make accurate measurements of output possible. In the second place, even if goals are precisely defined, their number, variety, and nature are such that measurement is not easy.

Fourth, it should be emphasized that the new planning techniques represent a special way of thinking and a rigorous approach to problem solving. The techniques have their roots in such disciplines as economics and mathematics. Therefore, they should not be viewed as simplistic pro-

---

[36] See Leonard Lecht, "The Changing Occupational Structure with Implications for Education." In The Emerging Role of State Departments of Education, with Implications for Vocational Education, Columbus, Ohio. The Center for Vocational-Technical Education (in press).

cedures which will produce incontestable conclusions. Rather, *they require a highly disciplined way of thinking and the courage to examine assumptions and to respect empirical data.*

Finally, educational planning based upon manpower requirements emphasizes the instrumental aspects of education. Education is seen, in other words, as a means to achieve important economic and social goals, usually of a national character. *The full development of the unique talents of individuals, as an educational goal, would be considered only incidentally in the manpower requirements approach.* Consquently, *fundamental educational goals,* which are not so easily defined, *could be neglected by planners using this approach.*

Even though the planning techniques have limitations, they will assuredly be applied and tested in education. Their promise is such that they will likely be found useful. By or before 1980, leaders will undoubtedly make judgments about the use of the techniques in education similar to that which Charles Hitch made recently with reference to defense:

> I would certainly agree that systems analysis is still in a very early stage of development, and much remains to be done in refining and making more efficient the tools of the trade . . . and even in devising better tools. But I am confident that it has passed the point in its development which medicine passed late in the nineteenth century where it begins to do more good than harm.[37]

NEW STATE AGENCIES TO FACILITATE EDUCATIONAL PLANNING

If educational planning is to flourish at the state level and if it is to serve educational institutions effectively, organizations will need to be adapted or created which will provide a setting to which competent planners will be attracted and in which they can function effectively. Since the nature of any organization should be shaped by the functions it is to perform, the first step in arriving at an organizational strategy to facilitate planning is to make explicit the state planning functions which will best serve education. The following functions are judged to be among those which state planning agencies should perform:

1. Determining through analysis and assessment those educational objectives for a state which should receive highest priority for given time periods;

2. Developing multi-year master plans designed to ensure the effective attainment of high priority and other educational objectives for pre-school, K-12, and higher education;

3. Creating various program alternatives designed to achieve high priority objectives, performing cost-benefit analyses of these alternatives, and translating the results into specific proposals;

4. Assessing state programs of financial support in order to determine their adequacy for ensuring investments needed to achieve educational goals and, when necessary, developing legislative proposals to correct inadequacies;

---

[37] *Op. cit.,* p. 76.

5. Examining school district, intermediate, and state department structures in order to determine their adequacy in relation to achieving established educational objectives, and, when necessary, developing alternative recommendations designed to improve these structures; and

6. Serving as an interpreter of quantitative data on education and of important state and national studies which bear upon and have implications for educational planning.

In considering the problem of what organizational arrangements will ensure the effective performance of functions such as those just noted, the following question becomes significant: Can existing organizations be adapted to perform these functions or will it be necessary to create new organizations especially designed to meet the challenge of state planning? The writer believes that, if state planning efforts are to be achieved which are commensurate with the educational challenges of today, new organizations will need to be developed and refined in most states. The argument is offered here that states should create and experiment with new organizations especially designed to facilitate educational planning. To introduce the argument let us examine briefly current planning arrangements.

Among existing organizations, state departments of education would perhaps be viewed as the state agency now most responsible for state planning in education. In this regard Fred Beach, as early as 1950, made the following observation: "Planning ranks at the top among the functions of the state departments of education. . . . It is the very essence of the leadership function. . . . Only through planning can the program of the state department of education have purpose and direction. No program of the state department can go much beyond the vision of its leaders as expressed in their plans."[38]

Some state departments have demonstrated a capacity for effective planning. One department, for example, has projected school and higher education enrollments for a 20-year period and has broken these enrollments down into a number of categories for special planning purposes. Important societal trends related to scientific and technological developments, economic conditions, and the international field have been identified and implications for education have been set forth by this department. It has also identified a number of important targets associated with such areas as urban education, integration, the administration of ESEA, expanding opportunities in higher education, accountability in education, computers in education, business involvement in education, and research on the process of change. With reference to the various target areas, the personnel, capital, and physical requirements needed by the state education agency to carry out its program responsibilities are set forth. Similar treatments by this department have been made of more traditionally defined programs such as vocational rehabilitation, elementary and secondary education, continuing education, and educational finance and management services.

[38] Fred Beach, *The Functions of State Departments of Education* (Washington, D. C.: The United States Government Printing Office, 1950), p. 4.

Even though a number of state departments have demonstrated planning capacities—and all of them should undoubtedly be encouraged to strengthen these capacities—it is suggested here that, if the far-reaching and long-range planning challenges facing the various states are to be met, new organizations will need to be created. More specifically, it is recommended that state legislatures, possibly in some cases with the aid of foundations, create state-supported agencies specifically responsible for educational planning. Such agencies might be established for a five-year period with renewal dependent upon the results achieved.

These state planning agencies would concentrate upon the total system of education in the state from pre-school through university education. While concentrating on education, the agency would have liaison with other state agencies—such as those concerned with labor, health, and welfare—which have interests in education. The products of the agency would be used by various institutions including state education departments, state boards of education, local and intermediate school districts, state legislatures, and the executive branch of state government. *The agency should be relatively free to concern itself with master planning for five- to fifteen-year periods;* therefore, the immediate pressures and processes of political decision making should not be allowed to affect its efforts in negative ways. This should not be interpreted to mean that it should not serve existing agencies and groups responsible for aspects of education in the state. The following illustrations are indicative of the contributions which a state planning agency might make to groups and agencies interested in education.

State legislators could benefit from the agency by obtaining carefully developed planning data, being alerted to special legislative needs, receiving legislative proposals for evaluation and having a better base for evaluating legislative alternatives initiated outside the agency. State departments would have specially developed planning data basic to their role in helping local school districts to establish better planning capacities or to cope with long-range planning problems. The data provided would also be useful to state departments in projecting their own planning and in making biennial requests to legislatures. The executive branch of government and state boards of education should have a source of ideas and better bases for making decisions about educational programs. Leaders in the executive branch would also be encouraged to think and plan within a longer-range time period.

The agency would constitute a staff resource for state planning. The plans, program proposals, and supporting data developed by the agency, in other words, would not be legally binding. However, a special body would provide advice and give some direction to the planning. The special body might consist of personnel such as the following: chairmen of state boards of education and higher education in the state; the governor; the chief state school officer; and other persons such as the following who might be appointed by the governor: a few key legislators; selected public school and non-public school personnel; selected higher education personnel; a few state government personnel; and a few leading citizens of the state not immediately related to state government or to formal educational institutions.

The state planning agency would need a variety of personnel with skills which complement one another. In addition to educators, there would be a need for urban planners, economists, specialists in population projection, systems analysts, computer experts, lawyers, and other specialists. While considerable staff help with planning problems might be obtained from personnel in universities, government agencies, or industrial firms, on an *ad hoc* basis, any substantial and continued effort would require a number of relatively permanent staff members, if it were to be effective. The identification and recruitment of a competent person who has the necessary vision, education, and coordinative skills to give leadership to such an effort should obviously be crucial.

It is believed that investments by states in educational planning agencies would result in substantial returns. This belief derives in part from the fact that billions of dollars are now being invested in education and that education requires more funds than any other state function. Even small improvements in the over-all allocation of resources should bring substantial returns. Such returns could be calculated in terms of efficiency (i.e., funds saved through better planning) or they could be estimated in terms of effectiveness (a higher quality and/or greater quantity of educational outputs). On either or both of these counts, the case for responsible state planning for education, and special organizations to support such planning would seem to be a strong one.

SOME IMPLICATIONS OF THE THRUST TOWARD PLANNING IN EDUCATION

As educational planning develops and expands, a variety of groups and agencies will be affected. For this reason there are various implications stemming from the planning movement.

Unquestionably, there are important implications for universities, regional laboratories, and other organizations responsible for training educational personnel who will engage in, or be affected by, planning. New, short-term training arrangements are needed to familiarize leaders in educational institutions and in education-related agencies with the nature and scope of the new approaches to planning. Such arrangements should provide personnel with sufficient understanding to enable them to communicate intelligently with planning leaders in government and other organizations about PPBS, operations research, and other planning traditions. After the training experiences, these personnel should also be able to see some of the implications of the new methods for educational planning in their own states.

Short-term, continuing education arrangements will not be sufficient to meet all of the emergent training needs. In addition, resident, on-campus experiences will be needed to prepare substantial numbers of personnel in sufficient depth so that they can actually use the new planning methods in education. Such work will entail one or more years of study, appropriate internship, and other field study relationships. As resident programs are refined, scholars will need to develop new knowledge about input-output relationships in education and invent new tools for measuring these relationships.

There are also important implications for state legislators and governors which stem from the new planning movement. In the first place, *they have an important responsibility to see that states achieve needed planning capabilities.* This will mean providing special financial support to strengthen existing planning agencies, in some cases, and the creation of specially supported planning agencies in others. It will also likely mean that governors and legislators with special interests in education will need to add planning experts to their own staffs to serve a liaison function with those engaged in educational planning or in giving direction to educational and related planning efforts.

There is a deeper meaning for state officials of the effort now underway to achieve greater rationality in educational decision making and planning. *If planning is to be effective, a different kind of political behavior will be required.* Undoubtedly, there will be some conflict between: (1) the more traditional patterns of compromise, bargaining, informal agreements, and private communications where the deciding values in legislative decision making are often implicit, and (2) the emergent patterns of weighing the costs and benefits of a given legislative proposal, arriving at decisions based upon carefully developed data, and systematically engaging in open and public discussion during the decision process. *This means that there may be substantial conflict at times between planners and responsible representatives of the people.*[39]

There are also significant implications for every professional organization interested in education. Traditionally, these organizations have had great influence on legislators and the development of legislation. They have done this in part because they have had full-time staffs who could gather, organize, and present pertinent information to legislators. However, the information presented has usually been in the form of needed financial input without clear relationships to educational output. With the increasing demand for planning data based upon some relationships between input and output, professional organizations—if they are to continue to be effective—will need to change their approaches. It may be pertinent to note that when the Department of Defense initiated systems planning, the Navy and other services soon established systems planning units to generate their own proposals and to assess program proposals of the Defense Department. It is possible that professional organizations will themselves acquire new kinds of staff and adapt newer planning methods before 1980.

---

[39] For a discussion of this problem within the federal context see *Hearings Before the Joint Committee on the Reorganization of Congress, Part 12,* August 31 and September 9, 1965 (Washington, D. C.: U. S. Government Printing Office, 1965), pp. 1856-61.

For those heading school districts, state departments of education, and institutions of higher learning, adjustments will also be required. Some of the larger school districts, state departments of education, and universities are already beginning to adapt newer planning methods in their own organizations and the likelihood would seem strong that this trend will continue. Since systematic planning always involves a careful look at existing practice and the assumptions underlying it, educational leaders and others intimately identified with education will certainly experience discomfort at times. For this reason there will inevitably be some defensiveness associated with national and state efforts to assess education. However, responsible educational personnel will undoubtedly adjust in a mature fashion as the emergent planning and assessment movement develops.

Finally, there are important implications for democratic decision making in the more general sense. Some would argue that more centralized planning arrangements will make for less participation on the part of citizens generally. However, this conclusion does not necessarily follow. *The new planning methods can provide citizens with more educational options to consider and more adequate data with which to examine these options.* To ensure this condition it will be necessary to provide citizens the necessary information and the necessary opportunities for evaluating the information. Recent studies by large foundations and recent recommendations by President Johnson suggest that by 1980 educational television will be much more widespread and much more capable of providing needed information to citizens than is the case today. Certainly, there will be many other media for disseminating pertinent information. *The challenge facing leaders will be to see that propositions and information concerning education are intelligently examined and interpreted by the general citizenry.* With an increasingly educated citizenry which places more and more value upon education, we can be optimistic about the analytical and constructive role citizens will play in education both before and after 1980.

*   *   *

SUPPLEMENTARY STATEMENT

J. R. RACKLEY*
AND
DONALD M. CARROLL, JR.**

What should states plan for in education? How can needed changes be determined? Planning and effecting needed changes in education should be based upon answers to these questions.

In the early history of public education in the United States, "planning"

* *State Superintendent of Public Instruction, Commonwealth of Pennsylvania.* Formerly, Dean of the College of Education and Professor of Education, University of Oklahoma (1949-56); Dean of the College of Education and Professor of Education (1956-62), and Vice President for Resident Instruction (1962-65), The Pennsylvania State University.
** *Director, Bureau of Curriculum Development and School Evaluation, Pennsylvania Department of Public Instruction.* Formerly, Curriculum Planning Specialist (1961-62), and Director, Bureau of Curriculum Planning (1962-66), Pennsylvania Department of Public Instruction.

for education by states can be described easily. An arrangement was needed which would furnish sufficient funds to construct small buildings, provide teachers better educated than pupils, obtain a few simple instructional materials, and present a modest curriculum to develop basic mathematical and literacy skills and to impart moral and cultural values. The methods used were correspondingly simple. Legislatures created school districts and delegated some authority to these school districts to enable them to meet limited responsibilities.

As the nation developed, the demands of people for a better and more extensive education also grew. A simple system of planning did not meet new demands. State education agencies were created to help plan and to manage the evolving state program of education. Planning strategies were not often changed significantly, however. State education agencies relied heavily upon legislatures for laws to regulate everything from the construction of schools and the qualifications of teachers to the detailed description of courses to be taught. The state agency became the enforcer of laws and regulations and only on rare occasions did it become a leader in a more advanced type of planning. The void in leadership was often filled by organized pressure groups exerting their influence on those who could make educational decisions. Comprehensive, coordinated and realistic educational planning was not characteristic of the times.

State boards of education composed of lay citizens were created to make general policies for the operation of the state school system. These boards came to rely increasingly on professional educators to provide them with staff assistance in making decisions. As schools were staffed with better educated faculty and administrators, it became less essential for state education agencies to concentrate on enforcing laws. Opportunity was thus provided for the state agency to change its role and to provide for the state board and other policy making groups, the information, proposals and alternatives required for sound educational decisions.

State education agencies have accepted, in considerably differing degree, the responsibility to provide leadership. Some have responded well; others less so, for reasons frequently unique to the state. One common denominator, however, of educationally progressive states is a strong state agency. But there are those who assert that these states are too few in number. They believe that most state agencies have not changed rapidly enough, are staffed with mediocre personnel, are politically oriented, and for the most part are either dormant or dying institutions. A recent report on Title III, of the Elementary and Secondary Education Act of 1965—a program which uses the words "exemplary" and "innovation" liberally—supports this with the opinion that if the program is assigned to the states it will deteriorate. It seems that state education agencies have yet to overcome the negative image of the past. High quality leadership is required. An assumption of this paper is that state education agencies must accept their new leadership obligations through imaginative planning if they are to be a viable force in American education. *The primary responsibility for state educational planning belongs with the state education agency.*

This paper will describe some ways that a state education agency can identify and plan for needed changes. The discussion will be concerned with establishing goals, assessing the condition of education in a state, planning for change, and organizing the state education agency to facilitate change where and when it is needed.

ESTABLISHING GOALS

It has become trite in some educational circles to discuss the formulation of goals. A statement of goals is usually considered to be an academic exercise to be completed in connection with accreditation procedures or to secure a favorable reaction to a grant application. Stating goals is regarded as necessary lip service before taking a previously determined course of action. There are some, however—and we are among them—who regard establishing goals as an essential first step in a state educational agency's planning efforts.

How are the goals established? How will they be used? The answers to these questions are most important.

Establishing useful goals is difficult. Traditionally, educators develop goals through professional committees. The results of committee work are announced as statements of educational purpose. Often the statements fail to receive general support because they are considered biased, the work of a group with vested interests, or are considered impractical. As more and more segments of society become interested in education, they should be involved in helping to make educational decisions. *Lay and professional people, involved in establishing educational goals for a state, provide a firm base for support of public education.*

Goals should be stated as specifically as possible. It is easier to focus opinion about a precise statement than a vague or general one. Because goals for state educational planning have wide applicability, stating them concisely, however, is often difficult, but it must be accomplished.

A statement of goals should be attractive enough to receive the support of those who constitute the state's social and political power structure. Considerable effort should be made to obtain this support.

When these are established, the state board of education should publicize goals as statements of public policy.

A clear statement of goals serves as a cohesive force, focusing the work of the state education agency staff, and providing direction to their planning efforts. Where goals seem general, and success in meeting the goal difficult to measure, staff of the state agency must develop more precise, measurable sub-goals or objectives which, collectively, may be used for purposes of assessment.

ASSESSMENT OF PRODUCT AND PROGRESS

Once goals have been established, data are needed to determine the degree to which the state education program is meeting its goals. Assessment is necessary, but any attempt to conduct a state-wide assessment of education has a number of inherent difficulties. Some of these are: (1) information may be used to compare one district unfavorably with another; (2) assessment techniques may not be sufficiently advanced to provide reliable information; (3) an assessment program may lead to an undesirable standardization of the curriculum; and (4) varying social conditions make it difficult to draw appropriate inferences from data about the pupils concerned. But a continuous assessment of education must be undertaken as a constant requirement for planning, and difficulties— whatever they be—must be overcome.

The National Assessment Project has made a good start in attempting to define techniques through which pertinent educational data can be collected on a national level. Instruments have been developed and sampling procedures proposed as part of this project. It is planned that National Assessment data be collected on a regional basis, reported by regions, and summarized nationally. Data are not to be presented state by state. While it is useful to know about the condition of education nationally and regionally, *state plans must be based upon conditions within a state.* States, therefore, cannot depend upon National Assessment to meet their own planning needs.

A state program of assessment has, as its purpose, the collection of information which can be used in formulating plans and policies at the state level. In this type of program the relationship of the product, or pupil, to the goals is studied.

Like the national program, a state program is not limited to achievement-type testing, and it should be clearly understood that assessment and testing, *per se,* are different. The most advanced measurement techniques should be used to obtain information not only about cognitive development, but also about attitudes, values, and psychomotor development of pupils. This information may then be used to determine how nearly the instructional program is meeting the established goals.

Where compatible with state goals, the state assessment program should be closely coordinated with the national program. If similar sampling techniques and common instruments are used, the ability of state education agency personnel to make more valid inferences is increased. In the final analysis, however, the state program must serve the state interests. Where other undertakings are inappropriate to the needs of the state, then techniques and instruments suited to these needs should be developed. Finally, a unit of the state education agency should manage the state assessment program.

PLANNING

As information from assessment becomes available it should be analyzed carefully. Attempts should be made to determine cause and effect relationships—not only for any weaknesses which are discovered, but also for strengths. The typical state education agency cannot, in all probability, conduct this analysis adequately with its own personnel. The interrelationship of factors is so complex that highly specialized personnel are needed. Social scientists and other scholars may, and should, be used as consultants to assist in the analysis.

Once cause and effect relationships have been determined with some degree of assurance, the development of alternative proposals can begin. Some procedures for developing and evaluating these proposals have been described well by Culbertson. Whether the planning-programming-budgeting-system (PPBS) or similar techniques are used does not seem particularly important. What does seem important is that: (1) strengths and weaknesses are determined as objectively as possible; (2) factors which seem to contribute to these conditions are identified; (3) research findings and informed opinion are used to formulate alternative methods of approaching the problem; (4) objectives, procedures, cost and personnel needed for each alternative are determined in detail; and (5) a decision is made as to the plan to be followed.

The chief state school officer, from the alternatives available, should recommend what appears to be the best one to the state board of education with supporting evidence. The state board should consider the alternatives and make the policy decision and the superintendent (or commissioner) should be responsible for carrying out the plan decided upon by the board. If a plan involves other agencies of government or a major policy decision of general state administration, the support of the governor is needed. If additional funds are needed, not only must the governor's support be obtained, but also the support of legislators. If the plan deals with some sensitive area of education, the support of school boards, professional education associations, and chief school administrators will be needed.

Coordinated planning—involving persons, agencies and organizations most likely to be affected—is the best guarantee of success in making the board's decision effective.

ORGANIZATION OF THE STATE EDUCATION AGENCY

One of the objectives of a state education agency is to determine and plan for needed educational changes, and the organization of the agency should facilitate this. When considering the organization of a governmental agency, there is a temptation to start by making charts, assigning designations, determining lines of authority and coordination, and listing personnel. Because of the variations among state education agencies it is difficult, if not impossible, to suggest one type of organization for all. It seems more practical, therefore, to describe the components of an organization, with specific details to be worked out by others. A basic consideration is that the organization should improve coordination of groups with related functions. A state agency to carry out the proposals described in this paper, should include the following components:

Educational Planning. Responsible for developing measurable educational objectives and using data collected from the assessment program to develop alternative plans for achieving objectives.

Educational Assessment. Responsible for developing techniques and instruments to measure the product of the state educational system, collecting and summarizing data and assisting in data analysis.

Research Administration. Responsible for managing a research program to test and analyze the effectiveness of specific plans which are adopted and for assisting in the development of assessment techniques and instruments.

Statistics. Responsible for collecting descriptive data about the state education system and relating these data to the development of plans.

Management Information. Responsible for designing data processing systems which permit the storage and rapid retrieval of planning data and for developing simulation models which permit the testing of various plans by computer before these plans are adopted.

Relating these components administratively in a functional manner should make possible a high degree of coordination in a planning effort. The specific planning activities of individual state education agencies would determine the size and type of staff needed, as well as the special equipment required.

IN SUMMARY

In this paper we have discussed a process by which a state education agency can determine and plan for needed educational change. Several points were developed:

Educational planning is a primary responsibility of the state education agency. While the educational effort is growing more complex and increasingly involves such other governmental agencies as health, welfare, the United States Office of Education, etc., it is the responsibility of the *state education agency* to coordinate the educational effort within a state.

Educational planning should be directed toward meeting clearly defined and generally accepted goals. Every effort should be made to state goals in terms of behaviors expected from pupils as a result of education. A determined effort must be made to clarify and describe goals susceptible of measurement.

Planning should be based upon accurate information. To obtain this information, a state educational assessment program is needed.

State educational planning should produce alternative methods of dealing with a problem. The decision as to which alternative should be followed is made at the policy level.

The state education agency should be organized to facilitate educational analysis and planning—both short- and long-range. Such an organization includes units for educational planning, educational assessment, research administration, statistics and management information.

CHAPTER 13

Planned Change, Public Education and the State

VIRGIL E. BLANKE*

Many new titles—such as "Designing Education for the Future," "Institute for the Development of Educational Activities," Title III Centers for Invention and Demonstration, Fifty million dollars in Title I funds for New York City and "The National Institute for the Study of Educational Change"—exemplify recent powerful attempts to change the field of education.

The key words are "designing," "innovation," "development," "demonstration," "invention," and "improvement." There seems little doubt now that educators throughout the nation are caught up with these new words. It is not a small or superficial interest that most of us feel, but a complete commitment. We are preoccupied and greatly impressed with change. In truth, it is our first real love affair since progressive education.

This emphasis on change is strange when one thinks about it, since the educational establishment has long been known as an element of our culture unlikely to shift its direction suddenly and dramatically. Why has this shift in emphasis taken place? What is change? In anthropology, cultural change is defined as a reformulation in human behavior. The opposite of reformulation (change) is persistence—the maintenance of *status quo*. Change and persistence, anthropolgists say, are universal features of any culture; furthermore, they are reciprocals of the same phenomena of cultural dynamics. Consequently, when one discusses change, he also considers persistence whether he realizes it or not.

If one weighs civilization, balancing persistence on one side of the scales and change on the other, the result would show that most of man's history has emphasized persistence and stability, rather than change. Cultural change has been, and still is, very slow in certain parts of the world. Most basic human values, as personified in the great religions of the world, condition man to accept his fate. Usually, he has accepted this concept because he "knew" he could not change his existence during his lifetime.

However, in the last few centuries, the scale has begun to tip, with more and more weight being added to the change side. Since the eighteenth

* Associate Professor and Director, Development Division, Ohio State University. Formerly, Superintendent of Schools, Massilon, Ohio; Staff Associate and Instructor, University of Chicago; Superintendent of Schools, Napoleon, Ohio; and principal and teacher in other Ohio school systems.

century, political, industrial and scientific revolutions have increasingly become the order of the day. These revolutions have many antecedents— the advent and maturation of scientific thought and applied science that have created industrial giants and improved the lot of the average man in many parts of the world; a marked decrease in the time lag between invention and use; more funds poured into planned technological change; developments growing out of three international crises (World War I, the 1930 depression and World War II); and especially in the United States, the creation of an educational system which produced mass literacy and an ever growing number of people who can plan and think critically.

As technological change, national planning, and mass education became accepted, men began to change even their basic values. More and more people in each succeeding generation believed that further technological and behavioral change was inevitable. More important still, they believed also that change was *better* than persistence.

Since education is crucial to this changing environment, is it any wonder that economists now talk about education as an investment, rather than as an expense, or that national planners emphasize education as the principal resource necessary to resurrect underdeveloped nations and poverty ridden communities?

A climate for change and its antecedents are the prime reasons we have had recent federal legislation providing substantial funds for education. The Elementary and Secondary Education Act (ESEA) and all of the other recent federal legislation are not the result of the "good guys" (educators) finally winning. Neither are they an example of more effective lobbying. We just happen to live in the generation which tipped the scales away from persistence, to change—both technological and behavioral.

So whether we like it or not—whether we accept the new generation and its climate for change—we in education are faced with new inventions and innovative mechanisms for bringing these new artifacts and ideas to our attention. Given a climate which promotes and rewards change, what kind of policies and procedures can a state utilize to ensure planned educational improvement, rather than random, reactive change which has characterized the educational scene for so long?

A System for Improvement

The need for a plan for improvement in the field of education has three starting points: (1) there are problems in existing teaching-learning situations—where a set of circumstances contradicts or impedes desired goals; (2) man has the tools for systematic inquiry (technology and methodology) necessary to solve such problems; and (3) in technologically advanced nations, men believe such change not only is necessary but right. Consequently, through government, private investment and foundations, man provides money, facilities, and personnel for such problem solving.

Development

The invention and design of better solutions to problems in teaching-learning situations will be called *development* in this paper. David Clark and Egon Guba[1] state that development has four objectives: (1) to identify operational problems, (2) to solve operational problems, (3) to design solutions to work in schools, and (4) to assess the effectiveness and efficiency of these solutions. The functions involved in reaching these objectives are: (1) gathering operational and planning data, (2) inventing solutions to operating problems, (3) engineering packages and programs for operational use, and (4) testing and evaluating the packages and programs.

Many teachers and educational administrators equate development with research. How often have we heard the statement, "Research should solve our problems, but it's too theoretical." However, the fundamental goal of research is not the solution of problems, as I have defined them.

> Science has achieved its great power by insisting on defining for itself the problems it proposes to solve, and by refusing to take on problems merely because some outside authority considers them important. But that power, and the precision of thought on which it depends, is purchased by a refusal to deal with many aspects of such problems.[2]

Scientific research is concerned with the production of knowledge through the projection and testing of theory. It designs and uses particular kinds of methodologies which establish the reliability and validity of the knowledge produced. Development, on the other hand, is the solution of practical problems. It often uses the knowledge produced by research and it can use research methodologies, but it *is not* research.

SOME FACTORS IN COMMON

Successful research and development, however, do have some factors in common. A clear articulation of a problem is mandatory in both activities. In development one articulates questionable relationships between means and ends; in research one questions and builds theory in an attempt to explain reality.

Most successful research and development activities are team efforts involving people who are expert in the content and methodology of the problem area. In addition to being expert they must be highly committed to solve the problem, because research and development require a high tolerance for frustration.

The agencies which house research and development teams must have money which can be made available at the instant committed people identify a problem. These agencies must also protect research and development (R & D) teams from other work. This particular requirement is a prime reason why little research and development goes on in individual school systems. Teachers cannot teach a full load and be involved in developmental activities also.

Last, but not least, successful research and development teams establish deadlines for reporting solutions or partial solutions. The process of

---

[1] David Clark and Egon Guba, "Effecting Change in Institutions of Higher Learning," UCEA International Visitation Program (Columbus, Ohio: October, 1966).

[2] Don K. Price, *The Scientific Estate* (Cambridge, Mass.: The Belknap Press, 1965), p. 105.

development is usually a non-programmatic activity, as Simon[3] uses that term. In such a non-structured environment, people constantly seek time to develop solutions more adequately. Since development builds on other research and development, teams must often report their progress before they would like to do so.

Figure 1: *An Educational Improvement System*

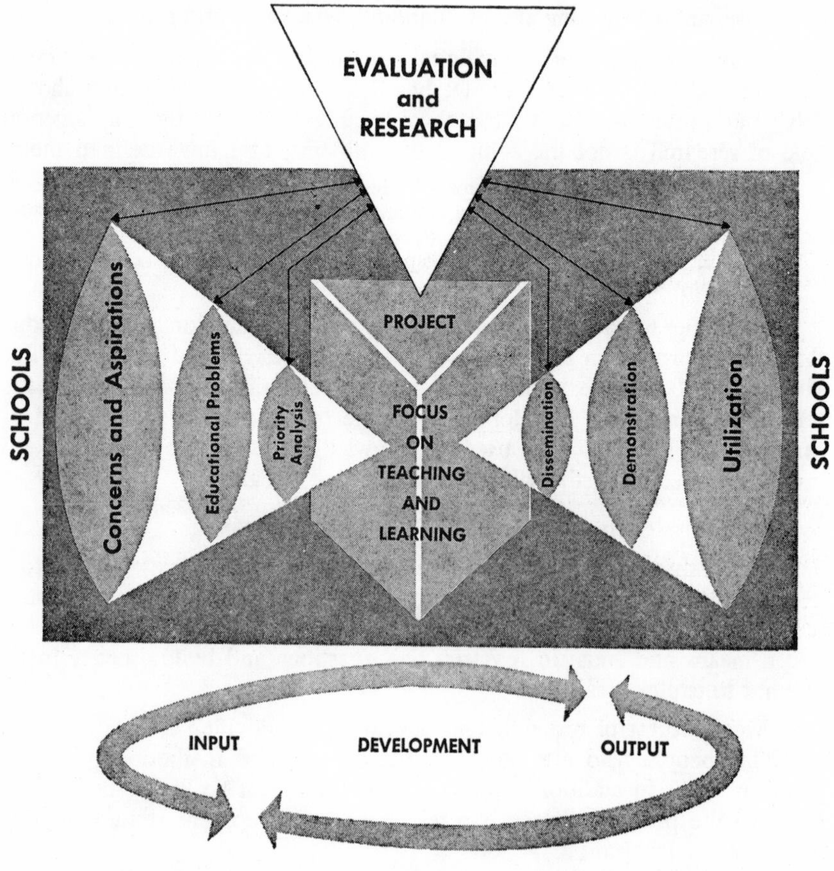

In the system described in this paper, development is the center (see Figure 1) because it is crucial to any state's attempt to improve its educational capability. However, development does not just happen. We have labored too long with the notion that teachers, local school systems and even state educational systems, can identify and solve their own problems. Ned Flanders[4] said recently that although the Association for Supervision and Curriculum Development has worked for 20 years to improve instruction by working with individual teachers and local school systems, his

[3] Herbert A. Simon and James C. March, *Organizations* (New York: John Wiley and Sons, 1958).
[4] Ned Flanders, "Interaction Analysis and Curriculum Development," a speech given at the Michigan Association for Supervision and Curriculum Development (Detroit, Michigan: December, 1966).

interaction analysis indicates that, in the classroom, students ask questions only 3 percent of the time and spend only 1 percent of the time in any activity which could be labeled inquiry.

ANTECEDENTS FOR DEVELOPMENT

Since the solutions to important problems do not just happen, what causes development activity to get underway? Sometimes the search for truth, be it scientific research or the work of artists, produces *knowledge* which leads to the design of innovation because man's conceptual power is increased. A particular piece of research or a particular theory may be so elegant that new solutions to problems just seem to spring from its concepts. Art forms are often the forerunners of architecture, for instance.

Another antecedent for development is the desire *for profit* or material gain. Market analysis (consumer research) is used constantly to see what problems consumers want solved. If they want a particular problem solved badly enough, someone is likely to develop a product or process that can solve it. In the academic environment, promotion, salary and tenure based on the "publish or perish" expectation are rewards which sometimes lead to development activities.

It is my opinion, however, that the single most important cause of development resides in the *problems* which plague individuals and groups of educators. The old adage, "necessity is the mother of invention," is not just a cliche. Here are examples of "practical problems" which have led to development activities: (1) Scientists and mathematicians in higher education discovered that even bright high school students were not being taught the logic and structure of mathematics and science. RESULT— Developments like SMSG, PSSC, Chemical Bond, etc. have dotted the American scene. (2) Economics has a logical structure which can be understood by junior high school students as well as by those in senior high school or college. RESULT—A curriculum developed by Meno Lovenstein is now ready for use. (3) Federal guidelines demand that recipients of federal funds evaluate their own projects. RESULT—Evaluation centers at Ohio State and Illinois and an R & D center for evaluation at UCLA have substantial assessment development underway. (4) Teacher behavior is changed little with in-service education based on telling or mimicry. RESULT—Techniques which will help teachers assess and change their own behavior are being designed in Cleveland by Professors Strom and Galloway of Ohio State University.

Figure 1 indicates that an educational improvement system must reflect an awareness that the concerns, aspirations, and educational problems in teaching-learning situations precede development. If problems in the schools, colleges, etc. are the single most important antecedent for development, how does one identify educational goals which actual circumstances contradict or impede? First, it seems only sensible to ask teachers, administrators, and other practicing educators, who are responsible for the daily activities in teaching-learning situations, what these problems are. It would seem wise also to solicit the clients in these situations—that is, the students and those citizens who are concerned about student growth. Any state improvement system should have a regular procedure for interviewing these people and identifying such problems. How many states do, however?

All of the regional educational laboratories were asked to conduct such a survey, but to my knowledge, very few took the charge seriously. The Michigan-Ohio Regional Educational Laboratory (MOREL) did try to assess its region for major problems and primary resources. An instrument was designed and 40 interviewers talked with nearly 1,000 educators and laymen during August and September. The information from these personal interviews was quantitatively analyzed by the research department in the Detroit Public Schools. These data were further reviewed by the 40 interviewers, and both analyses helped to establish priority for development projects.

BASES FOR PRIORITY DECISIONS

Even with such a concerted effort, however, the component parts of the problems were not articulated clearly. Problem articulation is necessary for any improvement system for political and scientific reasons. There are never enough resources to attack all problems simultaneously in any state, so political decisions must be made to establish priorities among the problems identified. Many criteria are used to establish such priorities. One criterion is the importance that society places on finding a solution to this problem. A second criterion in the establishment of political priority is the availability of resources which can be put to bear on these kinds of problems. No matter how significant a problem is, if the development resources are not available, it would seem politically unwise to place that problem high on the priority list. A third criterion focuses on the probability of a problem's solution. Not only must political leaders be assured that development resources for problem solving are available, but they must also be assured that these resources will, in fact, be likely to come up with a solution.

Administrators and policy makers in both the private and public sectors of society make such priority decisions. Private corporation managers constantly make decisions about how much profit should be plowed back into research and development. Most of the money now controlled by private foundations and endowments is used for some form of research and development so such priority decisions have to be made there, too. In the public sector, all levels of government are involved in this kind of decision making. The federal government has had more experience with this kind of decision making and this experience is documented brilliantly in *The Scientific Estate* by Don K. Price.[5] One of the major theses of this paper is that *state government, if it is to be influential at all, must become more knowledgeable about the research and development enterprise fairly quickly*.

---

[5] *Op. cit.* (footnote 2).

As Price points out in his book, administrators and politicians often use the wisdom of the professional (development) and scientific (research) communities. He goes on to say that this wisdom is always looked upon as advice and only as advice. According to Price, there is a clear separation in decision making between the political community (politicians and administrators) and the scientific community (researchers and developers). He documents a series of checks and balances which are emerging among and between politicians, administrators, professionals and scientists.

PROBLEM ARTICULATION AND SOLUTION

Within the professional and scientific communities there is another kind of problem articulation which is really the first step in any research or development project. In development it consists briefly of (1) stating the goal or goals concerned in action or behavioral terms, (2) listing all of the variables which contradict or impede goal accomplishment, (3) describing the relationship between and among variables and goals, and (4) choosing which variables and relationships are most contradictory or impending. Such careful problem articulation is crucial if the invention, design and assessment which follow in development are to be effective.

In addition, the ability of potential problem solvers to articulate problems, potential solutions and the methodology to be used in their solution, helps political decision makers to determine whether a problem is likely to be solved or not. Since administrators and politicians can seldom make sound judgments about the probability of problem solubility, they seek advice from professionals and scientists. This is one reason that development projects are presently written as proposals and evaluated by professional colleagues before the political decision makers take action one way or another. Having the professional read and evaluate development proposals before the political community makes priority judgments among the proposals is not just an intellectual exercise; it is absolutely essential. A present weakness in the field of education is that the professional readers of development proposals are either research oriented or practitioner oriented and neither group understands development well enough to evaluate such proposals effectively. The present lack of professional developers in the field of education does not allow political policy makers to receive the kind of advice they need in order to make effective priority decisions.

Robert Chin[6] says that little development is being done today in the behavioral sciences. Yet the national political and administrative community continually seeks professional counsel about educational problems from behavioral scientists. If Chin is correct, then neither behavioral scientists nor educators can provide the kind of wisdom needed to make effective priority decisions among development activities in the field of education. I would submit that the present unhappiness and frustration with programs financed under Titles I, III and IV of ESEA provide evidence of this breakdown.

---

[6] See Chapter 3 in this report, "Basic Strategies and Procedures in Effecting Change."

At the state level the situation is even more appalling. Not only is there little professional wisdom available, there is no organized system in any state within which that wisdom can be applied.

In spite of an inefficient improvement system nationally and in spite of a virtually non-existent system in states, solutions to problems in the field of education are being developed with increasing rapidity. The availability of different kinds of curricula alone is something many of us would not have predicted even five years ago. When one looks at these burgeoning curriculum developments, another problem appears. Most of the new curricula are not being used. If an improvement system is to be effective, it must have output as well as input and development. The invention of solutions to problems means nothing if they remain hidden in the development agency. Our improvement system must include some kind of merchandising whose function is the spread of innovations. Another name for the spread of innovations is diffusion, and diffusion is the output of our improvement system.

DIFFUSION AND UTILIZATION

Clark and Guba[7] have described the objectives of diffusion: (1) to make potential users aware of the existence of developed solutions, (2) to convince the user of the efficacy of these developments, (3) to develop a level of user competence with the new solutions, and (4) to complete the institutionalization of the invention. The functions which relate directly to these objectives in education are (1) informing schools about particular developments, (2) demonstrating their effectiveness, (3) training personnel in schools in the use of these developments, and (4) servicing and nurturing the innovations.

Although the Clark and Guba description of output has enabled me to complete a plan for educational improvement, I have found that many educators reject their notion as being too much one way. Teachers and administrators say, "I can't accept the Guba-Clark idea because it sounds as though I am going to be 'used' by the developer." It is true that their scheme does look at the improvement process from the developers' point of view. So rather than argue whether or not dissemination and demonstration are predominantly one way communication, I would prefer to ask a different question. How do the teacher, administrator, and teaching professor fit into an improvement system?

Each can, and should, use the essence of the plan in his own area of responsibility. Teachers should be able to diagnose classroom problems, articulate these problems and assign priorities to them. They should also be able to prescribe solutions for the problems and be able to put the solutions into action. This kind of teacher behavior is described very well in documents being produced at the Center for Research on the Utilization of Scientific Knowledge in Ann Arbor.[8]

---

[7] *Op. cit.* (footnote 1).
[8] Richard Schmuck, Mark Chesler, and Ronald Lippitt, "Problem Solving to Improve Classroom Learning" (Chicago: Science Research Associates, Inc., 1966).

Sometimes a teacher will develop his own solution to a diagnosed problem, but he should not try to invent all of his own solutions when other usable developments are already available. Every teacher ought to be able to find and use developed solutions which are relevant to the problem he has diagnosed. If the output segment in our educational plan were effective and if each teacher were educated so that he knew where and how to search, most teachers could become aware of the innovative possibilities open to them.

Brickell[9] suggests that search and knowledge are not sufficient. Without administrative support such analysis by teachers is academic. So perhaps each school or school system will have to create a new kind of position which we might call a "searcher". Another alternative would be to retrain principals and supervisors so they could fulfill this searcher role. Persons occupying these positions would be the local school system's complement to the development team's disseminator-demonstrator, and each of these positions could fill the crucial role of linkage between development and utilization.

With this addition to our improvement system, teachers could diagnose, prescribe and act on their prescriptions. For the first time teachers could behave as professionals in ways similar to medical practitioners. They would most often be adapters of innovations rather than adopters, but they could be adopters without feeling some unknown hand was manipulating them.

Since educators in teaching-learning situations are often adapters and inventors rather than adopters, our improvement system must provide opportunities for teachers and administrators to disseminate their own developments and adaptations. As inventions from development teams and adaptations from teachers increase in quality and quantity, we shall need a large number of demonstration centers in each geographic region. These demonstration centers would be located in public school systems and state universities. I.D.E.A. is contracting for such schools nationally to demonstrate a particular product line: team teaching, flexible scheduling, etc. Presently most curriculum development teams are working with schools in this way. (In fact, the evaluation component of development is often not accomplished because schools, originally designed as places for evaluation, become demonstration centers too soon.) Many Title III supplementary centers could become demonstration or shopping centers.

Figure 1 contains the words, "research and evaluation". Although this paper does not concern itself primarily with those aspects of an improvement system, a few brief comments may be helpful here. Since different objectives can be articulated for each component of the improvement system, each component can and should be evaluated separately. These separate evaluations should diagnose potential breakdowns and keep the system running more effectively. They should also identify improvements needed which will lead to developments on the system itself.

---

9 Henry M. Brickell, *Organizing New York State for Educational Change* (Albany, N. Y.: New York State Department of Education, 1961).

In the same way, each component should use the scientific research which is relevant to its domain and open up the system to scientists and researchers who want to use it as an environment for further inquiry.

DOES THE SYSTEM WORK?

The credibility of this plan has been established in at least three fields other than education. They are industry, the military and agriculture. The best example in industry is American Telephone and Telegraph,[10] where local telephone companies, Bell Laboratories, and Western Electric are linked to provide an improvement system. In one part of the military RACIC (Remote Area Conflict Information Centers) and ARPA (Advanced Research Planning Agencies) link problem with research and development. Since I have learned the inner workings of the system in agriculture better than those of the other two, I shall use a case to describe the agricultural improvement system. The analogy in the case useful to education is the system itself, not the product involved.

THE AGRICULTURAL IMPROVEMENT SYSTEM

This is a description of the process used by the Agricultural Extension Service to mobilize its resources to combat a new virus which was causing a loss in Ohio corn crops due to dwarfing corn. About two years ago, the county agent in Scioto County received a call from a farmer concerning dwarf corn in his field. The county agent visited the farm and observed the corn. Dwarf corn often occurs from causes which are hereditary, but the county agent noticed that the amount of corn affected surpassed any amount of corn in a single field that he had seen before. Therefore he surmised that there was something different and seriously wrong with the particular field in question.

The county agent returned to his office and discussed the matter with other corn growers in Scioto County by phone. These personal contacts confirmed his belief that there was something more seriously wrong than some of the hereditary problems in the corn of the past. All of the farmers had dwarf corn in their fields, and in most cases, more than they had ever had. The county agent, now alarmed, called an agronomy specialist in the agricultural extension service. The agronomy specialist visited a number of the fields containing the dwarf corn and declared he had never seen anything like it. Several samples of the corn and the soil in which it was growing were collected and brought to a plant pathologist on the staff at Ohio State University. The plant pathologist identified the problem as a new virus which had never been observed before. The extension agronomist then alerted other extension agronomists and county agents along the Ohio River. After checking a number of farms, the estimated extent of the infection was 25 to 30 percent of the corn crop in the affected counties. At this time the agronomists and the plant pathologists were also in communication with others like themselves in experiment stations in land grant colleges across the country.

[10] Ronald Havelock and Kenneth Benne, "An Exploratory Analysis of Knowledge Utilization" (Ann Arbor, Michigan: Center for Research on Utilization of Scientific Knowledge, October, 1965).

By this time the agronomy committees, consisting of farmers in each of the affected counties, had become aware through their county agents, of the seriousness of the problem. These committees then began to request help from the agricultural extension service to solve this problem. The county agents turned to the agronomy specialists who prepared, with the aid of the plant pathologist, a detailed report on the extent and nature of the problem. This report requested that certain emergency priorities be given to research and development for solving the corn dwarf virus situation in Ohio. The report was submitted to the Dean of the College of Agriculture, the state Director of the Agriculture Extension Service, and to the Director of the Agriculture Experiment Station. These three administrators met as a committee and reviewed the problem with the experts who have been named here.

After hearing the evidence concerning the problem and reading about the extent of the problem, the dean and the two directors appointed a committee of four men, consisting of an extension agronomist, an extension plant pathologist, a university agronomist, and a university plant pathologist, to prepare an experimental program to study the problem of control of the new virus. Emergency funds were appropriated from the federal sources under the administration of the three institutions involved. The extension service personnel set up experimental lots in the Ohio River bottom where the problem was first noted. The university personnel set up experimental and control plots containing the diseases in the greenhouses at Ohio State University. As a result, much progress has been made in identifying an effective control of the corn dwarf mosaic virus.

IS THE CASE RELEVANT?

The agricultural extension service is the overseeing agency responsible for linking the component parts of the total system. The organization has as its primary role the implementation of innovations needed on the farms. The leaders of the organization are committed to this task and are evaluated upon the efficiency and effectiveness with which they perform the task. The Extension Service carries out its task through the coordination of a number of institutions: the university, the experiment station, private industry, county experimental farms, and opinion leader farmers who consent to place demonstration plots on their farms. The extension service personnel are able to coordinate activities among these groups because the groups are tied to each other by a system of incentives and advisory committees which interlock and provide a source of mutual advantage for all.

Problem assessment is the responsibility of a farmer, or a group of farmers, whose product is being threatened. In long term development, there are county committees consisting of farmers, agricultural industrialists, agricultural retailers, etc., who systematically search for goals which are not being accomplished as well as they would hope. These county committees consist of "sophisticated searchers". The system has been in operation long enough so that many farmers know where and how to search for information, but the county committees and county agents assure that the search is not left just to individual farmers.

Problem articulation is the responsibility of the county agent. He and the farmer attempt to diagnose the problem which the farmer brings to him. If they cannot, the county agent sends for agricultural extension specialists. These three diagnose and search for a solution. If the solution is not to be found, the specialist may send the problem to scientists at the experiment station or the university.

Problem priorities are established in two ways. In an emergency the extension specialist submits a proposal for solution to the administrative heads of the extension service in a state. These three men have financial resources at their disposal provided by the federal and the state governments, and the three men decide whether the problem is important enough to warrant the use of these resources. In a long term development there is also a state committee which collects problems from the county committees and submits yearly proposals for development projects. This information forms, in part at least, the proposals which Congress receives each year for subsidies to agriculture. The federal extension maintains a manned force in Washington, D. C., which works on national problems and maintains a very effective reporting system to Congress.

Development in agriculture is the responsibility of either the experiment station or the university. Dissemination is the responsibility of the university, the high school and the county agent. Demonstrations, project plots, farm home shows, etc., are very well done in the agriculture environment. Agriculture extension is an outstanding example of an improvement plan such as we have described in this paper.

AN IMPROVEMENT SYSTEM FOR EDUCATION

Much of the recent federal legislation has been designed to produce an improvement system similar to those operating in agriculture, the military and industry. Although these funds have created new institutions—such as curriculum development projects, research and development centers, and regional educational laboratories—it is clear that any effective improvement system must include existing educational agencies like local school systems, intermediate school districts, state departments of education, state associations or unions, and state universities. What is the probability that these existing educational agencies will be able to join and use an improvement system such as the one described in this paper?

LOCAL SCHOOL SYSTEMS

Most individual school districts have never taken development seriously. Many individual educators have been concerned with invention and adaptation, but the school or the school system itself is concerned primarily with the teaching and processing of students—not with invention. Problem identification and articulation are accomplished on an expediency basis; putting out grass fires is the order of the day. Even when inventions or adaptations are designed in a local school system, there is practically no motivation to disseminate these new ideas to other school systems. Each district is a power unto itself.

Why has development not been accomplished in local school systems? First, very little money is spent on development. Most school districts do not have enough funds to teach students effectively; consequently, they can see no way to put a substantial portion of their money into development as agriculture or industry does. Many school administrators do not want to admit to their clients that problems even exist because they fear that problem admission will lead to community conflict which in turn will lead to non-support at the polls.

With this kind of attitude among school personnel it becomes almost impossible to have any sophisticated kind of problem identification and articulation. The attitude against problem articulation and solution is evidenced by the naive state of evaluation in the field of education and the negative stance against the presently proposed plan of national assessment taken by the American Association of School Administrators.

Problem articulation and solution requires highly trained specialists in many cases. Most school districts are not large enough to justify the use of specialists of any kind, let alone a new dimension of specialization. Reorganization and increased revenues through Titles I, II, III, and V of ESEA provide the potential for local school systems to design their own improvement system or become part of a larger improvement system —but the set against problem articulation and solution still persists. Many critics, especially those outside the field of education, deplore the lack of innovation and creativity in school system programs using these federal funds. However, criticism alone will not make for an improved system of education.

THE INTERMEDIATE UNIT

The intermediate school district's purpose is to provide certain services for local school systems which they cannot provide for themselves. In some cases, problem identification and articulation have been improved immensely; however, suggested solutions for the problems come primarily through the consultant advice of the supervisor or specialist. This provision of answers to problems does not often lead to the development of innovations. I am not saying that consultant activity is not necessary. I am saying that it is quite different from development. Federal and foundation monies have provided additional resources so that some intermediate units carry on development activity as well as service activities. In fact, some of the most innovative projects have grown out of intermediate units doing just that.

Intermediate units usually serve a particular geographic area, such as a county. Consequently, they are concerned primarily about the school districts in that area. Therefore, dissemination, when it does occur, occurs over a small geographic area. The geographic autonomy and responsibility of intermediate units and large school systems work against effective dissemination of exciting developments.

If intermediate units and large school systems could become as concerned about the spread of innovations among other districts as they are about the spread of innovations within, we would have a much more effective system. In order to accomplish that we must produce a cadre of diffusion specialists, either through new training programs or the reeducation of existing supervisors, and we must break down the feeling that intermediate school districts and large school districts are responsible only unto themselves.

STATE DEPARTMENTS OF EDUCATION

State departments of education could fulfill the monitoring role of an improvement system that agricultural extension plays. Agriculture is responsible for monitoring the entire improvement system for a geographic region and for the nation as a whole. It has perfected its way of operation so well that the linkage among components seems to be consummated with little threat to the people in any part of the system. It does this, I believe, because it is responsive to problems in all phases of the operation. The problems themselves are identified by the people working in each component, not by agriculture extension. It is here that the state department of education runs into a major conflict. State departments have been primarily enforcers of minimum standards in the elementary-secondary schools and in state universities through certification requirements for teachers. State supervisors do not often go to school systems and colleges of teacher education asking, "What are your problems?" Rather, they go with a code book and assess the program against the law and make suggestions as to how the minimum standards can and should be met.

State departments also assume fiscal responsibility. They account for the state taxes funds which go to local school districts and intermediate units. In addition, they communicate to the state legislature the financial needs of education. Because of this fiscal responsibility, administrators in state departments of education show the same fear of problem articulation that administrators of local school systems display. All of us would like to identify and recognize our problems, but we have to be careful how completely we articulate them because taxpayers and legislators may say "no" to requests for additional money if the problems we identify make the educational system seem ineffective. Furthermore, it has been my experience that many state legislators and individual taxpayers expect professional educators "to know the answers" to the problems we raise. These people do not realize that development is often necessary once one defines the problems. Since the legislator does not understand the necessity for problem articulation, invention, and dissemination, very little money is spent at the state level for development. At both the local and state levels, educators, especially administrators, have assumed that the taxpayer and the legislator would not support development. Consequently, we have not asked them to support it. *The behavior of Congress over the last 20 years challenges that notion to such a great extent that I think it is time we tested the idea with state legislatures.*

STATE EDUCATION ASSOCIATIONS

In most states, education associations have been much more effective at the identification and articulation of problems than the state departments of education. They have attempted to help state legislatures arrive at priorities for decision making. But often these associations are perceived as hindrances rather than aids by state legislators. There are at least two reasons for this perception. First, they are perceived as a special interest group lobbying for a particular group of people. Therefore, the professional wisdom that they can provide is often challenged by the legislators because of a built-in bias. Secondly, education associations, like state departments of education, have not understood the necessity and the power of development. Consequently, most of the legislative plans championed by associations request money to maintain the existing establishment rather than money to set up a system for the development of innovations.

This image as a special interest group is being further intensified for education associations by the territorial and membership fight they presently are waging with teacher unions. Both teacher unions and education associations could help their own cause in resource procurement from state legislatures if they would join forces in asking those legislatures to expend finances for the development of educational innovations at the state level in ways similar to procedures used by Congress in the areas of research and development. If associations and unions took this approach they could join with state departments of education, universities and school systems so that the totality of professional wisdom within the educational community could be brought to bear on decision making about development. Of course, all of these organizations must realize that the state legislature needs professional counsel beyond educators if development decisions are to be made wisely. Because of this, the associations and state departments of education should help the legislature procure that kind of advice.

UNIVERSITIES AND COLLEGES OF TEACHER EDUCATION

Much of the criticism leveled at local school systems can also be applied to teaching in colleges and universities. In the university, the kind of problem solving which is rewarded is that which is related to basic research or the arts. Neither of these is concerned primarily with problems in teaching-learning situations, so development activities are few and far between. The outstanding exception to this is agriculture and the other federally sponsored vocational programs. There has been some movement toward rewarding development in professional fields like medicine and engineering; however, even in those fields most development is carried on by institutions closely connected with the university, but not part of the university.

Although there is a reward system in large universities for research, many colleges of education do not have very competent researchers. Where such research does exist, the basic research model—usually psychology—is the one used, so little development is rewarded in colleges of teacher education anywhere. Professor Chin's comments are especially applicable in the field of education, I believe. Presently, colleges of teacher education could be viewed in Figure 1 as being similar to elementary and secondary schools in that they have teaching-learning problems and in that they should be users of solutions developed for these problems.

Recent federal legislation makes resources available so that universities can house development projects. In fact, some of this, particularly in curriculum development, is under way. However, it is clear that the planners of federal legislation were not at all sure that universities could switch their reward system to take advantage of these development funds, since outside institutions like regional laboratories were set up in the legislation to accomplish development and dissemination. It is interesting to note here that the successful curriculum developments in the physical sciences funded by The National Science Foundation began in universities like MIT but now are housed in agencies outside universities like Educational Development, Inc. Another very successful curriculum development operation is the Educational Research Council in Cleveland, and it has little or no university participation. Such is the case, I believe, because the *university sees itself as promoting basic research and not rewarding development.* If individual scholars in the university want to respond to practical problems, they are allowed to do so as individual consultants. However, this is construed as service within the university milieu rather than development.

IMPLICATIONS FOR STATES AND REGIONS

1. State Departments of Education should use ESEA Title I, III, or V funds to set up a regular system for problem identification.

- Teachers, students, and lay citizens should be asked to describe school situations where sets of circumstances contradict or impede goals. Our present problem identification techniques too often involve just school administrators. How many times is the North Central Accreditation report the work of principals or superintendents alone?

- Problem identification should include the teaching departments of colleges and universities as well as elementary and secondary schools.

2. Personnel from universities, research and development agencies, or elementary and secondary school projects financed with federal funds should be commissioned to translate the raw problem data into articulate problem statements.

- These people would search the environment for development work already underway on the problems articulated.

- Professional associations representing particular subject matter areas and disciplines should be deeply immersed in such problem articulation.

3. A special agency should be created in each region or state to assume several responsibilities including:

- Procure the funds necessary for development from state legislatures, federal sources, private foundations, local communities, industry and commerce, and philanthropic individuals.
- Provide the professional advice neecssary so that funding agencies or individuals can make priority decisions among problems.
- Coordinate a broad systematic attack on all educational problems that are given priority.
- Report the problems articulated and the development projects underway to all potential developers or users of solutions (the audience is much larger than our traditional concept of a school implies).
- Link educational problem solving with other social welfare problem solving.

4. This special agency need not be a new institution. It could very well be a joint responsibility of a board of regents and a state department of education.

- Some states might decide to use regional educational laboratories in this way.
- The Education Commission of the States may well become a national prototypic agency.

5. Individuals in universities and school systems should be encouraged to carry out their own development projects. The special agency should not control all funding for development; rather it should serve as a catalytic agent for increased funding and as a coordinating agency for development in a state or region.

- Incentive systems in both school systems and universities must be changed so that more individuals will consider development as a legitimate professional activity.
- University administrators should realize that the trend in federal funding is to spend a higher proportion of revenue for applied research (development) than for basic research. Consequently, personnel, expert in basic research, should be encouraged to spend at least part of their time and effort in the applied research field.

6. Development projects should be required to propose strategies for dissemination as well as for development.

- Special training programs for diffusion or dissemination specialists must be undertaken by the university community.
- These specialists would function as linkage agents between problems and solutions and vice versa. Examples already existing are county agricultural agents and the systems engineer in AT&T.
- State departments of education should set up a library or information retrieval center for all development projects in the state or nation. These centers might include personnel consultant services available in the state as well.
- Every school system of adequate size should finance school demonstration centers. This might be one school where many innovations are on display or many schools with a few innovations each. ESEA Titles I and III should be used to help finance such centers. Educators would view these centers in much the same way as a housewife views a shopping center.
- As with the Fair Food and Drug legislation, each center would be required to show the assets and liabilities of each innovation it demonstrates.
- Each innovation should be field tested in a school situation before it is put on display in the demonstration center.

7. The profession should increase its local capacity to articulate problems and search for solutions.

- Principals and key teachers in each school would be re-educated for this purpose. These people should be taught, at a minimum, how to learn to use the state department's information retrieval center.
- School system supervisors can help with this search task, but the focus of activity should be on the school and the classroom rather than on the school system.
- Department heads or elected faculty representatives should play this role in the university.
- State department of education supervisors should play the search role rather than continue to be primarily enforcers of minimum standards.

8. State departments of education should use their certification power to encourage teacher education institutions to explain this educational improvement system to all prospective teachers. Such courses should emphasize the benefits which will accrue to teachers who know how to make this improvement system work for them.

- Universities and the state department of education should combine to conduct in-service education about such an improvement system with all teachers who are already in service.

9. The entire improvement system should be monitored regularly by an independent evaluation team.

- Context, input and process evaluation appears to constitute a useful method for such an on-going assessment.[11]

IN SUMMARY

Problem solving, change and innovation are becoming part of every educator's daily pattern of living. This paper has described a system which should help people in a state or region to plan and use available change processes to improve teaching and learning. Such an improvement system appears valid and feasible because it is already being used in other fields like agriculture, the military and industry.

I have also tried to show that existing local and state educational agencies are not designed to effect such an improvement system but that they could be re-designed for such a purpose if the political and professional communities would use their wisdom and power jointly to accomplish such a task.

Although new development organizations like national curriculum projects, regional educational laboratories, research and development centers, and merging industrial complexes are already instituted, I have concentrated on the old line state and local educational organizations because, in the final analysis, they will decide whether any improvement system will work. The new institutions, however, should not be written off as unimportant or as failures because they *will become* instrumental in carrying out an improvement system such as the one I have described.

[11] Daniel L. Stufflebeam, "A Depth Study of the Evaluation Requirement," *Theory Into Practice,* Ohio State University, Vol. V, No. 3 (1967), pp. 121-133.

Last, but not least, the improvement system I have described is an evolving system. Our environment is changing so rapidly that no system for educational improvement can be considered final. Although the proposed system is a blurred snapshot of reality, such snapshots must be used as a basis for planning and implementing improvement programs in the field of education.

* * *

Some Strategies and Procedures in Effecting Changes

EWALD B. NYQUIST*

This paper will address itself to the role and functions of state education departments in effecting change. The assumption is that a strong state education department can be a powerful institutional agent of change, either by creating the requisite conditions for change or by directly effecting change.

One of the fashionable major strategies for effecting change is the development of structures for that purpose. This has come about because we have realized that—in a world of continuous change—change must be institutionalized if it is to be controlled. In other words, there must be in each major system today a segment that takes thought for tomorrow— that sees to it that needs are anticipated and prepared for. *The development of a competent state education department is, itself, a major example of a state strategy for effecting change.* A competent state education department's ministrations may well be instrumental in the social process which Daniel P. Moynihan has called the "professionalization of reform". How can a state education department be an agent of change?

LEGAL PROVISIONS AND ORGANIZATION

The first consideration is the constitutional and legislative provisions for educational leadership in the state. State constitutional provisions for organizational framework should be characterized by simplicity, leaving the fleshing out process to legislative enactment of statutory details. Constitutional mandates, once established, are difficult to change. Simple, broad and flexible provisions permit the legislature to make such changes in details as the times and the mood of the people dictate. An education department, its governing board of education and the chief state school officer selected by the board to serve at its pleasure should be provided for in the constitution, thus removing them from political manipulation and control. The protective autonomy of constitutional status guarantees the state board and its executive officer the opportunity and freedom

* *Deputy Commissioner of Education, The University of the State of New York, The State Education Department.* Formerly, Director of University Admissions, Columbia University (1948-51); Assistant Commissioner for Higher Education and Associate Commissioner for Higher and Professional Education, New York State Department of Education (1951-57). Member of numerous state, regional and national committees.

to interpret with clarity, perceptiveness and conviction to the public, the educational community and the political arena, the educational needs of a state without fear of political reprisal or the recriminations of special vested interest groups.

The appointment by the legislature or by the governor of outstanding citizens to a relatively small board has much to commend it. In a day when education has moved up in the ladder of priorities, only a prestige board, supported by competent professional staff, is capable of wisely interpreting the political instincts of the executive and legislative authorities and the educational needs of the people.

If state education departments are to provide effective state leadership and partnership with federal and local agencies, they must have the conditions of employment and the basic inducements to secure and maintain a highly skilled professional staff. A company is known by the people it keeps.

Such considerations as the following are relevant: (a) salaries and collateral perquisites continually competitive with those prevailing in the recruitment sources—either in or out of the educational community— from which professional personnel are usually drawn; (b) the creation and maintenance of pride and competence in a professional staff not subject to political control and manipulation; (c) a prevailing climate according generous hospitality to experimentation and innovation and a spirit conducive to the rapid promotion and accommodation of essential change; and (d) the allocation of high priorities to leadership activities rather than to regulatory and supervisory functions necessary as the latter are.

The posture, or intellectual stance, of a state board and its chief executive officer on innovation, experimentation and creative service, is overriding in importance. A conservative or incompetent board and a commissioner or superintendent of education who likes only riskless choices can be formidable obstacles to change in an educational system.

Before suggesting a few functions of state education departments which can bring about change, three assumptions should be stated:

1. A state agency must be acutely aware that this is a day of interlocking complexity, that education can no longer live in splendid isolation. Traditional forms of institutional autonomy are being displaced by emerging patterns at all levels which emphasize interdependence rather than independence in the expansion and improvement of education. Education is everyone's business, and the new era is one of "going steady".

2. It is assumed that a state education department considers education as a shared responsibility involving a federal-state-local partnership. Conversely, with the significant entrance of the federal government into the financing of education, no state can lead and still piously assert that in the American educational system, the state is *the* sovereign authority. Every dogma has its day. The dusty one of states' rights is no longer valid and

is being replaced with the concept of creative federalism. *Joint effort and mutual development of new activities enlarges the power of states and localities—not diminishes it.*

3. Since vast resources are being placed at the disposal of educational authorities, there is a heightened interest in the increased effectiveness which those resources are supposed to produce. A wise education department is one which is willing to give an accounting of its educational stewardship. Evaluation has become a major challenge to the profession.

EMERGENT FUNCTIONS OF STATE DEPARTMENTS

What are the emergent functions of state education departments which, if performed well, constitute a state strategy for effecting change?

THE ESTABLISHMENT OF GOALS AND OBJECTIVES

Comparatively few state education departments have gone through the process of defining broad goals to which state government, the local schools and citizens can commit themselves in allocating the combined state-federal-local resources available for their accomplishment. It is a painful process and one which—if well done—involves wide participation and consensus.

Requiring even more effort is the process of defining specific educational objectives to be achieved in the teaching and learning process. A recent book on the preparation of instructional objectives begins with an echo from Charles Dudley Warner's famous remark about the weather: "Everybody talks about defining educational objectives, but almost nobody does anything about it."

What are the desirable outcomes of the educational process, not only in terms of basic skills but including behavioral outputs as well? Each state must develop its own taxonomy of both cognitive and non-cognitive objectives.

LONG-RANGE PLANNING

Education is a complex mix of many shifting and interacting components. Simple and stable straightline relationships in education no longer exist. The rate of change requires that there be substantial provision for planning which is oriented toward tomorrow's needs rather than today's necessities.

Planning in some state education departments is now a year-round affair, not only to budget for the succeeding year's needs, but to make adjustments in long-range plans for unforeseen changes and needs. While it would be highly commendable if all operating heads in a department could be competent to plan in accordance with the new requirements, it is probably realistic for some major officer to be designated as the head of planning, with the function of coordinating and stimulating the planning of the entire department. At least one state education department is establishing an Office of Long-Range Planning for this purpose.

The growing practice for state governments to engage in program budgeting, following the example of the federal government, is certain to force periodic identification and assessment of needs and opportunities for educational programs, materials, and methods and the definition of the human and physical resources necessary to carry them out.

Long-range planning and the establishment of goals are interrelated. They force the designation of priorities—the relative urgency of various problems and issues—and the consequent allocation of resources to resolve them.

GUIDANCE AND COORDINATION

A strong state education department should carry on a number of activities designed to guide educational activities in a specific direction in line with broad goals and educational objectives. In this way, state education departments can effect change most directly. Examples are:

- the development of master state-wide plans for school district organization
- the development of regional and state-wide plans for improving and expanding vocational education and coordinating it with higher education
- the development of a state-wide plan for organizing supplementary educational centers and services, under Title III of the Elementary and Secondary Education Act of 1965 (ESEA), on a regional basis
- encouraging locally and collegiate sponsored in-service training programs for teachers and administrators with state aid incentives
- encouraging the development of foreign area studies in local curriculums with state assistance
- developing and promulgating curriculum and teaching guides in a number of subject matter areas, including vocational education, the basic disciplines, the humanities, advanced placement subjects, health education, etc.
- preparing a master plan for the establishment of community colleges (if departments have this function in higher education)
- encouraging local research, experimentation, and innovation through the establishment of categorical state aid programs for these specific purposes
- encouraging local school districts with state aid to correct critical areas of weakness such as the quality and opportunity of education for the disadvantaged; the identification of talent in depressed groups; the drop-out problem; the education of children of migrant laborers
- encouraging students to go on to advanced education through a state-aided scholarship program
- the development of state plans for the administration of federally aided programs, such as Titles III and V of NDEA; Titles I, II and VI of ESEA; the Vocational Education Act; Adult Basic Education; etc.
- encouraging the development of effective pre-school programs through state-aided programs for research and development
- encouraging the systematic development of educational television by the formation of a state-wide plan
- promoting the use of the various instructional technologies, including educational television and computer-assisted instruction, by providing state aid
- the development of a state plan, including a racial census, for desegregating schools and for accomplishing quality integrated education
- preparing and implementing a state-wide plan for the development and coordination of public and school library services

- preparation of a master plan for the orderly development of electronic data processing in the public schools, including the regionalized sharing of such services and the launching of demonstration programs on data-collecting and processing services
- the conduct of leadership state level and regional conferences on a variety of frontier developments in education, such as, pre-school education, new approaches to teaching the discipline subjects, and employer-employee relationships

The foregoing are only a few of the leadership functions which a state education department can perform. These activities become elements in an overall integrated plan, the development of which is in the mainstream of a department's planning activity.

A key feature and common element in many of these activities is the provision of state aid in order to stimulate local school systems to conduct programs for the purpose of increasing quality and opportunity. A major strategy in effecting change is the use of dollars. An emergent function of a state education department is to act more like a combined management consultant firm and philanthropic foundation, able to provide consultative services on a wide variety of problems and to make available money to bring about correction and change on the basis of formulated plans judged by adopted state criteria.

PROVIDING CONSULTATIVE SERVICES

A leadership department must be in a position to provide expert assistance and creative service to local school systems in helping them to solve local or regional problems, initiate new programs, establish complicated relationships, and develop their sophistication in strategies of constructive change. Local school systems should be able to solicit assistance from a state education department in a wide variety of areas, from the introduction of double entry bookkeeping and automatic data processing to solving problems of racial integration and employer-employee relationships.

Many states cannot afford vast professional staffs which can provide counsel on every problem area in education. There are other ways to achieve the same ends of improving quality, efficiency and educational opportunity. Colleges and universities can be called on to help local school systems. Regional or state-wide conferences can be conducted. Demonstration centers can be established. One state has inaugurated a Cooperative Review Service which employs staff personnel, supplemented by university consultants, as a task force to assist in evaluating programs, or even an entire school system.

INNOVATION AND DISSEMINATION

Ideally, of course, all professional personnel in a state education department should consider themselves as innovators and agents of change. This is too much to hope for in the short-run. The remedy over the long-run term lies in several specific activities and requisite conditions, some of which have already been discussed. Others are considered below:

Unit for Change. In a transition period, a state education department may find it expedient to establish one or more units charged with responsibility for change and for inducting department staff into the new role of the department. One department has established a Center on Innovation, modestly staffed, to provide a prominent focus for change and innovation. Its job is to "disturb the comfortable", internally as well as in the schools. Its purpose is to serve as a broker of ideas; to accelerate educational change on a state-wide basis in order to raise the quality of education through the design, evaluation and dissemination of new ideas and practices. It welcomes fresh ideas, encourages the trying out of new approaches in schools and colleges, evaluates the results, and passes these along to administrators and teachers throughout the state in an organized way.

Such a center, by providing a visible focus for change and innovation, can do much to promote throughout the state an attitude that favors and fosters research, experimentation, and innovation—not change for its own sake, but change carefully calculated to improve the level of learning and to lift the status of teaching. Such a center also has responsibility for developing strategies and structures for accelerating educational change and for the engineering of consent.

Dissemination System. A key provision in accelerating educational change is an organized dissemination system for desired new programs. As a minimum, this involves reporting through an information system, but it should go beyond this to a full-scale dissemination arrangement involving demonstration centers or techniques, in-service training, and adoption support.

Title III of ESEA provides funds for the establishment of supplementary educational centers which can perform this function. Properly developed and coordinated with state assistance and guidance into regional centers, such structures can bridge the gap between educational laboratories and Research and Development (R & D) centers on the one hand, and local school systems on the other.

Two-way Flow of Information. Providing for an information system that furnishes a two-way flow between the field and the department is essential to long-range planning and current decision making at all levels. The "information" stressed here is not statistical data but rather details of innovative programs and procedures.

The Education Research Information Center (ERIC) project established by the U. S. Office of Education is designed to establish informational clearinghouses and research documentation centers in specific programs with each center specializing in one specific area. State education departments should subscribe to these services, but they need to establish some supplementary intrastate system which solicits and redistributes information from their own schools and colleges.

An effective information system and the maintenance of a knowledge inventory of the most advanced thinking can go a long way in reducing wasteful duplication of effort and insuring that research and practice in mutual interaction build more quickly to ever higher levels of excellence.

Incentive Funds. The provision by a state legislature of funds to assist local schools, higher institutions, supplementary centers, regional educational laboratories, etc., in designing and establishing innovative programs, increases the force of a state education department's suggestions on the general need for change or on specific needs.

RESEARCH AND COLLECTION OF INFORMATION

Too few state education departments have either research capabilities or research obligations. A department's research interests should encompass (1) internal, departmental management concerns and (2) external, field needs and opportunities for educational programs, materials, and methods. There are many ways to lead and to effect change.

Staffing. A department should be so staffed that it can exercise some degree of leadership in organizing a state's total resources for engaging in educational research. In one state, the department took the initiative in creating an association of the state's educational research personnel, establishing formal liaison with key research personnel in the state's higher institutions, conducting annual research convocations, arranging for an inventory of research studies showing the gaps remaining, and then aggressively setting about to stimulate research needed. In short, *a community of educational research interests was created.*

Liaison. By joining or maintaining close liaison with the newly developed regional educational laboratories and R & D centers, state education departments can contribute substantially to research developments. They can suggest needed research and facilitate cooperation between higher institutions and local school systems. They can place the weight of their hegemony behind projects, thereby adding to the prestige of the outcomes and hastening the adaptation of results into regular school practice. Finally, by joining research groups and adopting a position of strong advocacy for research, state education departments are in good position to know when to suspend (at least temporarily) otherwise constraining state regulations, in order to create the most salutary climate for research and experimentation. This wise exercise of a regulatory function can, paradoxically, promote rather than inhibit change. At the very least, state education departments can get out of the way of school districts ready to make new departures.

Consultative Assistance. Departments should have research personnel available who can provide technical advice and consultative assistance on research design in the development of locally sponsored research and experimental programs.

Supplemental Funds. For a state education department to lead most effectively—in short, to have its suggestions adopted—it is helpful to have state funds set aside to supplement federal and other sources for experimental and research purposes. Considering the increasingly large investment being made in education by the people of any given state, it seems only prudent that—as a matter of state policy—a modest sum should be set aside each year for experimentation and research, as risk and venture capital for maintaining a constant and systematic search for new and better ways of doing the educational job.

Information System. A capable research unit is the proper setting for a highly developed information system for gathering basic educational data about elementary and secondary education. Statistical information is necessary for decision making and long-range planning, not to mention interpretation of the status and progress of education to the public, state legislative representatives, and the educational community.

EVALUATION

The educational community is being called upon to provide increased accountability to its many constituencies for the financial support received. Evaluative techniques will need to be employed in order to improve the decision making process in education for the sake of justifying additional support and of enhancing the educational process and its efficiency. Results of sound evaluation programs—especially if they depict marked weakness—are instrumental in bringing about change.

In judging the outcomes of the teaching and learning process, there are, of course, several nationally known testing instruments available. A state education department can exercise leadership by encouraging appropriate use of these, or by developing its own instruments for this evaluative purpose. Consultative services, in any case, should be available from a state department to help localities in developing locally used evaluative procedures and techniques. Such assistance is becoming more urgent in view of the encouragement given to local schools through federal funds to develop imaginative programs for educating the disadvantaged (Title I, ESEA) and for enriching the regular curriculum (Title III, ESEA).

But, all testing instruments currently available are normative in approach, and deal only with *relative* achievement. They furnish status studies which provide a basis for comparing schools with each other. One department is developing a different approach by intensively exploring whether reasonable standards of educational expectancy can be established, in view of school and student resources and conditions, *based not on what other schools have achieved, but on what schools with such resources and conditions ought to achieve.* This approach is based on economic theory of inputs and outputs.

Let us consider some of the uses to which a system of educational indicators might be put. Their primary value will be to help all of those responsible for education to do a better job. Good indicators will provide educators at each level from the classroom up, with warnings of changes that portend difficulty if not attended to. They will help these educators to assess relative need and the consequences of choosing various courses of action to meet those needs. When program decisions have been made, the indicators can help them to determine whether objectives are being realized and assist them in locating specific sources of difficulty when they are not. By relating changes in indicators to costs of producing the changes, some measures of cost effectiveness in education can be realized.

On the state level it should be possible to obtain detailed indicators of how the schools as a whole or any selected segment of them are doing. This information can then serve to guide the decisions of the state education department, the governor and executive departments and the legislature. A system of incentives might be devised to encourage systems to exceed expectations. Areas of severe weakness could be identified and corrective measures instituted.

Commissioner Harold Howe II suggested recently that states should set a "minimum level of quality for their schools." He is quoted in news reports as saying:

> Having determined that quality base line, the states must tax sufficiently to make sure that no school falls below it. If the local community wants to soar above that level, well and good.

A good system of indicators would provide that base line. Moreover, when persistent failure of a local school district to improve is the result of the failure of individuals to carry out their responsibilities, the indicators can provide the basis for appropriate action.